*From
Tradition
To
Commentary*

SUNY Series in Judaica: Hermeneutics, Mysticism, and Religion
Michael Fishbane, Robert Goldenberg, and Arthur Green, editors

From
Tradition
To
Commentary

Torah and Its Interpretation in the Midrash
Sifre to Deuteronomy

Steven D. Fraade

State University of New York Press

Published by
State University of New York Press, Albany

© 1991 State University of New York

For information, address State University of New York Press,
State University Plaza, Albany, N.Y. 12246

Library of Congress Cataloging-in-Publication Data

Fraade, Steven D.
  From tradition to commentary : Torah and its interpretation in the
Midrash Sifre to Deuteronomy / Steven D. Fraade.
    p.   cm. — (SUNY series in Judaica)
  Includes bibliographical references.
  ISBN 0-7914-0495-1. — ISBN 0-7914-0496-X (pbk.)
  1. Sifrei. Deuteronomy—Commentaries.   2. Bible. O.T.
Deuteronomy—Commentaries.   I. Title.   II. Series.
  BM517.S75F73   1991
  296. 1′4—dc20   90-9580
                                                      CIP

10 9 8 7 6 5 4 3 2 1

For Ellen

"'With the kidney fat of wheat' (Deut. 32:14): This refers to the laws, which are the body of Torah. 'And the blood of grapes' (ibid.): This refers to the narratives, which draw the heart of a person like wine."

Sifre Deut. §317

"' A fiery law unto them' (Deut. 33:2): Had law not been given with [the fire of Torah], a person would not be able to labor with it."

Sifre Deut. §343

Contents

Preface

Standing at the conclusion of the book that follows, I can barely recall when and how it began. I first engaged, in a serious way, the *Sifre's* commentary on the Book of Deuteronomy during the 1975–1976 academic year in a midrash text seminar taught by Judah Goldin at the University of Pennsylvania, where I was then a graduate student. We focused our attention on the *Sifre's* commentary on the lection *Ha'azinu*, or the Song of Moses (Deut. 32), several parts of which proccupy me again in the course of this book. Although I had and would study in like detail many other rabbinic texts, midrashic as well as nonmidrashic, the *Sifre* took a special hold on me that it has still not loosened. Why that was and continues to be I am not sure. My guess is that it has to do with two combined features of the *Sifre's* commentary to Deuteronomy, with which I trust the reader will soon become abundantly familiar: the beckoning depths of its teaching and the beguiling complexities of its text.

When, upon revising my doctoral dissertation as my first book (*Enosh and His Generation: Pre-Israelite Hero and History in Post-Biblical Interpretations,* SBLMS 30 [Chico, Calif.: Scholars Press, 1984]) I sought to set my sights on the next major project, I set them on the *Sifre*, turning from the history of tradition across many texts of biblical interpretation to the configuration of many traditions within a single text of biblical commentary. I have been pursuing this project now for eight years, leading from its first, tentative fruits ("Sifre Deuteronomy 26 [ad Deut. 3:23]: How Conscious the Composition?" *HUCA* 54 [1983]: 245–301) to the present, fuller harvest, having turned aside frequently along the way to till adjacent fields. Those adjacent fields, however, have been not only topical and textual but also methodological, and this book represents as much the fruits of such disciplinary cultivation, especially in the unabashedly eclectic intersection of historical and literary criticism. That restless intersection is best denoted as cultural history, and it is toward an as yet unattempted cultural history of ancient Judaism in general, and of ancient rabbinic Judaism in particular, that this study seeks to take a first step. Because of the length of time that I have thus labored both in the text of the *Sifre* and in the interdisciplinary honing of the methodological tools of that labor, many individuals and institutions have sustained me in my slow progress, and they are now to be thanked.

From the beginning I have been fortunate to receive the financial support from several institutions to allow me to pursue my studies in periodic freedom from my other academic responsibilities and to offset the costs of research and text processing: a National Endowment for the Humanities Summer Research Stipend in 1982, a Morse Fellowship from Yale University in 1983–84, an American Philosophical Society Research Grant in the summer of 1984, when I was a guest at Mishkenot Sha'ananim in Jerusalem, a sabbatical from Yale in the fall of 1986, a John Simon Guggenheim Memorial Foundation Fellowship for the whole of 1988, and grants from the Memorial Foundation for Jewish Culture and the Lucius N. Littauer Foundation for the same period, a fellowship during the fall of 1988 and the summer of 1989 at the Institute for Advanced Studies of the Hebrew University of Jerusalem, and several research grants from the A. Whitney Griswold Faculty Fund at Yale.

The following libraries and their keepers graciously provided me with photographs of manuscripts in their holdings, thereby permitting me to glimpse the interpretive fluidy of the *Sifre*'s own text that lies masked behind its printed pages: British Library (London). Bodleian Library (Oxford), Casanata Library (Rome), Hebrew Union College Library (Cincinnati), Jewish National and University Library (Jerusalem), Jewish Theological Seminary of America (New York) Staatsbibliothek (East Berlin).

Over the years I have had the opportunity to present parts of this book in far rougher oral form to scholarly audiences: two meetings of the Literary Study of Rabbinic Literature Group of the Society of Biblical Literature (December 1984 and December 1987), Judaic Studies faculty seminars at Yale (November 1984 and May 1985) and Wesleyan University (December 1985), a Midrash Colloquium at Yale (May 1988), a meeting of the Biblical Exegesis Group of the Institute for Advanced Studies at the Hebrew University (October 1988), and a seminar at the Seminary of Judaic Studies in Jerusalem (November 1988). The critical offerings of my colleagues on those occasions repeatedly led me to refine my arguments and reread my texts.

Many scholars in diverse fields and disciplines gave generously of their time to read earlier drafts of the chapters of this book and discuss with me the course I had set for myself. Whereas some reigned me in, others spurred me on. Whereas some drew my attention to small textual details upon which my larger arguments ultimately rest, others helped me to refine the larger cultural and conceptual frameworks within which I make sense of those details. They should excuse the faceless grouping and alphabetic listing of their names, conveying no sense of my personal appreciation of each one's particular blend of encouragement and candor: Esther Adler,

Marilyn Arthur, Marc Bregman, Michael Fishbane, Isaiah Gafni, Judah Goldin, Naomi Granot, Moshe Greenberg, Geoffrey Hartman, Martha Himmelfarb, Menahem Kahana, Wayne Meeks, Peter Ochs, David Ruderman, Richard Sarason, and David Satran.

Another group of readers, every bit as important as the preceding, but one that must here remain an anonymous aggregate, are the many Yale College students who over the past several years have studied with me the texts that are herein interpreted. Usually totally new to *Sifre* and with varying degrees of previous exposure to rabbinic literature, they revealed in their unencumbered readings unexpected faces to texts that I had turned over so many times before. Invariably, after a text seminar session I would rush to my study to revise once again the translation and explication of a section of the *Sifre* with which I had thought I was *finally* done. A *barayta* cited in the Babylonian Talmud (*Roš. Haš.* 25a-b; cf. *t. Roš. Haš.* 2:28) asks why the biblical elders, who shared with Moses the experience of revelation and the judicial authority to apply it to the life of Israel, are not individually named in the biblical record. The answer given: they stand in their inclusive anonymity for each successive generation of rabbinic authorities, including those yet to come. With no immodesty implied by this comparison, I would like my acknowledgement of the anonymous students who have worked with me through the pages of the *Sifre* to signify my hope that future "generations" of students will be empowered by the shared fruits of our labor to till for themselves the *Sifre*'s textual fields (as if) anew.

From the preceding, it may correctly be inferred that I intend this book as much for the neophyte student as for the veteran scholar of rabbinic writings in the hope that both will discover much new in the antique texts of traditional commentary herein presented for critical commentary. In part because of this dual audience, my own text is structured in two parts, the body of my commentary and the endnotes thereto. Novices may wish to read continuously, unencumbered by my extensive notes, unless, of course, their curiosity is piqued to dig deeper. But those who are prepared to forfeit an easier read to work for a greater textual pay, will find in those notes entrances to a vast network of bibliographic, text-critical, philogical, and intra- and inter-cultural strands that point backward to the labor-intensive foundations of my own commentary and forward to the seemingly endless possibilities for further study and commentary still.

To return to expressions of appreciation and to conclude these preliminary words, by far the greatest source of support in bringing this book to its completion has been my immediate family, my wife Ellen Cohen and our two children Shoshana and Nathaniel, who have shared me these recent years with a distant text that they understand even less than I. This book about ancient texts of teaching is for Ellen, who, in her own quite different pedagogic labors, has taught me that in the patient struggle of teaching someone/thing quite other than ourselves we draw that other both into and out of ourselves.

Transliterations

The transliteration of Hebrew and Aramaic follows the system of the *Journal of Biblical Literature* (107 [1988]: 582–83): *ʾbgdhwzḥṭyklmnsʿpṣ-qrśšt*. Spirants and *mappiq* are not indicated *Dāgēš forte* is indicated by doubling the consonant. Length of vowels is shown in citations of primary texts, but not necessarily in the titles of books, articles, tractates, etc. In the case of commonly used Hebrew and Aramaic terms or names (e.g., midrash), conventional spellings rather than true transliterations are often employed.

Greek transliteration follows standard practice (see *JBL* ibid.), but *iōta* subscript is not indicated; those who know Greek should be able to supply it where needed.

Note on the
Textual Basis of the Translations

*T*ranslations of passages from *Sifre Deuteronomy* are all my own and are based on what I have determined by consistent text-critical criteria to be the most authentic Hebrew text, this being of course a relative judgment. The commonly cited "critical edition" of *Sifre Deuteronomy* by Louis Finkelstein (*Siphre ad Deuteronomium* [Berlin 1939; reprint New York: Jewish Theological Seminary of America, 1969]) is an ecclectic edition that is problematic in its frequent choice of readings that, although "smoother," are contravened by the earliest manuscripts and attestations. See in particular the reviews by Saul Lieberman (*Kiryat Sefer* 14 [1937–38]: 323–36) and Jacob N. Epstein (*Tarbiz* 8 [1936–37]: 375–92). Therefore, instead of translating Finkelstein's text I have followed MS Vatican (Ebr. 32) where extant, which has repeatedly been shown to be the most reliable, though by no means perfect, witness to the text of the *Sifre* (both to Numbers and to Deuteronomy), on both stemmatic and linguistic grounds. For the former, see Menahem Kahana, "Prolegomena to a New Edition of the Sifre on Numbers," (Ph.D. dissertation, Hebrew University of Jerusalem, 1982), pp. 2–6, 116–227, 276 [Hebrew]; for the latter, see Moshe Bar-Asher, "A Preliminary Study of Mishnaic Hebrew as Reflected in Codex Vatican 32 of Sifre Bemidbar, "*Te'uda* 3 (1983): 139–64 [Hebrew]. Where MS Vatican is not extant, I rely on MS London (British Museum, Margoliouth 341), with the aid of MS Oxford (Bodleian, Neubauer 151), Cairo Geniza fragments, and early attestations. However, I always provide cross reference to Finkelstein's edition (cited by the standard section [*pisqā'*] number followed by page and line numbers preceded by the letter F in parentheses) as it remains the scholarly standard. Where my translation is based on a text significantly different from Finkelstein's text, I give its text-critical basis (primarily MS Vatican), plus significant alternatives, in the footnotes.

Because the other recent complete English translations (Reuven Hammer, *Sifre: The Tannaitic Commentary on the Book of Deutronomy* [New Haven: Yale University Press, 1986]; Jacob Neusner, *Sifre to Deuteronomy: An Analytical Translation*, 3 vols. [Atlanta: Scholars Press,

1987]) follow Finkelstein's edition, my translation will differ from them at least to the extent that I have not done so. A recent complete German translation (*Der tannaitische Midrasch Sifre Deuteronomium*, trans. Hans Bietenhard [Berlin, New York: Peter Lang, 1984]) came to my attention too late for me to employ or compare it systematically.

1 *Introduction:* *The Turn To Commentary*

This study comprises a series of critical commentaries to the earliest extant commentary to the biblical Book of Deuteronomy, the *Sifre (siprê děbê rab)*,[1] which is also one of our earliest compilations of rabbinic exegesis. Implicitly underlying the subsequent chapters with their close readings of discrete texts from the *Sifre* are questions of the nature, function, and purpose of this ancient commentary form: what, how, and with whom does it seek to communicate? Because, as we shall soon see, in antiquity, as today, there are many other ways to interpret a text, that is, to communicate what it is understood to mean, I shall also be asking implicitly: why choose commentary as the medium for such communication? Because I myself have adopted something of a commentary format (albeit very different from that of the *Sifre*) in explicating the commentary texts of the *Sifre*, these questions will ring doubly. My aim is to understand, in both literary and sociohistorical terms, the early rabbinic choice of scriptural commentary as a communicative medium, that is, to understand the dynamic workings of that medium as it was shaped by its rabbinic "authors" so as to engage its ancient (and I shall argue rabbinic) "readers" (by which I mean students). To do so I have chosen not to present the *Sifre* to you my readers as a panoramic whole, but to take you with me on a series of firsthand textual tours of some of its more striking landscapes, always with an eye to their broader cultural and sociohistorical settings, both within the larger text of the *Sifre* and without.[2]

Let me begin with a working definition of commentary as "a systematic series of explanations or interpretations (as of a writing)."[3] Of course, this definition tells us nothing of the methods or forms employed by such interpretations, how closely and in what manner they adhere to the text being interpreted or to one another, or the attitude of their authors toward that base-text or their intended audience. For all of these we can imagine many possibilities. But all commentaries so defined can be said to exhibit the following structural traits: they begin with an extended base-text, of which they designate successive subunits for exegetical attention, to each of which they attach a comment or chain of comments, which nevertheless remain distinct from the base-text, to which the commentary sooner or later returns (that is, advances) to take up the next selected subunit in sequence. Thus, the overall movement of the commentary follows to some degree, depending on how much of the base-text it comments upon, the progression of the base-text to which it attends. Herein lies what might be viewed as commentary's paradoxical nature: of necessity it fragmentizes its base-text in order to consider its parts in isolated detail, even as that base-text provides the overall structural framework in relation to which a collection of otherwise discrete and sometimes discordant comments acquire a *degree* of progressive continuity and at least external coherence.

Although today we might take for granted the commentary form as a way of interpreting a text, especially of Scripture, in postbiblical but prerabbinic varieties of Judaism, if we may judge from the extant literary evidence, it does not appear to have been the favored mode of scriptural interpretation. The majority, by far, of that interpretation (as of inner-biblical exegesis) takes the form of what has been called *rewritten Bible,*[4] which paraphrases the biblical text, whether as story or as law, in such a way as to blur the distinction between that text and its interpretation. It is *as if* the biblical text itself is replaced by its interpretive retelling. In some cases the "rewritten Bible" may follow the order of the biblical text upon which it appears to be based, filling in what are understood to be its gaps, clarifying what are understood to be its ambiguities, and leaving out what is deemed unneeding of retelling (e.g., the so-called *Genesis Apocryphon*, Pseudo-Philo's *Biblical Antiquities*). But in other cases the "rewritten Bible" may substantially rework the biblical order, blending together biblical texts from different locations even as those relocated biblical citations are exegetically paraphrased, thus concealing both the words of the Scripture and its order within its retelling (e.g., *The Temple Scroll* from Qumran).[5] Often the authority for such retelling is pseudepigraphically attributed to an inspired biblical figure (e.g., Enoch) or to God Himself (as, implicitly, in the *Temple Scroll*), thereby claiming for what to us appears as a retelling the status of actual revelation.[6]

Another form that also needs to be distinguished from the commentary is that of the homily or sermon. A preacher or teacher would begin with a particular biblical verse, story, or motif and weave round it a web of biblical citations, allusions, and interpretations, the organizing and unifying principle of which would be the thematic message he sought to convey. Although such a homily might depend heavily on biblical language and image for its rhetorical force, it would not direct its audience's attention to any successive biblical text per se. This may have been the dominant form of oral preaching and teaching in prerabbinic (Second Temple) times, say in the synagogues of Palestine.[7] These homilies may subsequently have been collected (or recollected) and edited so as to provide some of the materials out of which *literary* commentaries were later fashioned, but that is a different matter, and one for which we have little prerabbinic evidence, except as will soon be discussed.[8]

Similarly, the books of the New Testament contain,as is well known, extensive interpretations of the Hebrew Bible (Old Testament). However, their outer structure is not that of commenting on Scripture, but rather, in the case of the Gospels, of telling the story of Jesus' life and death, or, in the case of Acts and the Pauline Letters, of relating how his teachings were spread and the Church established after his death. This is not to minimize the role of scriptural interpretation in these writings but rather to stress that fragmented biblical interpretation and imagery is here incorporatied into the structure of a story, rather than fragmented stories incorporated into the structure of scriptural commentary, as is often the case in rabbinic commentary.[9]

Against this backdrop and in preparation for our study of the *Sifre*'s commentaries it is important to examine briefly the *only* two extant models of prerabbinic biblical commentary: the Dead Sea Scroll *pĕšārîm* and Philo's allegorical commentaries. Note that among the Dead Sea Scrolls the *pĕšārîm* represent a rather small, albeit important, part of the whole, whereas among Philo's extant writings, only about half of his treatises employ the commentary form, the others being no less exegetical but taking the form mainly of homiletical treatises on biblical motifs structured systematically rather than scripturally.[10]

The continuous *pĕšārîm* are commentaries to prophetic texts of Scripture (Habakkuk, Nahum, and Psalms being the most extensive and important).[11] They interpret the actual words of those books, sentence by sentence or phrase by phrase in succession, as signifying the events, groups, and persons that play key roles in the sacred history of the Dead Sea sect, some part of which presumably produced and studied these texts. The group's understanding of the revealed nature of these commentaries is best expressed in the following piece of *pēšer* commentary: "And God told Habakkuk to write down the things that are going to come upon the last generation, but the fulfillment of the end-time he did not make known to him. And when it says, 'So that he can run who reads it' (Hab. 2:2), the interpretation of it concerns (*pišrô ʿal*) the Teacher of Righteousness, to whom God made known all the mysteries of the words of His servants the prophets."[12] From this we see why the *pĕšārîm*, as continuous commentaries, apply to prophetic Scriptures.[13] These Scriptures, understood to communicate God's salvific plan for history, were thought to be veiled in mysterious language whose full meaning had not been disclosed to the prophets and their contemporaries but only subsequently to the Teacher of

Righteousness. He in turn, it is presumed, communicated them in the form of *pēšer* commentaries to his sectarian followers. These commentaries would enable the sectaries to understand their recent history and present circumstances as confirming rather than denying their elect self-understanding and to prepare for the "end of days," in which they thought themselves to be living and during which they expected, as God's chosen, soon to be vindicated for their exile and sufferings.[14] To give just one example (1QpHab (9.3–12):

> [A] When it says, "For you have plundered many nations, but all the rest of peoples will plunder you" (Hab. 2:8a), the interpretation of it concerns (*pišrô ʿal*) the last priests of Jerusalem, who amass wealth and profit from the plunder of the peoples; but at the end of days their wealth together with their booty will be given into the hand of the army of the Kittim [= the Romans]. For they are "the rest of the peoples."
>
> [B] "On account of human bloodshed and violence done to the land, the city, and all its inhabitants" (ibid., 8b). The interpretation of it concerns the [W]icked Priest, whom—because of wrong done to the Teacher of Righteousness and his partisans [or, council]—God gave into the hand of his enemies to humble him with disease for annihilation in despair, beca[u]se he had acted wickedly against his [= God's] chosen ones.

By dividing the verse (Hab. 2:8) into two halves and providing different significations for each, the *pēšer* enables the verse to refer both to the officiating Jerusalem priests of its own time ("the last priests of Jerusalem") and to the Wicked Priest in the time of the sect's "founder," the Teacher of Righteousness. By adjoining these two interpretations according to the scriptural order (the preceding interpretation took 2:8a to refer to the [Wicked] Priest as well), the *pēšer* implicitly enchains them, thereby associating, if not equating (1) the wickedness of the present priests with that of the Wicked Priest, (2) the expected punishments of the present priests with the already realized punishment of the Wicked Priest, and, more implicitly, (3) the sufferings of the *pēšer*'s audience with those of the Teacher and his associates (God's "chosen ones").

Many scholars have noted that both the term *pēšer* and the exegetical methods employed by the *pēšārîm* suggest an activity similar to that of dream, vision, or oracle interpretation, in which each symbolic detail in sequence is decoded; that is, assigned its concrete signification in the life of the dreamer or society for whom the oracle is intended.[15] In other words, the enigmatic terms of the original narrative, here the words of the prophet, are "translated" into the manifest language of a new narrative, here the life of the sect as revealed to their prophetic leader. Neither of these narratives is presented as a continuous whole, but each is fragmented so as to be systematically *interrelated*, but not integrated, point by point, with the other. The commentary form serves this successive decoding function well, for it *performatively* demonstrates, over and over again, the complete and absolute correspondence between the *words* of the original prophesy and its decoded fulfillment in the details of the sect's "story," through a terminology ("the interpretation of it concerns" and the like) that repeatedly connects the one to the other without collapsing the space between them.[16] Although the movement is from Scripture to the sociohistorical world of the sect (but then back again), it is as much the latter that is given deeper meaning by this interconnection as the former. If we presume, as I believe we can, that these texts functioned as part of the sect's "curriculum" of studies,[17] then this commentary structure would have the effect of repeatedly shuttling its students between the scriptural prophecies and their sociopolitical fulfillment in their collective life. Such engagement in the very activity of commentary would affectively reinforce the message that the *pĕšārîm* repeatedly convey: that the sectaries are justified in viewing and experiencing themselves as God's elect, for whose sake history, as foretold in the scriptural prophecies, was rapidly approaching its messianic consummation, when they would be vindicated and their enemies vanquished. This is very different from the converse procedure, whereby the sacred story of the sect might have been told, spiced with prophetic citations or allusions, to lend that story teleological significance as the final fulfillment of biblical prophecies.[18]

Given the above understanding of the function of the *pĕšārîm*, it is not surprising that these commentaries usually keep their interpretations short, returning without too much digression to the next unit of the prophetic base-verse. Also related to the oracular nature of the *pĕšārîm* is the fact that secondary verses, taken from entirely different parts of Scripture, are *not* drawn into the commentary, either to prove the interpretation of the prophetic lemma or to provide the exegetical basis for an associated point.[19] The exegetical focus is entirely on the prophetic base-verse and its equally prophetic decoding. This is in striking contrast with scriptural interpretation found elsewhere in the sectarian Dead Sea Scrolls, where the citation and interpretation of one verse may be enchained with that of another, often from a different part of Scripture.[20] As we shall soon see, this is also in contrast with the commentaries of Philo and with early rabbinic commentaries such as the *Sifre*. Finally, and perhaps most important, the oracular nature of the *pĕšārîm* requires that each phrase of the prophetic base-text usually receives a single, authoritative, declarative interpretation, for it is in that interpretation alone that the ancient prophecies are

understood to find their *completion*. The following threefold interpretation
therefore is an unusual exception (1QpHab 1.16-2.10), but one which
nevertheless proves the rule:

> "[Look, O traitors, and see; wonder and be amazed, for I am doing a deed in
> your days that you would not believe if] it were told" (Hab.1:5):
>   [A] [The interpretation of the passage concerns] the traitors together with
> the Man of the Lie, for [they did] not [believe the words of] the Teacher of
> Righteousness (which were) from the mouth of God.
>   [B] And it concerns (*wĕ'al*) the trai[tors to] the new [covenant,] f[o]r they
> were not faithful to the covenant of God, [but they profaned] his holy name.
>   [C] Likewise (*wĕkēn*), the interpretation of the passage (*pēšer haddābār*)
> [concerns the trai]tors at the end of days. They are the ruthless [ones of the
> coven]ant who will not believe when they hear all that is going to co[me up]on
> the last generation from the mouth of the priest into [whose heart] God put
> [understandi]ng to interpret (*lipšōr*) all the words of his servants the prophets
> by [whose] hand God enumerated all that is going to come upon his people and
> up[on his congregation].

The three enchained interpretations appear to represent not three separate
alternatives, but a chronological *sequence* in which the prophet's words are
applied to three groups of "traitors," or to one group at three times in the
sect's history: one at the time of the Teacher of Righteousness (A), one at a
time subsequent to that of the Teacher of Righteousness but prior to the
present of the commentary (B), and one at the end of days, yet before the
final judgment (C). In each case the "traitors" were/are oblivious to the
truth of the sect's understanding of Israel's covenant and sacred history.
The prophet's words not only foretell the history of the sect, but foretell a
threefold, repeated pattern, the last stage of which (C) has either already
begun or is imminent. Thus, the fact that the three interpretations are
presented in chronological order is not coincidental. By this structure the
commentary does not simply convey the base-text's meaning to its students
but conveys those very students, as it were, through the history of the sect
from its beginning through its more recent past to its imminent ending,
even while unifying that history in relation to the prophetic base-verse.
Although the lemma receives three distinct interpretations, presumably the
last interpretation is the final one to which the lemma is understood
principally to point. Having reached this final signification the *pēšer* closes
off the possibility of any others. Such a progressive movement of
commentary through a sequence of interpretations, although uncommon
in the Dead Sea *pĕšārîm* because of their oracular nature, provides a fitting
transition to the second major antecedent to the commentary of the *Sifre*,
the allegorical commentaries of Philo of Alexandria.[21]

Although the Dead Sea Scroll *pĕšārîm* are often adduced as the closest antecedents to midrashic (rabbinic) commentary,[22] in many ways the commentaries of Philo of Alexandria (ca. 20 *B.C.E.*–ca. 50 *C.E.*) offer a more important corpus for purposes of comparison and contrast, in part because of their greater volume, but also because they attend, as do our earliest rabbinic collections of commentary, not to prophetic books (the sole focus of the continuous *pĕšārîm* commentaries) but to the Torah (Pentateuch).[23] That Philo is our most prolific early Jewish writer of biblical commentaries is most likely related to the fact that Alexandria in his time was a major center of textural scholarship, much of which took the form of running commentaries (*hypomnēmata*) to classical Greek texts, as it had been for at least two centuries earlier.[24] That Philo focuses entirely on the books of the Torah is related to his highest regard for the divinely inspired, philosopher-lawgiver Moses, whom he understands to have deeply impressed in his writings the original and most complete imprint of the divine logos.

I would like to focus briefly on three structural features of Philo's commentaries that distinguish them from the *pĕšārîm* and that are shared, mutatis mutandis, by early rabbinic scriptural commentary, as we shall soon see in our studies of the *Sifre*.

First, Philo's commentaries are dialectical in style and form. Often, after the lemma is cited a rhetorical question or problem is raised regarding one of its "literal" (i.e., physical, external) meanings. The body of the commentary advances one or more allegorical (i.e., spiritual, internal) interpretations of the lemma as either an answer to the question or an obviation of the problem. This form is especially evident in Philo's *Questions and Answers on Genesis* and *Exodus*, but has been shown to form the underlying structure of the more complex allegorical commentaries as well. This is not to deny that Philo employs deictic exegesis, that is, the demonstrative linking of a biblical word or phrase with its meaning ("that is," "this means," etc.). Rather, it is to stress that this form does not define the structure of his commentaries overall as it does the Qumran *pĕšārîm*. The question and answer structure, even if wooden, at least creates the impression of dialogue between the author and Scripture, as well as between the author and the readers. It opens the lemma to interpretation and draws the reader into that activity. It is of course a common rhetorical device in Greek philosophical literature,[25] as in early rabbinic commentary.[26]

Second, Philo's allegorical commentaries, but not his more succinct *Questions and Answers on Genesis* and *Exodus*, frequently cite other verses from the Pentateuch in addressing an exegetical question or problem initially raised with respect to the lemma or in supplementing an initial interpretation of the lemma. The link between the lemma and the other verse may be verbal or thematic. But unlike contemporary philosophical texts, where Homer may be cited to interpret Homer or Plato to interpret Plato, these secondary verses themselves often become the objects of Philo's interpretation, sometimes in the form of another question or problem. Such concatenation or enchaining of interpretations can at times be extreme, appearing to lead the reader far from the base-verse and its initial interpretation(s). But this practice is clearly understood by Philo as necessary to uncovering, if not completely, the more profound hidden meanings that lie deeply embedded within the lemma, to which he eventually returns.[27] Although this procedure of interpreting Scripture with Scripture is completely absent from the continuous *pěšārîm*, it is, as we shall see, a common feature of early rabbinic commentary.[28] In all of these cases (Philonic, philosophic, and rabbinic) the practice of interpreting one text with its canonical kin both presumes and seeks to prove the overall unity and self-reflexivity of the textual corpus being commented upon, thereby affirming its complete and self-contained authority. This practice also presumes and seeks to cultivate in its audience a familiarity and competence with that corpus.

Third, Philo's allegorical commentaries commonly give multiple interpretations of the lemma. In his most basic form of commentary these multiple senses, or levels of meaning, comprise the literal, or physical, and the allegorical, or spiritual, usually presented in that order. Very often, but not always, the adduced literal meaning is either mundanely clear and hence insufficient or problematic and hence improbable, in either case requiring Philo, in his commitment to the Scripture's revelatory purpose, to uncover the text's deeper, under-sense (*hyponoia*). Sign posts to this under-sense are to be found in the Scriptural text itself. In other words, the lemma's literal meaning is often considered by Philo not to tell the whole story but to point beyond itself to it. Therefore, the search for the symbolic or allegorical level of meaning cannot begin until the biblical text is first engaged and questioned at its literal level of signification. In the more complex forms of his allegorical commentary, Philo often suggests multiple meanings, *both* at and beyond the literal levels, often enchaining them in hierarchical order, ascending as might the soul from most physical to most metaphysical levels. But Philo sometimes simply sets such alternative literal and symbolic meanings alongside one another as equal, even contradictory alternatives, attributing them sometimes to different *anonymous* exegetes ("some say," "others say").[29] However, even with such concatenation of interpretations, or levels of sense, Philo never claims to have exhausted the biblical text's possible meanings. Even when he clearly favors his own, final allegorical interpretation over those that have preceded it, he leaves open the possibility of still other, yet deeper meanings to be uncovered, or better ways to express what has already been uncovered. Both of these concessions are related not so much to Philo's personal modesty as to his view of the inadequacy of language to represent in direct correspondence the truth that the inspired soul, whether that of Moses or of Philo as the interpreter of his words, can apprehend.[30] This open-ended practice of multiple interpretations and levels of interpretation, the product of a succession of biblical interpreters to whom Philo acknowledges his debt even while claiming superiority for his own added level of nonworldly interpretation, contrasts sharply with what we witnessed of the Dead Sea *pĕšārîm*, with their presumption that the words of the biblical prophets had been directly, univocally, and finally decoded so as to point to a particular set of "historical" (sectarian) referents. In many ways Philo's practice of multiple interpretations is closer to that of the early rabbinic commentaries (such as that of the *Sifre*), but with the following crucial difference: Philo's privileging progression from literal to allegorical interpretations, as well as among the latter, finds no simple rabbinic analogue.[31]

The structural complexity and diversity of Philo's allegorical commentaries make it more difficult than with the *pĕšārîm* to exemplify economically the preceding characterizations. The following passage, by containing something of each of these above features and by being relatively succinct, is as good an example for our purposes as any.[32] It comments on Gen. 15:15, wherein God promises to Abraham: "Thou shalt depart to thy fathers nourished with peace, in a goodly old age."

> After "thou shalt depart" come the words "to thy fathers." What fathers? this is worth inquiring. For Moses could not mean those who had lived in the land of the Chaldeans, who were the only kinsfolk Abraham had, seeing that the oracle had set his dwelling away from all those of his blood. For we read, "the Lord said unto Abraham 'depart from thy land and from they kinsfolk and from the house of thy father unto the land which I shall shew thee, and I will make thee into a great nation'"(Gen. 12:1, 2). Was it reasonable that he should again have affinity with the very persons from whom he had been alienated by the forethought of God? Or that he who was to be the captain of another race and nation should be associated with that of a former age?[33] ... No; by "fathers" he does not mean those whom the pilgrim soul has left behind, those who lie buried in the sepulchres of Chaldaea, but possibly, as some say, the sun, moon and other stars to which it is held that all things on earth owe their birth and framing, or as others think, the archetypal ideas which, invisible and intelligible *there*, are the patterns of things visible and sensible *here*—the idea in which, as they say, the mind of the Sage finds its new home.
> Others again have surmised that by "fathers" are meant the first principles

and potentialities, from which the world has been framed, earth, water, air and
fire. For into these, they say, each thing that has come into being is duly
resolved. Just as nouns and verbs and all parts of speech which are composed
of the "elements" in the grammatical sense are finally resolved into the same, so
too each of us is composed of the four mundane elements, borrowing small
fragments from the substance of each, and this debt he repays when the
appointed time-cycles are completed, rendering the dry in him to earth, the wet
to water, the cold to air, and the warm to fire. These all belong to the body, but
the soul whose nature is intellectual and celestial will depart to find a father in
ether, the purest of the substances. For we may suppose that, as the men of old
declared, there is a fifth substance, moving in a circle, differing by its quality
from the four. Out of this they thought the stars and the whole of heaven had
been made and deduced as a natural consequence that the human soul also was
a fragment thereof.[34]

What is of interest here is the way in which the commentary
dialectically progresses from the first rejected meaning (*fathers* as
Abraham's biological ancestors), through a series of more symbolic but not
yet allegorical meanings suggested by other exegetes (*fathers* as, successively, the heavenly bodies, the archetypal ideas, and the physical
elements), and finally to what we must presume is Philo's own allegorical
preference (*fathers* as the heavenly ether from which the perceptible world
was born and to which the soul seeks to return). This exegetical progression
through multiple interpretations parallels, in a sense, the journey of the
soul itself as it leaves its physical confines to return to its spiritual source.
Put differently, the "breaking-open"[35] of the text of lemma, initiated by a
questioning of its literal probability, is necessary in order to begin the
process whereby its deeper sense will eventually be disclosed, just as the
final dissolution of the body at death into its constitutive elements is
necessary in order to release its soul for return to its ethereal source. In both
cases the progression is of necessity by stages. Philo does not so much reject
the interpretation of his predecessors as step upon them to arrive at his own
interpretation. Even in this progression the chain of interpretations
oscillates between physical and spiritual poles until it finally reaches its
destination: from heavenly, but still physical, bodies to archetypal ideas,
and from the mundane elements to the purest of elements, ether. It is not, in
the end, that Abraham is promised a return to the heavenly bodies, as first
suggested, but that his soul alone should return to its ethereal origins, the
origins as well of the heavenly bodies. If there is something circular in this
interpretation, beginning and ending with the heavenly bodies, then
commentary is circular in yet another way, for the return of the soul to its
ethereal source is suggested but not quite realized when Philo must return,

as the commentary form demands, to the text of Scripture, to confront its literal sense once again.[36]

We see, if not experience, here something of the performative aspect of Philo's employment of commentary: the overall progression in each unit of commentary from literal to allegorical, whatever its internal delays, is facilitated by the succession of alternative interpretations. This exegetical movement is by a series of steps, like the spiritual progression from fleshly trappings to ethical and spiritual perfection, with each such step, whether through the text or through being, requiring atttentive effort. This interpretive struggle must be repeated over and over again, even if on the broader plane of scriptural commentary there is net progress, as symbolized for Philo by the chronological progression of biblical characters, each of whom represents an ever higher virtue and state of the soul.[37]

Even though Philo clearly favors the allegorical level of interpretation, it cannot be attained without first engaging the text of Scripture and its literal meanings, whose validity Philo acknowledges even as he finds them insufficient. This is the exegetical equivalent of the tension Philo acknowledges between the observance of the commandments and the apprehension of their metaphysical significance. In a famous passage in which he criticizes those whose preoccupation with the allegorical interpretation of laws leads them to neglect their literal sense as requiring observance, Philo counsels dual aims: "[to give] a more full and exact investigation of what is not seen [= the allegorical] and in what is seen [= the literal] to be stewards without reproach."[38] After giving as examples the observance of Sabbath, festivals, circumcision, and Temple worship he concludes:

> Nay, we should look on all these outward observances as resembling the body, and their inner meaning as resembling the soul. It follows that, exactly as we have to take thought for the body, because it is the abode of the soul, so we must pay heed to the letter of the laws (*phētoi nomoi*). If we keep and observe these, we shall gain a clearer conception of those things of which these are the symbols; and besides that we shall not incur the censure of the many and the charges they are sure to bring against us.

It is impossible, according to Philo, for one to *bypass* the body, observances, or the literal meanings of Scripture in striving to move beyond them in pursuit of virtue and wisdom: in a sense, one must move *through* them.[39] We may infer that just as observance of the commandments is *necessary* to comprehending and attaining the virtues for which they sympolically stand, so, too, directly engaging the text of Scripture and its literal interpretations is a *necessary* prerequisite to progressing to the deeper levels of meaning embedded therein. Such literal engagement, over and over again, as the necessary first step in the scriptural-spiritual journey of the soul, can be achieved through the structures of commentary, especially in its atomization of the text of Scripture and subsequent concatenation of interpretations, as not in other, more distilled forms of exegesis, which Philo practices as well. Scriptural commentary in its practice would appear parallel to observance of the commandments in its performative power and necessity, seeking to make of Philo's readers "stewards" of the text even as they looked and moved beyond it.

Thus far I have stressed the performative and transformative functioning of Philo's allegorical commentaries vis-à-vis his individual reader, reflecting I believe Philo's own preoccupation with the intellectual, ethical, and spiritual progress of the individual soul toward perfection and completion. Nevertheless, the *sociohistorical* functioning of such commentary structures should not be ignored. Philo seeks to convince his fellow Alexandrian Jews that the two cultures, Jewish and Greek, which compete (however equally or unequally) for their attention are in essence one. Moses alone, the supreme philosopher and lawgiver, had the divine logos imprinted upon his soul, which he in turn has imprinted within the text of his Torah, which in turn can leave its imprint on the soul of the individual and the life of the community that exegetically and performatively engage it.[40] All other expressions of wisdom, however profound or pleasing, are mere shadows of that of Moses' Torah. But because this might not be obvious to those who have no guide in uncovering these teachings hidden beneath the letters of Scripture's laws and narratives, Philo offers himself as the supremely qualified guide for his time, endeavoring to demonstrate to his audience that whatever surrounding Greek culture has to offer can be obtained in purer and more original form in Israel's own scriptural heritage. To sustain this argument, Philo undertakes what amounts to a major translation project, rendering Scripture into the best cultural vernacular (as he regarded it) of his hellenistically educated or exposed public. And because his argument is not simply about the contents of Scripture, but about the status of its text as that central symbol which defines Israel and distinguishes the Jewish community from its neighbors, that translation had to take, at least in part, the form of dialogical engagement with the text—and not simply a distilled paraphrase of it—as well as with the received local traditions of its interpretation. In other words, Philo sought in the structure of commentary, itself *adapted* from wider Greek usage,[41] a performative instrument with which to link for his readers the language of Jewish Scripture to the language of high Greek culture (primarily philosophical) as he understood it, without dissolving the difference between them and while asserting the primacy of the former and the *derivativeness* of the latter.[42]

Returning to our earliest rabbinic commentaries, and to the *Sifre* in particular, we see that when compared to their *only* two Jewish antecedents—the commentaries of *pēšer* and Philo—they display common as well as distinctive traits, it being important not to stress one in desregard for the other.[43] Both deictic and dialogical forms of exegesis, the former characterizing overall the *pěšārîm* and the latter Philo's allegorical commentaries, are found in the *Sifre*. Although they often appear alongside one another in comments to adjacent lemmata, they are also frequently combined in the commentary to a single lemma. For example, the *Sifre*'s commentary may definitively proclaim what a word or phrase signifies, and then question that assigned meaning or set another, even discordant, meaning dialectically alongside it.[44] Still, the dialogical mode typically characterizes the *Sifre*'s commentary, even as it frequently employs the deictic. In this way the structure of the *Sifre*'s commentary is closer overall to that of Philo than to that of *pēšer*. Not surprisingly, therefore, two other dialogical features of Philo's (and non-Jewish philosophical) commentaries, absent from the *pěšārîm* commentaries, are also found in the *Sifre*, albeit with important differences: the interpretation of Scripture with Scripture and the concatenation of multiple interpretations.[45] But it is precisely with regard to multiple interpretations that the *Sifre*'s commentary, and early rabbinic commentary more generally, are significantly different from those of Philo. In the *Sifre*, as we shall repeatedly see, multiple interpretations or their sub-groupings may be ordered editorially so as to be encountered in progression, but not according to any standard hierarchical principle or plan (e.g., literal followed by symbolic, or ascending levels of symbolic). Before turning to this difference, however, there is something else to be learned from our brief look at the commentaries of *pēšer* and Philo as antecedents to that of the *Sifre*.

Ancient scriptural commentaries—and others may wish to extend this point to other kinds of commentary but I am ill-equipped to do so—even as they closely scrutinize the particles of the text to which they attend, are always about that text as a *whole*. By this I mean that they not only seek for the text to he held in high regard by its interpretive community, but for the interpretive community to regard *itself* in relation to that text as mediated by its commentary. In other words, such a commentary is not simply a series of declarative assertions about the meanings of words or clusters of words in a text but an attempt to *effect* a relationship between that text overall and those for whom it is "scripture," predicated on the assumption not only that that text needs and deserves to be interpreted, but that the community for whom it needs to be interpreted itself needs to be engaged in tha activity of interpretation to understand itself and *transform* itself into what it ought to be. Ancient scriptural commentaries are not simply constative conduits of meaning—and I in no way wish to deny this function—but also performative media by which the polymorphic "world" of the text and that of its students are transformatively brought toward each other, while never fully merged, so as to confront each other through the double-dialogue of commentary.[46] By *double-dialogue* I mean that the commentary simultaneously faces and engages the text that it interprets and the society of "readers" for whom and with whom it interprets. I employ the term *dialogue* here somewhat fictively, as we do not simply have in commentary two voices equally present and responsive to one another. Rather I intend the term to denote the dynamic, interrelational ways in which commentary creates and communicates meaning. Such meaning is not simply inherent in the text being interpreted and brought to the surface by the commentary, nor is it simply produced by the commentary and conveyed monologically to its readers, nor is it simply produced by such readers in their reading of the commentary. Rather, it is to be found in all three, and especially in the in-between working space, or socially situated discursive universe, that the commentary progressively constructs by inter-responsively drawing together and engaging the polyphonic world of Scripture with that of its students—divine will and presence with human society.[47]

By focusing attention on this *double-facing* character of ancient scriptural commentary (and I shall shortly indicate a third facing) I wish to avoid, in the following chapters, two tendencies in scholarly understanding and employment of such commentary: what I would call the hermeneuticist and historicist fallacies. The former tendency is to see the commentary primarily in its facing toward Scripture and to view hermeneutical practice as if conducted within a sociohistorical isolation booth into which only the commentator and the chosen text, or self-contained corpus of texts, are allowed entrance. The latter tendency is to see th commentary primarily in its facing toward the events or circumstances of its time, and to view its response to and representation of those events as being only slightly veiled by the formal guise of the scriptural exegesis in which it is wrapped. The former claims to have explained the commentary when it has identified hermeneutical pressures within Scripture and the commentary's responses to those. The latter claims to have explained the commentary when it has identified historical pressures outside of Scripture and the commentary's responses to those.[48]

These two tendencies, even as they face, and view commentary as facing, opposition directions, are really two sides of the same coin. That is the coin that presumes that the hermeneutics and historicity of scriptural commentary can conveniently and neatly be detached from one another, in the first case by viewing the hermeneutics of commentary's *interpretations* apart from the sociohistorical grounding of its performance and in the second by viewing the historicity of commentary's *representations* apart from the hermeneutical grounding of its performance. One consequence of this common position is the view that such a text, whether as a whole or in its parts, is either hermeneutical or historiographic, either facing in upon itself and the texts with which it intersects or out upon history and society. The former kind of text is of interest to the student of literature, the latter to the student of history.[49] The former kind of text is detached from or indifferent to history, the latter is directly engaged with it.[50]

I wish to deny neither of these facings or groundings, but to assert their inextricable interconnection. The following chapters presume, and I hope will demonstrate, that their bifurcation, although perhaps useful for the self-confirming maintenance of our disciplinary boundaries, reductively distort the *Sifre's* hermeneutical and historical aspects by viewing them in isolation from one another. Such a text of scriptural commentary may be seen as reflecting on and responding to its sociohistorical setting no less significantly, even if less directly and more complexly, than a continuous narration of the same. Such a text's form of discourse, when viewed in temporal relation to its antecedents as well as to the sociocultural circumstances of its creation and reception, may represent as much of an event as any event it could represent.[51]

Let us return then to the characteristic of early rabbinic commentary that is most distinctive when viewed in comparison with its antecedents and most significant, I shall argue, when considered it relation to its sociocultural context, that being its multiplicity of interpretations. I shall be intentionally brief here to allow the argument to unfold in relation to specific texts of the *Sifre* that we will examine at close range in the following chapters.[52]

The feature of the *Sifre's* multiple interpretations of scriptural words and phrases needs to be viewed in relation to its anthological or collective nature more generally. Not only are multiple interpretations often provided for a given lemma, but even within a single interpretation diverse types of materials are often combined in such ways that the unspecified nature of their interconnections is unlear. For example, a verse other than that being commented upon may be introduced and interpreted without it being stated how that verse and its interpretation relate to the primary verse and its interpretation. Similarly, a parable, story, saying, or rule may be adduced in relation to the interpretation of a verse of Scripture without it being clear exactly how what has been added fits or contributes to the exegetical context. Even where a verse is minutely divided and a different brief interpretation is offered for each of its atomized parts, the student of the text is left uncertain whether or not, and if so how, those interpretations should be understood in relation to one another. There can be no question that rabbinic commentary's practice of providing a multiplicity of meanings for a given scriptural fragment raises a distinctive set of theological-hermeneutical issues, to be treated in the subsequent chapters. However, this phenomenon must be seen in relation to the more general character of the commentary as a collective combining of heterogeneous and at times discordant traditions, some clearly editorially interconnected and others simply (it would seem) juxtaposed. What is the balance between these two manners of editorial combination, of both of which we shall see many examples? To what extent do we have a collection of independent exegetical assertions and traditional recollections that have been strung together for no appartent reason other than to preserve them, and to what extent do we have, as we saw in *pēšer* and in Philo, the editorial enchaining of traditions and interpretations for other purposes, presumably rhetorical, as well? Our difficulty in answering this question lies in part in our frequent lack of an authorial voice to tell us how to proceed from one such assertion to the next, how as interpreters of the commentary, to fill the connective gaps between the traditions set before us.

In this regard, let us return briefly to our two Jewish commentary antecedents. The Dead Sea *pěšārîm*, as we saw, present themselves as the authoritative decodings of scriptural prophecies, having been revealed by God to the Teacher of Righteousness, who in turn passed them on to his followers. The editorial voice that repeatedly links each lemma to its historical signification in the life of community is assumed to be, or at least to have the authority of, the Teacher.[53] The pattern is so standard, that even if we cannot discern what precisely in the lemma is "producing" its interpretation, or how one interpretation specifically relates to its neighbor, the overall relation of prophetic Scripture to its commentary, and of that commentary to its community of students fits within an overarching hermeneutical plan that is self-evident: together the commentary's interpretations add up to the prophetically prefigured and now disclosed sacred history of the sect as God's elect in the end of days. Similarly, but somewhat differently, Philo's allegorical commentaries are presented as the work of a single author, even though he incorporates the interpretations of "others."[54] Philo is clearly our tour guide, who tells us when he is moving from one level of interpretation to another, and why he is citing another scriptural verse and its interpretation. We often may wonder why Philo leads us so far afield, and how to connect our tour of one verse with that of the next, but at least we know that it is he who is leading us. Once again, there is degree of predictability, albeit less so than with the *pěšārîm*, as he repeatedly takes us from lemma, to questioning its literal meaning, to providing a chain of symbolic meanings, often in ascending order. That the overall route of the commentary is also that of the journey of the soul to moral and spiritual perfection is likewise clear.

By contrast, the *Sifre*'s commentary presents itself, implicity to be sure, as the *collective* and *cumulative* teachings of the class of rabbinic sages, even as those teachings are understood to originate in the revelation at Sinai. Already in the *Sifre*, sinaitic revelation is re-presented as being twofold: that which was immediately inscribed as Scripture and that which as oral teaching achieved its socially available expression only over time.[55] Between Sinai and the time of the text's redaction (mid-third century C.E.[56]) there stands no single individual who is said to have authored the commentary or to have authorized its interpretations. In other words, the commentary lacks an identifiable narrating voice.[57] Certainly, individual interpretations are often, but not usually, attributed to named sages, living between the first and early third centuries C.E. Someone (or a group or series of someones) redacted the text as we have it, collecting, selecting, ordering, and subtly reshaping the interpretations that were to be included, but that redactor (or series of redactors) intentionally, we must presume, hid his (their) identity, precisely to maintain the impression that the text before us is a collective, traditional one, constituting "words of Torah." Thus, whereas in the *pĕšārîm* and Philo the overall commentary is attributed to a single authoritative voice and the constitutive interpretations are unattributed, in the *Sifre* precisely the reverse occurs. We have no overall tour guide to tell us why we are moving from one interpretation or tradition to the next or where we are heading. Nor do the succession of enchained or juxtaposed interpretations and traditions, and the variety of formal structures and discursive modes by which they are expressed, follow a standard pattern that would simply allow for a self-guided tour. Likewise, unlike the commentaries of the *pĕšārîm* or of Philo, early rabbinic midrashic commentaries such as the *Sifre* do not permit the identification of a single, totalizing hermeneutical principle (or "mastercode"), whether typological or allegorical, under which to subsume the text's formal and interpretive pluralities.[58]

This collective nature of the *Sifre*'s commentary gives the impression not of a single commentator standing face to face with the text of Scripture in the unmediated work of interpretation (as if such were ever fully possible), but of a collector and subtle shaper of received *traditions* who creates a commentary out of such traditions by configuring them not only in relation to the atomized texts of Deuteronomy but also in relation to one another. This is the third facing to which I alluded earlier. To what extent did such a redactor, or series of redactors, feel constrained by the authority of the traditions he inherited—understood as tracing back ultimately to the revelation at Sinai—and sought to transmit, and to what extent did he feel free to pick and choose among them, to rearrange them, and to transform them, even if subtly, in his work of commentary? This is the dialectic of continuity and innovation that characterizes the stance of a sociohistorically grounded traditionality, one to which we will repeatedly return in the following chapters. Here I simply wish to stress that if we view scriptural commentary as dialogically engaging a biblical text from the past with the present society of its students, then in the case of the *Sifre* (and other early rabbinic commentaries) what mediates between the multivocality of the former and that of the latter is not the single guiding voice of an authoritative interpreter (such as Philo or the Teacher of Righteousness) but the multivocality of a received yet restless tradition.[59]

I also wish to stress something else: the collective and hence multivocal nature of the *Sifre*'s text is not just a matter of its authoring or redaction, but also of its audience. I shall argue that the implied audience of that text was first and foremost the collectivity or class of rabbinic sages and their disciples of mid-third century Palestine, even as the creators of our commentary hoped that it would have a life extending well beyond such time and place.[60] The *Sifre* uses several metaphors to describe the study activity of such sages and their disciples. They are to attend constantly to "words of Torah" (both scriptural and rabbinic), working and reworking them like a farmer does his field or vineyard, lest they go to ruin (be forgotten or confused with false teachings).[61] Thus, the first task of the sage is to maintain the words of Torah that he has learned by continually reviewing them, poring over them, to the point of fully absorbing them into his person (i.e., memory).[62] Then, having them ever ready in his "mouth," he can disseminate them as needed.[63] In this activity the sage is compared to a well, that constantly gathers waters (teachings) from all sides, so that once full he can disperse those waters to his disciples. Alternatively, the sage is a sponge, who absorbs *everything*, and not only what he needs for the moment or what his own teacher teaches.[64] Note the two-step procedure: gathering and disseminating, joining and dividing. Water is a particularly apt image for this activity because it can be collected, and hence kept and even transported in bulk, while remaining ever ready to be dispersed in smaller, more manageable quantities.[65] Similarly, the collectivity of rabbinic teachings, some of which may directly contradict others, are compared to a mixture of flour, bran, and meal, which the disciple sorts out with a sieve. Here the disciple has the *active* role of sorting and weighing the incommensurate rabbinic teachings that are gathered before him. Interestingly, the disciple in this tradition does not so much correspond to the person who does the sorting as to the *sieve* itself, as if to say that the disciple sorts and weighs teachings as they pass *through* him.[66].

These descriptions of rabbinic study can be taken to describe the "production" of the text of commentary before us, wherein diverse rabbinic traditions—diverse in form as well as in content—have been gathered, sorted out in exegetical relation to the verses of Deuteronomy, arranged in juxtaposition to one another, and often subtly reshaped in the process. Only so contained could their preservation and availability *through continuous study* be ensured. But to the extent that these gathered, arranged, and reshaped traditions still do not fully cohere or concord with one another, or for that matter with the verses of Deuteronomy to which they are attached, then the preceding descriptions of rabbinic study can be taken to describe as well the dialogical "consumption" of the text of commentary by the plurality of its students. They, the rabbinic disciples in particular, in dynamically working their way through the collected traditions of the commentary in relation to one another as to Scripture, continue the interpretive process of gathering and weighing, connecting and differentiating, that the redacted text itself has set in motion *but not completed.* These students, in socially enacting the text through their engaged study of it, advance its unfinished work by filling out (but never finally) the anonymous narrative voice that is only partially present in the text itself. The dialectical dynamic of such study leads to the transformative internalization and actualization of the commentary's interplaying network of traditions (and perspectives) within its students, who, like their text of study, thereby become one notwithstanding plurality. In a sense, as they work through the commentary the commentary works throught them.

We gain here a glimpse of the literary face of an otherwise oral circulatory system of study and teaching by whose illocutionary force disciples became sages and sages became a class that could extend their teachings, practices, and view of the world into Jewish society more broadly.[67] But that larger world—in its recalled past, experienced present, and desired future—was neither simple nor static, itself comprising a dangerous complex of discordant strands or voices in need of sense-making configuration. As we shall repeatedly see, the rabbinic work of dynamically configuring the heterogeneity of tradition is related to the rabbinic work of postitively positioning Israel as a whole within the heterogenious web of history and nature. If the work of commentary was to contribute to the solidification of a society of sages that desired to constitute Israel's leadership, then it needed to provide those sages not only with a performative medium for their own shared self-understanding, but also with one by which they could effectively fashion for larger Israel a supple self-understanding that would make sense in and of the world, both presently and across time.[68]

Such a medium requires that heterogeneous traditions (whether legal, exegetical, or anecdotal), whose oral origins we can only guess, be contained but not congealed within the structural framework of ongoing scriptural commentary. Thus rendered accessible but remaining fluid these traditions might be dynamically absorbed by the students of the commentary as they pore over it in their own repetitive acts of interpretive study, or transformative re-cognition. These students, in turn, might return the rabbinic "words of Torah" that they have absorbed back out into the oral circulatory system of rabbinic society and beyond in new combinations and reshapings, which might eventually be collected and configured once again to form another literary work of commentary, whether to Deuteronomy or to another text altogether.[69]

This circulatory view of the *Sifre*'s commentary requires that we ourselves, in the following chapters, comment upon discrete texts of the *Sifre* from two converging perspectives, that of their formation and that of their reception. By the first I mean attention to how otherwise discrete and sometimes discordant traditions have been redactionally combined and to varying degrees configured to form a running commentary to the text of Deuteronomy. There are two ways to discern such activity. The first looks *within* the immediate text for editorial signposts, such as linguistic, structural, or thematic links and repetitions that connect adjacent traditions beyond the mere fact of their physical juxtaposition. The second looks *without* the text to other rabbinic texts of the same vintage (and in some cases chronologically proximate nonrabbinical texts) in which related traditions have been differently combined and subtly reshaped to produce different rhetorical effects. Through such comparison and contrast it is possible to see both the relative freedom and the limits to that freedom by which *Sifre*'s editors were able to fashion commentary out of tradition.[70]

The second perspective that we shall adopt is that of the rabbinic student of the text of the *Sifre*, putting ourselves in the position of one who in progressively working through the text of commentary seeks to understand its contained traditions in relation both to one another, fore and aft, and to the text of Scripture, both fragmented and continuous, upon which it comments. In a sense, such a student of our text is drawn into the work of its commentary so as to provide the missing voice that variously joins together *and* differentiates between what has already been gathered and arranged before him. If we assume that the *Sifre* in describing the study activity of the sages and their disciples also describes how its own text of Torah teaching ought to be studied by its students, then we cannot understand the social work of that commentary without attempting to pose ourselves in the place of such students, even as we employ the distancing tools of the first perspective of intra- and intertextural critical analysis as controls.

This, of course, is a dangerous task, but no less so than the task of any historian who tries to understand an ancient society by viewing it from "within," even while acknowledging and maintaining his or her distance from it. Here I wish to strike a cautionary note. By heuristically posing ourselves in the position of the ancient students of the text we cannot pretend to *be* such students, exhaustively uncovering in any simple way what would have been its single "original" meaning to them. Our distance from the ancient text of the *Sifre* and its sociocultural setting, as well as the ambiguities of its own anthological multivocality, precludes such certainty and closure.[71] What we *can* seek is a self-consciously modest understanding of what and how that text might have communicated within the broader paramaters and paradigms of meaning and discourse defined by the ancient linguistic and sociocultural matrices of which that text is a part and in which and by which it would have been understood—even as we admit the hermeneutical circularity of our *reconstructing* of those matrices through our reading of such texts. This is simply to acknowledge that any discrete text of tradition and commentary might "mean more than it says" once it is encountered within such broader interassociative frames, beginning with those of the surrounding *Sifre* commentary and extending to other proximate rabbinic collections and configurations of tradition, midrashic as well as nonmidrashic.[72] This is not to suggest a harmonizing approach, but simply one that recognizes that no discrete text is ever understood monologically "in its own terms," but always dialogically in terms of the larger matrices of signification in which it is set and to which it contributes, however complexly. For us foreigners, that setting—in all its diversity and discordancy—is accessible to us mainly in the wider range of rabbinic texts, which like a succession of concentric yet interlocking circles frame the discourse of any particular text and thereby shape our expectations of it, even as those expectations are continually challenged by it.[73]

Thus, my own commentary to that of the *Sifre* will be seen to be somewhat dialogical, alternating between the perspectives of the text's formation and reception, as between that of the ancient student of the text and the modern critic of it. By means of this perspectival shuttle I will seek to make both hermeneutical and historical sense of the *Sifre*'s commentary in relation to its ancient setting without claiming reductively to have exhausted or mastered either. If, as I will argue, our commentary's chief "intent" (or purpose) was to engage dialogically its ancient rabbinic students in the reconstructive and redemptive work of its interpretation, then my own intent is not only to disclose something of how the *Sifre*'s commentary interprets Scripture, but also to demonstrate how it involves the interpretive collaboration of its students in the ongoing advancement of that work in such a way as to advance their own socioreligious self-understanding.[74] I see no way out of the methodological difficulties of this task, at least not if we wish to ask how the *Sifre*'s commentary might have *functioned* as such, that is, how it would have performed its transformative work of interpretation not only in relation to the text of Deuteronomy but also in relation to the society of interpreters whom we know as the rabbinic sages and their disciples. The social construction and solidification of that subculture, in significant measure through its collective self-representing work of Torah study, was regarded by the rabbinic shapers of the *Sifre*'s commentary as a necessary precondition for their command, in turn and in time, of a similar transformation of Israelite culture and society overall. The rabbinic creators of our commentary sought not simply to transmit correct interpretations of Scripture, but to instruct by engaging their students, deeply and dialogically, in a particular way of Torah study that they considered to be of sacred-historical consequence.

From this it should be clear why I have chosen not to speak reductively either of midrash or of the *Sifre* in the lump, but rather to present for patient commentary a sizable selection of the *Sifre*'s commentary texts.[75] My own intent is not to close those texts to alternative interpretations but to open them through such commentary to a particular way of critical study that I consider to be of cultural-historical consequence. Roland Barthes, in introducing a very different sort of commentary to a very different sort of "classic" text (Balzac's *Sarrasine*), writes as follows:

> If we want to remain attentive to the plural of a text (however limited it may be), we must renounce structuring this text in large masses.... The commentary on a single text is not a contingent activity, assigned the reassuring alibi of the "concrete":...the one text is not an (inductive) access to a Model, but entrance into a network with a thousand entrances; to take this entrance is to aim, ultimately, not at a legal structure of norms and departures, a narrative or poetic Law, but at a perspective (of fragments, of voices from other texts, other codes), whose vanishing point is nonetheless ceaselessly pushed back, mysteriously opened: each (single) text is the very theory (and not the mere example) of this vanishing, of this difference which indefinitely returns, insubmissive. Further, to study this text down to the last detail is to...assume the power (the time, the elbow room) of working back along the threads of meanings, of abandoning no site of the signifier without endeavoring to ascertain the code or codes of which this site is perhaps the starting point (or the goal): it is (at least we may hope as much, and work to this end) to substitute for the simple representative model another model, whose very gradualness would guarantee what may be productive in the classic text;...it is, finally, in the very writing of the commentary, a systematic use of digression (a form ill-accommodated by the discourse of knowledge) and thereby a way of observing the reversibility of the structures from which the text is woven; of course, the classic text is incompletely reversible (it is modestly plural): the reading of this text occurs within a necessary order, which the gradual analysis will make precisely its order of writing; but the step-by-step commentary is of

necessity a renewal of entrances to the text, it avoids structuring the text *excessively*, avoids giving it that additional structure that would come from a dissertation and would close it: it stars the text, instead of assembling it.[76]

Barthes's meditation on the medium of nontotalizing commentary to a single "classic" text provides an apt conclusion to my own attempt to characterize earliest rabbinic commentary in some but not absolute contrast to its historical antecedents in *pēšer* and Philo. But Barthes's meditation also provides me with the opportunity to conclude with a final word about what we have learned from such a comparative characterization of this commentary about our own study of it: as modern critical students of ancient rabbinic commentary, who seek not simply to master its forms and messages but to understand and even experience a modest something of how it works, we need ourselves to become practitioners of commentary.

The discrete texts of the *Sifre* that I have selected for such attention are virtually all those that themselves deal with motifs of Torah and its interpretation in relation to Israel and its sages. In this way, I wish to continue the discussion, begun in this introduction, of how what the *Sifre* says about these themes might inform our understanding of the *Sifre*'s own three-faced practice of interpretation. Each chapter focuses on a particular section of commentary (Chapters 2 and 4) or a sizable selection of commentaries (Chapter 3) in terms of a larger methodological issue or cluster of issues that have already been touched upon here. Chapter 2 treats the revelation of the Torah at Sinai in relation to the question of the way the commentary's representations extend simultaneously along three interconnected vectors (scriptural text, received tradition, historical time). Chapter 3 treats the place of the sage and his Torah within the commentary of the *Sifre* and focuses on ways in which the commentary's representations and discursive practices transformatively empower the class of sages—its primary audience—in its collective self-understanding as Israel's authorized teachers, leaders, legislators, and judges. Chapter 4 treats the tension between Torah and nature as witness to Israel's covenant with God, in the context of extending our discussion of multiple interpretations and their editorial configuration in relation to the temporality of commentary's own forward movement. Although the whole of the *Sifre*'s commentary could not be treated here in like concentration (but a broader cross-section is less intensively represented in the notes), close textual attention to the theme of Torah and its sagely study of interpretation, which afterall defines the structural design of the text as a whole, provides the best first entrance to and guide through many of its interconnecting halls and chambers.

2 Re-Presenting Revelation

Introduction

*T*he title of this chapter is intended doubly. Its subject is both the re-presenting of the received *text* of Scripture, rabbinically understood to have been divinely revealed, through the practice of rabbinic commentary to that text, and the re-presenting of the past *event* of God's revelation of Torah to Israel at Mt. Sinai, rabbinically understood to be the signified subject of several verses of Deuteronomy, again through the practice of rabbinic commentary to those verses.[1] In particular, I will focus on the *Sifre*'s commentary to Deut. 33:2–4,[2] which verses introduce Moses' final poetic blessing of the twelve tribes before his death and their entry into the Land of Canaan (33:1: "This is the blessing with which Moses, the man of God, bade the Israelites farewell before he died"):

> [2] He said:
> The Lord came from Sinai;
> He shone upon them form Seir;
> He appeared fro Mount Paran,
> And approached fro Ribeboth-Kodesh,
> Lightning flashing at them from His right.
> [3] Lover, indeed, of the people(s),[3]
> Their hallowed are all in Your hand.
> They followed in Your steps,
> Accepting Your pronouncements.
> [4] When Moses charged us with the Teaching [= Torah]
> As the heritage of the congregation of Jacob.[4]

The mention of Sinai, the "lightning flashing," the people's acceptance of God's pronouncements, and of Moses' charging them with the Torah are all suggestive of God's revelation of the Torah to Israel at Sinai, and it is in relation to this event, broadly speaking, that the other more open and enigmatic scriptural expressions of these verses are rabbinically understood, often in multiple ways, in the course of commentary. Put differently, it is with respect to the sign of Sinai in the opening clause that all the others are interpreted.

But these verses, although the principal focus of the section of the *Sifre*'s commentary here to be considered, do not constitute the principal biblical description of the event of sinaitic revelation. Rather, they themselves may be considered to be a poetic allusion to, and an intrabiblical interpretation of, the fuller narrative account of the event of revelation found in Exod. 19–24, which our commentary will cite or presume. Still other biblical verses are rabbinically understood to refer to that revelatory event and hence will similarly be woven exegetically into the *Sifre*'s commentary to Deut. 33:2–4: Judg. 5:4; Hab. 3:3; Ps. 29:4–11; 138:4.[5] Thus, our commentary's refiguring of the biblical text of Deut. 33:2–4 in relation to the event of revelation is achieved, at least in part, through the lifting of scriptural verses from other scriptural contexts and *their* refiguring in the newly created context of commentary to Deuteronomy. In this way the *Sifre*'s mode of commentary, like that of rabbinic commentary more generally, may be said to be "inter- (or intra)textual": it interprets Scripture with interpreted Scripture.

But the matter is not nearly so simple. For whoever—and we may be speaking of a succession of whoevers—created the commentary before us was not just the heir to a manifold biblical text, but to a manifold *tradition* of biblical interpretation, apart from which the biblical texts themselves could no longer be read, which is to say, understood. Were we to imagine the creator of commentary sitting in his workshop, as it were, we would have to picture that his malleable raw materials were not just the principal biblical text upon which he worked, nor other biblical texts that he exegetically worked into it, but a rich body of extra-biblical traditions (largely exegetical but not soley so), the origins and preliterary forms of which we are generally unable to reconstruct. On the one hand, these traditions predisposed and therefore constrained our commentary maker in his reading of the verses before him. Yet on the other hand, paradoxical as it might seem, by recombining and subtly reshaping such traditions in relation both to each other and to his biblical texts, our commentary maker could exercise the freedom to re-present revelation—both as received text and as past event—in ways that were simulataneously familiar and fresh.[6] How do we know this? We will see that many of the same traditions that have been creatively combined in the present commentary to Deuteronomy are also found, but differently positioned and shaped, in the approximately contemporaneous commentary of the *Mekilta* to the narrative account of revelation in the Book of Exodus, sometimes with significantly different meanings and rhetorical effects.[7]

Finally, there is a third type of re-presentation in the work of commentary, more subtle and difficult to identify, to be sure, than those of biblical text and accompanying tradition, that being the commentary's re-presentation of its own sociohistorical setting and circumstances in the context of its re-presentation of revelation. In particular, Israel's problematic relations with the "nations of the world," both as oppressors and competitors, find repeated and heightened (in comparison with their parallel expressions in other documentary settings) expression. These expressions take the form, among others, of a seemingly present *dialogue* in which the nations taunt Israel and Israel spurns the nations, and of a *story* about the visit of Roman officers, disguised as Jewish converts, to the "school" of the Palestinian rabbinic Patriarch. Although both of these encounters, I shall argue, are rhetorical "fictions" and hence relatively indeterminate in their historical referents, they ring true to the historical setting and social circumstances of the *Sifre's* time of composition, whatever the history of their prior transmission, being in a sense "historical fictions" and "fictional truths." Another type of recurring sociohistorical re-presentation, one to which I shall return with greater concentration in the next chapter, is that of the producers-consumers of the commentary text itself, that is, the rabbinic sages and their disciples. They appear at several unexpected junctures in the re-presentation of revelation as the leaders and potential leaders of Isreal, distinguished among Israel while suffering on their behalf. I shall argue that both types of collective *self*-representation—of Israel in relation to the nations and of the sages in relation to Israel—should be viewed in part as subtle forms of rhetorical self-*realization* (and -*justification*).

It needs to be stressed that none of these three types of re-presentation—of biblical text, of accompanying tradition, and of sociohistorical time[8]—takes the form of a continuous narrative. Each one is fragmentary. We have no rabbinic Josephus to provide us with a narratively continuous account of the biblical event of revelation as told from a postbiblical point of view by blending the biblical text with its subsequent traditions of interpretation as part of an even larger narrative continuum that extends to the author's present.[9] Just as the biblical text is here atomized so as to provide an exegetical base for its closely read re-presentation in rabbinic commentary, so, too, the re-presentations of rabbinic tradition and time appear as textual fragments that have been combined but not blended in the associative network of commentary, a network of heteromorphous "petits récits" or "historiettes."[10] It is precisely the paratactic interweaving of these three types of fragmentary re-presentation that may be said to constitute the work of commentary, which repeatedly shuttles, as it were, between splintered and resited biblical texts, their accompanying traditions, and the sociohistorical circumstances of the commentary's own study. In a sense, each type of re-presentation is rhetorically mediated to the student of the text by the others, even as that student himself is drawn into this work of filling out the lines of interrelation, both structural and topical, between the assembled fragments of text and tradition. Precisely this mediational interweaving makes it so difficult, as we will repeatedly see, to identify with certainty a particular interpretation's generative "stimulus"—whether in biblical text (exegesis) or historical time (eisegesis), as the alternatives are commonly posed. This complexity of commentary also means that to approach it for the sake of uncovering only one of its re-presentations—whether of biblical text, of rabbinic tradition, or of historical time—is to view it reductively, and hence illusively. Better than to hastily unravel this threefold re-presentation is to critically observe and even enter the complex and dynamic textures of its interweaving—its very world of representations.[11]

Sifre Texts and Commentary

The Lord Came from Sinai (§343)

[A1] He [Moses] said: The Lord came from Sinai; He shone upon them from Seir" (Deut. 33:2): Scripture tells that Moses began not with the needs of Israel but with the praise of God.

[A2] A *mashal* (parable): To what may this be compared? To an advocate (Greek: *rhētōr*) standing on the podium (Greek: *bēma*), hired by someone to plead his case, who does not begin with the needs of his client but with the praise of the king: "Happy is the world of which he is king. Happy is the world of which he is judge.[12] Upon us shines the sun [for his sake]. Upon us shines the moon [for his sake]." And others would then join him in praise. Only afterwards does he turn to the needs of that man [= his client], and concludes by again praising the king. Similarly, our teacher Moses did not begin with the needs of Israel but with the praise of God, as it is said, "And he said: The Lord came from Sinai," and only afterwards did he begin with the needs of Israel: "May there be a king in Jeshurun" (33:5). He concluded by returning to the praise of God: "O Jeshurun, there is none like God" (33:26).

[A3] So too King David began with the praise of God, as it is said, "Hallelujah! Sing unto the Lord a new song [His praise in the assembly of the pious]" (Ps. 149:1), and only afterwards did he begin with the praise of Israel: "For the Lord takes pleasure in His people" (ibid., 149:4). And then he concluded by returning to the praise of God: "Praise God in His holiness" (ibid., 150:1).

[A4] Similarly, Solomon his son began with praise of God: "There is no God like You in heaven or on earth, who keeps the covenant and mercy with Your servants" (2 Chr. 6:14), and only afterwards did he begin with the needs of Israel: "If there be a famine in the land" (ibid., 6:28). And then he concluded by returning to the praise of God: "Arise O Lord God to Your resting-place" (ibid., 6:41).

[A5] Similarly, regarding the eighteen benedictions which the early sages [13] established for Israel to pray daily, they did not begin with the needs of Israel until they had begun with the praise of God: "The great, mighty, and awesome God, You are holy and Your name is awesome." And afterwards [petition]: "Who releases the bound." And afterwards: "Who heals the sick." And afterwards [they conclude with praise]: "We are grateful to you."[14]

The commentary begins its explication of Moses' final prayer-blessing by dividing it into three units: introductory praise of God (verses 2-4), the body of the blessing read as a petition for Israel's needs (verses 5-25), and the concluding praise of God (verses 26-29). Although we shall focus only on the *Sifre*'s commentary on the first unit, it is useful to see the larger framework within which the commentary places it.

On the face of it, the words of Deut. 33 would appear to contain the words of blessing pronounced by Moses as God's agent (expressed through the phrase "man of God" in 33:1) *to Israel*. The analogy to the practice of a *rhētōr*, presumably modeled on common (non-Jewish) Greco-Roman practice[15] turns this about: Moses, as the people's agent, addresses God in petitioning for their needs. However, because blessing is implicitly an invocation of divine power to fulfill its words (compare the priestly blessing of Num. 6:24-26), and because Moses in addressing his blessing to Israel also refers to God in the second person (verses 3, 8-10), the apparent reversal is not as radical as it might at first appear. That reversal is necessary if Moses' blessing is to serve as a model for subsequent human petitionary prayer to God. However, in still another way the practice of the *rhētōr* differs from that of Moses, as it does from that of David and Solomon: after the *rhētōr* opens with praise of the king, others present join him in praising the king. As is often the case, the *mashal* (parable) does not neatly fit its *nimshal* (application).

The comparison and association of Moses and David can be seen elsewhere in the *Sifre*, where the two are portrayed as model leaders (*parnāsim*), representing respectively the prophetic and monarchic roles that the rabbinic sages claimed, in their own way, to have inherited.[16] The transition from David to Solomon, from father to son, is natural enough. From Solomon, commonly identified with the Temple that he built, we move to contemporary (that is, post-Temple) prayer established bu the "early sages" for recitation by the people.[17] They, too, in their arrangement of the Eighteen Benedictions, followed the order established by Moses' final prayer: praise, petition, praise.[18] Whereas the earlier exempla were inspired individuals who prayed to God on Israel's behalf on specific occasions, the practice establisched by the "early sages" was one that was to be performed daily by the people as a whole.

In this current practice, with which the commentary concludes, the paradigm of the *rhētōr* finally finds, albeit implicitly, its fullest analogue. For the public recitation of the Eighteen Benedictions is performed by a skilled *šāliaḥ ṣibbûr* ("public emissary") who, standing before the Holy Ark, recites the prayer's words of praise, petition, and praise of God on the people's behalf, even as they responsively join in that praise. Thus, the *mashal* of the *rhētōr* finds it most complete *nimshal* ("application") not in the past liturgical practices of Moses, David, or Solomon, but in the current liturgical practice (ideally at least) of Israel as a whole as ordained for them by the Second Temple antecedents of the rabbinic sages. The chain of biblical antecedents justifies current practice, even as that practice moves beyond its biblical antecedents via the linking metaphor of the *mashal's rhētōr*. Performatively viewed, the commentary may be said dialectically to transfer its students from the words of Moses to their fulfillment in the rabbinically authorized liturgical practice of their own culture. Finally, just as Moses is understood to *praise* God through his poetic re-presentation of God's past self-disclosure to Israel at Sinai (understood to be the subject of the following verse), the commentary's own interpretive re-presentation of Moses' words may be understood as a responsive prolongation of that praise into the present.

> [B] Another interpretation: When the Holy One, blessed be He, revealed Himself in order to give the Torah to Israel, he did not speak to them in one language but in four languages, [as it is said,] "He said: The Lord came from Sinai": this is the Hebrew language. "He shone upon them from Seir": this is the Roman language.[19] "He appeared from Mount Paran": this is the Arabic language.[20] "And approached from Ribeboth-Kodesh": this is the Aramaic language.[21]
>
> [C] Another interpretation: "He said: The Lord came from Sinai": When the Holy One, blessed be He, revealed Himself in order to give the Torah to Israel, He revealed Himself not just from one direction but from [all] four directions, as it is said, "He said: The Lord came from Sinai; He shone upon them fro Seir; He appeared from Mount Paran." And what is the fourth direction? "God comes from Teman" (Hab. 3:3).[22]

Deut. 33:2 poetically describes God's manifold self-disclosure to Israel in the desert. It uses four phrases to do so, each including a different place along the route of their wilderness journey: Sinai, Seir, Paran, and Ribeboth-Kodesh.[23] The *Sifre's* commentary, by contrast, subsumes all four under the first, understanding them all as expressions of what took place at or around Mt. Sinai. But, as these four phrases cannot be simply repetitive (that is, redundant), they are variously understood to denote the fourfold nature of God's self-disclosure at Sinai.

The first interpretation of this fourfold revelation (B) takes each of the four phrases to refer to another language. Whereas in other rabbinic texts it is said that God revealed the Torah at first in seventy languages, seventy (seven times ten) being the *total* number of human languages (and nations) in the world according to rabbinic conception,[24] here the same sense of totality of linguistic expression is symbolically expressed by the number four. Note that our text states explicitly that it was to *Israel* that the Torah was revealed in these four languages and not that each one was directed to a different nation.[25]

The second interpretation (C) takes the four scriptural phrases to signify four directions, from which God came simultaneously to Israel, thereby *surrounding* them with His presence at the moment of revelation.[26] Because the fourth phrase, "And approached from Ribeboth-Kodesh," is not taken to signify God's approach from a geographic location,[27] but the "holy myriads" (angels) that *accompanied* God at the time of revelation,[28] the commentary must rhetorically ask about the missing fourth direction. This is supplied from the related verse of Hab. 3:3, where it is said that, in addition to coming from Mt. Paran, God comes from Teman (South). Thus, the Habakkuk verse is understood to supplement the Deuteronomy verse that it parallels in its language. Interestingly, there is no need here to identify each of the four locations (Sinai, Seir, Paran, and Teman) with a specific direction.[29]

Taken together, these two sets of interpretations (B and C) complement each other in conveying a sense of the manifold totality, both spatially and linguistically, and the encompassing nature of God's self-disclosure to Israel at the time of revelation.[30] Both begin by stressing that God's self-disclosure was not, as may have been expected, uniform (one language or one direction) but multiform, as is the lemma itself. But it is precisely in the manner of parsing the lemma that the two interpretations part company. The first interpretation (B) simply divides the lemma and deictically assigns a definitive meaning (one of four languages) to each of its four parts, leaving to the student of the text to ascertain the associations that lie behind those assignments of meaning. The second interpretation (C) similarly divides the lemma into its parts, but without assigning to each its meaning, moving immediately to its hermeneutical crux, posed as a rhetorical question to the student of the text: the lemma signifies only three directions; whence can we derive the fourth? For a moment, the fourfold exegesis of the lemma is jeopardized, until a closely related verse from elsewhere in Scripture is provided as the answer to the question, thereby allowing the twofold fourfold exegesis to reach its conclusion. Thus, the commentary may be said to move (and to move its students) from "deictic" to "dialogical" commentary, the latter being marked, as discussed in Chapter 1, by three features: rhetorical question and answer, the interpretation of Scripture with Scripture, and the enchaining of multiple interpretations. In the present case, multiplicity of revelation marks both the structure of the commentary and its re-presentation of what took place as Sinai. This is expressed as well, but even more complexly, in the following interpretation, which now weaves the non-Israelite nations into the commentary's web:

[D1] Another interpretation: "He said: The Lord came from Sinai": When the Holy One, blessed be He, revealed Himself to give the Torah to Israel, He revealed Himself not to Israel alone but to all the nations.

[D2] He went first to the descendants of Esau and said to them, "Will you accept the Torah?" They said to Him, "What is written in it?" He said to them, "You shall not murder" (Exod. 20:13). They said, "This is the very essence of this people, and their [=our] forefather was a murderer, as it is said, 'Yet the hands are the hands of Esau' (Gen. 27:22), and his [=Esau's] father assured that he would be so, as it is said,[31] 'By the sword you shall live' (Gen. 27:40)."

[D3] He then went to the descendants of Ammon and Moab and asked them, "Will you accept the Torah?" They replied, "What is written in it?" He said, "You shall not commit adultery" (Exod. 20:13). They replied, "Aldultery is their [=our] very essence, as it is said, 'Thus the two daughters of Lot came to be with child by their father' (Gen. 19:36).

[D4] He went next to the descendants of Ishamael and asked them, "Will you accept the Torah?" They replied, "What is written in it?" He said, "You shall not steal" (Exod. 20:13). They replied, "[Theft is] their [=our] very essence [and] their [=our] forefather was a thief, as it is said, "He shall be a wild ass of a man' (Gen. 16:12)."

[D5] And there was not a single nation among the nations with whom He did not speak, knocking on each one's door to ask if they wanted to receive the Torah, as it says, "All the kings of the earth shall praise You, O Lord, for they heard (*šāmĕʿû*) the words you spoke" (Ps. 138:4). Could it be that they heard and accepted [His offer]? Scripture teaches, "In anger and wrath will I wreak retribution on the nations that have not obeyed (*šāmĕʿû*)" (Mic. 5:14).

[D6] Rather, they were not even able to observe [lit.: withstand] the seven commandments that the children of Noah had accepted as incumbent upon themselves, and finally cast them off and gave them to Israel.[32]

[D7] A *mashal*: [This can be compared to] a man who took his donkey and his dog to the threshing floor and loaded the donkey with a letek [of grain] and the dog with three seʾahs.[33] The donkey went along [easily], but the dog began to pant. He [= the man] removed a seʾah from him [= the dog] and put it on the donkey, and so too the second and the third [seʾah].

[D8] Similarly, Israel accepted the Torah according to all of its explications and fine points, as well at those very seven commandments that the descendants of Noah [at first] accepted but were unable to observe [lit.: withstand] until finally they cast them off and gave them to Israel.[34] Therefore, it is said, "He said: The Lord came from Sinai, and shone upon them from Seir."[35]

Once again, the lemma is interpreted so as to stress, contrary to what might have been expected, the fourfold nature of revelation: not to Israel alone did God disclose himself at Sinai, but to all of the nations. His self-disclosure to the nations was for naught, however, since they declined to receive His Torah. The lemma is understood to mean that God came to Israel with the Torah only after having sought out the other nations, beginning with Seir/Esau.[36] Although God begins with Seir/Esau, the order in which he approaches the other nations is not so much determined by the order of the lemma as by the order of the three universal prohibitions in Exod. 20:13 (murder, adultery, and theft). This determines the progression from the descendants of Esau (Seir), to those of Ammon and Moab (not specifically alluded to in the lemma), and then to those of Ishmael (Paran). Thus, the fourfold structure of the exegesis, so clearly seen in the preceding two interpretations, is loosely retained (Esau, Ammon and Moab, Ishmael, Israel), with the added element that God went to every other nation before finally ending up with Israel.[37] A widely attested tradition relating God's offering of the Torah to the nations of the world before giving it to Israel has been adapted, but not entirely smoothly, to the present commentary context.

In comparing the present version of that tradition with its closest parallels, especially the one found in the *Mekilta of R. Ishmael*, we can see how subltly yet significantly our commentary has reworked received traditions, especially with regard to the "nations of the world."[38] Here is the text of the *Mekilta*, drawn from the context of its commentary to the first commandment, "I am the Lord thy God" (Exod. 20:2):

[1] It was for this reason that the nations of the world were asked [to receive the Torah], so that they would not have an opportunity to say, "Had we been asked we would surely have accepted it." Behold, they *were* asked and they did not accept it, as it is said, "He said: The Lord came from Sinai," etc.

[2] He revealed Himself to the descendants of the wicked Esau, saying to them, "Will you accept the Torah?" They said to Him, "What is written in it?" He said to them, "You shall not murder" (Exod. 20:13). They said to Him, "This is the inheritance that our forefather passed on to us: 'By the sword you shall live' (Gen. 27:40)."

[3] He revealed Himself to the descendants of Ammon and Moab, saying to them, "Will you accept the Torah?" They said to Him, "What is written in it?" He said to them, "You shall not commit adultery" (Exod. 20:13). They said

to Him that they were all the children of adulterers, as it is said, "Both of the daughters of Lot were with child by their father" (Gen. 19:36).

[4] He revealed Himself to the descendants of Ishmael, saying to them, "Do you accept the Torah?" They said to Him, "What is written in it?" He said to them, "You shall not steal" (Exod. 20:13). They said to Him, "This was the very blessing which was pronounced on our forefather, 'And he shall be a wild ass of a man, with his hand upon everything' (Gen. 16:12). And it is written, "For surely I [Joseph] was stolen away [by the Ishamelites] out of the land of the Hebrews" (Gen. 40:15).

[5] And when He came to Israel, "From his right hand was a fiery law to them" (Deut. 33:2), they all opened their mouths and said, "All that the Lord hath spoken we will do and obey" (Exod. 24:7). And thus it says, "He stood and measured the earth. He beheld and released (*yattēr*) the nations" (Hab. 3:6).

[6] R. Simon b. Eleazar (ca. 200) says: If the descendants of Noah were unable to withstand [=obey] the seven commandments which were enjoined upon them, how much less would they have been able to endure all the commandments in the Torah.

[7] A *mashal*: [This can be compared] to a king who appointed two administrators. One was appointed over a store of straw and one was appointed over a store of silver and gold. The one who was appointed over the store of straw was suspected [of mishandling it], but [nevertheless] complained that he had not been appointed over the store of silver and gold. They said to him, "You good for nothing! If you were suspected in connection with the store of straw, how could anyone trust you with the store of silver and gold?

[8] Behold, one can reason a fortiori: If the descendants of Noah were unable to withstand the seven commandments enjoined upon them, how much more so [would they have been unable to withstand all the commandments in the Torah!][39]

Each version of the story comprises two editorially juxtaposed parts, the first describing God's attempt to offer the Torah to the nations (A–D5 in the *Sifre* and 1–5 in the *Mekilta*), the second, in each case employing a *mashal*, stressing the nations' failure to observe the seven Noahide (universal) commandments that they had previously received or been commanded (D6–D8 in the *Sifre* and 6–8 in the *Mekilta*). In the first part of each the sequence is essentially the same, except that the *Sifre*'s version stresses that God disclosed Himself to each and every nation in actively seeking that they accept His Torah, whereas the *Mekilta* stresses that God offered the Torah to the nations already knowing that they would not accept it, to prevent their later claiming that they would have accepted it had it been offered to them.[40] In the two versions the rejection of the Torah by the nations is related in similar terms, except that whereas the *Mekilta* stresses that the reason the nations rejected the Torah was because their sinful behavior had been predetermined by their ancestors, the *Sifre* goes even further in stating that the very essence, that is, character, of these people rendered them incapable of accepting the Torah. In both texts, the three commandments that the nations are unable to obey may be said to be those that constitute the minimal ethical norms of social behavior—not to murder, commit adultery, or steal— these being counted both among the Ten Commandments and the seven Noahide laws.

In the *Mekilta* version, after God fails with the specified nations He comes directly to Israel (signified by Deut. 33:2), as He presumably had planned all along. They accept the Torah without hesitation, thereby providing a climax and conclusion to the first part of the tradition. The *Sifre* at this point stresses how God made an extra effort to offer the Torah to each and every nation, knocking on their doors (D5). By juxtaposing Ps.138:4 and Mic. 5:14, the *Sifre* suggests that all the nations of the world heard God's words of revelation (presumably more than the single commandments mentioned earlier), but nonetheless failed to take them upon themselves. Thus, the nations' rejection of God's Torah is stated even more negatively in the *Sifre* than in the *Mekilta*; because according to the *Sifre* God intended for them to receive His Torah, their rejection of it is all the more a repudiation of both. God's subsequent offering of His Torah to Israel and their acceptance of it is not stated at this point in the *Sifre*'s commentary, as it is in the *Mekilta*, being left to be expressed only at the end of the second part (D8) with the concluding citation of the lemma (33:1). Instead, the *Sife* moves directly to the question of the nations' failure to obey *even* the seven Noahnide commandments, which in the *Mekilta* is set off from the first part by the attribution to R. Simon b. Eleazar. According to the *Sifre* version (D6), the descendants of Noah *rejected* (*pērĕqu*, lit.: removed) these commandments that they had previously, presumably at the time of Noah, *accepted* as binding (*qibbĕlû ʿălêhem*), finding them now, at the time of Sinai, too much to bear. The *Mikilta* version (6), by contrast, simply states that they were unable to bear these commandments that had been *enjoined* upon them (*niṣṭawwû ʿălêhen*).[41] Thus, once again, the *Sifre*'s rebuke of the nations appears to be even sharper than that of the *Mekilta*, for in the latter they reject what they had formerly accepted, being guilty not simply of moral weakness but of renunciation of their formerly accepted obligations.

There is also something incommensurate between the two parts of the commentary, both in the *Sifre* and in the *Mekilta*, but even more so in the former. In the first part the nations reject the Torah because of command-ments about which they appear to learn for the first time, whereas the second part implies that they had previously been subject to these very commandments, and in the *Sifre*'s version had accepted them as binding, long before they were approached at Sinai. In both commentaries the addition of this tradition stresses that even had the nations received the Torah at Sinai, they would never have been able to obey it, not simply because they were morally unsuited to it, but because of their past history of failing to fulfill the more minimal, universal covenant established by God with Noah.

This tension, and the difference between the *Sifre* and the *Mekilta* in its regard, becomes even more evident when we compare the two *meshalim*. In the *Mekilta*'s *mashal*, the man appointed over the straw (the nations, responsible for the seven noahide commandments) envies the man appointed over the silver and gold (Israel, responsible for the Torah). As the former cannot be trusted to fulfill the responsibility with which he has already been charged, how dare he complain that he has not been entrusted with a store of greater value? Applied to the nations, they are presumed to *envy* Israel's favored position, even though, because of their own previous actions, they cannot be taken seriously as contenders for that position.

In the *Sifre*, the force of the *mashal* is different. There Israel and the nations are represented as two animals to whom have been assigned loads to carry. The dog (the nations), carrying the *lighter* load, not only is unable to withstand its assigned load, but causes that burden to be transferred to Israel, which is already carrying a normal load. There is a curious disparity between the *mashal* and its *nimshal* (application): in the former it would appear (although this is not explicitly stated) that the dog's load is transferred to Israel by the master of both (God), whereas in the latter the nations themselves remove the Noahide commandments and transfer them to Israel. Who then is responsible for the extra burden borne by Israel as a consequence of the nations' moral failure, God or the nations or the two together? Against whom does our commentary implicitly protest? The jagged justaposition of *mashal* and *nimshal* evoke such questions without providing their answers. We are instead returned to the lemma ("The Lord came from Sinai, and shone upon them for Seir"), which in light of the preceding may be understood in a double sense: (1) God favored Israel with the Torah only after it had been rejected by the nations (Seir). (2) God placed upon Israel an additional load (the seven Noahide commandments) that had previously been accepted by the nations but had since been cast off by them. In other words, Israel is justified in its favored status as the sole recipient of the Torah, even as it protests, subtly to be sure, the extra burden that it bears as a consequence.[42] The first motif is shared by the *Sifre* and the *Mekilta*, whereas the second is particular to the *Sifre*'s distinctive choice and configuration of traditions.

I would not have made so much of these subtle differences between the *Sifre* and the *Mekilta* were it not for the fact that the motifs of Israel's suffering, self-justification, and future retribution in relation to the nations recur both individually and in interrelation elsewhere within the *Sifre*'s commentary, but particularly in its re-presentation of the event of revelation, as the following sections attest.[43]

> [E] When the Holy One, blessed be He, revealed Himself to give the Torah to Israel, He shook the entire world, together with its inhabitants, as it is said, "The voice of the Lord is over the waters, the God of glory thunders"(Ps. 29:3). When they heard the thunderous voices [of revelation], all the nations gathered together and came to Balaam, saying to him, "It seems to us that the Holy One, blessed be He, is about to destroy the world with water." He said to them, "It has already been said, 'The waters shall never again become a flood' (Gen. 9:15)." They said to him, "What then is this thunderous voice?" He replied, "The Lord will grant strength to His people"(Ps. 29:11)—and "strength"must refer to Torah, as it is said, "With Him are strength and sound wisdom"(Job 12:16). They said to him, "If that is so, 'May the Lord bless His people with peace' (Ps. 29:11)."[44]

This interpretation begins with the same formula, "When the Holy One, blessed be he, revealed Himself to give the Torah to Israel," as do the previous three. Ps. 29:3 shares with the lemma ("The Lord came from Sinai") the tetragram YHWH (here translated "Lord").[45] But the word *voice* (*qôl*) is of particular significance here, taken to signify God's revelatory voice, which at Sinai issued as thunder (cf. Exod. 20:15). The seismic effects of this thunderous communication are felt throughout the world, whose inhabitants fear that God is about to destroy it as He did in Noah's time. When the gentile prophet Balaam reassures the nations by telling them, in the words of the first half of Ps. 29:11, that what they hear is God giving the Torah to His people, they are so relieved that they wish Israel God's blessing of peace, in the words of the second half of the same verse.[46] Although the present passage opens with the same language as that which preceded it, the two are somewhat incommensurate: there the nations are participants in God's self-disclosing act of revealing the Torah, being the first ones to be approached by God, whereas here they are removed from the scene, albeit experiencing it indirectly, needing to be told by one of their prophets what is happening.[47] The tone here, as previously, is mocking, especially when, in their relief that they are not in danger, the nations complete the verse cited to them by Balaam, thereby invoking upon Israel a blessing of peace. Note also that the revelation at Sinai is exegetically made to point explicitly back to the primordial deluge and implicitly, through the blessing of peace, forward to Israel's eventual redemption from the rule of the nations. This positioning of Sinai between "urzeit" and "endzeit" recurs, but now even more forcefully, in the commentary's continuation:

[F] Another explanation: "He said: The Lord came from Sinai [and shone upon them from Seir]": In the future, when the Holy One, blessed be He, is about to punish Seir, He will shake the entire world, together with its inhabitants, as He did at the giving of the Torah, as it is said, "O Lord, when You came forth (*bĕṣē'tĕkā*) from Seir, [advanced from the country of Edom, the earth trembled, the heavens also dropped water, yea, the clouds dropped water]" (Judg. 5:4). And it says, "Then his brother emerged (*yāṣā'*), holding on to the heel of Esau; so they named him Jacob" (Gen. 25:26). The Holy One, blessed be He, said to Israel, "No nation will be able to come between you [and Esau]."[48]

The progression from Seit to Israel at the time of revelation, as the lemma is understood to signify, is now understood to signify as well the succession of Seir (= Esau = Rome) by Israel in the messianic future. However, to make this connection between revelation and redemption, two other verses must be drawn into the commentary's web of associations. Just as God's progression from Seir to Israel at Sinai was accompanied by a shaking of the entire world (as already expressed in E), so, too, in the messianic future. The idea that the whole world shook at the time of revelation is established from Judg. 5:4, which in speaking of God having come from Seir/Edom (the next verse, Judg. 5:5, explicitly mentioning Sinai), adds the detail of the earth having trembled. But that verse includes another detail not found in Deut. 33:1, that being the use of the verg *yṣ'* ("go forth") to describe what is understood as God's progression from Seir to Israel. That detail facilitates an association in turn with Gen. 25:26, which relates the birth (expressed with the same verb) of Jacob *immediately* following that of his twin brother Esau (= Seir), whose heel he clutches so nothing could come between them. By that verse, in its present juxtaposition with the lemma, God announces to Israel (note the direct dialogue) that when the final shakeup comes, they will succeed Esau (= Rome) directly, with no other nation rising to rule in between.[49] In terms of the lemma, God will in the future shine upon Israel (immediately) after Seir.

The interpretation is clearly political, and one might say "apocalyptic" (although not in the specifically visionary sense). At a time when Israel was ruled by Rome, and perhaps signs were beginning to appear of the Roman Empire's decline and dissolution, it could be hoped, on the model of Dan. 7, that Rome would be the last of the empires and that its fall would be succeeded *immediately* by Israel's messianic redemption and ascension to power.[50] As is so often the case, speculation about the end of history is modeled after its beginnings, which for Israel could be associated *both* with the birth of Jacob, the progenitor of the twelve tribes, as well as with the sealing of the covenant at Sinai, when Israel's life as a covenantal people could be said to have truly begun. Both of these originary moments, through their scriptural interassociation, are made to point beyond themselves to the messianic future when Israel will succeed Seir/Esau for the last time. Stated differently, Israel's relation to the nations, especially Esau, at Sinai is made to point back to its origins with the birth of Jacob and forward to its conclusion at the end of time. It should be noted that even after Roman rule ended without Israel's ascension following, the midrash could remain hermeneutically and rhetorically viable without alteration because Esau was understood subsequently to refer to Christendom as Rome's successor.[51]

The significance of Jacob for Israel's relations with the nations in relation to revelation is pursued as well in the next comment:

> [G] Another interpretation:[52] A *mashal*: [This may be compared to] a king who wished to present a gift to one of his sons, but feared [the reaction of] the son's brothers, of his close friends, and of his relatives. What did that son do? he adorned himself[53] and cut his hair, whereupon the king said to him, "To you I am presenting this gift." Similarly, when our father Abraham came into the world he had unworthy children, Ishmael and the children of Keturah, who turned out to be more evil than the first [generations]. When Isaac came along, he had an unworthy child, Esau, and all the princes of Edom turned out to be more evil than the first [generations]. But when Jacob came along, he had no unworthy children, for all of his children were perfect, as it is said, "Jacob was a mild [= perfect] man, dwelling in tents" (Gen. 25:27). Whereupon the Holy One, blessed be He, said to him, "To you shall I give the Torah." Hence Scripture says, "The Lord came from Sinai, and shone upon them from Seir."[54]

As in the previous comment, the revelation of the Torah to Israel is linked to the person of Jacob, Israel's namesake. Skipping the *mashal* for the moment, the commentary would seem to ask why the Torah was not given earlier to Abraham and his children or to Isaac and his children, at the time when a covenant was established or reaffirmed with them. The reason suggested is that both Abraham and Isaac had unworthy children, who would have inherited a portion of the Torah.[55] God waits, therefore, for the perfect Jacob (as suggested by Gen. 25:27), so as to give the Torah to him and his wholly worthy descendants. The lemma is cited to the effect that God passed over Esau (Seir), Isaac's unworthy son, to give the Torah to Jacob (= Israel).

The *mashal*, however, does not fit smoothly within this interpretation (that is, with its *nimshal*) and must itself be interpreted for it to make sense in its presently redacted context. If the favored son of the *mashal* is Jacob and the king is God, then the brothers who do not receive the gift and whose reaction God fears represent not Abraham and Isaac (Jacob's grandfather and father) of the *nimshal*, but the other nations (especially Seir/Esau, Jacob's brother). In the *mashal* the father does not immediately give the present to his favored son but must wait for him to physically prepare himself to be worthy of it, thereby obviating, if only somewhat, the other sons' envy.[56] Similarly, God does not immediately give the Torah to Abraham or to Isaac, whose offspring (the progenitors of Israel's neighbors and chief competitors) were unworthy, but waits for Jacob. Thus, the nations appear in the *mashal* as the brothers or relatives of the favored son, and in the *nimshal* as the unworthy offspring of Abraham and Isaac. Taken *together*, the *mashal* and its imperfectly suited *nimshal* suggest that God in giving the Torah to Jacob and his descendants chose *both* not to give it to Abraham and Isaac and not to give it to the nations, for had He given it to the former it would have been inherited by the latter. Thus, God's coming (shining) to Israel/Jacob from Seir/Esau is taken to signify not only His not having given the Torah to the nations, but also His not having given it to Abraham and Isaac as their progenitors. Israel's receiving of the Torah is, once again, an implicit rebuke of the nations. But if earlier (D) the nations did not receive the Torah because having been offered it they rejected it, here it is God who determines that they are simply not worthy to have the opportunity of a share in it.[57] Yet here, too, there seems to be some discomfort with the exclusion of the nations even as it is justified. The *mashal* would appear to project that unease onto the king (God), who does not immediately give his gift to his favored son out of concern for the reactions of his sons' brothers, friends, and relatives, who afterall are also the king's offspring and subjects. Curiously, it is up to the son (Israel), sensitive to the king's ambivalent feelings, to make it easier for the king to give him the gift, by demonstrating in public view that he is (they are) worthy of it. We have witnessed our commentary's ambivalent view of Israel's and God's relations to the nations before and will encounter it further along as well.

The next comment returns to revelation's eschalogical foreshadowing of redemption:

> [H] "He appeared from Mount Paran": There are four "appearances" [referred to in Scripture]. The first was in Egypt, as it is said, "Give ear, O Shepherd of Israel who leads Joseph like a flock. Appear, You who are enthroned upon the cherubim" (Ps. 80:2).[58] The second was at the time of the giving of the Torah, as it is said, "He appeared from Mount Paran." The third will occur at the time of Gog and Magog, as it is said, "God of retribution, Lord, God of retribution, appear!" (Ps. 94:1). The fourth will occur in the days of the Messiah, as it is said, "From Zion, perfect in beauty, God appear!" (Ps. 50:2)[59]

We have here an example of what has been called *scriptural enumeration.*[60] The lemma, in referred to God's appearance to Israel at Mt. Sinai, occasions the enumeration of other instances of God's appearance to Israel, all scripturally denoted by the same verb. Note that the number four, figuring so prominently in earlier interpretations (the four parts of the verse understood to denote four directions, four languages, and four nations), now denotes four junctures in Israel's sacred history, of which the lemma signifies the second. The progression is clearly chronological: moving from Israel's national enslavement, to its receiving of the Torah as its collective charter, to the final divine retribution against Israel's enemies, to Israel's final redemption and restoration. Because the second "appearance" at Sinai is the focus of attention in the present context of the commentary, it may be that this appearance is understood to be a symmetrical prefiguring of the fourth and final "appearance," an association that we have previously seen. The present list includes neither all biblical occurances of the verb *hôpîaʿ*, nor all biblical occasions upon which God is rabbinically understood to have appeared to Israel, but rather the intersection of the two, intentionally ordered according to a chronological progression.[61]

The commentary next turns to the fourth strophe of the lemma, which, as previously noted, is taken to refer not to a place, and hence not to one of the nations, but to God's angelic entourage.

> [I] "And approached from Ribeboth-Kodesh": The way of the Holy One, blessed be He, is not like that of [a man of] flesh and blood. When a man arranges a banquet for his son in celebration of the son's wedding, he displays all his treasures and all his possessions. But He who spoke and the world came into being is not like this. Rather, "With him were some of the myriads holy," and not "all myriads."[62]

The commentary understands the Aramaism *wĕ'ātâ* as though it were *wĕ'ittô* (which simply requires reading the consonants *w'th* as *w'tw*), meaning "with him."[63] Once Ribeboth-Kodesh is understood to refer not to the name of a place but to the holy angels ("myriads holy") that accompanied God, the prefixed *mem* can be taken not as a locative but as a partitive "from": at Sinai God only brought with him a part of his angelic corps, not needing to flaunt them all.[64] There may be here a mocking not so much of the average "man of flesh and blood" as of the gentile (Roman) kings (and their local agents) with their ostentatious public displays of wealth and might.[65] It should also be noted that while in some traditions the angels played an important *intermediary* role in revelation, conveying God's word to Moses or to the people, here and in what follows the angels simply *accompany* God as He Himself reveals His will to Israel.[66]

[J1] Another interpretation: "And approached from Ribeboth-Kodesh": When a king of flesh and blood sits among his entourage,[67] there are present among them men who are [more] beautiful [than he], men who have [more] beautiful hair (*qĕwûṣîm*) [than he], and men who are more heroic than he.[68] But He who spoke and world came into being is different. Rather, "And approached (*wĕ'ātā'*) from Ribeboth-Kodesh": He is an ensign ('*ôt hû'*) amidst the myriads holy.[69]

[J2] And when He revealed Himself at the Sea, they [Israel] immediately recognized Him, as it is said, "This is my God and I will glorify Him; the God of my father, and I will exalt Him" (Exod. 15:2).

[J3] Similarly, the nations of the world would ask Israel, "How is your beloved better than another" (Cant. 5:9), that you are killed for His sake, as it is said, "Therefore do maidens (*'ălāmôt*) [= unto death do they] love you" (Cant. 1:3)?[70] And it also says, "It is for Your sake that we are slain all day long" (Ps. 44:23). You are all beautiful, you are all heroic. Come and mingle with us."[71] And Israel replied, "Let us tell you only a part of His praise and you will recognize Him:[72] 'My beloved is clear-skinned and ruddy... His head is finest gold... His eyes are like doves by watercourses... His cheeks are like beds of spices... His hands are as rods of gold... His legs are like marble pillars... His mouth is delicious, and all of him is delightful' (Cant. 5:10–16)." When the nations of the world heard of the beauty and the praise of the Holy One, blessed be He, they said to Israel, "Let us come with you,[73] as it is said, 'Wither has your beloved gone, O fairest of women? Whither hath thy beloved turned? Let us seek him with you' (Cant. 6:1)." What does Israel reply? That they [the nations] have no part of Him:[74] "I am my beloved's and my beloved is mine; He browses among the lilies" (Cant. 6:3).[75]

Section J1, like section I that preceded it, speaks of God's having been *accompanied* by His angelic host when He came to disclose Himself at Mt. Sinai in order to give the Torah. An additional word play on *wĕ'ātā'* (MT: *wĕ'ātâ*) is now provided by dividing the word in two: a sign ('*ôt*) is He (*hû'*) [standing out] from (*mē-*) the myriads holy (*ribĕbōt qōdeš*).[76] Whereas section I stressed that God, not having to show off all of his angels, only brings with him some, section J1 stresses that even amidst this elite angelic escort God stands out, head and shoulders, as it were, above the rest. This theme occasions a shift to a tradition (J2) concerning God's physical self-disclosure at the time of His splitting of the Sea of Reeds, when Israel immediately recognized and emphatically pointed out their God, presumably again among His angelic entourage.[77] This in turn is related to a dialogue between the nations and Israel (J3), the words of the dialogue being taken almost entirely from the Song of Songs.[78] First, the nations try to entice, through flattery, Israel to abandon her lover, because of whom she suffers unto death (another word play) and to mix among them. Israel, by relating to the nations only a *part* of their lover's qualities (to reveal any more would be to share their intimacy with God with the nations), hope to have the nations recognize why Israel is so attracted, and hence committed (even unto death), to Him. The ironic twist comes when Israel succeeds at this too well, causing the nations to reverse themselves, now seeking to join Israel in pursuit of God. But Israel jealously rejects the nations' suggestion, arguing that God is Israel's lover alone. For the nations to join Israel in pursuit of her lover would spell Israel's loss of identity no less than for Israel to join the nations in abandonment of her lover.

The Song of Songs, which is overall construed by early rabbinic exegetes as a lovers' dialogue between God and Israel, and by early patristic exegetes as a lovers' dialogue between Jesus and the Church (or the soul of the individual Christian), is here construed as a jealous dialogue between Israel and the "nations of the world" (the "daughters of Jerusalem" of Cant. 5:8, 16).[79] But it is not said when this dialogue occurs, whether at Sinai or at the sea, both of which are rabbinically understood as times when the Song of Songs was revealed to Israel as part of God's self-disclosure.[80] However, in all likelihood the dialogue is specific to neither of these past events but is timeless, in a sense occurring in the extended, seemingly eternal present (note especially that modif of Israel's suffering and the nations' attempt to lure Israel away from her commitment to God). The dialogue is positioned here because it is *similar* to (note the transitional "similarly" [*kāk*]) what occurred at the sea and at Sinai in Israel's "recognition" of God's singularity.

The tradition of Israel's dialogue with the nations is found elsewhere.[81] But only in the *Sifre* is it combined with the preceding interpretations (I, J1, and J2) in such a way as to connect that dialogue not only with the splitting of the sea (its usual association) but with the revelation at Sinai (not found elsewhere). It is particularly interesting to note how, as a consequence of the *Sifre*'s placement and subtle reshaping of this tradition, the dialogue is made to intersect, both thematically and verbally, with the preceding interpretations of Deut. 33:2. First, just as in section I God, unlike the father of the bridegroom, displays only a part of his majesty, so too in J3 Israel only has to recount to the nations a part of her lover's praises. If in J2 (at the Sea), and implicitly in J1 (at Sinai), Israel immediately "recognized" (*hikkîrû*) God among His angelic entourage, in J3 she wishes for the nations to recognize (*makkîrîm*) Him as well, albeit not as fully. Similarly, the nations in J3 use two terms to praise Israel ("beautiful" [*nā'îm*] and "mighty" [*gibbôrîm*]) that were used in section J1 to describe the king's entourage.[82] But if Israel reveals to the nations only a part of God's praises, by citing *selectively* from Cant. 5:9–16, it is precisely in two uncited phrases from there that the verbal links between Israel's dialogue with the nations and its encounter with God at Sinai are the strongest. Cant. 5:10 reads in ful: "My beloved is clear-skinned and ruddy, prominent among a myriad (*dāgûl mērĕbābâ*)," the unquoted second half being almost identical to "ensign (*ʾôt*) among the myriads (*mēribĕbôt*) holy," as Deut. 33:2 is rendered in section J1.[83] Similarly, Cant. 5:11 reads in full: "His head is finest gold, his locks (*qĕwuṣṣōtāyw*) are curled and black as a raven." Israel's lover is described with the very same term previously used awkwardly in section J1 to describe the king's *familia*.[84] As already noted, the other two terms used there to describe the king's *familia* are used by the nations to describe Israel. Through such metaphoric slippage, the divine family is now understood to include, ideally at least, Israel itself. Finally, the motif of Israel's suffering, presumably at the hands of the nations, for the sake of her marriage to God and the sudden reversal of Israel's relation to the nations (wherein the latter come asking to join Israel) echoes previous interpretations (especially, D–G), here as there with a tone of mocking sarcasm.

By noting the verbal and thematic connections between this interpretation and those that preceded it, I do not mean to suggest any simple correspondences between them or to eclipse their differences, but to suggest that the present placement and shaping of this tradition of dialogue between Israel and the nations in the context of commentary on Deut. 33:2–4 produces a somewhat different set of resonances than in other redacted contexts. Here Israel's complex conflict with the nations is set in relation to the mutual and exclusive recognition that God and Israel bestowed upon each other at Sinai.[85] By means of such an editorial juxtaposition, the lemma triggers an enchainment of interpretations. To begin with, at Sinai God stood out among the divine beings (angels). By combining this idea with the interpretation of Exod. 15:2, it is suggested that at Sinai as at the Sea Israel immediately recognized God's singularity. The tradition of Israel's dialogue with the nations indicates that Israel pays a price for her singular attachment to God, which is her separation from the nations, which the nations seek to undo. But by revealing to the nations something of the nature of God's singularity, Israel's separation from the nations is transformed, in the very course of the dialogue, from a matter of negative consequence to one of positive choice. Just as God stands out among the angels, so too Israel in its recognition of God stands out among the nations (angels often representing nations), even as Israel dialogically engages those nations, at some risk of being absorbed by them, so as to communicate to them a *part* of God's praises. Here again we may detect some ambivalence regarding Israel's relation to the nations: she wishes for the nations to have some notion of the grounds for her intimacy with God, without wishing to share fully that intimacy with the nations.

The commentary next shifts its attention to the scriptural image of fiery revelation, in the dual sense of the one-time event at Sinai (K) and the eternity of Torah teaching that originates from that event (L–M):

> [K] "Lightning flashing at them from His right" (33:2): When [each] word[86] would go forth from the mouth of the Holy One, blessed be He, it would go forth from the right side of the Holy one, blessed be He, to the left side of Israel, encircle the camp of Israel twelve miles by twelve miles, and return by the right side of Israel to the left side of the Lord. The Holy One, blessed be He, would receive it in His right hand and engrave it upon the tablet. His voice[87] would travel from one end of the world to the other, as it is said, "The voice of the Lord kindles flames of fire" (Ps. 29:7).[88]

The Hebrew phrase *ʾēšdāt* (just translated as "lightning flashing") is a hapax legomenon that here and elsewhere is understood to comprise two words: fire (*ʾēš*) and law (*dāt*).[89] The divine utterance or command is understood to be both audible and visible, like the lightning and thunder that is described as accompanying revelation in Exod. 20:15. Each utterance was perceived as a flame or bolt of lightning that left God's right hand, encircled Israel as a whole, thereby marking its boundaries, [90] and returned to God's right hand, with which he then burned its commandment (law) onto the tablets. But each commandment also reverberated as a voice that could be heard (and felt) throughout the world.[91] Thus, while each divine utterance (*dibbûr*) as fire encompassed Israel collectively, thereby defining it as *separate* from the other nations, God's voice (*qôl*) as thunder extended *beyond* Israel to the nations, who, as we have previously seen (sections E and F), also experienced revelation, albeit less directly.

The tradition here expressed may be compared and contrasted with the much more widely attested one, found elsewhere in the *Sifre*, in which it is said that as each divine utterance or commandment issued forth it struck each Israelite individually with such force as to thrust him or her back twelve miles (to the edge of the camp), whence they had to return twelve miles before receiving the next one.[92] In our present commentary context the scriptural image of the fiery law being given to Israel from the *right hand* of God generates the midrasic image, found only here and in dependent texts, of each divine utterance engaging not each Israelite *individually* but encompassing them all as a *collectivity* before cutting its letters into the tablets. This understanding of revelation having encompassed Israel at Sinai was earlier encountered in the idea of God having spoken to Israel from four directions (§343 C), and will be met with again later (§313 C). So encompassed by divine speech/command, Israel is defined apart from the nations in engagement with God.

The image of Torah as fire, from the first half of *ʾēšdāt*, is next elaborated, but now in transtemporal terms:

[L1] "Lightning flashing at them from his right": Scripture tells that the words of Torah are likened to fire.

[L2] Just as fire was given from heaven, so were the words of Torah given from heaven, as it is said, "You yourselves saw that I spoke to you from the very heavens" (Exod. 20:19).

[L3] Just as fire [brings] life to the world, so do the words of Torah [bring] life to the world.[93]

[L4] Just as with fire, whoever gets [too] near to it is burned, while whoever gets [too] far from it is chilled, so it is with words of Torah: as long as a person labors with them, they [bring] life to him, but if he departs from them, they kill him.[94]

[L5] Just as fire is used (*mištammĕšîn bāh*) both in this world and in the world to come, so the words of Torah are used both in this world and in the world to come.

[L6] Just as fire leaves a mark upon the body of whoever uses it, and people who labor with it are recognizable among other people,[95] so too the disciples of the wise [sages] are recognizable by their speech, by their manner of walking, and by their dress in the market.[96]

[M] "A fiery law": Had law (*dāt*) not been given with it [= the fire], a person would not be able to labor with it.[97]

The association of revelation with fire in the scriptural expression *ʾēšdāt* occasions a list of five (or six according to some variants) ways, all of them positive, that the words of Torah, scriptural as well as rabbinic, can be compared to fire.[98] The first two interpretations (L2, L3), taken together, stress that such words of Torah, like fire, link heaven and earth: they originate in heaven and bring life to the world.

The third comparison (L4), however, does not fit smoothly within this positive view of Torah. The metaphor of scorching fire should suggest the following more ambivalent conclusion: get close enough to be warmed but not so close as to get burned. This, however, is very different from the *Sifre*'s wholly positive applications of the metaphor to Torah: for those who labor in Torah (no matter how close they get), it is a source of life, whereas for those who depart from Torah, it is a source of death: all or nothing.[99] The awkwardness of this juxtaposition may be highlighted by comparing it with the similar but smoother formulation in the *Mekilta*, in its commentary to the account of revelation in the Book of Exodus: "Because the Lord descended upon it in fire" (Exod. 19:18): This tells that the Torah is fire, was given from the midst of fire, and can be compared to fire. As it is the way of fire that whoever gets [too] near to it is burned, [whereas] whoever gets [too] far from it is chilled, [so too with Torah,] one should only warm oneself opposite its light."[100] The *Mekilta* differs from the *Sifre* in two respects:

1. It includes only one comparison of Torah and fire, omitting the other more positive ones.[101]
2. It states explicitly the more logical conclusion of the comparison, which is notably absent in the *Sifre*: warm yourself by the words of Torah but do not get too close.

It would appear, therefore, that the comparison of Torah to scorching fire originates in a context where its conclusion was more cautionary than in the *Sifre*.[102] What might that context have been? The *Mekilta*'s more cautious use of the comparison of Torah and scorching fire appears in the context of its commentary on Exod. 19–20, where it consistently denies that Moses ascended to heaven or that the divine Glory descended onto Mt. Sinai. Although the divine voice and heavenly fire crossed from heaven to earth, the barrier between heaven and earth remained intact; Moses and God communicated across that barrier but did not cross it. What was beheld was not so much a vision of God as God's word made visible.[103] This view, not necessarily consistent with rabbinic interpretations of the theophany elsewhere,[104] is best understood as an attempt to discourage an interpretation of Exod. 19–20 in terms of Ezekiel's ecstatic vision of the divine chariot (Merkabah), and ecstatic scriptural exposition more generally. Such an interpretation may have been particularly prevalent when Exodus's account of revelation was the synagogue lection for the festival of Shabuʾot (Pentacost) together with the Merkabah vision of Ezekiel as its prophetic accompaniment (*hafṭarah*).[105] In fact, the cationary association of Torah with the metaphor of scorching fire is elsewhere found in early rabbinic texts that warn of the dangers of too deeply engaging in the exposition of the Merkabah: "To what may the matter [of Merkabah exposition] be compared? To a highway that passes between two roads, one of fire (ʾôr) and one of snow. If a person inclines this way, he is burned by the fire. If he inclines that way, he is burned by the snow. What must one do? Walk in the middle, inclining neither this way nor that."[106]

Thus, the mystical exegete must exercise great caution lest overly intensive, unmediated exposition of or exposure to revelation (or at least certain parts of it) consume him.[107] If in the *Mekilta*, in the context of commenting on Scripture's account of the theophany at Sinai, the image of fire and snow has been slightly transformed so as to apply to *Torah as a whole*, then in the *Sifre*, in the context of its interpretation of Torah as that which positively distinguishes Israel from the nations, that image has been even more radically transformed so as to yield a wholly positive comparison: engagement with the Torah produces life, separation from it results in death. Still, this wholly positive conclusion sits uneasily alongside the more ambivalent comparison itself, adapted, as I have argued it is, from another context where other exegetical concerns were foremost.[108]

Yet, notwithstanding this internal strain, the reworked comparison of Torah to scorching fire makes sense overall within the larger context in which it is now set. Whereas the preceding comparison (L3) states that the words of Torah bring life to the world, the present interpretation (L4) stresses that such life is a reward to those who labor in the words of Torah. As the next interpretation (L5) adds, the world in which such life is granted to those who occupy themselves with ("use") the words of Torah is both this world and the world to come.[109] Implicitly, then, laboring with the words of Torah provides both a foretaste of and a bridge to the world to come.

In the final interpretation of Torah as fire (L6), attention shifts from words of Torah to the disciples of the sages, who by virtue of their constant laboring with the words of Torah are recognizable among the people more generally. This metaphoric slippage is subtly expressed by the fact that the final "so too" is not followed by "words of Torah," as previously, but by "disciples of the sages." Just as those who work with fire are physically marked and recognized, so too are the disciples of the sages distinguishable.[110] Their very manner of speech, walk, and dress are public signs of the deeply transformative effects of Torah learning and discourse upon their characters.[111]

Although this final interpretation represents a significant shift it also signals something of a return to an earlier motif, as suggested by the repeated use of the verb *hikkîr* ("to recognize," here in the passive). Just as Israel recognized God at the sea (J2) and implicitly at Sinai (J1), and just as Israel sings God's praises so that the nations might recognize Israel's lover among the other lovers (J3), now the disciples of the sages are recognizable among the crowd in the market. This final interpretation of the fire metaphor metonymically echoes the interpretation of the previously interpreted part of the lemma: just as God stands out like a "sign" (or mark) among the divine "family" and Israel among the nations, so, too, the disciples of the sages are marked among Israel. If Israel by recognizing God at the time of revelation is distinguished among the other peoples, then within Israel the sages, through their constant laboring with revelation, similarly are marked apart.[112]

Finally (M), having focused on the fire aspect of Torah as triggered by the word *'ēšdāt*, the commentary concludes by returning to its combined sense of fire (*'ēš*) and law (*dāt*). Were it not for the latter, it would be impossible for a person to labor with (that is, study) the former. In a sense, this conclusion brings us back to the internal incommensurability of the third interpretation of the analogy between fire and Torah (L4). *Unlike* fire, it is possible to labor with the Torah to acquire through it "life" without needing to keep a distance from it in fear of being burned. This is because the Torah contains *within* itself a mediating shield against the heat of its own fire: its laws, or very discipline of *collective* life.[113]

Lover, Indeed, of the People(s) (§344)

The next verse (33:3) presents several problems for understanding and interpretation, both because of its hapax legomena and because of the irregularities of its syntax.[114] Although no longer speaking specifically of God's self-disclosure to Israel in the wilderness, it continues the theme of the special relationship between God and Israel. The commentary, while understanding the verse as a general (timeless) statement about Israel's relationship to God, extends and interconnects motifs previously enunciated in relation to God's revelation of the Torah to Israel at Sinai: God's favor for Israel vis-à-vis the nations, the distinctive place of Israel's (rabbinic) leaders in the covenantal scheme, Israel's sufferings, and Israel's conditionless acceptance of the Torah. The biblical verse comprises four strophes (two lines of two parts each). The commentary attends to each of these in turn, and does so three times. Its first series of comments is as follows:[115]

> [A1] "Lover, indeed, of the people(s)" (33:3): This teaches that God loved Israel [more] than he loved any other nation or kingdom.
>
> [A2] "Their hallowed are all in Your hand": This refers to the leaders (*parnāsîm*) of Israel, who stand over Israel and give their lives (*napšām*) for them.[116] Of Moses what is said [in this regard]? "Now, if You will forgive their sin [well and good]; but if not, erase me from the record which You have written" (Exod. 32:32). Of David what is said [in this regard]? "I am the one who sinned and have surely acted wickedly, but what have these sheep done? [O Lord my God, let Your hand fall upon me and my father's house, and let not Your people be plagued]" (1 Chr. 21:17).
>
> [A3] "They follow in Your footsteps": Even though they are persecuted, even though they are smitten, even though they are despised.[117]
>
> [A4] "Accepting Your words": They take upon themselves the yoke of the Torah, as it says, "All that the Lord has spoken we will do and obey" (Exod. 24:7).[118]

Although the first lemma speaks literally of the "peoples" (*ʿammîm*) in the plural, the commentary understands the primary object of God's love to be Israel, for which there is a long and broad tradition.[119] However, the plural *peoples* still enters the commentary, for God's love for Israel is contrasted with that for the other nations.[120] This may be occasioned by the word *ʾap*, which, although usually understood emphatically ("indeed"), may also be understood to mean "also": "He also loves the nations [but not as much as He loves Israel]."[121] Thus, the first clause is understood not simply as an expression of God's love for Israel, but of Israel's distinction in this regard from the other nations. Whereas the commentary could easily have understood the lemma to refer to God's love of Israel *alone* (taking ʿ*ammîm* to refer to Israel as a collectivity), it does not do so. Instead, it chooses to express the idea of God's love for Israel in relation to the *foil* of the nations, thereby acknowledging, even if begrudgingly, that they, too, are the objects of divine love, but less so.[122]

The interpretation of the second clause (A2) moves from Israel as a whole, distinguished among the nations, to their distinguished leaders or *parnāsîm*, who not only devote themselves to Israel's welfare but forfeit their lives on Israel's account. I will discuss these *parnāsîm* in greater detail in the next chapter.[123] But here it simply needs to be said that, although they are associated in the past with Israel's biblical leaders (here and elsewhere with David and Moses, elsewhere also with Joshua), in the *Sifre*'s own sociohistorical context they are associated with those *rabbinic* sages who merited appointments to judicial and administrative paid communal positions.[124] As the lemma is interpreted, these are Israel's "hallowed" (*qĕdōšāyw*), whose lives are in God's hands (*bĕyādekā*). Perhaps they are God's hallowed because they hallow His name (*qiddûš haššēm*) by giving their lives in His service. Just as earlier (§343 J3), Israel as a whole is said to give its life in its dedication to God, here its leaders are said to give their lives in their dedicated leadership of the people.[125]

The interpretation of the third clause moves outward again from Israel's leaders to Israel as a whole, while continuing the theme of suffering. Apparently, the image of being under God's feet[126] (like being in his hands previously), elicits images of suffering and being spurned (presumably by the nations) for His sake. There are two ways to understand this interpretation. The first is to view the third clause together with its interpretation as two parts of a complete thought: even though they suffer, they [still] follow in your steps (or sit at your feet). Alternatively, we may find the completion (apotasis) of the interpretation of the third clause in the interpretation of the next clause: even though they suffer, they accept the God's words (the commandments) unconditionally. Here and in the following interpretations I favor the second alternative, understanding the commentary to enchain its interpretations of the third and fourth clauses.[127]

When we look at this first series of atomizing interpretations of Deut. 33:3 as a whole, we see that it is textually *framed* on one side by God's special love of Israel (A1) and on the other by Israel's unconditional acceptance of His Torah (A4). Within that frame is placed Israel's sufferings (at the hands of the nations) for the sake of the Torah (A3) and Israel's (rabbinic) leaders' self-sacrifice for the sake of Israel (A2).[128] Thus, the suffering both of Israel and its leaders is "justified" by the bond of divine love and human obedience within which it is editorially configured. As we shall see, this pattern is repeated twice, albeit with some important variations, in the next two sets of interpretations:

[B1] Another interpretation: "Lover, indeed, of the people(s)": This teaches that the Holy One, blessed be He, did not dispense love to the nations of the world as He did to Israel. Know that this is so since they [= the sages] have said: "What has been stolen from a gentile is permitted, while what has been stolen from an Israelite is forbidden." It once happened that the government [of Rome] sent two officers, instructing them as follows: "Go and disguise yourselves as converts,[129] and find out what is the nature of Israel's Torah." They went to Rabban Gamaliel at Usha,[130] where they recited Scripture and studied Mishnah: Midrash, Halkhot, and Aggadot.[131] As they [= the officers] were taking their leave, they said, "All of the Torah is pleasing and praiseworthy, except for one thing, and that is your saying, 'What has been stolen from a gentile is permitted, while what has been stolen from an Israelite is forbidden,' but we will not report this to the government."

[B2] "Their hallowed are all in Your hand": These are the great ones (gĕdôlîm) of the Land of Israel who are seized in place of all of Israel,[132] as it is said of Ezekiel, "Then lie on your left side, and let it bear the punishment of the House of Israel, for as many days as you lie on it you shall bear their punishment.... When you have completed these, you shall lie on your right side" (Ezek. 4:4–6).

[B3] "They follow in Your footsteps": Even though they anger [You].[133]

[B4] "Accepting Your words": They take upon themselves the yoke of Your Torah,[134] "All that the Lord has spoken we will do and obey" (Exod. 24:7).[135]

Although the second interpretation of the first clause (B1) is similar to the first interpretation of the same clause (A1), it states negatively what had previously been stated positively: not that God loved Israel more than the nations, but that God did not love the nations as much as He did Israel. This more negative emphasis is demonstrated by a rabbinic rule, implicitly understood to be backed by divine authority, that permits gentile stolen property to an Israelite, but not the reverse.[136] This rule occasions the telling of a story of two Roman officers who are sent surreptitiously (perhaps as spies) to study with the rabbinic Patriarch so as to report to Rome on the nature of rabbinic teaching.[137] In the end, they are so impressed with their rabbinic studies that they praise the Torah (written and oral) to the Patriarch, as presumably they will to the government, notwithstanding the single rule that they found objectionable but would not report.

This story is reminiscent of two earlier fictional dialogues in our commentary, one (§343 E), in which the nations, at the time of revelation, are so relieved that the world is not being destroyed that they express the hope that God will bless Israel with peace, and the other (§343 J3), in which the nations, first seeking to entice Israel to mix with them, are so impressed by Israel's praises of her lover-God that they seek to join Israel instead. In the latter story, much the same language is uses as here to describe the positive impression made by Israel on the nations.[138] In all three cases the nations (here represented by Roman officers) end up praising or blessing Israel despite their original intentions or inclinations to the contrary, and despite the fact that these very texts are so negative toward the nations. In other words, the nations are made to extol or bless Israel even as they are being mocked.[139]

This aspect of the present story can best be seen if we compare it to its closest parallel in the Palestinian Talmud (*B. Qam.* 4:3 [4b]).[140] There the context is the interpretation of the mishnaic rule (*B. Qam.* 4:3) that an Israelite is not culpable if his ox gores the ox of a gentile, whereas a gentile whose ox gores that of an Israelite must pay full damages regardless whether or not the gentile's ox was a habitual gorer.[141] To explain this discrepancy between the treatment of the property of a gentile and an Israelite, several justifications are offered, the first two based on scriptural verses understood to refer to the gentile nations' rejection of the Torah, and especially of the seven Noahide laws, at the time of revelation. First, Rab (ca. 240) cites Hab. 3:6 "[God] stood and measured the earth; He saw and loosened the nations," interpreting it to mean that God loosened the bounds on the property of the gentile nations.[142] Next, R. Hezekiah (ca. 240) cites a part of Deut. 33:1, " He appeared from Mt. Paran," to mean that God turned his face against the gentile nations. R. Jose b. Ḥanina (ca. 280) interprets this verse to mean that God "lowered them from [= reduced their claims to] their possessions." [143] Another interpretation is attributed to R. Abbahu in the name of R. Joḥanan (ca. 270): in such matters gentiles should be judged according to their own norms, wherein no distinction is made between an ox that habitually gores and one that gores for the first time.[144] But this latter point does not address the seeming unfairness of not holding culpable the Israelite owner of an ox that gores a gentile's ox.[145] It is in this context that the Palestinian Talmud cites its version of our story:

It once happened that the government [of Rome] sent two officers to learn Torah from Rabban Gamaliel. They learned from him Scripture [and] Mishnah: Talmud, Halakhot, and Aggadot. At the end they said to him: "All of your Torah is pleasing and praiseworthy, except for these two things that you say: An Israelite woman cannot serve as a midwife to a gentile woman but a gentile woman can serve as a midwife to an Israelite woman, and an Israelite woman cannot nurse the child of a gentile woman but a gentile woman can nurse [the child of] an Israelite woman with her permission.[146] [Second,] the stolen property of an Israelite is prohibited while the stolen property of a gentile is permitted." At that moment, Rabban Gamaliel decreed that the stolen property of a gentile be forbidden because of the profanation of the divine name [in the eyes of the gentiles]. [The Romans continued: "Regarding the rule,] 'The ox of an Israelite which gored the ox of a gentile, [the Israelite owner] is not culpable, etc.,' we will not report the matter [to Rome]."[147] Even so, they did not get so far as the Ladder of Tyre when they forgot everything they had learned.

It is clear from the Palesitnian Talmud's version of the story that of all the rules that apply a different legal standard to the gentile than to the Jew, the most problematic was the one governing the stolen property of a gentile. Whereas the version in the Palestinian Talmud has Rabban Gamaliel decree that that law (but not the others) be changed as a consequence of the officers' demurral, the *Sifre* commentary takes the rule for granted.[148] It is precisely because this law would have been particularly offensive to a gentile, and hence more likely to result in a "profanation of the God's name," that the Romans' decision to report favorably on the Jews' Torah without reporting this one is so striking in the *Sifre*'s version of the story. In the parallel version in the Palestinian Talmud, the Roman emissaries end up with nothing to report to Rome, because they forget everything they learn. Furthermore, the *Sifre*'s detail of the Roman's having feigned being converts, not found in the other versions of the story, strengthens the striking reversal at the story's end.[149] The Roman officers who begin by deceiving their Jewish hosts, presumably with some negative intention, end by deceiving the gentile authorities that sent them, presumably to Israel's benefit. In a sense, they are like Balaam (compare earlier, §343 E), who when charged to "curse" Israel, ends up "blessing" them. Once again (compare above, §343 J3), the subtext of the *Sifre*'s commentary is one in which Israel desires that the nations praise them and their (rabbinic) Torah, even as the latter provides the basis for Israel's self-understanding as being distinct among the nations as God's especially beloved.

The second interpretation of the second clause (B2) returns again from Israel as a whole to their leaders, here referred to as Israel's "greats" (*gědôlîm*), who give themselves as pledges for Israel. These would seem to be similar to the *parnāsîm* who give their lives for Israel in A2, and perhaps again refer to rabbinic sages who, in assuming leadership duties, represent their communities before God and suffer on their behalf as a consequence.[150] The present interpretation understands "in Your hand" to mean that Israel's leaders are like a pledge held in God's hand—like a pledge held as collateral for Israel's proper conduct. If the people of Israel sin, their leaders are held in their stead, at least until such time as the Israelites themselves pay in full. This *vicarious* nature of the leaders' sufferings is expressed in the citation from the prophet Ezekiel.[151] The example of Ezekiel may be compared to those of Moses and David in the previous interpretation of this clause (A2), where Israel's leaders are said to suffer, or at least to be prepared to suffer, on Israel's behalf. Although Moses is understood to offer his life in atonement for Israel's sin, God rejects this suggestion of vicarious punishment. Similarly, although David suffers as Israel's leader, it is for his own actions. Only Ezekiel of the three is actually said here to have suffered for Israel's sins.

As before, the interpretation of the third clause (B3) finds its apotasis in the interpretation of the final clause: even though Israel sins and thereby provokes God's anger, it still accepts the yoke of His Torah.[152] Perhaps Israel is being contrasted to the nations, who, according to earlier parts of the commentary, rejected the Torah as a whole (that is, in principle and not just in some of its particulars). Taken together with the previous set of interpretations, the verse is understood to mean tht even though Israel suffers on account of the covenant and even though it perpetually violates it, the covenant remains intact, both with respect to God's special love for Israel and with regard to Israel's acceptance of the bonds of His Torah. Both God's love for Israel and Israel's acceptance of the Torah are unconditional, notwithstanding the continual strains of suffering and sin.[153]

Finally, the commentary presents a third set of interpretations, which contain many familiar but also some fresh elements:

[C1] Another interpretation: "Lover, indeed, of the people": This teaches that the Holy One, blessed be He, loved Israel [more] than He loved any other nation or kingdom.
[C2] "Their hallowed are all in your hand": This refers to the souls of the righteous, which are kept with Him[154] in [His] treasury, as it is said, "The life of my lord will be bound up in the bundle of life in the care of the Lord" (1 Sam. 25:29).
[C3] "They follow in Your steps": Even as they are shoved back twelve miles and return twelve miles [to receive each commandment].
[C4] "Accepting Your words": [They take upon themselves the yoke of your Torah, saying,][155] "All that the Lord has spoken we will do and obey."[156]

The final interpretation of the four clauses retains the original framework of God's special love for Israel (C1) and their ready acceptance of the Torah (C4). However, the interpretation of the second clause (C2) shifts from the self-sacrifice of Israel's leaders (previously *parnāsîm* and *gĕdôlîm*) in the extended present, to the eternal protection by God Himself of the souls of the righteous (*ṣaddîqîm*). Now Israel's "hallowed" are their righteous, and it is their souls that are in God's "hand"."[157] If in this world Israel's (presumably rabbinic) leaders suffer and even give their lives for Israel's sake, then beyond this world the souls of the righteous are eternally entrusted to God's own care.[158]

If the second interpretation (C2) points beyond time and implicitly toward the world to come, then the next interpretation (C3) points back again to the event of revelation at Sinai, while moving outward again from Israel's leaders to Israel as a whole. What in the previous interpretations was understood as Israel's suffering in the extended present, is now understood in relation to the originary struggle of the Israelites as each one steadfastly received each divine utterance or commandment at Sinai.[159] The final scriptural clause of the lemma is interpreted identically as twice before, having become the commentary's refrain: notwithstanding the struggle and suffering involved, Israel (then as now) accepts God's word and will unconditionally.

Although it would be a mistake to harmonize reductively the three sets of interpretations of the four clauses of Deut. 33:3, that is, to make of them a single interpretation, it is clear that the various interpretations dynamically interconnect with one another as well as with what has preceded them in the commentary. In particular, the framing motifs of God's special love for Israel, as distinguished among the nations (A1, B1, C1), and of Israel's unconditional acceptance of His Torah (A4, B4, C4), echo (which is to say, they repeat but with a difference) the *Sifre*'s earlier commentary to Deut. 33:2. This repetitive framing pattern varies only at one point, in B1, where the nations themselves (as represented by the Roman officers) are eager to sing the praises of Israel's Torah (as rabbinically taught), even to the extent of consciously overlooking a part of that Torah that would appear to discriminate against them.[160]

Within the frame of God's love for Israel and Israel's unconditional acceptance of (if not complete fidelity to) His Torah, recurs another theme that we had previously encountered (see 343 L7): the distinctive place of Israel's political and religious leaders and models (successively referred to here as *parnāsîm, gĕdôlîm,* and *ṣaddîqîm*), who are understood as Israel's "hallowed ones" who are in God's "hands" (A2, B2, C2). This latter expression is taken to signify both the suffering that Israel's religio-political leaders endure on Israel's behalf, as well as the reward of eternal life with God that awaits the righteous.[161] The related theme of larger Israel's ignominious suffering at the hands of the gentile nations also finds its expression once again (A3), but tempered perhaps by its paratactic juxtaposition with two related themes: Israel's own provocation of God's anger through transgressing His commandments (B3), and the recollection that at Sinai too they took a pounding in receiving God's words and commandments (C3).[162] Yet despite these covenantal strains, the commentary concludes three times (A4, B4, C4), in identical language, with the assertion of Israel's originary and continually repeated acceptance, in dialogical deed and study, of God's Torah.

The Heritage of the Congregation of Jacob (§345)

The next verse (33:4) gives fresh expression to Moses' transmission of the Torah to Israel, with the commentary paying close attention to the details of its language and juxtaposition of its two halves:

> [A] "Moses charged us with the Teaching" (33:4): This charge is only for us, only for our sakes, as it is said, "I have built the House for the name of the Lord, the God of Israel" (1 Kings 8:20). For what is this House?[163] "And I have set a place there for the Ark, [containing the covenant which the Lord made with our fathers when He brought them out from the land of Egypt]" (ibid. 8:21). Behold, this charge is only for us, only for our sakes.[164]

The commentary focuses on the word us, which in Hebrew means literally "to us" or "for us" (lānû), expanding on the latter sense as "for our sakes."[165] In other words, Moses did not command the Torah to Israel for his own sake or for God's sake, but for Israel's sake alone. This is compared to Solomon's Temple, which, according to 1 Kings 8:20, might be thought to have been built for the sake of God, whose presence (or "name") would therein dwell. The next verse, however, clarifies that the Temple was built as a house for the ark, in which were kept the terms of the covenant that God established with Israel when He liberated them from Egypt. Thus, just as the Temple was built for the sake of the ark of the covenant, the Torah was commanded to Israel for their sake (and not God's).[166] Implicitly, therefore, Temple and Torah (and perhaps Temple worship and Torah study) are metonymically linked.

The next interpretation asks about Moses' role as Torah giver (now taking lānû as "to us"), in relation to the appearance of Jacob in the second half of the lemma:

> [B] Another interpretation: "Moses charged us with the Teaching (Torah)": Is it from our teacher Moses that we inherited the Torah? Is it not that our forefathers had merited it?[167] For it is said, "The heritage of the congregation of Jacob" (33:4)? From this I might learn that it is an inheritance [only] for the children of royalty (lit.: kings).[168] [Is it not also][169] an inheritance for the children of commoners (qĕṭanîm)? Scripture teaches, "You stand this

day, all of you, [before the Lord your God: your heads, your tribes, your elders, and your officers, even everyone of Israel]" (Deut. 29:9).[170]

This comment responds to a seeming ambiguity in the verse: if Israel acquired the Torah at Sinai from *Moses*, why does the verse conclude by referring to the Torah as the inheritance of the descendants of *Jacob*, who preceded Moses? Although the Torah was acquired by the intermediacy of Moses, it was because of the merits of the patriarchs, here represented by Jacob, that their descendants received it.[171] But the citation of the second half of the lemma to answer a question occasioned by the first raises in turn a new question: if the Torah is the inheritance of the *descendants* of Jacob, are we to think that the Torah is the domain of a privileged aristocracy.[172] Another verse is then cited to emphasize that Moses charged the Torah to *all* of Israel, then and now, and not to a select group among them. Here, as elsewhere in the *Sifre*, the text expresses an "egalitarian" Torah ethic: because the Torah was commanded to all of Israel, all of Israel (in principle at least) have an equal share in it. The rejected distinction between royalty and commoners, it seems to me, is a figurative rejection of the claims of any subgroup within Israel who would claim a superior status vis-à-vis the Torah on the basis of genealogical lineage. Two possibilities come to mind: those who could claim no converts in their lineage, and those of priestly stock.[173] Although the rabbis considered themselves to be an elite, authoritative class of Torah teachers, unlike the priestly class they drew their members from all of Israel regardless of genealogical pedigree and sought to transform all of Israel in their image.

The commentary next offers a radically different understanding of Deut. 33:4 by exploiting the plasticity of just one word of its second half:

[C] ["The heritage of the congregation of Jacob":][174] Read not "heritage" (*môrāšâ*), but "betrothed" (*mĕʾôrāsâ*):[175] the Torah is betrothed to Israel and is like a married woman with respect to the ations of the world. And so it says, "Can a man rake embers into his bosom without burning his clothes? Can a man walk on live coals without scorching his feet? It is the same with one who sleeps with his fellow's wife; none who touches her will go unpunished" (Prov. 6:27–29).[176]

Although, according to the preceding interpretation (B), the Torah is the inheritance of *all* of Israel, regardless of genealogical lineage,[177] it is still not the inheritance of the nations. Thus, the previous inclusive interpretation of the lemma, facilitated by reading it in combination with Deut. 29:9, is followed by an exclusive one, facilitated by a re-reading of its awkward word for *heritage*. The two interpretations, however, need not be contradictory: Torah is for *all* of Israel, but *only* for Israel. According to the latter interpretation, graphically reinforced by the citation from Proberbs, the nations are prohibited from "touching" the Torah, just as a man is prohibited from touching another's wife. The fire metaphor recalls the earlier (§343 L–M) comparison of Torah to burning fire. There it was said that it is only because of the laws that accompany the Torah's fire that it is possible to labor in it without getting burned. Therefore, only those (Israel) who accept the obligations of the Torah (§344 A4, B4, C4) can engage it without being burned. Whereas in the Proverbs verse *fire* is employed as a metaphor for adultery, in the *Sifre's* commentary *adultery* is employed as a metaphor for the nations' relation to the Torah (fire). Here, however, the fire metaphor is subordinated to that of betrothal: if, at Sinai, Moses acted as God's agent in delivering His wedding contract (the Torah) to Israel, then the monogamous nature of the relationship of Israel to God (previously expressed in our commentary in §343 J3), can also be expressed as an exclusive one between Israel and the Torah.[178] For the nations to seek the textual pleasures of the Torah outside a *legally* defined commitment to it is comparable to one who seeks the sexual pleasures of another's wife. Who might such "nations" be? Either Christians who engage in the study of the Hebrew Bible (Old Testament) without submitting to its (rabbinically understood) covenantal stipulations, or pagan "fellow travelers" who attend synagogues to hear the Torah taught without formally converting to Judaism, that is, without committing themselves to its commandments.

The commentary next returns to the lemma to reconsider Torah as "heritage" (*môrāšâ*), again in an inclusive sense (within Israel), but now in some tension with what has preceded:

> [D] "The heritage of the congregation of Jacob":[179] A *mashal*: [This may be compared] to a king's son who when young is taken captive to a country across the sea. Should he desire to return after a hundred years, he need not be embarrassed to do so because he can say, "I am returning to my inheritance."[180] [Therefore it is said,] "The heritage of the congregation of Jacob."[181]

The previously expressed idea that the Torah is Israel's exclusively betrothed mate poses a problem. What if an individual or group within Israel is separated or estranged from the Torah, can it at a later time return to the Torah? If we adopt the model of monogamous marriage, we would have to answer no, especially if the separation or estrangement involved embracing other sources of wisdom or types of practice, as may be presumed.[182] Thus, the former, inclusive interpretation of Torah as "inheritance" is *reinstated*, but now in a new sense: whereas previously the commentary stressed that all classes of Israelites, regardless of genealogical lineage, have a share in Torah, now it stresses that all Israelites, no matter how long or how far they been separated from Torah, can forever return to it as it is inalienably theirs. Unlike the betrothal metaphor (*mĕʾôrāsâ*), the inheritance metaphor (*môrāšâ*) asserts that all of Israel have an *unconditional* share in the Torah.[183]

But this midrashic return does not obviate the preceding understanding of *môrāšâ* ("heritage") as *mĕʾôrāsâ* ("betrothed"). Rather, the two understandings may be said to coexist within the redacted structure of the commentary, even as they are in some tension with one another. The commentary's (and hence its students') oscillation between inclusive and exclusive understandings of Israel's relationship with the Torah is accomplished through two exegetical strategies: interpreting the two halves of Deut. 33:4 in relation to one another and other verses (A, B), and finding both understandings in the dual word *môrāšâ-mĕʾôrāsâ* of the second half (C, D). At Sinai Moses *commanded* the Torah to *all* of Israel for *all* times, defining their relation to the Torah in legally obligatory terms that precluded a similar relationship to Torah on the part of the nations (B, C). This may be said to be the *mĕʾôrāsâ* aspect of the relationship. Yet even when the Israelites depart from the Torah it is always theirs to which to return, for it is theirs not by virtue of their own conduct (for which nevertheless they are held accountable according to the Torah's terms) but by virtue of the conduct of their originary ancestors, from whom, in a sense, they have inherited the Torah (B, D). This may be said to be the *môrāšâ* aspect of the relationship. These two aspects may also be contrasted, but not absolutely, in temporal terms. On the one hand, Torah as *mĕʾôrāsâ* binds Israel "on this day" as on the day they received it at Sinai, thereby transcending history in the perpetual present of Israel's engagement with it. On the other hand, Torah as *môrāšâ* is passed on through time, inherited from the past, having a history, in a sense, of its own. Thus the Torah is continually *commanded by Moses* yet successively inherited by all who are *congregated to Jacob*.

This dual interpretation is a fitting vantage point from which to look back briefly upon much of what has preceded it in the commentary. If the Torah in encompassing Israel defines Israel by defining its boundaries, it does so simultaneously in inclusive and exclusive ways, that is, by inclusively defining what is contained within (all of Israel) in exclusive relation to what lies without (the nations). Such a dialectic requires that hermeneutical (no less than historical) attention to one is never far removed from attention to the other. This is in part because the constructer of the boundary (God) is understood, in some problematically irreducible way, to be the creator and caretaker both of what is within and of what is without. To put it in terms of a central paradox posed by the paratactic juxtaposition of traditions within the commentary: God is the exclusive lover of His favored Israel, yet still somehow the "lover of the peoples." Israel must continually engage and confront these peoples, even as they did when their boundary and its creator were first revealed to them at Sinai.

He Encompassed Him and Instructed Him (§313)

Before concluding, let us look at one other verse that the *Sifre* commentary interprets as signifying the revelation at Sinai. Although not contiguous with the sections of the commentary that we have examined, it expresses some of the same ideas and draws upon some common traditions. The verse is Deut. 32:10, which like 33:2 poetically recounts Israel's encounter with God in the wilderness. But here the image is of Israel as a foundling, discovered alone and cared for by God in the midst of a wasteland:

> He found him in a desert land,
> And in a howling wasteland;
> He encompassed him, he cared for him,
> He kept him as the apple of His eye.

The *Sifre* provides four sets of interpretations of these poetic images, the first relating them to Abraham, the second relating them to Israel at the time of the revelation at Sinai, the third relating them to the period of Israel's wanderings through the wilderness, and the fourth relating them to the messianic future, which is viewed as a return to the idealized period of God's care and protection of Israel. Note once again the chronological progression as well as the symmetrical pairing of revelation and eschatology (as in §343 H). I shall examine here only the second set of interpretations, but it is important to keep in mind the larger chronological sequence in which it is set. The motifs and even some language will be familiar, even as their exegetical and rhetorical juxtaposition is fresh:

[A] Another interpretation: "He found him in a wilderness land": This refers to Israel, as it is said, "I found Israel like grapes in the wilderness" (Hos. 9:10).[184]

[B] "And in a howling wasteland": In a place of distress, in a place of marauding troops, in a place of robbers.[185]

[C] "He encompassed him" (*yĕsōbĕbenhû*) : Before Mt. Sinai, in connection with which it is said, "You shall set bounds for the people round around (*sābîb*), saying..." (Exod. 19:12).[186]

[D] "He cared for [=instructed] him" (*yĕbônĕnēhû*): With the ten commandments. This teaches that when [each] divine utterance [= commandment] went forth from the mouth of the Holy One, blessed be He, Israel would observe [187] it and would know now much midrash could be inferred from it,[188] how many laws (*hălākôt*) could be inferred from it, how many a fortiori arguments (*qôlîm wahămûrîm*) could be inferred from it, how many arguments by verbal analogy (*gĕzērôt šawwôt*) could be inferred from it.[189]

[E] "He kept [= protected] him as the apple of His eye": They went twelve miles [back] and returned twelve miles for each and every divine utterance, but they were not startled[190] either by the voice of the thunderings[191] or by the voice of the lightnings.[192]

With the previous set of interpretations having taken the lemma to refer to Abraham, Hos. 9:10 is now cited so as to identify the unspecified direct object of the verb *to find* with Israel. The Hosea verse serves this purpose well as it shares two words with the lemma: *found* and *wilderness*. The image of finding sweet and juicy grapes in the hot and dry desert also expresses the sense of relief with which God "found" Israel.

In B, although the lemma appears to stress the *natural* hardships of Israel's condition in the wilderness (dry and windy), the commentary, here as in the other sets of intepretations, stresses the risks of *human* violence. Thus, the divine protection envisioned during the time of Israel's sojourn in the wilderness of Sinai seems to be a retrojection from later, more settled but socially insecure circumstances. In particular, the time and place of the *Sifre*'s editing in the mid-third century Palestine is known to have been one of particular economic hardship, lawlessness, and abuse of the local population by Roman troops.[193]

In C, God's encompassing of Israel is said to refer to His having gathered them around Mt. Sinai. Although the context of Exod. 19:12, which is linked to the lemma be the use of the word *sābîb*, refers to God's having set a boundary about the mountain, preventing the people from getting too close to it, the verse literally speaks of God's having bounded the people, perhaps here taken to refer not only to their inner boundary vis-à-vis the mountain, but to their outer boundary as well.[194] We have previously (§343 C, K) encountered the idea of God's revelation having defined Israel's outer boundary, whereby they are distinguished from the nations round about them.

The verb *yĕbônĕnēhû* of the lemma is generally understood by biblical scholars as a *polel* form of the root *byn*, the only occurrence of this form of the verb in the Hebrew Bible. As such, it is thought to mean here to "bestow (mental) attention on" or to "consider (kindly)," but that understanding is derived largely from the sense of the scriptural context.[195] In D, our commentary also construes the word in relation to its scriptural context, that context now being taken to refer to God's revelation of the Torah to Israel at Sinai, understanding the verb in terms of its root meaning to split or descern.[196] But even so, the verb is read doubly, first as God's instruction of Israel with the ten commandments (with God as the verb's subject and

Israel as its object), and second as Israel's discerning of the multiple possibilities of interpretation of each commandment (with Israel as the verb's subject and each divine commandment as its object).[197] Thus, even at the very moment of revelation, the people of Israel were not simply passive *receivers* of the divine word, but already empowered by God as the active *perceivers* of its multiple hermeneutical (and performative) potentialities. Israel's polymorphic *vision* at Sinai, according to this formulation, was not so much of God as of his words.[198] Although the present commentary is not one of legal interpretation per se, the context in which it sets this interpretation is itself one of multiple (four) interpretations of a single verse.

In E, we find a tradition previously encountered (§344 C3) but differently expressed: each Israelite was thrown back to the edge of the camp by the powerful thrust of each commandment.[199] Whereas elsewhere the *Sifre* emphasizes Israel's readiness to accept God's commandments unconditionally, notwithstanding the shock and struggle involved, here it stresses the divine *protection* accorded to Israel, whereby what might have been the intolerable shock of revelation was ameliorated.[200]

The biblical image of God's loving, protective care for the abandoned infant Israel (cf. Hos. 9:10; Ezek. 16:3-14) is commonly understood to refer ideally to the period of Israel's wandering in the wilderness, during which time God provided for their physical needs and shielded them from physical harm. In the *Sifre*'s commentary that image has been refigured in relation to the time of God's revelation of His Torah to Israel at Sinai. It was then and there that God took Israel to Himself, enveloping them and protecting them with his loving care from the ravages not so much of nature as of violent society without. It was then and there that He gave them their first real nourishment, words from His mouth, helping them to receive each one directly without ill consequences and enabling them to get the most out of each morsel. Such a synthetic restatement, while not doing justice to the rhetorical dynamic and dialectic of the *Sifre*'s atomistic commentary, at least conveys the richness of images therein juxtaposed and thereby demanding of interpretation.

Conclusions

Having completed our tour de textes, what are we to make of them, especially in relation to the question, raised at the outset of this chapter? Two modes of exegetical operation have been evident throughout, precisely those that in Chapter 1 I delineated as characteristic of the *Sifre*'s commentary overall (as of "dialogical" commentary more generally):

1. The fracturing of the biblical text to facilitate close and sustained

attention to the details of its expression, often in relation to atomized fragments relocated from elsewhere in Scripture.

2. The redactional assembling of multiple interpretations of the resulting scriptural fragments.

As we have frequently seen, such discrete interpretations may themselves be constructed of several relocated and subtly reshaped shards of tradition, here refigured through their paratactic juxtaposition with one another and with the fractured base text of Deuteronomy. This dual procedure results in such a proliferation of meanings and perspectives—a complex interplay of texts, traditions, and their associative links—that we may no longer be able to recall Scripture's own continuity of narration or to substitute for it, in any simple sense, and alternative narrative continuity produced by its commentary. It is impossible to present the *Sifre*'s re-presentation of revelation, both as received text and as past event, in summary fashion without leveling the lively contours of its formal and substantive heterogeneity. Let it suffice for me to recall here two examples, one in which a biblical word is given two meanings and the other in which a postbiblical tradition appears in two different shapes: *Torah* of Deut. 33:4 is *both* Israel's "heritage" (*môrāšâ*: §345 B, D) *and* Israel's "betrothed" (*mě^ɔôrāsâ*: §345C). Each fiery divine utterance-commandment that issued from God's mouth at Sinai *both* encompassed and thereby defined the boundaries of Israel as a whole, twelve miles by twelve miles, before returning to God (§343 K) *and* struck each and every Israelite so powerfully as to thrust each one back twelve miles from whence each had to return twelve miles to receive the next one (§344 C3)?[201] When we ask our commentary the questions "What does the biblical text really say?" and "What really happened?" we receive a plethora of answers that cannot easily be assimilated to one another.

That rabbinic midrash frequently attributes multiple, even seemingly incommensurate, meanings to a single scriptural word or phrase is a commonly recognized and discussed characteristic of its mode of biblical interpretation.[202] Less often acknowledged, however, is the corollary of this textual phenomenon for historical re-presentation: if Scripture is the divinely authored record of Israel's sacred story, then the midrashic multiple interpretations of that record of necessity adduce multiple versions of that story. But to the extent that the biblical text is rabbinically understood to point not just to the distant time of the events it narrates but to all times—from the originary past of Scripture to the extended present of rabbinic discourse and practice to the awaited future of messianic redemption—then all such times are open to multiple transformations as they are repeatedly re-presented and interwoven in commentary's reshaping and resiting of Scripture and tradition.[203] For example, we saw that the visit by two Roman officers to the academy of the Patriarch Rabban

Gamaliel is narrated in the *Sifre*, in the context of commenting for the second of three times on a atomized Deut. 33:3, in a fashion strikeingly dissimilar from its narration in other early rabbinic sources. One could say that these differences simply reflect the existence, either at different times or in different circles, of different versions or memories of a single, original story or event. This may well be. But my examination of the different versions of this story, like similar examinations of other variant traditions, suggests that our imagined commentary maker did not simply represent mimetically the version of the story with which he was familiar. Rather, he appears to have *fashioned*, however unsmoothly, the story as we here have it, perhaps out of multiple versions with which he was already familiar, to suit the rhetorical moment of his commentary. In the *Sifre*, unlike the other rhetorical contexts in which the tradition appears, that moment is one of incessant preoccupation with distinguishing Israel from the nations in relation to Israel's receiving and accepting of God's revelation at Sinai.[204]

From such multiple re-presentations and repositionings of biblical texts and postbiblical traditions it is important not to generalize too hastily about the rabbis having had a radically different conception either of language or of time overall from "ours."[205] Rather, just as within the discursive network of scriptural commentary the fixities of biblical text are transformatively refigured in terms of the fluid undercurrent of their multiple meanings, so, too, and perhaps concomitantly, the seeming fixities of received tradition and historical time are multiply transformed, with no implied devaluation of any of these. It is precisely the multiple fractures of text, tradition, and time that enables their interweaving—like that of scriptural past, rabbinic present, and messianic future—in the complex fabric of commentary. However, an important, previously noted difference between the fracturing of biblical text and that of received tradition and historical time must be emphasized. The fixed, continuous, textual context from which the fragments of Scripture have been lifted to be transformed can be assumed to have been a commonly held cultural possession, providing a common point not only from which to depart but also to which to return repeatedly in the work of commentary. In other word, biblical text remains whole notwithstanding, and perhaps even thanks to, its repeated fission and consequent fusion. The same cannot be presumed either for extra-biblical tradition or for history. We have no *continuous* early rabbinic retold Bible (like Josephus' retelling of the story of revelation, for example),[206] nor any continuous early rabbinic historical or biographical narratives (nor for that matter coherently articulated rabbinic theologies or mythologies),[207] from which we may assume the componenets of our commentary to have been lifted to be reshaped. It may be precisely for this reason that the rabbinic fragmentation and re-presentation of tradition and time are to be found within the network of rabbinic commentaries to fixed, commonly accepted, and (to the rabbis) divinely authorized and hence authorizing texts, here that of Scripture but elsewhere that of the Mishnah (in the commentary of the Talmuds). In place of what in other cultures is the continuous narration of history, or mythology, or biography as autonomous discourses, we find in rabbinic commentary to Scripture the interweaving of heterogeneous historio-graphic, mythological, and biographical fragments, together with those of Scripture, all on the loom of Scripture itself. This is a cultural network that the student of the commentary does not so much passively receive as transformatively engage and enter. That network is *timely* to the extent that it is rhetorically configured so as to engage a historically located society of students. But it is also *timeless* to the extent that its configuration of tradition remains restlessly uncongealed, open to subsequent reconfigu-rations in the continuous dialogic of transmission and reception.[208]

As irreducible as this web of midrashic re-presentations may be, several of its recurring themes and their repeated interassociations, whether facilitated by strutural juxtaposition or linguistic interconnection, cannot but strike us. To the *limited* extent that our commentary may be said to display qualities of coherence, such coherence lies in those repetitions—often with differences—and interassociations as they are structured into the text in such a way as to engage its students in the continuing work of connecting and differentiating between them.

The first such set of repeated juxtapositions that I would like to highlight concerns both the nature of the event of revelation and its textual expression. At several points our commentary stresses that God's revealed word encompassed the people of Israel, thereby defining them as a unity, even as proximate interpretations depict Israel as having perceived or received that word as a multivocal (in language and in meaning) communication.[209] This combination is most succinctly expressed in the juxtaposition of the words *yĕsōbĕbenhû* and *yĕbônĕnēhu* as rabbinically understood (§313): at Sinai God encompassed the Israelites to enlighten them to perceive the multiplicity of hermeneutically to be derived meanings contained within each divine word. The heterogeneous polyphony of revelation was socially circumscribed by the parameters of the people of Israel that received it, even as those very parameters were defined by that revelation. If each divine utterance in encompassing the Israelites as they accepted *and* interpreted it bound them together, it also bound them to the single God from whose "mouth" that multivocal word issued.[210] After Sinai, or at least after the cessation of prophecy and the canonization of Torah, collective access to the interpreted word of God continues through the redacted texts and social institutions of rabbinic Torah study, which similarly circumscribe and configure the human and hermeneutical polyphony they contain.[211]

In revealing the Torah to Israel at Sinai, God intimately and exegetically encouraged and engaged them with His word, thereby drawing them close to Him in mutual recognition and commitment.[212] But this romance is not all sweet, displaying recurring elements of struggle and strain, partly because of the inherent shock of human exposure to the fiery divine word,[213] partly because of Israel's inability to fulfill fully its obligations,[214] but most notably because the obverse of Israel's encompassed intimacy with God and His Torah is their struggle for self-definition (not to mention survival) vis-à-vis the "nations of the world." Here we encounter some remarkable tensions among the traditions: God first discloses Himself to the nations so that they might accept His Torah,[215] even though He knew long before Sinai that they were unworthy to have any part in it;[216] Israel rejects the overtures of the nations to intermingle with them, even as Israel desires to relate to the nations the virtues of her lover-God;[217] Israel protests her suffering at the hands of the nations for the sake of her commitment to God and His Torah,[218] even as that suffering is understood to confirm her closeness to Him and her distinctive identity vis-à-vis the nations;[219] Israel claims an exclusive intimacy with God and His Torah,[220] even as she cannot absolutely deny that He loves the nations, too.[221]

As much as the nations become through the commentary very much present at Sinai, the commentary's ambivalent preoccupation with the nations and Israel's sufferings at their hands brings Scripture, and in a sense Sinai, into the perpetual present of the commentary's discourse and audience.[222] Another motif from the commentary's present that is repeatedly woven into its re-presentation of the past event of revelation is that of Israel's rabbinic leaders, who, on the one hand are distinct among Israel for the mark that Torah study leaves upon their characters,[223] and on the other, suffer especially on Israel's behalf.[224] If their righteous behavior, distinctive character, and closeness to God epitomize, in a concentrated way, the transforming effects upon Israel of close engagement with God's Torah, then they also epitomize in their sufferings (presumably, once again, at the hands of the nations) the obverse consequences of Israel's exclusive bond to God and Torah.

Just as the commentary draws together through its interassociations revelation as a past event with the present consequences of the revealed text for Israel's corporate condition, the commentary repeatedly points forward in time toward Israel's future expectations as they relate to both aspects of revelation. The conflict with the nations at Sinai points forward toward God's eventual blessing of Israel with peace (§353 E), even as it prefigures

Israel's eventual succession of Esau (Rome) in political dominion (§353 F). Similarly, God's direct appearance to Israel at Sinai prefigures His future appearance to them in messianic times (§343 H).[225] However, the bridge between this life and the next, as between this world and the next, is Israel's, and especially her sages' present "laboring" in the fiery law of Torah (§343 L5–6).

In many ways, what is most striking in the *Sifre*'s network of images of Torah revelation is its recurring preoccupation with the "nations of the world." In comparing several traditions with their parallels in other commentary settings, I have argued that the nations are viewed even more negatively in the relocating and refiguring of those traditions here than elsewhere.[226] If we assume, as I have, that this negative preoccupation with the "nations of the world" reflects (or should we say refracts?) something of the present time and circumstances (third-century Palestine) of our imagined commentary maker, can we identify those nations more specifically? Although Rome is clearly indicated in some sections (§343 F; §344 B1), and the Church is perhaps alluded to in others (§343 J3),[227] in most instances the rubric "nations of the world" can easily refer to either or both or to a broader transhistorical, and hence indeterminate, reality (or perception thereof) still.[228]

However, if by pulling on this recurring thread in the fabric of the commentary we are not drawn to any clearly identifiable historical exigency as its stimulus, perhaps by pulling in the other direction we will be drawn to such exigencies within the text of Scripture? Clearly, the language of Deut. 33:2–4, with its juxtaposition of Seir (Esau) and Paran (Ishmael) with Sinai (Israel) and with its statement of God's love for the "peoples" (plural) might have been sufficient to introduce the theme of the nations of the world into our commentary or to spur the more negative re-presentation of traditions that already related the theme of revelation to Israel's relations with the nations. Perhaps as a response to Scripture our commentary maker wished to assert that Sinai is not the equal of Seir and Paran and that God does not love all the peoples equally. But a broader look at the *Sifre*'s commentary, especially to the lections *Haʾăzînû* and *Zōʾt Habběrākâ*, suggests that its preoccupation with and especially negative attitude toward the nations of the world extends way beyond these particular scriptural barbs, significant as they may be.[229] It seems certain that our commentary maker shaped and interwove the traditions available to him in relation to the scriptural passages before him in such a way as to accenturate both the conflict and the difference between Israel and the nations, even while retaining a degree of ambiguity regarding the place of those nations within the covenantal scheme, here centered on Sinai.[230] We need not reduce our commentary to a pointed polemical response to a specific party or set of events to appreciate its sociohistorical force in relation to Israel's ongoing work of defining itself both in distinction from and in relation to "the nations." The complexity and irreducible ambiguity of Israel's historical self-perception in relation to the nations is, in a sense, represented by our commentary's web of fractured re-presentations of the text and event of revelation. Israel's view of the nations, like that of its past and future, cannot be conveyed through any single view, but through the restless intersections of a proliferation of petits récits.[231]

These questions and their indeterminate answers are simply to suggest that our commentary progressively yet dialogically unfolds among the crisscrossing axes of biblical text, rabbinic tradition, and historical time in such a way as to make it inadvisable to privilege or overdetermine any one of their re-presentations. What is most striking in the end is the way in which the commentary engages the attentive student as a participant in its timely yet timeless network. Through the textured fabric of that work, biblical writ (and the event of its revelation), inherited tradition (in all its fluidity), and historical time (including its expected messianic reversals) are all made transformatively *present* in the social world of its *performative* study.

That social world was one in which Israel had continually to confront the "nations of the world," whether in the burdensome rule of Rome or in the burgeoning presence of the Church, whose own sacrohistorical claims to have replaced the old Israel with a new one were increasingly buttressed by the argumentation of scriptural interpretation. Israel needed to distinguish and separate itself from both, even as they were forced by historical circumstances to relate and respond, whether directly or indirectly, to both. The rabbis' own hopes of becoming and providing Israel's religious and political leadership depended, in no small measure, on their ability to provide the discursive and performative media by which Israel might execute, and eventually complete, that delicate balancing act of self-understanding. According to the texts of biblical commentary that we have examined, Israel needed to understand itself as that people who alone among the nations were divinely distinguished at Sinai, when it immediately recognized God in His singularity and unconditionally accepted His Torah. But just as significantly, such a self-understanding was grounded in the *continuity* of that mutual recognition and intimate relationship between God and Israel through Israel's constant engage-ment—both in study and practice—with the "words of Torah" in the seemingly perpetual present. The nature of that worshipful engagement, and the role of the sages and their disciples as the masters of its dialogical media of textual enactment, is the subject to which we next turn.

3 The Early Rabbinic Sage and His Torah in the Text of the Sifre

Introduction

At the heart of rabbinic Judaism, as of the vast rabbinic literature in which it finds its expression, is the rabbinic sage (Hebrew, *ḥākām*).[1] That literature, spanning close to a millennium and comprising several complex genres, contains, scattered about, various kinds of information about the rabbinic sage, all of which are found in the *Sifre:* legal and nonlegal teachings attributed to individual sages or groups of sages; stories about individual sages in their dealings with one another as well as with nonsages, both Jewish and non-Jewish; statements prescribing attitudes and conduct appropriate to the sage; references to the institutions within which the sages worked or upon which they sought to exert their influence. Several studies have culled rabbinic texts for these sorts of information out of which to fashion a synthetic, narrative portrayal of the rabbinic sage, in some cases typologically or chronologically differentiated.[2] But in such work of distillation another, equally important type of information about the rabbinic sage is often ignored: the discursive practices of those very texts, which in and of themselves, I shall argue, give expression to who the rabbinic sages were or sought to become—the two often being difficult to differentiate.

But these two types of information, that which is *in* the text and that which is *of* the text, are not as separable as the preceding paragraph might seem to suggest. For our understanding of such texts' discursive practices and purposes must condition the historiographic manners in which we employ the information that they contain. Essential to our understanding of the way rabbinic texts work, and therefore to the social and historical reconstructions that we base on those texts, must be the recognition that rabbinic literature is a medium dedicated *both* to transmission and to transformation: its texts not only transmit received traditions from an earlier time, but simultaneously and often subtly transform—for purposes of their own place and program in time—what they seek to transmit.

Let me illustrate this point, and at the same time introduce the texts and topic of this chapter, with a well-known rabbinic passage from a collection not much anterior to the *Sifre:*

> *Moses received (qibbēl)* Torah from Sinai and transmitted *(māsar)* it to Joshua, and Joshua to the elders, and the elders to the prophets, and the prophets transmitted it to the men of the Great Assembly. They said three things: Be thorough in judgment, raise up many disciples, and make a fence around the Torah. Simeon the Just (ca. 200 B.C.E.) was among the last of the Great Assembly. He used to say: . . . Antigonus of Soko received [Torah] from Simeon the Just. He used to say: . . . (*'Abot* 1:1-3)

This "chain of tradition" continues with five pairs of techers, each of whom adds one or more teachings to what he has received before transmitting the newly transformed Torah to the next link in the chain. The last pair is that of Hillel and Shammai (ca. 30 B.C.E.-10 C.E.), who in turn (despite some kinks in the chain) transmit what they have received and taught to Rabban Johanan ben Zakkai (2:8), who together with his five students establishes, at the time of the destruction of the Second Temple in 70 C.E., the first specifically rabbinic center for learning at Yavneh (Jamnia).[3]

In this genealogical chain each "link" (explicitly beginning with the men of the Great Assembly, but implicitly for their predecessors) transforms as it transmits Torah. That which is newly added at each successive link in the chain is no less Torah than that which precedes it as it takes its place within the cumulative tradition, which is said to originate in the divine revelation at Sinai.[4] Presumably, each teacher, or generation of teachers, taught more than is here explicitly credited to him and thus transformed what he received more complexly than is here schematically expressed. Furthermore, we have no way of verifying whether the named teachers actually said what is credited to them, the attributions themselves being a product of the tradition's complex history of transmission and transformation.[5]

But the transformative quality of this passage, and of the collectivity of sages for whom it serves as self-confirming pedigree, is as much historiographic as it is literary. In historiographic terms this chain is most significant for what it omits: the class of priests. Like other rabbinic texts, and many modern scholars,[6] it presumes that protorabbinic (that is, pre-70 C.E.) sages had primary responsibility for the transmission and elucidation, not to mention judicial implementation, of Torah texts and traditions during the Second Temple period. However, a very considerable body of evidence (analyzed in detail by me elsewhere[7]) indicates that it was the priesthood, whether centralized or separatist, who in Second Temple times were most commonly associated with the authority to transmit, teach, and adjudicate Israel's covenantal laws and traditions.

One might conclude from this seeming contradiction that, although our text is not a correct representation of that earlier period of the history of Torah transmission, it *is* symptomatic of the situation in time when sages and not priests as a group filled such roles in Israelite society. This text may then be thought of as the creation of such sages who wished retroactively to transform the past from the vantage of an *already* transformed present.[8] But, lacking external evidence to the contrary, one could just as easily argue that this text was created at a time when the priesthood still filled, or claimed for itself, such a role and that the creators of this text, *critical* of that present situation, sought, perhaps in part through the very force of their discourse, to *transform* it. And finally, but not necessarily independent of the preceding possibilities, we might consider this text, and the wider body of rabbinic texts for which it stands, to be transformative in still another way: disciples of sages, through their engaged study and hence interpretation of this text,[9] might be *empowered* to view the very activity of *their* study as part of an unbroken, living chain of Torah and tradition extending back to and deriving from Sinai, with themselves as its latest links.[10]

This is by no means to suggest that the previously cited text or rabbinic literature more generally can be dismissed as pseudepigraphic fabrication. Rather, it is to caution that the representational employment of such a text, not only for periods anterior to the time of its redaction but for that time as well, needs to be conditioned by considerations of the dialectical intertwining of transmission and transformation so central to the self-understanding of the rabbinic sages, who claimed the status of "words of Torah" for their own teaching discourse, both exegetical and nonexegetical.

The critical history of the rabbinic sage confronts a sizable obstacle not unrelated to the above concerns: the chronology of the sources at our disposal. The earliest rabbinic texts date from the third century C.E.[11] All of these texts are anthologies, some ordered topically, others exegetically, in each case with an intermixture of the other. Such collections undoubtedly incorporate traditions and the literary crystallizations of traditions that antedate, and may in some cases considerably antedate, the time and circumstances of their formation into the continuous texts in which we now find them. But the process of textual redaction has left such a deep mark on the constituent parts that the extraction of those parts—not to mention the distillation and synthesis of their traditions—for purposes of historical representation of a time much earlier than that of the texts' redaction is fraught with difficulties.[12] Systematic, controlled methods for the unsplicing of such texts have not been (and, we may have to admit, cannot be) developed.[13]

From shortly after the destruction of the Second Temple (70 C.E.) until our earliest rabbinic texts in the third century—precisely that period during which the rabbinic movement took root and presumably underwent significant development—we do not have a single datable rabbinic text. Nor do we have much in the way of pertinent archeological or extra-rabbinic literary evidence from that period with which to fill the gap. Therefore, we have little way to measure the historical reliability of rabbinic accounts of the lives and teachings of the sages of that time (the tannaim).[14] The situation is very different for the late Second Temple period, from which we have a relative abundance of evidence of different sorts and from different settings against which to measure the rabbis' claims to be the successors to an uninterrupted authoritative chain of sages extending back well into Second Temple times (and untimately to Sinai), and from which to fashion, albeit not easily or completely, an alternative picture of the antecedents to the post-70 rabbinic sage.[15]

It is as though we enter a historiographic tunnel shortly after the destruction of the Second Temple from which we do not emerge until the early third century. We can put together "before" and "after" pictures (however blurry and partial), but we can be much less certain of how much of the transformation in Jewish learned circles that occurred within that tunnel occurred near its beginning (at Yavneh after the destruction of the Temple), around its middle (in the Galilee following the failed Bar Kochba revolt), or not until its end a century and half later (with the ascendancy of R. Judah as patriarch). It should not surprise us if our earliest texts of rabbinic transmission and transformation, appearing in the third century at the end of what might historiographically be termed the tannaitic tunnel, project some of the most significant transformational aspects of rabbinic Judaism back onto its foundational figures and their times: R. Akiba, R. Johanan B. Zakkai, Hillel, and their presumed antecedents.[16]

It is often suggested that by the time the Second Temple was destroyed in 70 C.E. its replacement by the Pharisaic-rabbinic sages and their "democratizing" program of lay Torah teaching and study had been long in preparation. These sages, it is argued, had already articulated and organized an alternative to the Temple worship and its priestly oligarchy, had won widespread popular support for their program, and now simply moved from side stage to center stage with the exit of the obsolete sacrificial system and its priestly supporters. Other groups that had previously challenged the legitimacy of the Jerusalem priesthood but on the grounds of an *alternative* priestly leadership or ideology (e.g., the Qumran sectaries) likewise found themselves suddenly without ground to stand on and quickly left the scene, leaving the nascent rabbinic movement without competition for national leadership.[17]

The evidence that I have presented elsewhere[18] suggests that this conventional picture is problematic as it views the late Second Temple period and the aftermath of the Temple's destruction largely through the eyes of third century—if not later—rabbinic texts. The extant Second Temple evidence suggests, rather, that at least until 70 C.E. scribal authority, both didactic and judicial, for Israel's Scriptures and laws remained mainly in priestly hands, and when that authority was delegated downward it was to quasi-priests (e.g., Levites) or to others associated with the priests (e.g., Pharisees). Similarly, those who had questioned or denied the legitimacy of the officiating Jerusalem priesthood of their time could not conceive of anything other than a priestly "constitution" for the Jewish people.[19]

Although the destruction of the Temple meant the end of a centralized sacrificial cult, it should not be assumed, as is often done, that the priesthood's social status and claims to be the authentic guardians and interpreters of Israel's Scriptures and laws, rooted as these both were in Scripture and in a long history, necessarily terminated, thereby creating a complete leadership vacuum. This is not to minimize the political, religious, and social trauma and dislocation caused by the destruction of the Temple, but to suggest that it need not have meant the sudden end of the paramount position of the priesthood as Israel began to reconstitute its life without a Temple, especially as long as Jerusalem remained accessible and hopes for the rebuilding of its Temple remained alive (in both cases until 135 C.E.). The example of the Samaritans, who maintained (and continue to maintain until this day) the religious, social, and intellectual paramountcy of their priesthood long after *their* temple was destroyed in the late second century B.C.E. suggests that a similar *possibility* for the Jews should not be dismissed out of hand. In fact, several kinds of evidence suggest that priestly status, and perhaps authority, continued to be a factor in Jewish communal life long after 70 C.E.[20]

How long priestly authority continued in noncultic realms of public life and how long it took for the nascent rabbinic movement to establish itself as the new national leadership is impossible to say, because we have very little direct evidence from the period between 70 and 200 C.E. and because our first documents, rabbinic texts of the third century such as the *Sifre,* come from the rabbinic "victors." As I have already suggested, the extent to which rabbinic portrayals of earlier times can be taken as historically representational is a serious and complex question. But we may also ask whether we can assume that these texts are at least directly symptomatic of social conditions at the time of their redaction, which is to ask whether, in fact, the rabbis were already at that time the "victors," or whether the religious and social transformation that eventually established the rabbis as the successors to the priests as the national leadership was still in progress. If the latter, then these texts, when viewed in the historical context of the time of their creation, might be seen not so much as *reports* of a transformation already completed as part of the very *work* of that transformation—as the discursive media of their *will* to socioreligious power and its self-justification.

A cardinal rule of critical historiography is that the stories of the past that our sources permit us to tell may not be those we would most like to tell or others would have us tell. In this chapter I shall gather a wide array of commentary texts from the *Sifre* that both in their topics and in their discursive practices touch upon, whether explicitly or implicitly, the rabbinic sage and his Torah and the relation of each to its biblical antecedents as well as to the sociohistorical situation of third century Palestine. The critical history of the sage much before the creation of such commentary in the early third century is, unfortunately, one that our extant sources and present critical tools do not permit us to recount.

The *Sifre* is especially interesting in this regard because the Book of Deuteronomy to which it provides the earliest extant commentary is the most didactic of the books of the Pentateuch—in its rhetorical style, in its narrative framework, and in its frequent admonitions to Israel to teach and learn God's words. Narratively set on the eve of Moses' passing from leadership, it is particularly concerned with designating institutions for the *continued* transmission and adjudication of God's word in Israel's social midst. But the Book of Deuteronomy is also the most explicit of the books of the Pentateuch in stressing the role of the priests, here being the descendants of Levi, as the authoritative teachers of God's revelation and as the judicial authorities for the implementation of Israel's convenantal laws.[21] Deuteronomy, thus, presents the early rabbinic exegetes and the redactors of the *Sifre* with numerous opportunities to assert the importance of study of Torah as a central religious obligation upon which Israel's covenantal fortunes rest, while challenging them to express their claims to be the paramount authorities in matters of Scripture and Jewish law in exegetical engagement with a biblical text that associates that authority with the hereditary priesthood. This is a challenge to advance the rabbinic work of collective self-representation and legitimization in engagement with a scriptural text that, perhaps like social reality, offered some resistance to that work.

The following explications of *Sifre* texts will not seek simply to extract from those texts information about the rabbinic sage and his practice of Torah study as if those texts were linguistically autonomous of the sages who both produced and studied them. Rather, it will seek to engage critically the discursive practices of those texts as the best guides to who the rabbinic sages were and were working to become—successors to the priests, prophets, and elders of earlier times—through the medium of their own self-defining and transforming work of Torah study and teaching.

Sifre Texts and Commentary

Ask Your Elders and They Will Tell You (§310)

In the "chain of tradition" passage cited earlier the biblical elders *(zĕqēnîm)* serve as an important link between Joshua and the prophets, who in turn transmit the Torah tradition to the men of the Great Assembly, with whom are associated the first extra-scriptural teachings of Torah.[22] As we shall repeatedly see, the rabbinic sages identify themselves as the descendants of those nonpriestly elders, who are portrayed both as the predecessors and as the successors to the classical prophets (Samuel through Malachi) in the authoritative chain of Torah transmission. This identification is important to the rabbis because it is the biblical lay elders who both accompany Moses onto Mt. Sinai (according to Exod. 24:1, 9) and are assigned leadership and judiciary functions by him (Exod. 18:13-26; Num. 11:16-25; Deut. 1:9-18). It is in part their link to these elders that allow the rabbinic sages to claim both to have inherited the authority to transmit the Torah (written and oral) received at Sinai and to be the authoritative adjudicators of its terms. The significance of these elders for rabbinic self-understanding is well exemplified in the *Sifre's* commentary to Deut. 32:7. That verse is part of the "song" that Moses delivered to the people shortly before his death, in which he rehearsed their sacred history to prepare them for entering promised land. The verse comprises two parallelistic doublets:

> Remember the days of old,
> consider the years of each and every generation;
> ask your father and he will inform you,
> your elders and they will tell you.

The *Sifre* divides the verse in order to explicate its parts, and does so twice:

[A] "Remember the days of old": [God said to them:] Take heed of what I did to the earliest generations: what I did to the people of the generation of the Flood, and what I did to the people of the generation of the Dispersion [the Tower of Babel], and what I did to the people of Sodom.
[B] "Consider the years (*šĕnôt*) of each and every generation": You can find no generation without people like those of the generation of the Flood,

and you can find no generation without people like those of the generation of the Dispersion and like those of Sodom, but each and every individual is judged according to his deeds.[23]

[C] "Ask your father and he will inform you": These are the prophets as it says, "When Elisha beheld it he cried out [to Elijah], 'Father, father'" (2 Kings 2:12).

[D] "Your elders and they will tell you": These are the elders, as it is said, "Gather for Me seventy men of the elders of Israel" (Num. 11:16).

Another interpretation:

[A'] "Remember the days of old (ʿôlām)" [read as: "Remember the days of eternity"]: He [= Moses] said to them: Whenever God brings sufferings to you, remember how many good and consoling things He will give you in the world (ʿôlām) to come.

[B'] "Consider the years of each and every generation": This is the generation of the Messiah, which will last for three generations, as it is said, "Let them fear You as long as the sun shines and the moon lasts, for a generation and generations" (Ps. 72:5).[24]

[C'] "Ask your father and he will inform you": In the future Israel will be able to see and hear as if hearing from the Holy One, blessed be He, as it is said, "Your ears shall hear a word behind you" (Isa. 30:21), and it says, "Your teacher [= God] shall not hide himself any more, and your eyes shall see your teacher" (Isa. 30:20).

[D'] "Your elders and they will tell you": What I [= God] revealed to the elders on the mountain, as it is said, "And to Moses He said, 'Ascend to God, [you and Aaron, Nadab, Abihu, and the seventy elders of Israel]'" (Exod. 24:1).[25]

At the most basic level, the commentary wishes to identify and distinguish between the verse's parallel and seemingly similar, and hence potentially redundant, parallel elements: "days of old (eternity)" and "each and every generation"; "your father" and "your elders." The commentary begins by identifying "days of old" (literally, "days of eternity") with the very earliest generations of human history, in particular with three generations that are understood by the rabbis to have been thoroughly wicked and rebellious in their behavior.[26] It is these specific generations that God Himself (A) urges Israel to recall in the commentary's paraphrastic restatement of the lemma. This interpretation of "days of old" as referring to the early rebellious *generations* anticipates the interpretation of the next clause, with its "each and very generation." According to that interpretation, Moses urges his audience to differentiate (bînû) between the earliest rebellious generations whose members were entirely wicked, and later generations, including that of the present, whose moral make-up is more mixed. These later generations are no longer judged en masse, but their individual members are judged each according to his or her own deeds.

Next, the terms *father* and *elders,* appearing in parallel construction in the biblical text, are understood as signifying not one's own biological father and the elderly of one's family or community as sources of wisdom, as would seem to be the scriptural sense, but *inspired biblical leadership classes.* The word *father* is deictically interpreted, but with the aid of another verse, to signify "prophets." The world *elders* is similarly interpreted as signifying "elders": not simply those of advanced age within one's community but those nonpriests who were divinely authorized to share in Moses' leadership and judiciary functions (Exod. 18:13-26; Num. 11:16-25; Deut. 1:9-18).[27] In the *Sifre,* as in other rabbinic collections, the rabbinic sages view themselves as the present-day extension of this biblical class of lay elders, especially in their inspired authority and appointment to positions of judicial and administrative responsibility over the larger Jewish community.[28]

The commentary's juxtaposition of *prophets* and *elders* may also serve subtly to associate the two, as they are associated in the sequence of the "chain of tradition" in *m. ʾAbot* 1:1.[29] But elsewhere in the Mishnah *(Yad.* 4:3) it is stated that the successors to the prophets (after Ezra) were also "elders," who are akin in their legal authority to the rabbis.[30] This association and sequence is also expressed in *Seder ʿOlam Rabba* 30, which locates the transition from prophets to elders during the rule of Alexander the Great (having telescoped the Persian period), and cites Deut. 32:7 in a way similar to the *Sifre,* but more clearly identifying the elders in that verse with the sages (*ḥăkāmîm*):

> Until here prophets would prophesy through the Holy Spirit; from here on, "Incline your ear and hear the words of the wise (*ḥăkāmîm*). . . ." (Prov. 22:17-21). So too it says, "Ask your father and he will inform you, your elders and they will tell you" (Deut. 32:7). (You might think that this refers to the elders of the market, but Scripture says, "And they will tell you." Thus, you learn that this is an elder who has acquired wisdom.)[31]

Thus, according to rabbinic historiography, whereas the biblical elders preceded the classical prophets in the "chain of tradition," the latter were succeeded by the postbiblical elders, or proto-rabbinic sages of Second Temple times, who in turn are succeeded by the rabbinic sages themselves.

Returning to the *Sifre's* commentary to Deut. 32:7, we see that if the first set of interpretations (A–D) focuses on the biblical past, beginning with its earliest times, but with implicit extensions into the present, the second set (A′–D′) focuses on the ultimate future, but again with connections to the present. This second set of interpretations, demarcated by "another interpretation," begins with the sufferings of the present and then shifts our attention to the distant, messianic future. In the midst of such present sufferings, the righteous (we may presume) are told by Moses to consider the *future* "days of eternity," wherein they will finally be rewarded. Similarly, the generations referred to in the verse's second clause, earlier interpreted as signifying the three rebellious generations at the beginning of time, are now deictically interpreted as signifying the three generations of the Messiah at the end of time. Thus, in both sets of comments the "days of eternity" are defined in relation to the next biblical clause as referring to three generations: primeval and messianic. Similarly, the verse's *father,* first interpreted as signifying the prophets, is now interpreted less directly as signifying God, who in the messianic future will be the teacher of *all* of Israel, obviating then the need for mediating prophets. Note how the order of the prooftext verses from Isaiah have been reversed (30:21 followed by 30:20): not only will Israel hear the word of their teacher but they will see Him. This reversal permits the commentary to ask implicitly, What will be the nature of that direct vision of God? This implicit question is answered by the citation and interpretation of the final clause of the lemma (D′), with which the commentary concludes, once again (cf. A) relaying the interpretation in God's own voice: in the future all of Israel will directly behold Me, as did the inspired biblical elders upon Mt. Sinai (as related in Exod. 24:9-11).

Because each of the *Sifre*'s two commentaries to Deut. 32:7 comprises a set of four interpretations, some of them more deictic and some more dialogical, how we perceive the effect of their overall juxtaposition is related to how we perceive the nature of the internal links between their parts. At the outermost level, the fact that the first set of interpretations moves from the distant past to the present whereas the second moves from the present to the distant future, suggests that the editorial ordering of these two commentaries is not as accidental as might first appear: textual order, as encountered in the chronology of "reading," bears some relation to "historical" chronology. Let us review some of the more obvious structural links that enhance the overall temporal framing of this collection of eight discrete interpretations: The three "prehistorical" rebellious generations are set opposite the three messianic generations. In the former the wicked are punished whereas in the latter the righteous will be rewarded. In the delicately suspended "time-between," the righteous are punished for their own deeds, even as they can look forward in consolation to their future rewards. Whereas in biblical times Israel obtained knowledge of God's will through the intermediacy of divinely authorized prophets and elders, in the messianic future Israel will hear and behold God directly. But what of the "time-between"? How is God's will to be known and His presence experienced in the here-and-now, when there are neither prophets in the biblical sense nor possibilities for direct knowledge of God? This question, implicitly asked by the commentary's juxtapositions, is also implicitly answered: the rabbinic successors to the biblical elders presently fulfill this mediating function.[32] In this regard it is significant that the elders alone remain constant both between the lemma and its interpretation and between the two sets of interpretations. Thus, *father* is taken to signify first prophets and then God, *days of eternity* is taken to signify first the beginning of time and then its end, and *each and every generation* is taken to signify first early rebellious generations and then the final messianic generations. But *elders* are always the elders—the inspired class of elders that is—whose biblically assigned roles in revelation and its societal adjudication remain operative (unlike those of the prophets) throughout time, or until such time as Israel's direct hearing and seeing of God, itself modeled on the experience of the biblical elders, will make their mediating functions unnecessary.

Finally, it may be noted that the two-part commentary is framed overall by one other inclusio: in the very first interpretation (A) and the very last (D') God Himself addresses Israel directly, whereas in the intermediary interpretations (as in the "time-between") either Moses (A') or the anonymous voice of the rabbinic commentary does the speaking.

In noting these configuring aspects of the commentary's structure and details I do not wish to claim that the two sets of interpretations, as well as their internal elements, could not have stood alone in some other contexts, but simply that as they are here combined in this configuration rather than some other, they engage the students of the commentary in the dialogical (both in relation to fractured scripture and interconnected tradition) practice of a socially grounded hermeneutic.

That I Command You Today (§41)

If the rabbinic sages view themselves as the latest link in the horizontal "chain of tradition," they also view themselves as an essential link in the vertical chain that connects Israel to God. Once again the rabbinic association with the biblical elders proves critical to the chain:

[A] "[If, then, you (plural) obey (*šāmōʿa tišmĕʿû*) the commandments] that I [Moses] command you today" (Deut. 11:13): Whence can you derive that if a person learns (*šāmaʿ*) a teaching from one of little learning (*qāṭān*) within Israel, he should consider it as if he had learned it from a sage (*ḥākām*)? From the words, "That I (*ʾānōkî*) command you (plural) today."

[B] And is not one who learns from a [single] sage like one who learns from [the collectivity of] sages, as it is said, "The words of sages are like goads"

(Eccl. 12:11)?[33] Just as a goad aligns the cow in its furrows so as to bring life to its masters,[34] similarly the words of Torah align a person's mind (*da'at*) with that of God. And is not one who learns from [the collectivity of] sages like one who learns from the Sanhedrin, as it is said, "Masters of assemblies (*'ăsuppôt*)" (ibid.)? "Assemblies" must refer to the Sanhedrin, as it is said, "Assemble (*'espâ*) for Me seventy men of the elders of Israel"(Num. 11:16). And is not one who learns from the Sanhedrin like one who learns from Moses, as it is said, "They were given by one shepherd" (Eccl. 12:11)? [And furthermore it says,] "They remembered the ancient days, the days of Moses [. . . the shepherd of his flock]" (Isa. 63:11). And is not one who learns from Moses like one who learns from the Mighty One, as it is said, "They were given by one shepherd"? [And furthermore it says,] "Give ear, O shepherd of Israel [. . . You who are enthroned on the cherubim]" (Ps. 80:2). And furthermore it says, "Hear, O Israel, the Lord is our God, the Lord is one" (Deut. 6:4).[35]

Deut. 11:13, the first verse of the second paragraph of the liturgical recitation of the Shema, is interpreted to mean that because it is to all of Israel that God's commandments (Torah) were conveyed by Moses, then, ideally at least, all of Israel is in possession of Torah and from each and every one of them Torah might be learned. Such a teaching, even from an Israelite of low status, can be thought of as if coming, after a sequence of steps, from Moses, and ultimately from God, from whom it originally derives.[36] Although this is probably occasioned most immediately by the plural word *you* (*'etkem*) in the lemma, there are other parts of the verse that might also have triggered the interpretation overall. The doubling of the verb *šm'* (*šāmō'a tišmě'û*), although usually understood to denote obedience, may here be understood to denote a twofold hearing or learning, from the actual person and from the next rung up the revelatory ladder.[37] Furthermore, the word for *I* (*'ānōkî*) may imply an identification of Moses with God, because this is the word by which God identifies Himself in the first of the Ten Commandments. Because in Deut. 11:13-21 Moses switches several times between the first and third persons in communicating God's words (the next verse beginning, "I [God] will grant the rain for your land in season"), it is somewhat unclear who the *I* is here: Moses or God.[38] Finally, the word *today* may be understood to mean that all of Israel (even "commoners") are as much recipients of the Torah today, in the perpetual present of the commentary, as at Sinai.[39] In any case, a biblical verse that seems to state that all of Israel must obey the divine commandments of the Torah is radically transformed into a statement that all of Israel are recipients of Torah and, hence, potentially at least, teachers of Torah.

But the commentary does not stop here. Rather, by atomistically and successively interpreting the words of a seemingly unrelated verse, Eccl.

12:11, it inserts between the Israelite of little learning and Moses as God's communicative agent several intermediary steps: the individual sage, the collectivity of sages, and the Sanhedrin,[40] identified with the inspired biblical elders. Notice that the last part of Eccl. 12:11 must be interpreted twice, first with *shepherd* referring to Moses and second with *one shepherd* referring to God in His oneness, to reach the desired end. Through the editorial combining of commentary to these two verses (Deut. 11:13 and Eccl. 12:11), the second found with variation in other early rabbinic sources independent of any interpretation of Deut. 11:13, a vertical reverse teaching chain is established, beginning with a single simple Israelite and ending with a single supreme God.[41] The distance between these two single figures is filled first by the individual sage, and then by the collectivity of sages who, although not being genealogically distinct from the people, trace their intellectual ancestry back through the seventy elders of the Sanhedrin to Moses. By stressing, on the one hand, that, ideally at least, all of Israel are teachers of Torah, all having been equally commanded by God, yet on the other, that the sages in particular have inherited the role of the elders (Sanhedrin) to mediate between Israel and God, the text expresses two views of the sage that cannot but be in some tension with each other: the sages are of the people, yet distinct from (and implicitly superior to) them.

What is striking here is the way in which this view gradually and dynamically unfolds through the dialogical dissection, interpretation, and unexpected interrelation of several scriptural verses. It would be a mistake, it seems to me, to collapse the middle of this text to reduce its message to the simple statement, "Even if you learn it from a lesser teacher, it is as if it comes from God."[42] For the intermediary position of the sage finds its expression in the unfolding exegetical discourse by which the text's middle transports its students from the single simple Israelite (*qāṭān*) with which it begins to the single supreme God (*gĕbûrâ*) with which it ends. As the opening interpretation of Eccl. 12:11 states, the words of Torah (here understood as scriptural as well as rabbinic) guide a person's mind to the will of God. By concluding with the Shema, which is liturgically connected to the lemma, the commentary, in a sense, also completes a circle. Note in particular the symmetrical pairing that results: single Israelite opposite single God, single sage opposite single Moses, and collectivity of sages opposite the elders of the Sanhedrin.

By stressing that that which a humble Israelite teaches might be regarded *as though* it comes from a sage, and successively from God Himself, our text does not equate, and certainly not in normative terms, that which one of little learning teaches with that which a sage teaches, but rather emphasizes that the sages presently fill the communicative place that

according to Scripture was previously occupied by Moses and the inspired
elders in mediating God's will and teaching to the people. This intermediary
role of the elders and the sages is confirmed by the commentary's
continuation, which takes up still another, seemingly unrelated verse:

> [C] Behold [Scripture] says, "Your eyes are like pools in Heshbon, by the
> gate of Bat-rabbim" (Cant. 7:5b). "Your eyes": These are the elders who are
> appointed over the community. And so [Scripture] says, "For the Lord has
> spread over you a spirit of deep sleep, and has shut your eyes, [the prophets,
> and covered your heads, the seers] (Isa. 29:10). "Pools": Just as a person
> cannot know what is in such a pool, so too a[n average] person cannot
> understand the words of the sages. "In Heshbon": In caluclations (*ḥešbônôt*)
> which are completed through counsel and thought. And where are [these
> calculations] completed? In the houses of study (*bātê midrāšôt*), [as it is said],
> "by the gate of Bat-rabbim."[43] And furthermore, Scripture says, "Your nose
> [= countenance] is like the Lebanon tower that looks toward Damascus"
> (Cant. 7:5c)? If you have performed (*'āśîtem*) the Torah,[44] you may hope for
> Elijah, to whom I said, "Go back by the way you came, to the wilderness of
> Damascus" (1 Kings 19:15), and [Scripture] says, "Be mindful of the Torah of
> My servant Moses [whom I charged at Horeb with laws and rules for all Israel.]
> Lo, I will send [the prophet Elijah to you before the coming of the awesome,
> fearful day of the Lord.] He shall reconcile [fathers with sons and sons with
> their fathers, so that, when I come, I do not strike the whole land with utter
> destruction" (Mal. 3:22-24).[45]

The words of Cant. 7:5, uttered by the male to the female lover, is
understood as God's praise of Israel. Israel's "eyes" are the elders appointed
to positions of public authority, presumably judicial.[46] This would link the
present interpretation to the preceding interpretation of Eccl. 12:11, with
its reference to the Sanhedrin. The supporting citation of Isa. 29:10 is
interesting because that verse associates eyes with prophets and "heads,"
the latter being understood, elsewhere in the *Sifre,* as elders appointed to
judicial positions.[47] The "pools" of Cant. 7:5 are taken to signify the
teachings of the sages, thereby making the association of elders with sages
explicit. If in the previous part of the commentary (A-B) it is stressed that
the teaching of an Israelite of little learning may be thought of as deriving
from a sage, here it is stressed that such an Israelite is unable to fathom the
teachings of the sages. These elders sit in the rabbinic houses of study,
where they weigh and tally the various rabbinic views and establish norms
of behavior according to the majority view. Finally, if Israel wishes to look
toward Damascus, that is, toward the coming of Elijah the harbinger of the
Messiah, it needs to perform the Torah as defined in the rabbinic houses of
study.

Whereas Deut. 11:13 speaks of Israel's welfare being dependent on its observance of the commandments revealed to it by God via Moses, the *Sifre*'s commentary stresses instead, through its atomistic interpretation of a network of verses, the place of the elders and rabbinic sages, as judges and as scholars, in mediating that revelation to Israel and in sustaining Israel's hope for eventual redemption.

Or the Magistrate in Charge at the Time (§§152-153)

The preceding "chains," like the " chain of tradition" of *m. ʾAbot* 1, conspicuously omit the priesthood, both horizontally as the authorized transmitters of Torah and vertically as the intermediaries between Israel and God. Yet Scripture, and the Book of Deuteronomy in particular, assigns primacy of place to the priesthood in these two regards, and especially in the realm where they join, that is, in effecting God's will within Israelite society through the implementation of Scripture's system of justice. Deut. 17:8-13 prescribes that when a local court is unable to decide a civil or criminal case, it is brought before a centralized tribunal located at the place designated by God and composed of levitical priests and a (presumably) lay magistrate. The biblical text in full reads as follows:

[8] If a case is too baffling for you to decide, be it a controversy over homicide, civil law, or assault—matters of dispute in your courts—you shall promptly repair [lit.: arise and ascend] to the place which the Lord your God will have chosen, [9] and appear before the levitical priests, or[48] the magistrate in charge at the time, and present your problem. When they have announced to you the verdict in the case, [10] you shall carry out the verdict that is announced to you from that place which the Lord chose, observing scrupulously all their instruction to you. [11] You shall act in accordance with the instructions given you and the ruling handed down to you; you must not deviate from the verdict that they announce to you either to the right or to the left. [12] Should a man act presumptuously and disregard the priest charged with serving there the Lord your God, or the magistrate, that man shall die. Thus you will sweep out evil from Israel: [13] all the people will hear and be afraid and will not act presumptuously again.[49]

S. R. Driver comments:

Judgment in ancient Israel, even on secular issues, seems often to have been adiministered at a sanctuary: the priests would thus possess an hereditary knowledge of civil and criminal law not less than of ceremonial law, which, especially at a time when Hebrew law was still imperfectly codified, would naturally give them an advantage over either the local "elders," or the ordinary lay judges. Hence they would be properly represented on a tribunal, appointed expressly for the purpose of dealing with difficult or serious cases.[50]

Let us now look at the *Sifre's* commentary on the requirement to bring difficult cases to a central tribunal made up largely of priests:

[A] "If. . . too baffling (*yippālē*')": This teaches that Scripture speaks of a *mûplā*' (senior legal authority).[51] "For you": This refers to [one qualified to give] legal counsel (*'ēṣâ*).[52] "A case": This refers to a matter of *halakah*. "To decide" (*lĕmišpāṭ*): This refers to logical inference (*dîn*). "Homicide (literally, between blood and blood)": Between menstrual blood, the blood of birthing, and the blood of a flux. "Civil law (literally, between plea [*dîn*] and plea)": Between cases requiring material punishment (*dînê māmônôt*), cases requiring capital punishment (*dînê nĕpāšôt*), and cases requiring corporeal punishment (*dînê makkôt*). "Assault (literally, between stroke [*negaʿ*] and stroke)": Between plagues (*nĕgāʿîm*) [of "leprosy"] that affect humans, and plagues that affect houses, and plagues that affect clothing. "Matters (of)": These refer to valuations, and devotions, and consecrations. "Disputes": This refers to the bitter waters which the suspected wife is made to drink, the breaking of the heifer's neck, and the purification of the leper. "In your courts (literally, gates)": This refers to gleanings, the forgotten sheaf, and the corner of the field.[53]

The overall effect of this dissection and deictic specification is to transform the supreme tribunal from one that adjudicates difficult cases of intra-Israelite conflict, to one whose primary purpose is to decide between the conflicting views of the *sages* in matters of specialized legal exegesis and differentiation, especially with regard to proximate legal categories. We have here what might be thought of as the intellectualization (or rabbinization) of the functions of the central judiciary of Deuteronomy.[54] The commentary continues:

[B] "You shall arise": Immediately. "You shall arise": In court [where they sit]. ["And you shall ascend":] With regard to this it has been said:[55] Three courts were there: one at the gate to the Temple Mount, one at the gate to the Temple Court, and one in the Chamber of Hewn Stone. They would come to that [court] at the gate of the Temple Mount and [the elder] would say: "Thus have I expounded and thus have my colleagues expounded, thus have I taught and thus have my colleagues taught." If they [the court members] had a tradition [which would resolve the dispute] they told them, and if not they would proceed to that [court] that was at the gate of the Temple Court, and [the elder] would say: "Thus have I expounded and thus have my colleagues expounded, thus have I taught and thus have my colleagues taught." If they [the court members] had a tradition [which would resolve the dispute] they told them, and if not, they would all [including the representatives of the lower courts] proceed to the high court that was in the Chamber of Hewn Stone. For from there Torah emanates to all of Israel, as it says, "From that place which the Lord shall choose" (Deut. 17:10).[56]

[C] "You shall promptly repair (lit.: arise and ascend) to the place which the Lord your God will have chosen": This teaches that the Land of Israel is higher than all of the lands and the Temple is higher than all of the Land of Israel.[57]

This section of commentary, in its present context, is striking for the two ways that it transforms the biblical passage with which it is engaged:

1. It emphasizes, through its citation of a mishnaic tradition, that the central tribunal of Deuteronomy is in fact a series of *three* courts, all of them located in the Temple domain, to which local conflicts of legal *teaching and interpretation* are brought for adjudication. Through the repetitive detail and dialogical style of the text we are drawn into the very process of progressing, that is, ascending, by stages from one to the next of these three courts until finally we reach, as it were, the legal summit, the high court in the Chamber of Hewn Stone (where the Sanhedrin of seventy-one members is said to have sat). We are then told that from there Torah teaching emanates, presumably through such sages, to *all* of Israel. The double verb for ascending is here interpreted doubly: not only is the Temple the highest place within the Land of Israel, but the Land of Israel is higher than the rest of the world.[58] The pathos of such a text being created (at least in its present, redacted form) and studied at a time when that Temple had long ago been destroyed and its mount long ago desecrated, with little immediate hope for a reversal of that calamity, is fully experienced only upon arriving at the end of the section.

2. Once again, the intellectual and teaching role of the central courts is emphasized, rather than their strictly juridical function and authority. The central courts decide not so much between conflicting parties in a civil or criminal dispute as between *sages* who differ in their legal interpretations.

   Paradoxically, these two transformative strategies, when taken together, consign the central court(s) of Deut. 17:8–13 to a presently unrecoverable past, while contemporizing (rabbinizing) their functions. The Temple as the supreme source of Torah teaching has been lost, even as the pedagogic and judicial functions herein assigned to it are familiar enough to our text's rabbinic audience. The Temple although no longer standing continues to exist, in a sense, in the discursive world with which the student of the text is presently engaged.

The resolution of these seemingly contradictory exegetical moves comes in the succeeding section, set off, it would at first appear,[59] from what precedes it:

> [A] "And you shall appear (*ûbā'tā*)" (Deut. 17:9): [This is stated so as] to include the court at Yavneh.
>
> [B] "Before the levitical priests (*hakkōhăhîm hallēwiyyîm*)": It is required that the court include priests and Levites. This being the requirement, might we infer that if it [a court] lacks priests and Levites it is disqualified? Therefore, Scripture says, "or the magistrate (*šōpēt*)": Even though it lacks priests and Levites, it is [still] qualified.
>
> [C] "In charge at that time": R. Jose the Galilean said: Might you have thought [that it refers to your going to] a magistrate who is not living in your time? Rather, [it refers] to your going to a magistrate who is qualified and authorized [to serve] in your time. Thus, one who previously had been related [to one of the parties, and had been disqualified to judge], but has since ceased to be related, is [now] qualified. Therefore it says, "Do not say, 'How is it that the former days were better than these?'" (Eccl. 7:10).
>
> [D] "And you shall seek their decision, and they shall declare the verdict in the case (*dĕbar hammišpāṭ*)": These are detailed arguments of judgment (*diqdûqè mišpāṭ*).[60]

The verb *you shall appear* (literally, "come"), following the previous instruction, *you shall promptly repair* (literally, "arise and ascend"), could not, from the rabbinic perspective, be a mere repetition. While the preceding verse (Deut. 17:8) was taken to refer to *ascending* to the high courts in Jerusalem on the Temple Mount, the present verse (17:9), which does not mention ascending, is taken to refer to (or at least to include) something else: the successor court (and school) at Yavneh, which is not distinguished by its physical elevation. But does this court also require the presence of priests for it to have authority? The answer is no, for the magistrate of Deut. 17:8, 12 is understood, in *contrast* to the preceding priests (and Levites), to be a nonpriest, presumably a rabbinic sage, given the earlier reference to Yavneh.[61]

. The dialogical interpretation of the seemingly unnecessary phrase *in charge* [literally, "who will be"] *at that time* stresses that those who may not have been qualified to judge in the past may now be qualified. Our commentary, therefore, argues from Scripture that changing circumstances have necessitated both a move of the central court from Jerusalem to Yavneh (and, by implication, to the successor rabbinic centers) and also, perhaps more significantly, a change in the makeup of that court. The citation from Eccl. 7:10 acknowledges yet rejects the nostalgic tendency to compare the present (rabbinic) leadership with that of the past (presumably priestly).[62] Finally, the interpretation of the conclusion of verse 9 (D) once again intellectualizes or rabbinizes the function of the central court: one comes to it not so much to receive a specific legal *sentence* as to learn the fine points of legal *argumentation*.[63]

The combined impression of these adjoining units of commentary (§§152 and 153) is both a sense of deep loss caused by the destruction of the Temple with its central judiciary and, almost conversely, a sense of continuity between that institution and its rabbinic successors, including the present text, through which it lives on. The Chamber of Hewn Stone may be tragically gone, but the Torah that once went forth from it now goes forth from "Yavneh." This dual sense of continuity despite rupture is exegetically achieved both by portraying the work of the central tribunal of Temple times in rabbinic intellectual terms, and by loosening the scriptural requirements for its location (Temple Mount) and makeup (priests) "in that day" (the commentary's perpetual present). But these two senses are less combined editorially than juxtaposed as Scripture is broken open for its parts to be atomistically yet successively interpreted. In working through the fine points of these juxtaposed expositions, the rabbinic student of this text comes to experience the presence of the Temple even in its absence and, concomitantly, the illocutionary force of the rabbinic claim to be the legitimate successors to the priests who sat within the Temple precincts as guardians, expositors, and adjudicators of Israel's covenantal texts and traditions—as the central sources of Torah teaching for all of Israel.

They Shall Teach Your Statutes to Jacob (§351)

As the following text illustrates, the rabbinic sages also had to confront Scripture's assignment of didactic authority to the levitical priests:

[A] "They [the descendants of Levi] shall teach Your statutes to Jacob" (Deut. 33:10): This teaches that all decisions (*hôrāyôt*) can issue only from their mouths, as it says, "Every matter of dispute or assault is subject to their ruling" (Deut. 21:5): "Dispute" (*rîb*) refers to disputes concerning the [red] heifer (Num. 19), disputes concerning the heifer [whose neck is broken] (Deut. 21:1–9), disputes concerning the suspected wife (Num. 5:11–31). "Assault" (*nega^c*) refers to plagues (*něgā^cîm*) affecting a person and plagues affecting clothing and plagues affecting houses.

[B] "Your instructions (*tôrātekā*[64]) to Israel" (Deut. 33:10): This teaches that two Torahs were given to Israel, one oral and one written. Agnitus the [Roman] general once asked Rabban Gamaliel: "How many Torahs were given to Israel?" He replied: "Two, one written and one oral."[65]

The first part is very similar to what we encountered at the beginning of §152. Whereas the authority to teach (understood as issuing legal judgments) conferred upon the descendants of Levi by Scripture is confirmed, even emphasized, by the commentary, the introduction of a prooftext that itself becomes the object of commentary facilitates a narrowing of the scope of priestly instruction to specific areas of conflict and plague for which Scripture explicitly requires priestly supervision of the rites of expiation and purification.[66] But all of these are rites that were no longer practiced once the Temple was destroyed (it not being clear to what extent they were practiced before). Thus, the didactic role of the priests is affirmed, even while its scope is radically conscribed.

The commentary on the second half of the verse is even more radical. Either sensitive to the possible redundancy of the parallelistic doublet or reading "your Torah" as "your Torahs,"[67] the commentary shifts attention to what may be said to be the central tenet of the rabbinic sages' self-understanding: two Torahs were revealed by God to Israel at Mt. Sinai, one written and one oral, the latter containing the continually unfolding, *rabbinically* transmitted, yet divinely authorized explications of the former. By "deriving" this teaching from the details of the verse at hand— one of the most explicit identifications of covenantal instruction with the levitical priests—the midrash deflects attention from the question of *who* teaches Torah to the question, fictively posed by a Roman official to a rabbinic patriarch, *what* does that Torah comprise?[68] The exchange between Agnitus and Rabban Gamaliel, it would at first appear, does not add anything new to what has already been stated in interpretation of the lemma. This anecdotal dialogue, however, rhetorically functions in two ways in its present redacted configuration:

1. It draws our attention away from the lemma and its assignment of teaching authority to the priests.
2. By having the doctrine of the dual Torah expressed by the rabbinic patriarch in direct response to a Roman official, it identifies that doctrine implicitly with the Jewish people as a whole (whom the patriarch may be thought to represent in such official dealings) and more particularly with the status claims of the rabbinic sage movement (which the patriarch is understood to head).[69]

Thus, Rabban Gamaliel's official affirmation of the coequal status of written and oral Torahs is implicitly an affirmation of rabbinic teaching authority. Thus, the commentary moves overall from affirming the scriptural truth of priestly didactic authority, to exegetically delimiting the scope of that authority, to exegetically expanding the signification fo the lemma in such a way as to divert attention from priestly teaching authority to that of the sages (by whom the this text is studied), as the purveyors of the *dual* Torah (of which this text and its interpretative practices are a part).[70]

Serving Him with All Your Heart (§41)

The *Sifre* not only creates an exegetical space into which to insert the figure of the rabbinic sage, but does the same for the study of Torah (*talmûd tôrâ,* or just *talmûd*) as a central religious obligation.[71] If space for the former is created by conscribing the place of the priest, then space for the latter is created by conscribing, and even coopting, the place of sacrificial worship. Deut. 11:13-14 reads as follows: "[13] If, then, you obey the commandments that I enjoin upon you this day, loving the Lord your God and serving Him with all your heart and with all your soul, [14] I will grant the rain for your land in season, the early rain and the late."

The *Sifre*'s commentary dissects the verse and presents a series of explications of 13b and 14 as follows:

[A] "Serving Him (*ûlĕʿābĕdô*)": This refers to [the obligation to] study (*talmûd*). You say that this refers to study, but perhaps it refers to [the Temple] service (*ʿābôdâ*).[72] Behold it says, "The Lord God took the man and placed him in the Garden of Eden, to work it (*lĕʿābĕdāh*) and to tend it (*ûlĕšāmĕrāh*)" (Gen. 2:15). What kind of work (*ʿābôdâ*), and what kind of tending (*šĕmîrâ*) could there have been then? Thus, you must deduce that "to work it" refers to study, while "to tend it" refers to [the observance of] the commandments.[73] And just as service at the altar is called *service,* so too study is called *service.*

[B] Another interpretation of "serving Him": This refers to prayer. You say that this refers to prayer, but perhaps it refers only to [the Temple] service. Therefore it says, "with (= in) all your heart and with all your soul" (Deut. 11:13). But is [Temple] worship within the heart? Therefore, when Scripture says "serving Him" it refers to prayer. And similarly David says, "Accept my prayer as an offering of incense before you," etc. (Ps. 141:2). And it says, "When Daniel learned that the edict was signed he went to his house [where he prayed]" (Dan. 6:11) And it says, "As he approached the den he cried to Daniel in a sorrowful voice, the king saying to Daniel: 'Daniel, the servant of the living God, the God whom you served (*pālaḥ*) regularly, can He save you from the lions?'" (Dan. 6:21). But was there [Temple] worship (*pûlḥān*) in Babylonia? Therefore, when Scripture says "serving Him," this refers to prayer. And just as service at the altar is called *service,* so too prayer is called *service.*

[C] R. Eliezer ben Jacob says: "Serving Him with all your heart and with all your soul": This is a warning to the priests that their hearts not be divided at the time of [their Temple] service.

[D] Another interpretation: What does Scripture mean by saying. "with all your heart and soul"? For does not Scripture say elsewhere, "[You (sing.) shall love the Lord your God] with all your heart and with all your soul" (Deut.

6:5)? There (6:5) it refers to the individual, while here (11:13) it refers to the public. There it refers to study, while here it refers to performance (maʿăśeh).

[E] Since you have learned [of your obligation], now perform [it]. If you perform what is required of you, then I too will perform what is required of me: "I will grant the rain for your land in season" (Deut. 11:14).[74]

The commentary begins by seeking to define the meaning of *serving* God in the lemma in such ways that would *deny* its signifying sacrificial worship (ʿăbôdā). The first two interpretations (A and B) propose instead "study" and "prayer" respectively. In the aftermath of the destruction of the Second Temple study and prayer became, at least among the rabbis and their followers, increasingly regularized and ritualized as acts of worship in their own right. In both cases, the possibility that the verb ʿbd in the lemma refers to something other than sacrificial worship is established not from the verse itself but by analogy to another verse in which the same verb (or, in the case of Dan. 6:21, its Aramaic equivalent) could be interpreted to refer to nonphysical service or labor. By showing that this verb could denote study and prayer elsewhere in Scripture, in one case (Adam and Eve) at a time preceding the beginnings of sacrificial worship and in the other (Daniel) in a place where such worship was impossible, similar meanings are established by analogy for the same verb in Deut. 11:13. That verse, however, unlike Gen. 2:15 and Dan. 6:21, is not simply descriptive but *prescriptive*, and as such is understood to designate study and prayer as normative forms of worship or divine service.

The next interpretation (C), that of R. Eliezer ben Jacob,[75] in shifting attention from the expression *serving Him* to the phrase *with all your heart,* reestablishes surprisingly what had just been denied: *serving Him* may indeed refer to the priestly service in the Temple. Furthermore, this interpretation takes for granted what had previously been explicitly rejected: sacrificial worship involves the heart.[76]

The next interpretation (D) is more difficult to understand, especially in relation to its present context in the commentary. Noting tht the phrase *with all your heart and with all your soul* is used elsewhere in Scripture (Deut. 6:5), the commentary assigns different meanings to the two occurrences of this phrase so that neither could be construed as redundant. It does so twice. First, noticing that Deut. 6:5 has *your* in the singular, whereas Deut. 11:13 has *your* in the plural, the commentary understands the former to refer to the individual (yāḥîd) and the latter to the public (ṣibbûr). It is unclear, however, with regard to what activities this distinction is being drawn because the first verse speaks of loving God whereas the second speaks of loving and serving God.[77] Second, the phrase *with all your heart and with all your soul* in Deut. 6:5 is said to refer to study (*talmûd*), whereas the similar phrase in the lemma (11:13) is said to refer to performance (*ma'áseh*).

How might we understand these two interpretations of section D in relation to what preceded it as it is presently configured in the commentary? I would suggest that the commentary is returning to its two original interpretations of the lemma as signifying study (A) and prayer (B), but now in reverse order. Not only is Deut. 11:13 linked to Deut. 6:5 by nearly identical language, but also by the fact that the latter ("you shall love the Lord your God") in its larger scriptural context is also rabbinically understood to refer both to study and to prayer.[78] However, from a rabbinic perspective those two verses could not simply mean the same thing but must at least refer to different aspects of study and prayer. Thus, Deut. 6:4–7 when understood to refer to prayer refers to the individual's prayer, whereas Deut. 11:13 when understood to refer to prayer refers to collective, public prayer.[79] Similarly, study is divided into its two aspects, study proper and its dependent actualization in practice, with the former assigned to Deut. 6:5 and the latter to Deut. 11:13.[80]

So, in a sense we have come full circle with *serving Him* referring to study (as in A), but now to study in combination with practice. This return to the original emphasis on the obligation of study also serves to conscribe (without in any way negating) R. Eliezer ben Jacob's interpretation of *serving Him* as referring to priestly Temple service. Although study and prayer might take the place of Temple worship in present practice, it remains a scriptural and interpretive (not to mention messianic) presence.[81] But the commentary's return to study is not a full return to its original interpretation but an advance beyond it, in adding to study its concomitant complement of performance. This leads directly to the commentary's interpretation of the succeeding verse (11:14), with which the unit concludes. God addresses Israel: having learned (*šama'tā*), now perform (*'áseh*)[82]; if you perform as required, then I will perform as required, rewarding you with timely rain (measure for measure). Thus, Israel's covenantal welfare is directly dependent of its practice of Torah, which is in turn dependent on its study of Torah. Stated differently, human action, as informed by Torah study, can trigger divine action.

Although Deut. 11:13 does not itself speak of sacrificial worship, the *Sifre*'s commentary, recognizing an ambiguity in that verse's use of the verb *to serve,* raises the possibility that the verse could be understood to refer to such worship, only to deprivilege (albeit not absolutely) that possibility in preference for its replacements: study and prayer. But the indirect manner in which that argument unfolds through the juxtaposition of alternative possibilities and the surprising twist at its conclusion draws the student of the text into that very *work* of engaged intratextual study which, when fulfilled in practice (including prayer), is understood to be the central act of serving God with a full heart, now that sacrificial worship is no longer possible. As long as the Temple stood, Israel's welfare was considered to be dependent in large measure on the regularity of its sacrificial worship.[83] But with the Temple now destroyed, Israel's welfare is dependent, according to our commentary, on the regularity of their prayer and study of Torah, together with its concomitant fulfillment in practice. If in the first case the officiating priests, dedicated to the service of God, were viewed as the chief sustainers of Israel's sacred life and covenental fortunes, in the second case this officiating role is claimed by the rabbinic sages, dedicated masters and models of the sacred work of Torah study and practice. If by the former type of ʿăbôdâ (service and labor) God's presence could be experienced and favor obtained in the past, then by the present type of ʿăbôdâ God's presence and favor are still accessible, even though the sacrificial nexus of human and divine has been lost.

Holding Fast to Him (§49)

As we have seen, the rabbinic sages claimed not only roles that were formerly assigned to the priesthood, but that their self-defining activity of Torah study (*talmûd tôrâ*) was a paramount religious act, indeed an act of worship, not simply equal but superior to that of sacrificial worship.[84] But just as sacrificial worship had been a social practice, conducted under the leadership of the priests in the public arena of the Temple (*bêt hammiqdāš*), so, too, Torah study was to be a social practice, conducted in the company of sages in the public arena of the study house (*bêt hammidrāš*). As a form of worship, study was to be not simply a religious *obligation* but a religious *experience*, potentially of the highest order, as the following piece of commentary demonstrates:

[A] "[If, then, you faithfully keep all that I command you, loving the Lord your God, walking in all His ways,] and holding fast to Him" (Deut. 11:22): But is it possible for a person to ascend to heaven and to cleave to fire? For has it not been said, "For the Lord your God is a consuming fire" (Deut. 4:24), and it says, "His throne was fiery flames" (Dan. 7:9). Rather, attach yourself to the sages and their disciples, and I will account it to you as though you had ascended to heaven to receive it [Torah]—not that you ascended to receive it in peace, but rather as though you waged war in order to receive it. And thus it says, "You went up to the heights taking captives" (Ps. 68:19).

[B] The expounders of *haggādôt*[85] say: If you desire to come to know the one who spoke and the world came into being, study *haggādâ*, for thereby you will come to know the one who spoke and the world came into being and cling to His ways.

[C] If you have performed what is required of you, then I too will perform what is required of me: "The Lord will dislodge [before you all these nations]" (Deut. 11:23).[86]

    The idea of attaching oneself to God is understood literally, only for this understanding to be rejected as an impossibility.[87] Rather, by attaching oneself to the sages and their disciples, that is, by engaging in the study of rabbinic Torah, as the continuation of the passage suggests, this verse can be fulfilled.[88] The commentary appears to be saying, in God's voice, that if you attach yourself to the sages in study of Torah, I will account it to you as if you, like Moses, had ascended to heaven to receive it. And just as Moses, according to rabbinic interpretations of Ps. 68:19, had to wage war against the angels to reach heaven to receive the Torah, so too Moses' successors when they study Torah are considered to ascend to heaven in struggle and to return with Torah as their captive.[89] Thus, it is not simply that those who study Torah with the sages are like Israel as a people when they stood at the foot of Mt. Sinai to receive the Torah (which is also described in rabbinic traditions as having been a struggle[90]), but that they are like Moses himself when he alone valiantly ascended to the fiery heavens to acquire the Torah on Israel's behalf.[91]

    The teachers of that branch of rabbinic Torah to which the present text may be said to belong next raise their voices (B), to claim that it is only through the rabbinically guided study of the scriptural narrative of Israel's sacred history that God the creator can be known.[92] At this point God's voice reenters the discussion, implicitly linking the rabbinic interpretation of the scriptural protasis with its apodosis in the next verse: only when you, Israel, do your part—now understood as attachment to the sages in their study and practice of Torah—will "the Lord dislodge before you all these nations" (11:23). Such social attachment is the most realizable route not only to the mystical goal of attachment to God, but to the political fulfillment of God's promises to redeem all Israel from the rule of the nations.[93]

    The motif of ascending to heaven in struggle and risk is suggestive in another way as well. In Second Temple times, Jewish groups that were alienated from what they considered to be a defiled temple and priesthood, envisioned a heavnely temple in which God was enthroned and to which religious virtuosi might ascend. Stories of such ascensions, usually told of biblical heroes, frequently include vivid descriptions of the dangerous obstacles encountered along the way, including blazing barriers, through which the hero had to pass in order to attain his goal of reaching the heavenly palace and its fiery divine throne (e.g., *1 Enoch* 14). Thus, persons who, for whatever reasons, felt that God's presence was not adequately accessible to them on the horizontal plane of history and society, projected society, projected an ideal temple and their desire to reach it onto a vertical plane of heavenly ascent.[94] Similar motifs recur, long after the Temple had been destroyed, in the Hekhalot literature of rabbinic times, again presumably as a substitute for access to God's presence on the horizontal, earthly plane. Without necessarily regarding our text as a direct polemic against any specific group, we can understand it as advocating a scholastic alternative to the hope for or fantasy of direct, unmediated human access to God, whether on earth or in heaven. The radical idea that attachment to a community of sages whose central ritual was the study of humanly mediated divine words would be regarded as the closest one could approach God, may be seen as a response both to what had been lost and to what others sought to establish in its place. The experience of revelation could be obtained, that is, reenacted, in the here and now not through the ecstatic visions or ascensions of individuals, but through participation in the society and discourse of sages and their disciples. As the *Sifre* comments elsewhere: "'[You shall keep and you shall perform all the laws and rules] that I have set before you *this day*' (Deut. 32:11): Let them be as dear to you today as if you [yourselves] had received them today from Mt. Sinai; let them be as ready in your mouths (*rĕgîlîm bĕpîkem*) as if you had heard them today."[95] But our present passage goes even further. In citing the otherwise unnecessary Dan. 7:9, it subtly suggests that the ascension here spoken of is not simply to Sinai but to the heavenly divine throne (*kārsē'*). By an intertextual play between the flame (*šābîtā*) of that throne and the taking of Torah as captive (*šābîtā šebî* of Ps. 68:19), it suggests that in acquiring words of Torah, such as these, the rabbinic student acquires not simply an experience of Sinai, but a bit of God's fiery heavenly throne.

You Shall Hold a Day of Assembly (§135)

If the sages as expounders of "narratives" (*haggādôt*) claim to be intermediaries in the human search to know and to experience God (last passage examined), as expounders of scriptural laws they claimed to be intermediaries in the revelation and actualization of God's will within Israelite society. Approximately half of *Sifre* focuses on the rabbinic delineation, extension, and application of biblical rules.[96] It is a common feature of law in general that codes require regular reinterpretation as sociohistorical conditions change and as the intent of the original framers becomes increasingly unrecoverable (and perhaps irrelevant). The following passage implicitly claims that it was the very intent of the divine lawgiver to transmit through the sages written rules that would require their authoritative interpretation:

[A] "On the seventh day [of Passover] you shall hold a day of assembly (*ʿăṣeret*) for the Lord your God" (Deut. 16:8): Rabbi [Judah the Patriarch] says: Could it be that a person should be restricted (*ʿāṣûr*) to the house of study the whole day? Scripture teaches [elsewhere, regarding the day of assembly], "to [= for] you" (Lev. 23:35; Num. 29:35). Could it be that a person should eat and drink the whole day? Scripture teaches, "a day of assembly for the Lord your God." How is it possible [to reconcile these two]? Devote part [of the day] to the house of study and part to eating and drinking.

[B] R. Ishmael says: Since we have not learned [from Scripture] that work is forbidden on [intermediate] festival days, whence do we learn it? Scripture teaches, "For six days you shall eat unleavened bread and on the seventh day you shall hold a day of assembly" (Deut. 16:8). Just as the seventh day is a day of restriction (*ʿāṣûr*), so too the sixth day is a day of restriction. Or perhaps just as the seventh day is a day of restriction from *all* work, so too the sixth day is a day of restriction from *all* work? Scripture teaches, "For six days you shall eat unleavened bread and on the seventh day you shall hold a day of assembly." Only the seventh day is restricted from all work and the sixth is not restricted from all work. Thus, Scripture has been transmitted to the sages, for them to say on which days work is forbidden and on which days permitted, and which kinds of work are forbidden and which kinds of work are permitted.[97]

The first part of the commentary (A), attributed to R. Judah the Patriarch, contrasts two scriptural expressions relating to observance of the final day of a festival (and by implication, other festival days), each one leading to a different view of the purpose of that day and each undermined by the other. The commentary is left then to ask: how can the day be both "an assembly for the Lord your God," dedicated to the service of God (here interpreted in terms of study), and a day "unto you," spent in a self-satisfying manner (here interpreted in terms of eating and drinking)? The solution is to dedicate the day both to studying and to eating and drinking. But this solution leaves unspecified how much or what part of the day is to be spent in each type of activity.[98]

The second part of the commentary (B), in the name of R. Ishmael, deals with a similar ambiguity arising from the lemma: what is the difference, in terms of abstinence from work (still playing on *ʿăṣeret*), between the final holy day and the intermediate days (represented by the immediately preceding sixth day) of the festival?[99] The lemma is understood to juxtapose the seventh day with those that precede it in such a way as to *both* compare and contrast them.[100] Again, a compromise is reached: the intermediate days are like the seventh day in that *some* work restrictions apply to them, but they are unlike the seventh day in that *not all* work is forbidden on them.[101] As in the preceding section, even though the exegetical problem is solved and a legal principle established, the legal particulars remain to be determined. Our commentary concludes, there-fore, that the authority to determine these particulars has been entrusted to the sages; literally, that the written text of Scripture has been transmitted (*māsar*) to them (to interpret and to apply).

Taken as a redacted whole, this passage is an interesting example of the tension between scriptural exegesis and rabbinic authority in the deter-mination of law, particularly in the gray areas where legal principles ambiguously adjoin. On the exegetical axis, there is obvious delight in the close but free reading of the details of scriptural expression, both within the lemma and in related verses from elsewhere in Scripture. Similarly on the rhetorical axis, the dialogical question and answer, and the dialectical raising, rejecting, and reconciliation of antithetical possibilities engages the student of the text in the rabbinic interpretation of Scripture as a sacred practice in and of itself. But there is, in the end, the admission that exegesis of Scripture's words can lead (or be pushed) only so far, at which point practical legal determinations to suit changing social realities are predicted on rabbinical and not scriptural authority. Although Torah is given to all of Israel, its authoritative transmission (here understood dynamically as its applied specification and hence transformation) is in the hands of Israel's rabbinic sages.[102]

May My Discourse Come Down as Rain (§306)

By dedicating themselves to the continuous study and teaching of Torah texts and traditions, the rabbinic sages sought to be regarded not so much as techincians in the interpretation and application of its laws and teachings (although such expertise was essential), but as the discursive and practical *embodiment* of Torah as God's word and will in the midst of Israelite society. The sage was anything but autonomous of Torah texts and traditions, which he sought to master through their complete integration into his memory and life. This is part of what unfolds in the following exegetical juxtaposition of three related interpretations:

[A] Another interpretation of "May my discourse come down as rain" (Deut. 32:2): Just as rain falls on trees and infuses each type with its distinctive flavor—the grapevine with its flavor, the olive tree with its flavor, the fig tree with its flavor—so too words of Torah are all one, but they comprise *miqrā'* (Scripture) and *mišnâ* (oral teaching): *midrāš* (exegesis),[103] *hălākŏt* (laws), and *haggādôt* (narratives).

[B] Another interpretation[104] of "Like showers on young grass" (ibid.): Just as showers fall upon the young grasses and cause them to grow—some green, some black, and some white[105]—so too words of Torah include masters of Torah who are wise (*hăkāmîm*): some of whom are worthy (*kĕšārîm*), some of whom are righteous (*ṣaddiqim*), some of whom are pious (*hăsîdîm*).[106]

[C] Another interpretation [of "May my discourse come down as rain"]: Just as rain cannot be anticipated until it arrives, as it says, "And after a while the sky grew black with clouds [and there was wind and a heavy downpour]" (1 Kings 18:45),[107] so too you cannot know what a disciple of the sages is until he teaches: *mišnâ, hălākôt,* and *haggādôt;*[108] or until he is appointed administrator (*parnās*) over the public.[109]

These three interpretations appear to form a coherent cluster within a larger series of interpretations of the rain and dew metaphors of Deut. 32:2. Moses' appeal that his final words (the "Song of Moses") be eagerly received, are understood by the *Sifre* commentary to refer to words of Torah in general, both written and oral.[110] The implications of the metaphors of rain and dew for words of Torah are variously explored, each interpretation drawing on the image of rain or dew dividing so as to penetrate the ground and vegetation. In the first of the present cluster (A) it is noted that just as rain produces trees of diverse flavors (presumably the flavors of their fruits), so too the words of Torah (especially oral Torah) come in several flavors or forms. But just as all types of trees are sustained by the same rain, so too the different branches of Torah discourse (the rabbinic study curriculum) are one, deriving from a single source.[111]

In the second interpretation (B), commenting on the parallel second half of the lemma in which the showers give life to tender grasses of diverse colors, the metaphor is still taken to signify "words of Torah," but now understood to comprise not different types of Torah *discourse* but different types of *sages.* The structural similarity between this and the preceding interpretation (not exact to be sure) suggests that these two interpretations be read as complements to one another. The awkward statement in the second interpretation that words of Torah comprise types of sages, suggests an equation between sages in their variety and words of Torah in their variety, all of which are sustained by the same divine source, all of which are life giving. The metaphor of rain for Torah teachings has begun to slip.

This implied equation of sages with words of Torah is affirmed in the third interpretation (C), where the metaphorical image shifts from the way in which rain breaks up as it penetrates vegetation to the way in which it suddenly appears. Just as rain cannot be anticipated or, we might say, its qualities cannot be known until it actually comes, so too the sage cannot be known until he teaches.[112] The variety of what he teaches is the same (with slight variation) as that of the branches of Torah discourse that we encountered in the first interpretation. In a sense, then, the sage *is* the Torah he teaches. Whereas in the first two interpretations the rain is analogous to (*kak*) "words of Torah," now it is analogous to "disciples of the sages"; the metaphoric slippage begun in the preceding interpretation is now complete. This becomes even more significant when we try to apply the commentary's interpretation back to the biblical image: if Moses hopes that his words will penetrate the people as rain does the herbage, the commentary suggests not only an equation of those penetrating words with rabbinic teachings but with rabbinic sages as Torah teachers. Note finally how in each of the three examples a threefold division is adduced: between three types of oral Torah, between three types of sages, and between three types of teachings of sages, all of which, like the rain, are ultimately one.[113]

Because of this relative tightness and circularity of structure the concluding words of the third interpretation, added as though an afterthought ("or") yet part of our text in all of its attestations, stand out so boldly: an alternative way of telling whether someone is a sage is by his having been appointed (presumably by a rabbinic authority) as a public administrator (*parnās*). The term *parnās* appears several times in the *Sifre* to denote figures, both biblical (Moses, David, and Joshua) and rabbinic (Hillel, R. Jōḥanan ben Zakkai, R. Akiba), who are said to have denoted themselves as leaders to providing for Israel's welfare.[114] Other evidence suggests that in rabbinic times in Palestine the *parnās* was a village administrator with general responsibility for the oversight of village affairs, in particular finances, including the distribution of public charity and the supervision of building projects.[115] Two *Sifre* passages draw connections between the *parnās* and the biblical king,[116] and another suggests that the position of *parnās* was passed from father to son.[117] But our present passage is the most significant of all for its explicit *identification* of the *parnās* with the rabbinic sage and his learning. The appointment of a person to the position of *parnās* and his conduct in that position is understood to be as sure an indication of his learning as hearing him teach rabbinic Torah. In other words, Torah learning is the chief qualification for such appointments.[118]

Other scholars have suggested that it was only in the mid-third century C.E. (around when the *Sifre* as a redacted text was created), with the political and religious authority of the Patriarch firmly established and the size of the rabbinic class expanding, that the rabbinic movement assumed, or at least sought, central authority for the appointment of local magistrates (including *parněsîm*) and judges. This was a way of gaining influence for the rabbis' program within broader Jewish society and as a way of providing financial support for the sages so appointed.[119] The appointment of sages to positions of public responsibility, both judicial and administrative, met with initial opposition, it appears, from communities that had in the past considered such appointments to be a local prerogative, from a wealthy (and perhaps priestly) local landed aristocracy that feared being displaced by the rabbinic newcomers, and even from some rabbis who either were reluctant to undertake public roles to which they were not accustomed or suited or were opposed to the growing centralized authority of the Patriarch and the professionalization of the rabbinate. The sage movement as a whole, however, needed to argue, whether to convince themselves or others, that they constituted not just Israel's intellectual and religious elite, but the social and political leadership of the Jewish people at both the national and the local levels. From a rabbinic perspective these two claims, ideally at least, needed to go hand in hand. If rabbinically defined Torah learning and performance were to be the central religious obligations the fulfillment of which would, in covenantal terms, sustain Israel's life and determine its future fortunes, then the judicial and administrative leadership of Israel's corporate life would have to rest in the hands of rabbinic sages who were learned masters and living exemplars of Torah. It should not be surprising, then, to find the issue of such appointments as a recurring theme in the *Sifre*'s commentary, as the following two sections attest.

When the Heads of the People Are Gathered (§346)

[A] "He [God] became King in Jeshurun" (Deut. 33:5a): When Israel are united in one counsel below, His great name is praised above, as it is said, "He became King in Jeshurun." When? "When the heads of the people were gathered" (33:5b). And *gathering* here must refer to "heads of the people," as it says, "God said to Moses, 'Take all the heads of the people [and have them publicly impaled before the Lord, so that the Lord's wrath may turn away from Israel]'" (Num. 25:4).

[B] Another interpretation [of "He became King in Jeshurun"]: When the Patriarch appoints elders to a court below,[120] His great name is praised above, as it is said, "He became King in Jeshurun." When? "When the heads of the people were gathered." And *gathering* here must refer to "elders," as it is said, "Gather for me seventy of Israel's elders" (Num. 11:16).[121]

The two interpretations are clearly parallel in their structures and in their broad understanding of the lemma: God's greatness is established above by Israel's unity below, that unity being a function of the "gathering" of Israel's leaders.[122] But despite these outward similarities, a closer reading reveals that the two interpretations are different. The first begins as an implicit call for unity among Israel, especially among Israel's leaders. But then we find the awkward statement that "*gathering* must refer to 'heads of people'," followed by the citation of Num. 25:4. However, the identification of *gathering* with "heads of people" is already found in the lemma, without any need for recourse to Num. 25:4, where we find the latter expression but not the former.[123] The citation of Num. 25:4 therefore must serve another purpose: to define what is meant in this interpretation by *heads of the people*. Although Num. 25:4 might be understood to say that the "heads of the people" are themselves to be executed for the promiscuity and idolatry of the Israelites at Shittim (whom they joined, encouraged, or failed to restrain[124]), rabbinic interpretations of this verse consistently understand the "heads of the people" to be the same as the "judges of Israel" (*šōpĕtê yiśrāʾēl*) of 25:5, who themselves *carried out* the executions.[125] Thus, the "heads of the people" of the lemma are understood by the commentary to be Israel's *judges*, through whose collective judgments God's wrath is "turned away from Israel" (Num. 25:4). Who these judges are remains to be defined.

In the second interpretation the *heads of the people* are defined as elders, that is, the rabbinic elders who are appointed by the Patriarch to serve on courts, following the model of Moses's gathering (at God's command) of the seventy elders (Num. 11:16). Thus, the Patriarch corresponds to Moses and the rabbinic appointees to the biblical elders, the latter being an association that we have seen before, the former being one we shall encounter later.[126] The editorial juxtaposition of the two interpretations, linked by their similar structures, results in a twofold statement: (1) The "heads of the people," whose "gathering" causes Israel to be united in counsel, and thereby God's name to be praised, are Isrsael's judges (from Num. 25:4), (2) who are the elders (sages) appointed by the Patriarch (from Num. 11:16). The Patriarch's appointment of sages to such positions resounds both "horizontally" back to Moses and "vertically" up to God.

I Will Appoint Them as Your Heads (§13)

The analogy between the authority of the Patriarch and that of Moses to make judicial appointments, as well as popular opposition to such appointments, is suggested in the *Sifre*'s commentary to Deut. 1:13. The scriptural context of that verse is Moses' decision to distribute leadership responsibility, especially in judicial matters, to a select group of *lay* tribal leaders (the "elders" elsewhere).[127] That verse reads (with Moses speaking to the people): "Get for yourselves men who are wise, discerning, and experienced, from each of your tribes, and I will appoint them as your heads." There is an ambiguity here between the people's role in selecting their "heads" and Moses' role in appointing them.[128] There is also the question of the meanings of the three stated qualifications for those to be appointed. The commentary begins as follows:

[A] "Get for yourselves (*hăbû lākem*)": "Get" must refer to "counsel" (*ʿēṣâ*), as it says, "Give (*hābû*) your counsel what we shall do" (2 Sam. 16:20), "Come (*hābâ*), let us take counsel (*nitḥakmâ*) against them" (Exod. 1:10).[129]

The opening comment stresses that the people's function in selecting their "heads" is merely advisory and not determinative. Moses and not the people are to select their leader-judges.[130] Because the first verse cited employs the imperative of the verb *yhb* in conjunction with "counsel" (that is, "advice"), the imperative of the same verb in the lemma is similarly construed. The second verse cited also usses the imperative of *yhb*, and is also understood to denote counsel, but more subtly. Pharaoh is understood to take the initiative against Israel, but turns to the Egyptian people for their counsel before proceeding.[131]

The commentary continues:

> [B] "Men": Did you think it would say "women"? Why then does it say "men"? To indicate men who are experienced and many-sided [in their learning].[132]

In a patriarchal society it is presumed that men and not women would serve in such leadership roles. Why, then, need Scripture state the obvious? Not to denote the gender of the leaders but to indicate their depth and breadth of learning, anticipating what will next emerge as the privileging of their attribute of wisdom (as sages).

> [C] "Select from each of your tribes persons who are wise (*ḥăkāmîm*), and discerning (*nĕbōnîm*), and experienced (*yĕdū'îm*), and I will appoint them as your heads" (Deut. 1:13). With regard to this Arios[133] asked R. Jose (ca. 150 C.E.): "Who is a wise person (*ḥākām*)?" He replied to him: "Whoever maintains (*mĕqayyēm*) his learning." [Arios asked:] "But is this not a discerning person (*nābôn*)?" He replied to him: "'[Persons who are] discerning' has already been mentioned."
>
> [D] What is the difference between a wise person and a discerning person? A wise person resembles a rich money changer. When someone brings him [money] to examine he examines it, and when no one brings him [money] to examine he takes out his own and examines it. A discerning person resembles a poor money changer. When someone brings him [money] to examine he examines it, and when no one brings him [money] he sits waiting anxiously.[134]

According to the lemma, the lay leaders are to be selected according to three intellectual qualities. The discussion launched by Arios' question and R. Jose's reply revolves around the difference between two of these, the *ḥākām* and the *nābôn*, now representing not simply two intellectual qualities but two types of intellectuals.[135]

The midrashic passage as a whole (if not R. Jose) clearly favors the *ḥākām* over the *nābôn*. R. Jose defines the *ḥākām* as one who, unlike the *nābôn*, not only learns Torah, that is, acquires a knowledge of it, but maintains it through constant review.[136] Is this not true for the *nābôn* as well? asks Arios, to which R. Jose responds that the *năbôn*, being separately mentioned, cannot be identical to the *ḥakām* (lest Scripture be redundant).

What follows (D)—the metaphorical comparison of these two types of learned men—may be seen either as R. Jose's further response or as an editorial juxtaposition to the preceding dialogue, the latter being my preference. The contrast between *ḥakām* and *nābôn* as two different types of scholars is now illustrated through comparison with rich and poor money changers, the preference for the *ḥakām* now becoming manifest, even though the precise difference between the two requires interpretation on the part of the student of the text. Like the rich and poor money changers, the *ḥakām* and the *nābôn* provide a service to those who come seeking their expertise, most likely in legal matters.[137] But the difference between the two is that the former preoccupies himself with the examination and evaluation of his wealth of acquired rules and traditions whether or not his services are sought. In other words, he spends his time absorbed in study *for its own sake*, and not, like the *nābôn* (poor money changer), only when his expertise is sought for a practical application.[138]

There is in this subtle juxtaposition of two interpretations of the *ḥakām* a tension (evidenced elsewhere in the *Sifre*, as we shall see): the sage is someone who serves the public, yet who is preoccupied with Torah study for its own sake. But there is another, even more important social thrust to this seemingly simple passage with its privileging of the *ḥakām*. Although several qualities are mentioned in Scripture as criteria for the selection of men to share leadership with Moses,[139] that which is singled out for favored treatment by our commentary is the one by which the rabbis call themselves, as if to suggest, once again, that they view themselves as the successors to the anonymous *lay* leaders (*zĕqēnîm*) who shared the burden and honor of leadership with Moses.

By contrast, the *ḥakām* and *nābôn* are also distinguished from one another in the *Damascus Document* of the Dead Sea sectaries, where the *nābôn,* and not the *ḥakām,* is privileged. There it is said that God raised up the elect community, comprising "from Aaron men of discernment (*nĕbônîm*), and from Israel men of wisdom (*ḥăkāmîm*), and made them hear [his voice]" (CD 6.2–3). Whereas, discernment is associated with the priests of the community, who are considered the prophetic conduit through which God makes his will and the proper interpretations of prophecies known to the community as a whole, the community's *laity* are characterized by the attribute of wisdom.[140]

This is not to suggest, as one scholar has, that our *Sifre* passage be read as an antisectarian polemic.[141] Rather, agianst a background in which some associated the authoritative teaching and adjudication of covenantal law with an inspired priesthood, the *Sifre* text wishes to downplay relatively the *nābôn* in relation to the *ḥākām*, whose genealogy extends back to Moses through the anonymous lay elders and whose pedagogic and juridical authority is predicated upon his incessant engagement with a wealth of divine texts and traditions for their own sakes. The *ḥākām*, unlike the *nābôn*, according to this formulation, is not simply a privileged *source* of sacred wisdom, but, as we have previously seen, its very *embodiment* through his *life* of constant Torah study and review for its own sake.

The commentary continues by explaining the last of the three qualities to be sought in Israel's leaders:

> [E] "Experienced (*yĕdūʿîm*), from each of your tribes"[142]: That they be well known (*yĕdūʿîm*) to you. For when each one wraps himself in his cloak and comes and sits before me, I do not know from which tribe he comes, but you recognize him, for you grew up among them. Therefore it says, "Known to each of your tribes": that they be well known to you. R. Simeon ben Gamaliel says: As soon as every court is seated [appointed], people complain about it, saying, "What makes so-and-so fit to be appointed, and what makes so-and-so unfit to be appointed?" Therefore it is said, "Known to each of your tribes": that they be well known to you.[143]

The third quality (*yĕdūʿîm*) is interpreted not in relation to the two that precede it, that is, not as a third and separate intellectual quality, but in relation to the phrase that follows it, thereby returning to the earlier social issue of the relation of the appointees to the people from whom they are drawn (A). The appointees should be familiar to the people over whom they will have judicial authority. The two issues of the relation of the leaders to the people and the qualities for which they are chosen by Moses are then linked in a statement attributed to a rabbinic patriarch, thereby associating his authority to make such appointments with that of Moses: if the appointees (and their merits) are known to the people, they will not question such appointments and implicitly the authority by which they are made. Our commentary is *unique* among its close and equally early parallels in raising to an explicit level the possibility of popular opposition to such patriarchal appointments.[144] Our text toes a fine line indeed: those who are appointed over the people should be of the people, even as they are not appointed by the people. This latter point is even more emphatically stated in the commentary's continuation:[145]

> [F] "I will appoint them as your heads" (Deut. 1:13): Is it possible [that Moses would have said], "If you appointed them, they would be [legitimately] appointed, but if not, they would not be appointed"? [No, for] Scripture teaches, "*I* will appoint them as your heads." If I [Moses] appointed them, they

are [legitimately] appointed, but if not, they are not appointed. Is it possible [that Moses would have said], "If you placed them in high positions (*gĕdaltem ʾôtām*), they would [legitimately] be in high positions, but if not, they would not be in high positions"? [No, for] Scripture says, "*I* will appoint them as your heads." If I [Moses] placed them in high positions, they are in high positions, but if not, they are not in high positions![146]

Whatever the people's advisory role in the appointment of their leaders (A) and however important it is that those leaders be familiar to the people (E), Moses alone has the authority to appoint and promote them. In view of the preceding passage that we examined (§346), in which Moses' appointments are explicitly linked to those of the patriarch and in view of the implicit association of the Patriarch Simeon ben Gamaliel with Moses in the preceding section (E) of this passage, it would appear that this passage serves to support the patriarch's claim to the authority to make such appointments in the face of local opposition to what may have been viewed as outside interference with long-established local jurisdiction in such matters.[147] The serious consequences of such (rabbinic) appointments, both for the people and for the appointees is stressed in the final two interpretations of this unit:

[G] Another interpretation [of "I will appoint them as (= over) your heads"]: If you keep [= obey] your leaders (*dabbĕrêkem*), your heads will be kept [from harm]; but if not, your heads will not be kept from harm.
[H] [Another interpretation: Read not "I will appoint them (*waʾăsîmēm*) as your heads," but "their guilt (*waʾăšāmām*) is upon your heads."][148] This teaches that Israel's guilt is upon the heads of their judges. And so it says, "Mortal man, I have appointed you a watchman for the house of Israel; and whenever you hear a message from My mouth, you must transmit My warning to them. When I say to the wicked man...and you have warned the wicked man...." (Ezek. 33:7-9).[149]

The first interpretation (G) understands the second person pronominal suffix (*your*) of the lemma to be addressed to Israel and through a play on the word *head* has the lemma say: your heads (covenantal well-being) depend on your obedience to your heads (appointed leaders).[150] The second interpretation (H) construes the second personal pronominal suffix (*your*) to be addressed not to Israel but to the judicial appointees themselves and, by another word play (a revocalization of the scriptural Hebrew) has the lemma say: the burden for Israel's guilt is upon your heads. The commentary's "audience" is presumed now to comprise such judicial appointees or at least potential appointees. The citiation from Ezekiel serves to protray the lay judges (heads) in prophetic terms. Like the prophets, they are understood to be conveyors of God's word to the people, bearing the moral burden of warning them, through their judgments, of the covenantal consequences of the people's behavior.[151] If in the first interpretation it is stressed that Israel should regard their judges with utmost respect, in the second it is stressed that those judges themselves need to view their work with utmost seriousness. In both cases, Israel's covenantal welfare is dependent on the proper appointment and functioning of their (rabbinic) magistrates.

The commentary as a whole, then, by atomistically focusing on an important biblical precedent for the *centralized* appointment of *local* lay magistrates, makes several interconnected points, all of which strengthen patriarchal claims to have inherited the authority for such appointments from Moses. But we need not assume that this text constitutes an extrarabbinic polemic, that is, an argument against those who challenged such rabbinic appointments from without (although such opposition appears to have existed). Rather, the text, as a specimen of intrarabbinic discourse (recall how the final interpretation turned the lemma into an address to the judicial appointees), more likely functions to strengthen support for such centralized patriarchal appointments among the sages themselves. In the very context of engaged rabbinic study this text subtly yet dynamically impresses upon rabbinic disciples the importance of appointments to public service as logical and necessary extensions of their intellectual vocation and prophetic self-understanding.[152]

Despite the recurring emphasis that the *Sifre* places on the appointment of rabbinic judges and magistrates, with its bold (perhaps wishful) statement that the very appointment of a person to such a position itself is a sign of his learning, what *defines* the sage is not such appointments, with their financial and social rewards, but a life *preoccupied* with the central ritual of study for the sake of the perpetuation of God's word in memory and in deed. How this ideal was in reality balanced against the demands of public service (with its possibilities for economic security and social influence) is impossible to determine from our text. But the tension itself finds ample expression, as we will shortly see, in the *Sifre*'s repeated warnings both against viewing rabbinic public service as an end in itself and against regarding study alone as self-sufficient.

If, Then, You Carefully Keep (§48)

The following complete, and rather extensive, editorial unit (§48) engagingly expresses, in its juxtaposition and enchaining of a multiplicity of interpretations of Deut. 11:22, many familiar motifs bearing on the rabbinic sage and his Torah study.

[A] "If, then, you carefully keep (*šāmōr tišmĕrûn*) all this command-ment": Why is this said? Because it is [elsewhere] said:[153] ["If, then, you carefully heed (*šāmōᶜa tišmĕᶜû*) the commandments" (Deut. 11:13). Might I understand this to mean that once a person has learned words of Torah he may sit idly and need not review them? Scripture teaches,] "If, then, you carefully keep all this commandment." Scripture hereby tells us that just as a person must be careful not to lose his money, so too he must be careful not to lose his learning. And similarly it says, "If you seek it [understanding] as you do silver" (Prov. 2:4). Just as silver is difficult to acquire, so too words of Torah are difficult to acquire. But could it also mean that just as silver is difficult to destroy, so too words of Torah are difficult to destroy? Scripture teaches, "Gold or glass cannot equal it [wisdom]" (Job 28:17): They are as difficult to acquire as gold and as easy to destroy as glass vessels. "Nor can it be exchanged for vessels of fine gold" (ibid.).[154]

This commentary responds to the similarity in expression between Deut. 11:22 and Deut. 11:13. Whereas the former uses the verb *šmr* (to keep), the latter uses the verb *šmᶜ* (to hear). Because, from a rabbinic perspective, these two verses cannot mean the same thing, each is understood to signify a different aspect of the obligation to study: hearing (learning) and keeping (retaining or maintaining what one has learned). The two verses, like the two aspects of study that they signify, complement rather than replicate one another. Lest one should think from Deut. 11:13 that having acquired learning he can relax self-assured in that learning, Deut. 11:22 comes to add the necessity of constantly reviewing what one has learned so as not to lose it. The comparisons of Torah with money and silver suggest both the difficulty of acquiring words of Torah and the value of retaining them.

But the analogy to silver when pushed a step further might suggest that Torah knowledge once acquired is difficult to destroy.[155] Hence, an additional metaphor, similarly drawn from Scripture, is required: Torah is also like fragile glassware that can easily be destroyed if it is not carefully maintained. This dual comparison, then, expresses not only the value of Torah learning once acquired but the ease with which it can be forfeited if not continually attended to.[156] Thus, the relationship between student and Torah is one of mutual benefit: through Torah learning the student acquires something of value and by constantly reviewing what he has learned he maintains it in his memory, thereby preventing its loss or destruction. This twofold idea is further developed in the succeeding interpretation of Deut. 4:9:

[B] R. Ishmael says: "Only take utmost care (*hiššāmēr lĕkā*) and watch yourself (*ûšĕmōr napšĕkā*) scrupulously [so that you do not forget the things that you saw with your own eyes and so that they do not fade from your mind as long as you live. And make them known to your children and to your children's children]" (Deut. 4:9). This may be compared to a king who snared a bird and handed it over to his servant, saying: "Safeguard this bird for my son. If you lose it, do not think that you have lost a bird worth an *ᵓîsār*,[157] but rather as if you had lost your life." And so it says, "For it is not an empty thing for you" (Deut. 32:47). For the thing about which you say "it is empty," "it is your life" (ibid.).[158]

Deut. 4:9 is linked to the lemma (11:22) by its double use of the verb *šmr*. The repetition of this verb in Deut. 4:9 is understood to signify two interconnected acts of guarding: by safeguarding (through constant study and review) the words of Torah the student of Torah actually safeguards his own life.[159] This understanding is further demonstrated in the juxtaposition of the phrases *it is empty* and *it is your life* in Deut. 32:47: do not think that the Torah is ever empty (of meaning), for it is the basis of your life (and therefore must be continually safeguarded through study and review).[160] Unique to this version of the tradition is the detail that the servant is asked by the king (God) to safeguard the bird (Torah) *for his son.* If the son is Israel, then the servant is the rabbinic sage or disciple, who stands in a mediate position between God and the people of Israel, who cannot by themselves assume full responsibility for the Torah that God has given them. Thus, although Deut. 4:9 and 32:47 are biblically addressed by Moses to all of Israel, they are here refigured by the *mashal* to be addressed especially to the class of sages: *their* life (raison d'être) depends on safeguarding the Torah for Israel through their constant study of it (and teaching it to their "sons"), upon which, in turn, Israel's life depends.

Although the preceding interpretations are couched in general terms (as though directed to all of Israel), what follows makes clear that the learning activity exegetically enjoined is that which characterizes rabbinic sages and their disciples in particular:

[C] R. Simeon ben Yohai says: This may be compared to two brothers who received inheritances from their father. One converted his to a *denar* and consumed it, while the other converted his to a *denar* and saved it. The one who converted his to a *denar* and consumed it soon found himself without anything, while the one who converted his to a *denar* and saved it after a while became rich. Similarly, a disciple of the sages who learns two or three teachings (*dĕbārîm*) a day, two or three chapters (*pĕrāqîm*) each week, two or three sections (*pārāšiyyôt*) each month, will after a while become rich. Concerning him it is said, "He who gathers little by little increases it" (Prov. 13:11). He who says, "Today I will learn and tomorrow I will learn [something new], today I will study and tomorrow I will study [something new]," finds himself in the end without anything. Concerning him it is said, "He who gathers during the summer [is capable, but he who sleeps during the harvest is incompetent]" (Prov. 10:5). And it says, "In winter the lazy man does not plow; at harvest time he seeks, and finds nothing" (Prov. 20:4). And it says, "One who observes the wind will never sow" (Ecc. 11:4).[161]

Here we find several additional metaphorical expressions for the importance of continuous study. Better to be constantly learning, a little at a time, and to be reviewing and delving ever deeper into what one has previously learned, than to learn each day something new and distinct, without integrating it into what was previously learned.[162] The learning of the former type of student will accumulate and be sustained, whereas that of the latter will not. The argicultural metaphor suggests the need to be constantly toiling in one's studies so as to ensure the future harvest of their fruits.[163]

The next prooftext and its commentary form what could be an autonomous unit, even though in context it develops the social implications of the positive and negative scholastic models previously advanced and is linked to what precedes by the scriptural "lazy man":

[D] And it says, "I passed by the field of a lazy man, [by the vineyard of a man lacking sense]. It was all overgrown with thorns; [its surface was covered with weeds, and its stone wall lay in ruins]" (Prov. 24:30–31). "I passed by the field of a lazy man": This refers to one who had already acquired a field. "By the vineyard of a man lacking sense": This refers to one who had already acquired a vineyard. Since he acquired a field and acquired a vineyard but did not labor in them, whence do we know that his end is to be called *lazy*? [Scripture teaches, "I passed by the field of a lazy man, by the vineyard of a man lacking sense."] And why is he called *lacking sense*? For he purchased a field and a vineyard but did not labor in them. [164] And whence do we know that in the end [a disciple like this] will overlook [*lĕhāniaḥ*, perhaps "forget"] two or three teachings in a section (*pārāšâ*)? As it says, "It was all overgrown with thorns." And whence do we know that he will seek the correct interpretation of the section and will not find it? As it is said, "Its surface was covered with weeds." And concerning him it says, "And its stone fence lay in ruins." Seeing that he does not retain [learning], he [nonetheless] sits and declares unclean what is clean and declares clean what is unclean, thereby breaking down the fences of the sages.[165] What in the end will be his punishment? Solomon came and referred to him in the tradition: "He who breaches a stone fence will be bitten by a snake" (Eccl. 10:8). Behold, whoever breaches the fence of the sages will be punished in the end.[166]

By dissecting and gradually interpreting Prov. 24:30-31, the following view unfolds. The disciple, compared to the owner of a field and vineyard, must continually cultivate the learning that he has acquired, lest it go to ruin. A disciple who is not continually active in maintaining what he has learned, yet who nevertheless presumes to render judgments based on his acquired but not presently engaged learning, poses a threat to the society of sages by breaking down its self-defining "fences" and will incur divine punishment.[167]

Without reducing their hermeneutical and rhetorical differences, we may note that the first four sections (A–D) of the commentary to Deut. 11:22 when viewed in their redacted succession cohere dynamically as a group. They progress from a concern with the value of Torah teaching and the importance of preserving it, both for its own sake and for the sake of the "life" of those who study it, to a practical emphasis on the importance of gradually acquiring Torah learning through the constant review of what one has already learned, to a warning to the disciples to conform to the values and practices that define the boundaries of rabbinic society and protect those within.[168]

In the following sections (E–M), several scriptural metaphors are interpreted to refer to Torah teachings and sages. Because the collection begins and ends with the metaphor of the honeycomb, I understand it to form a circular subunit of the larger unit, even as it echoes and develops several of the previous motifs.

[E] R. Simeon ben Menasya (ca. 200 C.E.) says: Behold it says, "A sated person [disdains a honeycomb]" (Prov. 27:7a): A disciple begins by not knowing anything. "To a hungry man anything bitter seems sweet" (27:7b): He only has what he has learned.[169]

In contrast to the bloated student who gloatingly rejects further learning of Torah (the sweet honeycomb), the properly humble disciple knows that having begun with nothing he still knows little and hungers for more, finding sweet even what is bitter. This accords with the commentary's earlier (C) admonition to the disciple to learn steadily, a little at a time, constantly reviewing and integrating what he has learned to establish a firm foundation for future learning.

The metaphor of the honeycomb, just employed to refer to Torah learning, is next taken to refer to the Torah sage himself:[170]

[F] "A sated person disdains a honeycomb": Just as a sieve[171] separates flour, bran, and meal, similarly a disciple of the sages sits and sorts words of Torah and weighs them: so-and-so permits while so-and-so prohibits, so-and-so declares unclean while so-and-so declares clean.[172]

The disciple might at first be confused and discouraged by the multiplicity of contradictory teachings of the sages. He is enjoined to attend to them *all* as words of Torah, taking them all in while learning to discern between them. The smug, satiated student disdains such painstaking study activity. The honeycomb, formerly understood to refer to Torah learning is now understood to refer to the student of Torah. Taken together with the preceding interpretation, we have here two aspects or stages in the learning of the disciple: gathering or accumulating learning, sorting out what he has learned.[173]

> [G] R. Judah [bar Ilai] says: A strong student (*šekkōḥô yāpeh*) is like a sponge that absorbs everything. His opposite is like a rag that only absorbs what it needs. The latter says, "I have enough with what I have learned from my master."[174]

This comment reiterates the idea that the student should never be satisfied with what he has learned, but should continually pursue Torah study for its own sake.[175] This pursuit may require that the student will eventually leave his master to study with others. This aspect of the master-disciple relationship is further developed in the next two comments:

> [H] R. Simeon b. Yoḥai (ca. 150 C.E.) says: Behold it says, "Drink water from your own cistern (*bôrekā*), [running water from your own well. Your springs will gush forth in streams in the public squares]" (Prov. 5:15-16): Learn from the one who is with you in your city (*šeʿimmĕkā bāʿîr*), and only afterwards disseminate (*haprēš*) [what you have learned] in all other places, as it is said, "She is like a merchant fleet, [bringing her food from afar]" (Prov. 31:14).
>
> [I] R. Simeon ben Menasya says: "Drink water from your own cistern": Drink the waters of the one who created you (*bĕrāʾkā*), and do not drink turbid waters, lest you be drawn to the teachings of heretics.[176]

Although a disciple should not be satisfied with the teachings of his master alone (see G), he must first learn what he can from his teacher in his own place (a word play[177]), establishing a solid foundation in learning before becoming a peripatetic scholar who disseminates Torah teachings in other places. A second interpretation (I) of the same verse states that the student must distinguish between the "waters of the one who created you" (another word play) and the "turbid waters" of heretics.[178] The juxtaposition of these two interpretations, with their two plays on the scriptural expression *your cistern,* suggests, on the one hand, an identification of one's teacher with one's creator, and, on the other, an association of travel to other places with exposure to "heretical" teachings. Discipleship to a single teacher provides an intellectual "home" from which a student can later venture into the world without being tempted by, what to the rabbis were, false teachings.[179]

Next, the commentary expands its interpretation of the cistern metaphor by contrasting it with the metaphor of a well, found in the continuation of the verse:

[J] R. Akiba (ca. 120 C.E.) says: Behold it says, "Drink water from your own cistern" (Prov. 5:15a): At first a cistern cannot bring forth a drop of water of its own, containing only what is in it. Similarly, a disciple at first does not know anything other than what he has learned.[180] "Running water from your own well" (5:15b): He can be compared to a well. Just as a well causes living waters to flow in all directions, so too disciples will come and will learn from him. And thus it says, "Your springs will gush forth," etc. (Prov. 5:16).[181]

The cistern and the well represent two stages in the intellectual career of the disciple. At first (the cistern stage), the disciple contains only what he has acquired from his master and does not bring forth learning of his own. Later (the well stage), as a master he produces on his own a constant flow of learning, sending it in many directions to his own disciples without fear of running dry.[182]

Sections E–J represent a somewhat circular subunit of the larger subunit (E–M) of the commentary. Although returning to the idea that the disciple begins without learning (E) and is totally dependent for what he knows on his master, it has moved forward (following the adopted lemma) in expectation that the disciple, if patient and persistent in his studies, can eventually become a master with disciples of his own.

The commentary continues by developing the analogy of Torah learning to water in many aspects:

[K] Words of Torah may be compared to water: Just as waters endure forever, so too words of Torah endure forever, as it is said, "they are life to him who finds them" (Prov. 4:22). Just as waters lift the unclean from their uncleanness, so too words of Torah lift the unclean from their uncleanness, [as it is said], "Your word is exceedingly pure and your servant loves it" (Ps. 119:140). Just as waters restore a person's soul, [as it is said,] "Like cold water to a parched throat" (Prov. 25:25), so too words of Torah restore a person's soul, [as it is said,] "The Torah of the Lord is perfect, renewing life" (Ps. 19:8). Just as waters are forever free, so too words of Torah are forever free, as it is said, "Ho, all who are thirsty, come for water" (Isa. 55:1). Just as waters are priceless, so too words of Torah are priceless, [as it is said,] "She [= wisdom] is more precious than rubies," etc. (Prov. 3:15). Or [might one think that] just as waters do not rejoice the heart, so too words of Torah do not rejoice the heart? [Scripture teaches,] "For your love is more delightful than wine" (Cant. 1:2).

[L] Just as wine rejoices the heart, so too words of Torah rejoice the heart, [as it is said], "The precepts of the Lord are just, rejoicing the heart" (Ps. 19:9). Just as you cannot discern wine's flavor when it is new, but the longer it ages in a vessel the better it becomes, so too the longer words of Torah age within a person the better they become, as it is said, "Wisdom is in the aged" (Job 12:12). Just as wine does not keep well in silver or gold vessels, but only in the lowliest of vessels, in vessels of clay, so too words of Torah do not keep well in one who regards himself as a vessel of silver or gold, but only in one who regards himself as the lowliest of vessels, as a vessel of clay. Or [might one think that] just as wine is sometimes bad for one's head and bad for one's body, the same is true of words of Torah? [Scripture teaches,] "Your oil yield a sweet fragrance" (Cant. 1:3).

[M] Just as oil is good for one's head [and] good for one's body, so too words of Torah are good for one's head and good for one's body, as it is said, "For they [= instruction and teaching] are a graceful wreath upon your head, a necklace about your throat" (Prov. 1:9), and it says, "She [= wisdom] will adorn your head with a graceful wreath" (Prov. 4:9). Words of Torah are compared both to oil and to honey, as it is said, "Sweeter than honey, than drippings of the honeycomb" (Ps. 19:11).[183]

Each analogy of Torah teachings to a valued liquid (water, wine, and oil) suggests several positive qualities shared by Torah teachings with that liquid, but each such analogy soon reaches its limit, at which point the metaphor turns potentially negative and needs to be replaced with another, until we arrive at oil, which is beneficial to a person's head and body (the whole person).[184] The final addition of the honey metaphor breaks the rhetorical pattern, because it is not occasioned by a potentially negative consequence of the preceding oil metaphor. This final shift is necessitated by the rhetorical need to return to the honey (*nōpet*) metaphor with which this unit began with its interpretation of Prov. 27:7 in section E, thereby providing an inclusio that allows the commentary to return to and proceed with its explication of the lemma of Deut. 11:22.[185]

[N] [Another interpretation of] "If, then, you carefully keep": Whence can you say that if a person [at first] learns a teaching of Torah and retains [*měqayyēm*] it [in his memory],[186] just as what he first learned is retained by him, so too what he subsequently learns will be retained by him? From that which is said, "If, then, you carefully keep (*šāmōr tišměrûn*)." But if he learns something at first and then forgets it, just as what he first learned is not retained by him, so too what he subsequently learns will not be retained by him. Therefore, Scripture teaches, "If you do forget (*šākōaḥ tiškaḥ*)" (Deut. 8:19). No sooner do you remove your eyes from it than it vanishes, as it is said, "You see it, then it is gone" (Prov. 23:5). And it is written in the Scroll of the Pious,[187] "If you abandon me for one day, I will abandon you for two days."[188]

The repetition of the verb *to keep* in the lemma is now interpreted as referring to early and late stages in one's learning: if a disciple in the early stages of his learning maintains (= fixes in his mind) what he has studied through continual review, then he provides a firm foundation for the retention of his future learning. Similarly, the repetition of the verb *to forget* in Deut. 8:19 is adduced in support of the converse: if a disciple learns initially without continual attention to what he has learned, he will not only forget what he has learned but be unable to retain future learning. The fragile nature of Torah learning and the constant attention necessary to preserve it is once again exegetically enunciated, as it is in the commentary's own continuation:[189]

[O] Another interpretation of "If, then, you carefully keep all this commandment": Perhaps you might say, "[Leave it to] those who are elders, those who are leaders (*gĕdôlîm*), those who are prophets" [to maintain the Torah]. Therefore Scripture teaches, "If, then, *you* (plural) carefully keep." This teaches that *all* are equal with regard to Torah. Similarly it says, "Moses commanded us Torah as an inheritance of the congregation of Jacob" (Deut. 33:4). It does not say "priests, Levites, and Israelites," but "congregation of Jacob." And similarly it says, "You stand this day, *all of you*, [before the Lord your God—your tribal heads, your elders and your officials, all men of Israel]" (Deut. 29:9).

[P] But for such who arose and preserved (*qiyyēm*) Torah in Israel, would not Torah have been forgotten?[190] Had not Shaphan arose in his time, Ezra in his time, and R. Akiba in his time, would not Torah have been forgotten in Israel? For it says, "A teaching (*dābār*) in its time, how good it is!" (Prov. 15:23). The teaching of one such as this is equal to all the rest together.[191]

By drawing attention to the plural form of address in the lemma, the commentary stresses that *all* of Israel, and not just a select class of leaders, are enjoined not simply to observe the Torah's commandments but to maintain the Torah through study. Other verses are adduced that are interpreted in the same way. Two types of special status are specifically rejected: acquired (elders, leaders, and prophets) and inherited (priests, Levites, and Israelites). Although the sages regard themselves as a distinct and elite class within Israelite society, they draw their disciples from that society as a whole, regardless of genealogical pedigree or social status.[192]

Notwithstanding the comment in the first section (O) that "all are equal with regard to Torah," the next section (P) stresses that certain individuals are "equal to all the rest together" because of their labors to preserve Torah teaching at times when the people as a whole might otherwise have forgotten it. The three individuals mentioned are presented in chronological order, constituting, in a sense, a chain of Torah preservers. They are significant for the fact (at least according to tradition) tht they all lived at times of crisis and restoration and either directly or indirectly were involved in the scribal activity of collecting and editing Torah. Shaphan was the scribe who read to King Josiah the newly discovered "scroll of the Teaching," resulting in Josiah's sweeping reforms (2 Kings 22:8–20; Chr. 34:14–28). Ezra, also a scribe, established the Torah as the constitution for the third generation of the restored community after the Babylonian Exile.[193] R. Akiba, one of the foremost early rabbinic sages and raiser of disciples, was active during the critical period between the destruction of the Temple in 70 C.E. and the Bar Kochba revolt in 135, and he is credited with having initiated the editorial compiling of the "oral Torah."[194] Although Shaphan held an official position in Josiah's royal court, and Ezra was a priest who acted with the authorization of the Persian empire, R. Akiba, as far as we know, enjoyed neither acquired nor hereditary status apart from his learning (attained, according to rabbinic lore, relatively late in his life). By placing R. Akiba on a par with the scribes Shaphan and Ezra, our text implicitly places R. Akiba's status on a par with theirs. Because they were responsible for preserving and establishing texts of written Torah and he for collecting and ordering the oral traditions of the sages, our commentary also equates the status of the latter (of which its text must be seen as part) with the former.

The special status claimed here for Shaphan, Ezra, and R. Akiba derives not from hereditary pedigree but from their work of preserving Torah in *their* own times of particular need, that is, of providing "a teaching in its own time" (Prov. 15:23).[195] All such preservers of Torah, whenever they may live, are understood to be included in the words, previously cited, of Deut. 29:9, "You stand *this day*, all of you," understood to signify the perpetual present of the commentary.[196] Implicitly, however, these three constitute a scribal chain of authority, by virtue of which they stand apart from and superior to the people as a whole. To the extent that Rabbi Akiba, the last link in this chain, represents the class of rabbinic sages, they, too, may be viewed both as deriving from the people as a whole, with whom they are "equal with regard to Torah," and as standing apart from and superior to them, by virtue of their dedication to maintaining Torah teaching through their constant engagement with it. The tension between thes two rabbinic Torah ethics—"egalitarian" and "elitist"—is not resolved by the commentary, which in juxtaposing them leaves it to the student of the text to struggle with their dialectical implications.

Despite the accomplishments of the rabbinic sages and their predecessors in preserving Torah, the *Sifre* text continues to express the anxiety that Torah learning could at any time be easily forgotten or abandoned:

[Q] Behold it says, "They shall wander about seeking the word of the Lord, but they shall not find it" (Amos 8:12). Our sages permitted (*hittîrû*)[197] going from city to city and from province to province to determine whether an insect that comes into contact with a loaf of bread renders it unclean in the first or second degree. Rabbi Simeon ben Yohai says: Does this [verse] come to say that the Torah will be forgotten in Israel? But has it not been said, "It will not be forgotten from the mouth of their offspring" (Deut. 31:21)? Rather, so-and-so prohibits while so-and-so permits, so-and-so declares unclean while so-and-so declares clean, and one cannot find a clear ruling.[198]

The lemma (Deut. 11:22, not cited here) was previously interpreted to enjoin the preservation of Torah teaching through its constant study and review for its own sake. Such activity, as we have amply seen, leads to a multiplicity of teachings and interpretations. Amos 8:12 is interpreted to refer to a time (presumably the *present* of the text) in which one may go from place to place inquiring of different authorities about a particular legal matter without receiving a definitive ruling. Juxtaposed with this interpretation is Rabbi Simeon ben Yohai's rhetorical question whether Amos 8:12 suggests that Torah teaching will eventually be forgotten (not found) in Israel. This possibility is denied by the citation of Deut. 31:21: multiple (even contradictory) scriptural meanings and rabbinic rulings may be confusing, and disconcerting, but they need *not* imply the loss of Torah from Israel's "mouths."

Let us consider this section in relation to what has preceded it. If the activities of collecting, sorting, and studying the full range of rabbinic words of Torah are necessary for the maintenance of Torah and in turn of Israel, then the resulting collectivity of rabbinic Torah teaching (like that of rabbinic society) will be marked by a degree of multivocal heterogeneity, even discordancy. Participants in that society and students of those traditions, including those of the *Sifre*'s commentary, may be dismayed by what they find, that is, when they *fail* to find (ready-made) the clear-cut normative rulings they seek.[199] Our commentary, through its metonymic linking of the "word of the Lord" with the multivocality of rabbinic teachings, suggests that the very act of dialogical engagement with such words of Torah, all understand ultimately as divinely authorized, is a religious and redemptive performance in its own right, irrespective of their performative applicability. This idea gains even more forceful expression in what follows:

[R] Another interpretation of "If, then, you carefully keep (*šāmōr tišmĕrûn*) [all this commandment]": Lest you should say, "Behold I will study a difficult lesson and not bother with an easy one," Scripture teaches, "For it is not an empty thing for you" (Deut. 32:47). For the thing about which you say "it is empty," "it is your life" (ibid.). For you should not say, it is enough for me that I have studied laws (*hălākôt*). Scripture teaches, "commandment," "the commandment," "all this commandment"[200]: study *midrāš, hălākôt*, and *haggādôt.*[201] And similarly it says, "Man does not live on bread alone" (Deut. 8:3). This refers to *midrāš.* "But on anything that the Lord decrees": This refers to *hălākôt* and *haggādôt.* And similarly it says, "Get wisdom, my son, [and gladden my heart]" (Prov. 27:11). And it says, "My son, if your mind gets wisdom, my mind, even mine, will be gladdened" (Prov. 23:15). R. Simeon ben Menasya says: I only know about one's father who is on earth. Whence do I know about one's father who is in heaven? Scripture teaches, "even mine," thereby including his father who is in heaven.[202]

Once again, the verb *to keep* (maintain) is interpreted as referring to continuous study for its own sake, and the doubling of the verb is taken to refer equally to a difficult as to an easy lesson. *All* of Torah is laden with significance and none of it should be presumed to be "empty" of meaning, or of little significance, for Torah as a whole is the foundation of Israel's life.[203] Similarly, the inclusive language of the expression *all the commandment* is understood to signify the three branches of oral Torah studies, all of which are of equal importance and together form a well-rounded scholar. In particular, one should not think that legal studies are more important than or exempt one from nonlegal studies.[204] Deut. 8:3 is similarly interpreted as enjoining a balanced program of study: one should not pursue only the intellectually challenging, dialectical exegesis of texts, but also the more straightforward mastery of legal and narrative traditions.

Such well-rounded studies of all of God's Torah, both written and oral, legal and non-legal, dialectical and apodictic, brings joy to the heart of one's father.[205] The redundant (emphatic) expression *even mine (gam-ʾānî)*, indicates that the father who is gladdened by his son's scholarly achievements is not only one's biological father but also one's heavenly father (God). The sage's and disciple's study of the complete rabbinic curriculum for its own sake is not only a holy act through which God's presence can be experienced, but a mythic act through which God Himself is affected.[206]

After having lavished its attention for so long on the initial words of Deut. 11:22 as enjoining continual engagement with Torah teaching for its own sake, the commentary *finally* proceeds to the continuation of the lemma:

> [S] "That I command you to perform it" (Deut. 11:22): Why is this said? Because it is [previously] said, "If, then, you carefully keep." I might think that once a person has kept [preserved in memory] words of Torah he can sit idly, and need not perform them. Therefore Scripture teaches, "To perform it": its own reply [to such a thought] is "to perform it." If a person has learned Torah, behold, he has fulfilled one commandment. If he has both learned and has kept [= preserved], behold, he has fulfilled two commandments. If he has learned and kept and performed, there is nothing greater than this.[207]

Although moving forward, the commentary also returns to the theme and rhetoric of the very first section of the larger unit (A). There, we will recall, it was said that were it not for the first part of Deut. 11:22, with its repetition of the verb *šmr* ("to keep"), one might have concluded from Deut. 11:13 that having learned (*šmᶜ*) Torah one could sit idly. Now the very same exegetical strategy is applied to the verb *šmr*: were it not for the succeeding phrase "that I command you to perform it (*laᶜăśōtāh*)," one might have concluded that having fulfilled the obligation to keep (repeatedly review) Torah one could sit idly and not be obliged to fulfill it through practice.

What emerges overall, then, through this dialectical juxtaposition of verses and parts of verses is a threefold obligation (*miṣwâ*), each part of which is signified by a different Scriptural verb: learning (*šmᶜ*), review (*šmr*), and performance (*ᶜśh*). Ideally, the three are inextricably bound to each other, and the greatest merit is acquired by the person who fulfills them all.[208] Whereas attention to the first (learning) and last (practice) obligations frames the unit as a whole, the commentary's own preoccupation is clearly with the middle obligation—to maintain and preserve words of Torah by repeatedly returning to the *same* scriptural words (*šāmōr tišmĕrûn*) through the *multiplicity* of their rabbinic interpretations. This, as we have repeatedly seen, is the persistent exegetical theme as well as the persistent discursive practice of the unit's own protracted middle, which dynamically engages the student of the text in the very activity that it repeatedly, although in many different ways, enjoins.

Finally, the commentary arrives at the last word of Deut. 11:22 with which it will deal in this unit (§48), the verb *to love*:

[T] "To love [the Lord your God]": Lest you should say, "I am studying Torah in order that I be called a sage, in order that I be appointed to a court,[209] in order that I be rewarded with length of days in the world to come," Scripture teaches, "To love." Study in any case [for its own sake], and in the end honor will come [by itself]. And similarly it says, "She [wisdom] is a tree of life to those who grasp her," etc. (Prov. 3:18); and it says, "They are life to him who finds them" (Prov. 4:22); and it says, "She [wisdom] will adorn your head with a graceful wreath" (Prov. 4:9): in this world. "Crown you with a glorious diadem" (ibid.): in the world to come. "In her right hand is length of days" (Prov. 3:16): in the world to come. "In her left, riches and honor." (ibid.): in this world.[210]

Addressing itself, presumably, to disciples of sages, the commentary stresses that they should study Torah not for the sake of thisworldly or otherworldly gains (including their appointments as sages), but as a religious act performed for its own sake—as an act of love of God—in faith that the honor due to a life of study will eventually be received, both in this world and the next, as the study of Scripture itself reveals. The point is not to deny the rewards of Torah study, but to stress that expectation of those rewards should not motivate such study.[211]

As we have repeatedly seen in other parts of the *Sifre*'s commentary, the rabbinic movement, especially in the third century, sought to increase its social influence and the economic security of its members by placing sages in judicial and administrative positions of authority.[212] These positions were awarded to disciples upon ordination as rabbis and were an important vehicle for patriarchal control of the rabbinic movement. They were also a way to extend rabbinic teaching, practice, and authority beyond the limits of rabbinic circles. Notwithstanding (and perhaps because of) the importance of such titles and appointments both to the rabbinic class and to its individual members, our commentary cautions against viewing the pursuit of Torah studies as an means to such ends. This idea is significantly amplified in the commentary's continuation, with which the larger unit (§48) concludes:

> [U] Rabbi Exeazar the son of Rabbi Zadoq[213] says: Perform deeds for the sake of doing them, speak of [= study] them for their own sake. He used to say: If Belshazzar, who used Temple vessels together with profane vessels,[214] had his life uprooted from this world and the world to come, how much more so will one who [mis]uses the vessel [= Torah] with which this world and the world to come[215] were created have his life uprooted from this world and the world to come.[216]

Torah study is not to be abused for the sake of worldly gain, because the Torah is a holy vessel, not just equivalent to the holy vessels with which Israel served God in the Temple when it stood but, as the argument a fortiori implies, superior to them: the Torah is that vessel by which this world and the world to come are created (and sustained). Herein lies a central paradox of the rabbinic view of Torah study and practice: one is rewarded for study and practice of Torah in this world and the world to come, but the "use" of Torah for the sake of such rewards causes one to forfeit both.[217]

The comparison of the improper use of the Temple vessels with that of Torah as a holy vessel, and the implicit argument that Torah study is the superior successor to the Temple rites, underscores the boldness of the sages' claim that such study—the intensive engagement with the multiplicity of rabbinically mediated echoes and shadows of scriptural meaning—constitutes the central religious act of Jewish life. Implied in this claim is the *concomitant* claim of the sages to be that class which, through its dedication to such study practice within Israel, now constitute the sole legitimate leadership—both religious and social—of the people of Israel.

Take to Heart All the Words (§335)

A similar comparison between Temple and Torah, but with a surprisingly poignant twist, is made in the following two-part commentary, the last one that we shall consider in this chapter:

> [A] "He [Moses] said to them: Take to heart [lit.: set your heart toward] all the words with which I have warned you this day" (Deut. 32:46): A person needs to direct his heart and his eyes and his ears toward the words of Torah, and so it says, "Then the Lord said to me: O mortal, mark well, look with your eyes and listen with your ears to what I tell you. . . . Note well [lit.: set your heart toward] the entering into the Temple" (Ezek. 44:5). We may argue a fortiori: If in the case of the Temple, which could be seen with the eyes and measured with the hand, a person needed to direct his heart and his eyes and his ears [toward it], then how much more should this be with words of Torah, which are like mountains suspended by a hair.[218]

God instructs Ezekiel to attend to the Temple entrance in the same language that Moses instructs Israel to attend to his words (of Torah). The commentary, however, is not satisfied simply with drawing this analogy, but argues a fortiori that attention to words of Torah needs to be even *more* intensive than to the Temple. Whereas the Temple was solid and seemingly secure, words of Torah, by which is meant here the rabbinic oral Torah,[219] are fragile and tenuous. The expression *like mountains suspended by a hair* is used by the Mishnah (*Ḥag.* 1:8) for specific areas of rabbinic law (Sabbath, festival offerings, sacrilege) in which many rules hang form few scriptural warrants. Our commentary, by contrast, so characterizes *all* "words of Torah," stressing that they all require the constant attention of ears, eyes, and heart, even as these tenuous "words of Torah" are associated with Moses.[220] This is a remarkable rabbinic admission, but also a bold rabbinic self-justification.

The analogy to the Temple building may be understood to extend another step forward. Notice that the *priestly* Ezekiel is instructed to observe those coming and going from the Temple, just as when the Temple stood the class of Levites devoted themselves to, among other tasks, guarding the Temple gates.[221] At these gates the line between sacred and profane, priests and people, was the thinnest and most breachable, requiring constant oversight. The rabbis viewed with similar anxiety the preservation and transmission of Torah teaching, given the thin and breachable line that secured it, on the one hand, within the text of Scripture and, on the other, within the society of Israel. As will become manifest in the continuation of the commentary as it progresses to the second half of the verse, the sages knew that their success or failure at maintaining that thread intact depended not so much on their own exegetical genius as on their ability to raise the next generation of sages that would carry on their exegetical work:

> [B] "That you may enjoin them [upon your children to keep (*lišmōr*)][222]" (Deut. 32:46b): He [Moses] said to them: "I would be most grateful if you would maintain (*těqayyěmû*) the Torah after me. Similarly, you should be grateful to your children if they would maintain the Torah after you." It once happened that when our Rabbi [Judah the Patriarch] came from Laodicea, R. Jose the son of R. Judah [bar Ilai] and R. Eleazer the son of R. Judah[223] entered and sat before him. He said to them: "Come close! I would be grateful to you if you would maintaim the Torah after me. Similarly, you should be grateful to your children if they would maintain the Torah after you." With all of Moses' greatness, had no one received his Torah [from him], it would not have been worth a thing.[224] How much more is this the case [for us]! Therefore it says, "That you may enjoin them [upon your children to keep]."[225]

As elsewhere in the *Sifre*'s commentary to Deuteronomy, the scripturally enjoined instruction of "children" is understood to refer to the transmission of Torah to the *disciples* of the sages.[226] R. Judah the Patriarch as redactor of the Mishnah, the first compilation of rabbinic oral teachings, stands in relation to his successor sages much as Moses stood in relation to those who received from him the Torah: the greatness of both as "lawgivers" was tenuously dependent on the ability of their followers (in both senses) to establish their "codes" as living texts through constant study, interpretation, and performance. The humility with which the disciple must stand before his master, from whom he has acquired his learning,[227] is matched by the humility with which the master now stands before his disciples, who alone will determine through their own engaged study of Torah texts and traditions the success and survival of his teachings.[228]

Conclusions

Sifre Deuteronomy, like other rabbinic collections, does not so much recount stories about heroic sages as construct a culture and society of sages and their disciples by engaging them together in the religious and redemptive practice of Torah study. The commentary of the *Sifre* is best approached for historiographic purposes as an artifact of that culture as it was socially cultivated in the rabbinic *bêt midrāš* ("house of study") of third century (and thereafter) Palestine. The sages and disciples who stand both behind and before the commentary of the *Sifre* understood themselves to be preserving and transmitting "words of Torah" that, through *rabbinic* mediation, could sustain, and eventually redeem, the life of Israel as a holy nation bereft of what had once been its holy and national center. The sages sought not only to replace that holy and national center but to establish themselves as its officiants *and* exemplars. To succeed in this compound task the rabbinic sages had to dedicate themselves to the central holy work of Torah study for its own sake while asserting and broadening their practical influence upon public and political affairs. In other words, they had to hermeneutically immerse themselves in the sacred texts and traditions of the past while rhetorically attuning them to the sociohistorical circumstances of the present. They had to claim being the *descendants* of Moses, the biblical elders, and the prophets and also the *successors* to Aaron, the priests, and the Levites. They had to understand themselves as being of the people and also distinct from and superior to them.

To what extent and at what pace did the sages achieve these somewhat contradictory goals? How much resistence, both internal and external, did they encounter to their ambitious agenda of socioreligious transformation? Who from wider Jewish circles were drawn to join or support them and why? These are important questions to which rabbinic texts such as the *Sifre*—being transformational in their re-presentations not only of Scripture and tradition but of their own sociohistorical contexts—do not provide easy answers. Although that text should not be read as a simple reflection of the sages' lives or times, it does provide an inside view of the literarily crystallized practices of Torah study and interpretation by which disciples of sages were to achieve entrance into and, as important, internalized identification with the still young but growing rabbinic class and culture. Especially in the continuous and collective practice of "maintaining" the words of Torah (both "written" and "oral") through dialogical commentary as a form of continuous religious service, the sages sought to transform *themselves* into a cohesive society whose discourse and deeds would make them worthy and capable of transforming, in turn and in time, the practices, structures, and self-understanding of Jewish society more broadly.

4 Polyphony and Plot: Torah as Song as Covenantal Witness

Introduction

As we have repeatedly seen, a distinctive characteristic of midrashic commentary is the multiplicity of interpretations that it often adduces for a single scriptural word or phrase. As discussed in Chapter 1, although multiple interpretations of Scripture can be found in extrarabbinic varieties of ancient Jewish exegesis (e.g., frequent in Philo and infrequent in *pēšer*), none of these evidence the degree of ungraded heterogeneity of multiple interpretations to be found in the *Sifre*, especially in its aggadic, but also in its halakhic parts.[1]

It should be stressed that the rabbinic recognition of Scripture's multiple meanings is not predicated on any sense of a lamentable gap between the ancient text, whose univocal meaning was once known, and its belated interpreters, who must grope undecidably after that lost meaning. Rather, multiplicity of scriptural meaning is rabbinically understood to be inherent in the very nature of the polyphony of divine communication and its human reception already at Mt. Sinai:[2]

> "One thing God spoke, two things have I heard, for might belongs to God" (Ps. 62:12). One scriptural passage issues as several meanings, but one meaning does not issue from several scriptural passages.[3] In the school of R. Ishmael it is taught: "[Behold, My word is like fire, declares the Lord,] and like a hammer that shatters rock" (Jer. 23:29). Just as a hammer divides into several shivers [or sparks], so too one scriptural passage issues as several meanings.[4]

The parallel in *b. Šabb.* 88b concludes: "So too each and every utterance which issued from the mouth of the Holy One, blessed by He, divided into seventy languages."[5] As discussed earlier, the multiplicity of voices at Sinai is understood by the *Sifre*'s commentary as a reflection both of the power of divine speech and of the divine empowerment of Israel to discern the multiple meanings already contained within each divine utterance: "When [each] divine utterance went forth from the mouth of the Holy One, blessed by He, Israel would observe it and would know how much midrash could be inferred from it, how many laws could be inferred from it, how many a fortiori arguments could be inferred from it, how many arguments by verbal analogy could be inferred from it."⁶ Thus, *from the very beginning*, revelation was perceived by Israel in terms of the synchronic multiplicity of its interpreted meanings.

From a historical perspective it may be said that such passages reflect an attempt by the rabbis to retroject the centrality, quality, and ideology of their work of scriptural exegesis back onto the event of revelation at Sinai. But viewed conversely—that is, from the perspective of what the rabbis conceived themselves to be doing in their interpretation of Scripture—it may be said that the rabbis understood their activity as both a continuation of and a participant in that originary event. As the *Sifre* exposits:

> "You shall keep and you shall perform all the laws and rules that I have set before you this day" (Deut. 32:11). "You shall keep": this refers to oral study (*mišnâ*). "You shall perform": this refers to practice (*maʿăśeh*). "All the laws": this refers to the interpretations (*midrāšôt*). "And rules": these are the regulations (*dînîm*). "That I have set before you *this day*": let them be as dear to you today as if you had received them today from Mt. Sinai; let them be as ready in you mouths (*rĕgîlîm bĕpîkem*) as if you had heard them today.⁷

Thus, the fracturing of a singular divine utterance into multiple voices as it engages Israelite individual and community characterizes as much the revelation of Torah at Sinai as the rabbis' ongoing exegetical engagement with that revelation through the medium of study. As the *Sifre* has God say: "Attach yourselves to the sages and their students and I will consider it as though you had ascended to heaven to receive it [Torah]—not that you ascended to receive it in peace, but rather as though you waged war in order to receive it."⁸ The ongoing dialogical struggle of interpretation is, in a sense, a continual re-enactment of the originary struggle of revelation at Sinai, as rabbinically interpreted.

In principle, then, the multiplicity of interpretations of Torah, like the words of Torah themselves, are synchronous, each deriving ultimately from the same transcendent moment of revelation. This, to repeat, is in principle. In practice, once the variety of interpretations assume the *textual* form of successive commentary and are so encountered by the students of those texts, atemporality must yield somewhat to temporality (and indeterminacy to determinacy).⁹ Textual temporality is, to begin with, a function of the progressive nature of the text's arrangement: one linguistic and literary unit is presented and perceived after the other. Unlike narrative or thematic texts, however, the outermost linear configuration of a scriptural commentary is not the chronological order of a story being narrated or the logical order of a theme being developed but the sequence of the scriptural text being commented upon: one word or phrase of Scripture is explicated after the other.[10] However, to the extent that a single unit of commentary to a particular scriptural word or phrase may be complex—containing an array of interpretations, proofs, exemplifications, stories, and so on—there are internal progressions of tradition within the external progression of the commentary overall. Thus, not only does the commented-upon biblical text (however conceived) have a beginning, middle, and end, along whose course the commentary proceeds, but the commentary to each part of that text, to the extent that it comprises multiple parts, advances from beginning, through middle, to end, even if each such end is inconclusive or simply a pause before a new beginning. In other words, the atemporal polyphony of scriptural intrpretation is textually *encountered* by the student of scriptural commentary in linear, and hence temporal succession, in relation to both Scripture and the collectivity of tradition configured by its commentary.

But the progressive nature of such study, like all reading, is not linear in any simple, unidirectional sense. Our understanding of a particular interpretation may be shaped in part by those that have preceded it, whether of the same lemma or of previous ones, even as that understanding prospectively points forward in anticipation of the interpretations that will follow. However, once we arrive at what follows, we may, retrospectively, alter our previous understandings, whether in small or large ways, before again advancing forward. Thus, all reading, no matter how linear its text, is a circular reading backward and forward.[11]

These two aspects of the temporality of a polyphonous text and its study—linear progression and the interplay of prospection and retro-spection—may be turned from textural necessity to rhetorical virtue by the editorial collector and shaper of its voices so as to draw and direct the text's students into a dialogical engagement with those voices. For example, by arranging a number of textural "events" in succession, an editor may take advantage of the linearlity of textural reading so that those events will be encountered as a chronological sequence, as a skeletal story or history, whose gaps or continuation need to be filled in by those students. Thus, we have seen on several occasions in our study study of the *Sifre*'s commentary that alternative interpretations of the same verse may be arranged in sequence so as to constitute a progression corresponding to historical chronology.[12] Similarly, even within a single interpretation, a series of exemplifications of an exegetical point may be arranged in chronological sequence so that in working through those exempla the student of the text traverses time in chronological sequence, whether from biblical times to messianic times or only from biblical times to rabbinic times.[13]

But the creator of a text can also take rhetorical advantage of the prospective and retrospective nature of the reading of such a text by relaying its "events" in such a way as to delay or accelerate, withhold or release, the forward movement of the text and its study, often thereby adding elements of suspense or surprise to what would otherwise be a predictable, and therefore not very engaging, progression. There are many methods for doing this, some of the most common being flashbackward (analepsis) and flashforward (prolepsis), summary and scene (including dramatic dialogue), and gaps and their filling. Thus, whereas a linear narrative elicits from its readers such a simple question s "What will happen next?" which it proceeds to answer, more complex narrative structures elicit questions that are not so immediately or self-evidently answered by its continuation: "We have been told where we are going but how will we get there?" "Why are we turning back?" "Why this delay?" "Where will this detour lead?" "How will we bridge this gap?" Such implicit (and sometimes explicit) questioning and answering occasioned by the textual-temporal continuum and its gaps serves to engage the reader (here student) of the text in the dynamic process of its interpretation. Such a reader must work, and wait, for his or her textual pay.[14]

This dynamic interplay of prospection and retrospection—in the very midst of forward progression—is as true of textual readings as it is of living in time.[15] Even as we move individually from birth to death, and collectively from urzeit to endzeit, our experience of and actions in the present are determined to a large extent by our memories and retellings of the past and our anticipations, whether in hope or in fear, of the future. As others have commented, this correspondence (by no means exact to be sure) between textual progression, or plot, and historical time is not coincidental, but is in the nature of the intertwining of the two. As Frank Kermode states: "In making sense of the world we...feel a need...to experience that concordance of beginning, middle, and end which is the essence of our explanatory fictions."[16] Similarly, Peter Brooks, defining plotting as the "logic or perhaps the syntax of a certain kind of discourse... that develops its propositions only through temporal sequence and progression," writes that it is "one central way in which we as readers make sense, first of the text, and then, as an interpretive model, of life."[17] Thus, in addition to the linear temporality of the continuous text and the disruptive temporality of its discursive practices, there is the lived temporality of its students, which, in a sense, is constantly being refigured through their interpretive engagement in the temporalities of the text and its discourse. The present, whether of reading or living, is not simply a midpoint en linear route from past to future, but an expansive continuum in which the subject perpetually slips and slides between past and future, even while progressing through that continuum toward its expected (and, as so often it turns out, unexpected) end. The dialectics of continuity and disruption, of progressive advance and circular return, are as much features of our textual studies as of our experiences in history.[18]

In what follows I wish to call attention to some plotting aspects of a particular section of the *Sifre*'s commentary, both as it has been structurally shaped by its redactors and as it might be dynamically engaged by its students. However, in so doing, I by no means wish to minimize the heterogeneity of the multiple traditions and interpretations so configured. On the one hand, the very plasticity of tradition in its polyphony enables the combination of exegetical "events" in the variety of dynamic ways just discussed. On the other hand, the configuration of such polyphony in the structure of commentary both facilitates and directs, however incompletely, the student's interpretive engagement with Scripture through the mediation of tradition. The polyphony of revelation is rhetorically configured by the commentary's redactors and further refigured in the progressive process of its dialogical reception by its students without in any way efacing the discontinuities or discordances of its multiplicity of meanings.[19]

The text of commentary upon which I have chosen to comment is particularly striking both for its extreme polyphony, which should soon become obvious, and for the force of its plot, which I hope to demonstrate. The commentary assembles thirteen interpretations of the opening words of the lection *Ha'azinu* ("The Song of Moses," Deut. 32),[20] which we shall first consider briefly in its own right.

The Song of Moses (Deut. 32)

The opening words of *Ha'azinu* form a parallelistic doublet, which translate without difficulty as follows:

Give ear, O heavens, and let me speak;
Let the earth hear the utterances of my mouth.

With this, Moses calls heaven and earth to give their attention to his penultimate address to Israel, in the form of a "song" (cf. 31:16–22) of teaching (32:2), which he hopes will penetrate his audience's consciousness as advantageously as rain showers do the tender grass (ibid.). That song begins as a retrospective survey of Israel's sacred history: a just and faithful God (verses 3–6), having bestowed blessings upon Israel in her pastoral youth (verses 7–14), confronts the people's subsequent ingratitude and lapse into idolatry (verses 15–18), which oblige Him to invoke the convenantal threats of national disaster, if not extinction (verses 19–25).

This, it would appear, is Moses' final warning to the people before his death and their entry into the Promised Land: if they fail to uphold the covenant they will surely suffer its curses (cf. 31:16–22).[21] But suddenly, as though Moses shifts from a review of Israel's history to a preview of its future redemption, God has second thoughts (verses 26–35), and turns his threat of doom into a promise of rescue from and revenge against Israel's enemies (verses 36–38), so that Israel and the nations might finally acclaim His providential power (verses 39–43). It is to this prophetic message of Israel's doom suddenly turned to salvation that heaven and earth, perhaps as representatives of all of nature, are called to witness.[22]

Sifre Text and Commentary

I have divided the *Sifre*'s commentary to Deut. 32:1 into three sections—beginning, middle, and end—for reasons that should soon become clear, and have numbered the interpretations, first through thirteenth.

Beginning

First Interpretation

"Give ear, O heavens, and let me speak" (Deut. 32:1):

[A1] R. Meir (ca. 150 C.E.) said: When Israel were blameless (*zakkayyîm*) they bore witness against (*mĕ'îdîm bĕ-*[23]) themselves, as it is said, "And Joshua said to the people, 'You are witnesses against yourselves'" (Josh. 24:22). But they became corrupt in relation to (*qilqĕlû bĕ-*[24]) themselves, as it is said, "Ephraim surrounds me with lies, and the house of Israel with deceit" (Hos. 12:1).

[A2] He called the Tribes of Judah and Benjamin to witness against them, as it is said, "And now inhabitants of Jerusalem[25] and men of Judah, judge between me and my vineyard, what more could have been done to my vineyard . . .?" (Isa. 5:3-4). But the Tribe of Judah became corrupt (*qilqĕlû*), as it is said, "Judah acted treacherously" (Mal. 2:11).

[A3] He called the prophets to witness against them, as it is said, "The Lord forewarned Israel and Judah by the hand of every prophet and seer" (2 Kings 17:13). But they [Israel] became corrupt in relation to the prophets, as it is said, "They mocked the messengers of God" (2 Chr. 36:16).

[A4] He called the heavens to witness against them, as it is said, "I call heaven and earth to witness against you today" (Deut. 4:26; 30:19). But they became corrupt in relation to the heavens, as it is said, "Do you not see what they do . . . the children gather wood and the fathers light the fire [. . . to the Queen of Heaven]" (Jer. 7:17-19).

[A5] He called the earth to witness against them, as it is said, "Hear, O earth, I am going to bring disaster [upon this people]" (Jer. 6:19). But they became corrupt in relation to the earth as it is said. "Also their altars shall be as heaps on the furrows of the field" (Hos. 12:12).

[A6] He called the roads to witness against them as it is said, "Thus says the Lord, stand upon the roads and see" (Jer. 6:16). But they became corrupt in relation to the roads, as it is said, "At the head of every road you built your high place" (Ezek. 16:25).

[A7] He called the nations to witness against them as it is said, "Hear well, O nations, [and know, O congregation, what is in store for them]" (Jer. 6:18). But they became corrupt in relation to the nations, as it is said, "They mingled with the nations and learned their ways" (Ps. 106:35).

[A8] He called the mountains to witness against them, as it is said, "Hear, you mountains, the case of the Lord" (Mic. 6:2). But they became corrupt in relation to the mountains, as it is said, "On the tops of the mountains they sacrificed" (Hos. 4:13).

[A9] He called the cattle to witness against them, as it is said, "The ox knows its owner [and the ass his master's crib, but Israel does not know]" (Isa. 1:3). But they became corrupt in relation to the cattle, as it is said, "They exchanged their glory [for the likeness of an ox that eats grass]" (Ps. 106:20).

[A10] He called the wild animals [and birds] to witness against them as it is said, "Even the stork in heaven knows his appointed times [. . . but my people does not know the ordinance of the Lord]" (Jer. 8:7). But they became corrupt in relation to the wild animals and birds, as it is said, "I went in and saw every detestable form of creeping thing, and beasts" (Ezek. 8:10).

[A11] He called the fish to witness against them, as it is said, "Or speak to the earth and it shall teach [. . . and the fish of the sea will declare to you]" (Job 12:8). But they became corrupt in relation to the fish, as it is said, "And made man like the fish of the sea" (Hab. 1:14).

[A12] He called the ant to witness against them, as it is said, "Go to the ant, sluggard; [Study its ways and learn.] Without leaders. . . it lays up its bread in the summer" (Prov. 6:6-8).

[A13] R. Simeon b. Eliazar (ca. 200 C.E.) says: How lowly is such a person who has to learn from an ant. Had he learned and acted accordingly he would have been lowly enough. But needing to learn from an ant, he did not even learn.

[B1] In the [eschatological] future the congregation of Israel will say before the Holy One, blessed be He: "Master of the universe, behold my witnesses still exist," as it is said, "I call heaven and earth to witness against you this day." God answers her: "Behold I am causing them to pass away," as it is said, "For I am creating new heavens and a new earth" (Isa. 65:17).

[B2] She says before Him: "Master of the universe, behold I see the places [in relation to which] I became corrupt and was ashamed, as it is said, "See your way in the valley, [know what you have done]" (Jer. 2:23). He says to her: "Behold I am causing them to pass away," as it is said, "Every valley will be lifted up" (Isa. 40:4).

[B3] She says before Him: "Master of the universe, behold my name still exists." He says to her: "Behold I will cause it to pass," as it says, "I will call you by a new name" (Isa. 40:4).

[B4] She says before Him: "Master of the universe, behold your name[26] is [still] attached to the names of the Ba'als." He says to her: "Behold I will cause it to pass," as it is said, "I will remove the names of the Ba'als" (Hos. 2:19a).

[B5] She says before Him: "Even so, my domestics (*bĕnê bayit*) will still mention it." He says to her: "And they shall no longer be mentioned by their name" (Hos. 2:19b).

[B6] And, again in the future, she will say before Him: "Master of the universe, you once wrote, 'If a man divorces his wife [and she leaves him and marries another man, can he ever go back to her?]' (Jer. 3:1)." He says to her: "I only wrote *man*. And is it not said, 'For I am God and not man' (Hos. 11:9)? And have you been [formally] divorced from me, house of Israel? For has it not already been written, 'Thus said the Lord: Where is the bill or divorce of your mother [whom I dismissed]?' (Isa. 50:1)."[27]

The first interpretation is a composite of many parts. It is the lengthiest and most complex of the interpretations, and, as we shall see, it sets the stage, although not in any simple sense, for what will follow. I have divided the first interpretation into two parts, the first (A) dealing with the "history" of Israel's relations with their covenantal witnesses from the biblical past until the present, and the second (B) dealing with the role of the witnesses in God's future (eschatological) judgment of Israel.

From the very beginning we see that the commentary assumes that heaven and earth are called by Moses to serve as *witnesses* to Moses' warning to Israel of the consequences of their violations of the covenant with God. Although the reason for Moses' call to heaven and earth is not specified in Deut. 32:1, earlier in Deuteronomy (4:26, 30:19, and 31:28) heaven and earth are explicitly invoked as witnesses. Therefore, the *Sifre*'s commentary, like most modern commentators, here, too, understands Moses' call to heaven and earth as a call to witnesses, thereby setting the theme for the subsequent twelve interpretations, all of which deal with aspects of heaven and earth's witnessing roles, variously construed.[28]

For the rabbis, as perhaps for the Book of Deuteronomy, the nature of such witnessing is twofold: legal and didactic. The witnesses not only testify (as before a court) to the guilty party's original acceptance and subsequent violation of the terms of the contract, thereby justifying their punishment, but, and perhaps more important, the witnesses have the responsibility of regularly reminding them of those terms, especially the stipulated penalties for their violation, in the hope of bringing the guilty party back into compliance. Thus, the witnesses as much bear witness before Israel concerning the covenant as bear witness before God concerning Israel's behavior.[29] The viability of the witnesses in both of these roles depends on their own inculpability with regard to the violations for which they are to provide witness.

The first part (A) of the first interpretation begins with primeval time during which Israel as a whole was so innocent that it could be its own witness, placed, as it were, on a covenantal "honor system." But this ideal situation did not last for very long as Israel soon became corrupted by its own deceitful behavior, and hence could no longer be trusted to witness against itself. A series of witnesses are next called upon. Note here that despite our commentary's repetition of the phrase *hēʿîd bâhem* ("he caused to witness against them") eleven times, it never specifies *who* summons these witnesses to witness: presumably it is God, in the case of heaven and earth through Moses.

Once Israel as a whole is unable to witness against itself, witnesses are sought among Israelite subgroups, beginning with the select tribe of Judah and then turning to the prophets. But each of these in turn fails as a witness. Unable to find suitable witnesses within Israel, the rest of creation is approached, mainly the elements of nature, beginning with the heavens and then the earth, the subjects of the lemma.[30] But once again these become disqualified as witnesses, having been implicated in Israel's idolatrous practices, becoming, in a sense, accessories to Israel's crimes. The search continues with the roads, the nations, the mountains, the domestic animals, the wild animals and birds, the fish, and finally the lowly ant.[31] It is only with the ant, here representing the lowest form of animate life, that the alternation of witness and corruption comes to a halt, as though here, finally, is a creature that has not been compromised by Israel's behavior. If only Israel would learn from the self-reliant, forward-looking work habits of the lowly ant! But as the seemingly appended statement of R. Simeon b. Eleazar suggests, even this is too much for a lethargic Israel. Having reached the end of this list of witnesses, presumably extending to the present time, we are left with the lowly ant alone as a possible witness, but a witness that seems hopelessly unable to affect Israel's conduct.

From this utterly depressed point the commentary jumps suddenly from the present to the eschatological future, while returning to an idealized (feminine) Israel (*kĕnesset yiśrāʾēl*), now portrayed in dialogue with God (B1). Although the time is future, employment of dramatic dialogue makes the encounter seem present. Israel begins by expressing the fear that heaven and earth still remain as witness to testify against her, thereby ensuring a negative divine sentence. God in response offers to remove these witnesses to Israel's past behavior. Once again Israel is disturbed by the earth with its valleys (and presumably high places) that remind her of her shameful past.[32] God offers to level these valleys. But, continues Israel, her very name is a constant reminder of her past. God responds by promising her a new name, or identity. But, Israel responds, God's name, having been applied by her to non-gods, is likewise tied to

Israel's shameful past.[33] In response, God proposes to remove these names from the idols. But, Israel continues, these theophoric idolatrous names will continue to be used by others (presumably non-Jews whom Israel has influenced), thereby reminding Israel of her past idolatrous practices. God agrees to remove *entirely* these names from use.[34]

The dialogue next (B6) shifts—and here we need to be reminded that we are still overhearing a *future*, hoped-for dialogue—from one about Israel's witnesses and memories, now having been disposed of by God, to one about the state of Israel's relationship with God: is it possible for a "man" (God) to accept back an unfaithful "wife" (Israel) whom he has divorced? In other words, can the covenant be restored once ruptured by such infidelity? This final barrier to Israel's reconciliation with God is no barrier at all, because God is not a man and since there never was a divorce, only a separation; the covenant was never ruptured, only strained.[35]

Scripture's notice of Moses' call to heaven and earth to hear his song is placed by the *Sifre*'s commentary within a new, broader temporal framework; that is, within a larger historical progression of witnesses. This chain of witnesses is emblematic of the history of Israel's covenantal condition, beginning with her original innocence, continuing with her corruption and sense of abandonment by God, and ending with her future reconciliation with God. Thus, the overall progression of the text is one of temporal advancement, even if the order of the intermediary points is determined by other considerations.[36] Contrary to Scripture, in which heaven and earth *alone* are invoked by Moses as *permanent* witnesses to the covenant (as Deut. 32:1 is most commonly understood), the *Sifre*'s commentary depicts them as only two among a sequence of twelve witnesses, each of which (except for the last, the ant) has been compromised by some association with Israel's unfaithful behavior, thereby becoming disqualified as a witness to God's covenant with Israel. The combination of heaven and earth in the lemma triggers the generation of an intertextual scriptural pattern of witnessing and corruption that runs through time as well as through nature as a whole, including, curiously enough, the nations. Heaven and earth now take their places as two points in that larger transscriptural and transhistorical pattern.

Juxtaposed to this past history of decline (A1–13) is a projected future of covenantal rehabilitation (B1–6). But in the middle, that is, in the present, there remains a rather significant temporal *gap*: between past disqualification and future removal of heaven and earth as witnesses, and between Israel's past degeneration and future restoration as God's direct covenantal partner. How is that gap to be filled?

Both structurally and thematically, A1–13, depicting Israel's past decline and B1–6, depicting Israel's eventual restoration, stand opposite each other, almost as inverse images. In the former we exegetically engage, stage by stage, Israel's past descent from initial innocence to present humiliation. In the latter we exegetically engage, again stage by stage, Israel's future ascent from humiliating memory to final reconciliation. The rhetorical effect of these two sets of repetitive prolongations is to instill in the student of this text not only an identification with the respective dynamics of past descent and future ascent, but a heightened awareness of the present hiatus between the two. But also note that exegetically this structural pattern mirrors the pattern of the biblical Song of Moses as a whole, with its progression from Israel's original innonence through decline to near abandonment and then, through a sudden reversal, to a future expectation of restoration as an act of divine grace. Although our commentary is here attending only to the opening words of the song, its interpretation anticipates the song as a whole.[37] Thus, both the commentary and the song leave their "audience" with the hope that God will bridge the gap between the past descent to present despair (A1–13) and future ascent to covenantal redemption (B6)—but how?

Middle

We turn now to the middle section of the *Sifre*'s commentary, which contains eleven more interpretations of Moses' summons to heaven and earth in Deut. 32:1. I shall present each such interpretation followed by a brief explanation, before taking up the section as whole and its relation to the beginning section.

Second Interpretation

Another interpretation of "Give ear, O heavens, and let me speak":
[A1] This can be compared to a king who entrusted his son to a tutor (*pêdāgôg*) who would constantly keep an eye on him. The son said, "Does father think that entrusting me to this tutor will do any good? I will keep an eye on him while he eats and drinks, and when he sleeps, I will leave to pursue my own affairs." His father said to him, "I have entrusted you to a tutor who will not allow you to move." Similarly, Moses said to Israel, "Do you think that you can escape from under the wings of the Shekinah or move off the earth?"
[A2] Furthermore, the heavens are keeping a record [of human deeds[38]] as it is said, "The heavens will reveal his sin" (Job 20:27). And whence do we know that the earth too makes known [human deeds]? As it is said, "And the earth shall rise up [to testify] against him" (ibid.).
[B] In the [eschatological] future the congregation of Israel will stand in judgment before God, saying to Him: "Master of the universe, I do not know who went bad (*qilqēl*) with respect to whom, and who was unfaithful (*šinnâ*) with respect to whom." Did Israel go bad with respect to God[39] or was God unfaithful with respect to Israel?[40] But when Scripture says, "The heavens

declare His righteousness" (Ps. 3:6), it is obvious that Israel went bad before God and God was not unfaithful with respect to Israel, as it is said, "For I the Lord change (*šānîtî*) not" (Mal. 3:6).[41]

Although thematically this interpretation belongs with those that follow, it echoes in important ways some of the language of the first interpretation.[42] It may be said to provide a transition, albeit a startling one, between the beginning and middle sections of the commentary. Here there is no suggestion that heaven and earth were ever disqualified or deprivileged as witnesses, nor that in the future judgment the heaven and earth that had witnessed Israel's misdeeds would be removed, so as not to remind Israel of her past. Rather, now we learn that Moses, corresponding to the king of the *mashal*, invoked heaven and earth as witnesses precisely because they are permanent, inescapable observers and recorders of Israel's behavior, and that when the future judgment comes they will make their reports. Should Israel, at the time of judgment, question who is to blame for the covenant going awry, the heavens will testify to Israel's guilt and God's faithfulness. In this portrayal of the future, yet perhaps pre-messianic, judgment God does not engage Israel in dialogue—she addresses Him but He does not respond—nor intercede on her behalf. Whereas in the first interpretation Israel became corrupt (*qilqēl*) in relation to heaven and earth, thereby disqualifying them as witnesses, here heaven and earth testify to Israel's having become corrupt (same verb) before God. The juxtaposition of this interpretation with that which precedes it is indeed striking, as much for the similarities of expression that link the two together as for the differences of understanding that distinguish them from one another. Whatever hope was instilled at the end of the first interpretation is here not to be found.

Third Interpretation

Another interpretation of "Give ear, O heavens": R. Judah (b. Ilai, ca. 150 C.E.) said: This can be compared to a king who had [two] state trustees (*ʾappôṭěrôpîn*) to whom he assigned [the administration of] his possessions, entrusting to them as well his son. He said to them: "Whenever my son fulfills my will, indulge him and pamper him and provide him with food and drink. But whenever my son does not fulfill my will, he is not to taste anything of mine." Similarly, when Israel fulfills God's will, what is said of them? "The Lord will open for you his good treasure, the heavens" (Deut. 28:12). And when they do not fulfill God's will, what is said of them? "For the Lord's anger will flare up against you, [and He will shut up the heavens so that there will be no rain and the ground will not yield its produce]" (Deut. 11:17).[43]

As in the previous interpretation, a *mashal* is used to compare Israel to the son of a king who is entrusted to the king's appointees. Note, however, that whereas in the previous interpretation the king of the *mashal* is understood in the *nimshal* (application) to represent Moses, here the king is understood, as is more common, to represent God.[44] Also changed is the role assigned to heaven and earth (the two trustees) as witnesses to the covenant: not only do they watch over Israel (as did the tutor in the previous example), but they reward and punish it by releasing or withholding God's provisions, serving as God's agents in enforcing the covenant's terms.[45]

Fourth Interpretation

Another interpretation of "Give ear, O heavens": R. Nehemiah (ca. 150 C.E.) says: This can be compared to a king, whose son got mixed up with bad company. [The king] began to complain about him to his brothers, then he began to complain about him to his friends, then he began to complain about him to his neighbors, and then he began to complain about him to his relatives. This father did not cease complaining until he said to the heaven and earth: "To whom can I complain about you [my son] except these?"[46]

The commentary presents a *mashal* in which a king turns in desperation to heaven and earth as the only audience that has not yet heard him complain about his son. Although the *mashal* is not provided with a *nimshal*, it might be presumed that the king represents Moses, but in light of the preceding *mashal* (third interpretation), in which the king represents God, the ambiguity of who summons heaven and earth as witnesses is maintained: did Moses do it on his own or on behalf of God? In any case, the imperative, cohortative, and jussive verbal forms of the lemma are understood as expressions of urgency and frustration on Moses' part as he is left with nowhere else to turn for an audience to his song except to heaven and earth. Note the contrast with the first interpretation in which heaven and earth are among the first witnesses summoned.

Fifth Interpretation

Another interpretation of "Give ear, O heavens": R. Judah (b. Ilai, ca. 150 C.E.) says: On the one hand, it is not enough for the righteous until they bring relief to the [whole] world in which they dwell. For what is said concerning Israel on account of the merit (*zĕkût*[47]) they acquire by fulfilling God's will? "The Lord will open for you [his good treasure, the heavens]" (Deut. 28:12). And *opening* is an expression for "relief," as it says, "He opened her womb" (Gen. 29:31). On the other hand, it is not enough for the wicked until they bring distress to the [whole] world in which they live. For what is said concerning Israel on account of the guilt (*ʿāwôn*[48]) they acquire by not fulfilling God's will? "For the Lord's anger will flare up against you, [and He will close up the heavens so that there will be no rain and the ground will not yield its produce]" (Deut. 11:17). And *closing* is an expression for "distress," as it is said, "For God closed fast [every womb]" (Gen. 20:18).[49]

A general principle regarding the righteous and wicked is applied to Israel in its relation to the world: it is not enough for the righteous to bring rewards to themselves alone nor is it enough for the wicked to bring punishments to themselves alone. Similarly, Israel through its fulfillment of God's will brings blessings to the whole world and through its violation of God's will brings suffering to the whole world. This idea is related to heaven and earth as the dispensers of Israel's covenantal rewards and punishments:[50] when the heavens open and close in response to Israel's behavior, relief or distress come to the world in general. At issue is not only the reward of rain or the punishment of drought in particular, but relief and distress in general, which the verbs *opening* and *closing* are said to signify. The whole world's well-being, for better or worse, depends on Israel's actions. This is the meaning of the call to universal heaven and earth to bear witness to the terms of Israel's particular covenant.[51]

Sixth Interpretation

[A] Another interpretation of "Give ear, O heavens": The Holy One, blessed be He, said to Moses: Tell Israel, "Look at the heavens which I created to serve you. Have they [ever] changed their [assigned] course (*middātām*)? Or has the sun said: 'I will not rise from the East to illuminate the whole world'? No, as it says, 'The sun rises and sets' (Eccl. 1:5). And what is more, it is happy to perform My will, as it is said, 'It is like a bridegroom [coming out of his chamber]' (Ps. 19:6)."

[B] "Let the earth hear the utterances of my mouth": Look at the earth which I created to serve you. Has it [ever] changed its [assigned] course? Have you sown seed in it which it did not cause to sprout? Or have you sown wheat and it brought forth barley? Or has the cow said, "I will not thresh and I will not plow today"? Or has the donkey said, "I will not carry or go"? And similarly, concerning the sea it says, "Do you not fear Me, says the Lord; [will you not tremble before Me, who set the sand for a boundary to the sea?]" (Jer. 5:22). For from the time that I decreed it [to remain within its boundaries], has it changed its ways, saying, "I will rise and flood the world"? No, for it says, "I broke it with my decree... and I said, 'This far you may come and no further; here your surging waves will be stayed'" (Job 38:10–11). Furthermore, the sea is distressed but is unable to do anything,[52] as it is said, "Though [its waves] toss, they cannot prevail" (Jer. 5:22).

[C] We can argue a fortiori: If these, which are not liable to gain or loss, which when worthy do not receive reward and when sinful do not receive punishment, and which are not concerned about sons or daughters, do not change their [assigned] course, then you, who when worthy receive reward and when sinful receive punishment, and who are concerned about sons and daughters, how much more so should you not change your [assigned] courses![53]

In this interpretation heaven and earth—the celestial and terrestrial creations—are presented as models of obedience to God's will. Now heaven and earth are not called upon to observe Israel to report its sinful behavior at the time of judgment, but Israel is called upon to observe heaven and earth, standing for nature as a whole, to learn from their exemplary compliance with God's laws.[54] Once again, there is no hint here, as there was in the first interpretation but not in any of the succeeding interpretations, of heaven and earth having been disqualified or deprivileged as witnesses.

The motif of nature, especially the heavenly bodies and the sea, providing a moral model for Israel, while having important roots in wisdom and prophetic writings of Scripture,[55] finds especially heightened expression in Jewish literature of the Second Temple period, as we shall see later when we examine an important "countertext" (1 Enoch) to our commentary. Note especially nature's animation: nature could choose to rebel against God's laws, but does not.[56] This personification of the elements of nature strengthens the a fortiori argument, according to which Israel should apply the example of nature's behavior to its own, and even more so. Here it is suggested that Israel should learn from nature to keep to its assigned covenantal course, whereas in the first interpretation it was stated that Israel was unable to learn from the lowly ant. Here the elements of nature remain viable as witnessing models.

Seventh Interpretation

Another interpretation of "Give ear, O heavens": R. Benaya (ca. 220 C.E.) said: When a person is found guilty, the first to lay a hand on him are his witnesses, as it is said, "The hands of the witnesses [should be first upon him]" (Deut. 17:7). And afterward [other] people come forward, as it is said, "And afterward the hand of all the people" (ibid.). Similarly, when Israel does not [perform God's will], what is said of them? "And the anger of the Lord will flare up [against you and He will shut up the heavens]" (Deut. 11:17). And afterward [other] punishments come forward: "And you shall perish quickly [from the good land]" (ibid.) But when Israel does perform God's will, what is said of them? "And it will come to pass on that day, says the Lord, that I will respond with the heavens and the earth shall respond. . . . And I will sow her unto Me in the earth" (Hos. 2:23-25)[57]

The idea, previously expressed implicitly, that heaven and earth as juridical witnesses implement the punishment in which their testimony results, is now expressed explicitly.[58] The cited verses stress the priority of place accorded to heaven and earth as witnesses in implementing God's punishments and rewards of Israel.

Eighth Interpretation

> Another interpretation of "Give ear, O heavens": R. Judah b. Ḥananiah[59] said: When Moses said, "Give ear, O heavens, and let me speak," the heavens and uppermost heavens stood still. [And when he said,] "Let the earth hear the utterances of my mouth," the earth and everything on it stood still. And if you are amazed by this, go see what is said of Joshua: "He said before the eyes of Israel: Sun stand still...and the sun stood still...and there was no day like that previously" (Josh. 10:12-13). From this we learn that the righteous have dominion over the entire universe.[60]

This interpretation represents a shift of attention from the eight that preceded it, all of them having focused on heaven and earth as legal and didactic *witnesses* to Israel's strained relationship with God. In this and the succeeding interpretations, our collection finds other significations in Moses' call to the heavens and earth. *Presumed* by this interpretation is the view that the heavenly bodies in their revolutions produce sounds. In other rabbinic texts, these sounds are understood as musical praises of God. For Moses's song to be heard, all of nature, must cease its movements and pay complete attention to what he is about to say.[61] And should one be amazed that Moses had the power to halt the movements of the heavenly bodies (not explicitly stated in Scripture), the explicit scriptural notice of Joshua's having halted the revolution of sun and moon will allay such doubt. Whereas in the previous interpretations heaven and earth have power over Israel as God's agents in overseeing the terms of the covenant, in this interpretation the righteous, as if playing God's part, have power over heaven and earth.[62] Whereas in the previous interpretation heaven and earth were exemplary for their adherence the rules set for them by God, now the righteous are exemplary for their power to command nature in violation of those rules. Implicitly and ideally, were all of Israel righteous (that is, sages[63]) its relation to nature would be inverted, no longer characterized by anxiety in the face of nature but by dominion over it.[64] The juxtaposition of this interpretation with those that have preceded it highlights a tension that, I shall argue, runs through the *Sifre*'s commentary to Deut. 32;1 as a whole.

Ninth Interpretation

> Another interpretation of "Give ear, O heavens": Since Moses was close to heaven he said, "Give ear, O heavens." And since he was far from the earth, he

said, "Let the earth hear the utterance of my mouth." Along came Isaiah and confirmed this usage:[65] "Hear, O heavens" (Isa. 1:2), for he was far from heaven, and "give ear, O earth" (ibid.), for he was close to the earth."[66]

This interpretation pays particular attention to the fact that Moses uses different but parallel verbs in summoning heaven and earth. This is no mere stylistic redundancy but expressive of Moses' status at the time he uttered these words. The suggested meaning is confirmed by a comparison of the lemma with its closest scriptural parallel, in which Isaiah uses the same verbs to summon heaven and earth but in reverse order: the verb *give ear,* used by Moses for heaven and by Isaiah for earth, denotes closeness, whereas the verb *hear,* used by Moses for the earth and by Isaiah for heaven, denotes distance.[67] The two prophets are portrayed as being somewhere between heaven and earth, with Moses being closer to the former and Isaiah to the latter.

Tenth Interpretation

[A] Another interpretation [of "Give ear, O heavens"]: Since the heavens are many, he addressed them in plural language (*ha'ăzînû*). And since the earth is less, he addressed it with lesser [= singular] language (*tišmaʿ*): "Let the earth hear the utterances of my mouth." Along came Isaiah and confirmed this usage: "Hear, O heavens, and give ear, O earth" (Isa. 1:2), using plural language (*šimʿû*) for the plural and lesser [= singular] language (*ha'ăzînî*) for the lesser.

[B] But the sages say: The matter is not so! Rather, when the [two] witnesses come to bear witness, if their words are found to be concurrent their testimony stands, and if not, their testimony does not stand. Thus, if Moses had said, "Give ear heavens," and Scripture had said no more [about addressing the heavens], the heavens would have said, "We only heard by 'giving ear.'" "Let the earth hear [the utterance of my mouth]": The earth might have said, "I only heard by 'hearing'." Along came Isaiah and confirmed [or, complemented] this usage, [by saying,] "Hear, O heavens, and give ear, O earth" (Isa. 1:2), thereby providing "giving ear" and "hearing" to the heavens and "giving ear" and "hearing" to the earth.[68]

We encounter here two more interpretations of the similarities and differences between Moses' call to heaven and earth and that of Isaiah, again stressing the complementary nature of their language choices. The first simply notes that Isaiah confirms Moses' use of a plural and singular verbal forms to address the heavens and earth respectively.[69] Thus, Moses and Isaiah concur in addressing heaven and earth differently as befits their plural or singular numbers respectively. This interpretation *may* in turn complement, by virtue of its juxtaposition, the preceding interpretation in which Moses is said to have been closer to heaven than was Isaiah: Moses being closer to the greater is himself the greater.

But the sages reject this interpretation (and perhaps the ninth interpretation as well), and in offering their alternative bring us back to the theme of the juridical *witnessing* functions of the heavens and earth, which had figured so prominently in earlier interpretations. First, an important mishnaic legal principle is invoked: in capital cases, the two witnesses are examined independently so as to determine the *concurrence* of their testimonies, thereby ascertaining their reliability.[70] But testimony can be concurrent only if it is based on identical modes of perception. Our commentary extends this principle one step further: even as the witnesses are given their witnessing assignments, they must be identically charged. Hence, the fact that heaven and earth are differently charged by Moses in Deut. 32:1 would appear to guarantee that their testimonies would not be concurrent and, as a result, would be invalidated in court. However, when Moses' charge is combined with Isaiah's, this legal obstacle is removed: each witness has been charged both to "give ear" and to "hear" (however we might understand the difference between the two, which is immaterial here).[71] Thus, the juxtaposition of Moses' and Isaiah's words to heaven and earth does not so much reveal any difference between Moses and Isaiah (as in the ninth interpretation) or between heaven and earth (as in the first part of the tenth interpretation) as the way in which their respective words conjoin, as if to constitute together a single twofold call that charges heaven and earth *identically*.[72] In the previous two interpretations of this juxtaposition, Isaiah's words are regarded as stylistically complementing those of Moses. But here the force of the juxtaposition is more substantive, for it ensures the very success of heaven and earth as reliable witnesses in the divine court to which they must bring their testimonies. But if the sages' explanation of the juxtaposition of Moses' and Isaiah's words is of greater legal consequence than the preceding two, it depends nevertheless for its rhetorical force upon them.[73]

Eleventh Interpretation

Another interpretation of "Give ear, O heavens, and let me speak": Because the Torah was given from heaven, as it is said, "You have seen that from heaven I spoke with you" (Exod. 20:19). "Let the earth hear the utterance of my mouth": For Israel stood upon [the earth] when they received [the Torah], saying, "Everything God has said we will do and obey (*nišmaʿ*)" (Exod. 24:7).[74]

Because the revelation at Sinai took place at the junction of heaven and earth, with Israel standing on the latter while receiving the Torah from the former, it is appropriate that heaven and earth, having framed that event, should continue to serve as witnesses to its terms. Although no verse is cited in support of the claim that Israel stood upon the earth, the citation of Exod. 24:7 would seem to associate Israel's promise to obey (*nišma^c*) with Moses' call to the earth to hear (*tišma^c*).

Twelfth Interpretation

[A] "Another interpretation of "Give ear, O heavens": For they did not perfom the commandments given to them from [=concerning] heaven. And which commandments were given to them from [= concerning] heaven? The intercalation of the year and the fixing of the new months, as it is said, "They [the heavenly lights] shall be for signs and seasons, and for days and nights" (Gen. 1:14).

[B] "And let the earth hear": For they did not perform the commandments which were given to them on [=concerning] the earth. And which are the commandments which were given to them on [=concerning] the earth? Gleanings, forgotten sheaves, corner crops, heave offerings, tithes, sabbatical years, and jubilee years.[75]

Just as the Torah was given from heaven and received on earth (the previous interpretation), so too the Torah requires Israel to attend to heaven and earth in observing its commandments. As in the previous interpretation, although a prooftext is provided for the commandments relating to heaven, none is provided for the commandments relating to earth. This interpretation implies that heaven and earth witness against Israel for its failure to fulfill the commandments relating to their respective domains.

This concludes the eleven middle interpretations of our lemma. Although it would be forced to argue that they cohere, in any simple sense, as a group—in fact we nave noticed some tensions among them—they share a concern for understanding the significance of Moses' call to heaven and earth as witnesses against Israel and the specific language therein employed by Moses. Heaven and earth keep a constant eye on Israel,[76] they serve as God's agents in rewarding and punishing Israel,[77] thereby bringing blessings or curses upon the world as a whole,[79] they listen to Moses' (or God's) complaints about Israel,[79] they serve as models to Israel of compliance with God's will,[80] they bear witness to Israel's original acceptance of the Torah,[81] and together they provide the necessary two witnesses against Israel for their failure to observe God's commandments.[82] This section repeatedly, but in different ways, stresses how appropriate it was for heaven and earth to have been assigned these witnessing roles, as well as how appropriate were the words with which Moses assigned them their charge.[83]

As a whole, then, notwithstanding its internal heterogeneity, this middle section stands in sharp contrast to the beginning section (first interpretation). There, it will be recalled, heaven and earth appeared to have been disqualified as witnesses, Israel in the present appeared to be without any effective witnesses, presumably estranged from God, while awaiting an eschatological future in which heaven and earth would finallly be removed and Israel would be reconciled directly and dialogically with God. Only one interpretation among the middle eleven, implicitly at least, questions the dominion of heaven and earth as God's sole witnessing agents, suggests an alternative to the repeatedly expressed *anxiety* of standing before heaven and earth (nature) as covenantal witnesses, and thereby retains a shiver of the hope expressed at the end of the first interpretation. That is the eighth interpretation with its assertion that Moses, in ordering heaven and earth to stand still, provides a model for the dominion of the (rabbinic) righteous over nature. The source of this power, however, has not yet been specified, except perhaps implicitly in Israel's obligation to observe the commandments relating to both heaven and earth.

End

Let us turn now to the concluding section of the *Sifre*'s interpretation of Deut. 32:1, keeping in mind the unfilled gap opened in the first interpretation and the unresolved tensions between that interpretation and the subsequent eleven interpretations.

Thirteenth Interpretation

[A] Another interpretation of "Give ear, O heavens": For they did not perform all the commandments which were given to them from [= concerning] heaven, and they did not perform all the commandments which were given to them on [= concerning] the earth.

[B1] Moses called two witnesses against Israel which would last for all eternity,[84] as it is said, "I call heaven and earth to witness against you this day" (Deut. 4;26–30:19). But the Holy One, blessed be He, called the song to witness against them, as it is said, "and now write for yourselves this song [and teach it to the people of Israel; put it in their mouths, in order that this song may be My witness against the people of Israel]" (31:19). We do not know whose testimony prevails,[85] that of the Holy One, blessed be He, or that of Moses. When it says, "This song shall respond (*wĕ⁽ānĕtâ*) before them as a witness" (Deut. 31:21), it indicates that the testimony of the Holy One, blessed be He, validates the testimony of Moses, and not that that of Moses validates that of the Holy One, blessed be He.[86]

[B2] And why did Moses call two witnesses against Israel which would endure for all eternity? He said: "I am flesh and blood and tomorrow I will die.

What if Israel will wish to say, 'We did not receive the Torah'? Who will refute them?" Therefore, he called two witnesses which would exist for all eternity. [B3] And God called the song to witness against them. He said: "The song will testify against them from below and I [will testify against them] from above."[87] And how do we know that God is called a witness? As it is said, "I will draw near to you in judgment, and I will be a swift witness" (Mal. 3:5). And it says, "I am He who knows and bears witness, says the Lord" (Jer. 29:23). And it says, "And let the Lord God be a witness against you, the Lord from his Holy Temple" (Mic. 1:2).[88]

This interpretation comprises two very different main parts. It begins (A) by repeating more briefly, or perhaps more severely, the preceding (twelfth) interpretation. Again it is stated that heaven and earth were chosen as witnesses because of Israel's failure to observe the commandments pertaining to their respective domains, but now it speaks of their failure to observe *all* the commandments, without specifying. It is difficult to know whether this is simply an abbreviated recapitulation of the previous interpretation or an even stronger indictment of Israel for failing completely in its covenantal obligations.[89] If the latter, then this would be the most negative assertion of the commentary thus far, stressing (like the first interpretation [A13]) just how far Israel has sunk in its covenantal malfeasance. In any case, its language is the most repetitive of any two adjacent interpretations in the entire series of interpretations. This repetition provides a rhetorical bridge between what I have called the *middle* and *end* sections: it repeats (either more succinctly or more severely) what precedes it before advancing to the commentary's surprising denouement. But we have moved ahead of our commentary.

It is next (B1) stated explicitly what had earlier been unclear: Moses called heaven and earth to witness against Israel. The phrase *hēʿîd bāhem* ("he caused to witness against them"), which last appeared eleven times in the first interpretation but without a specific subject, now reappears for the first time, but with Moses as its explicit subject.[90] Similarly, Deut. 4:26–30:19, the scriptural basis for understanding Moses' call to heaven and earth as a summons of witnesses, is cited here for the first time since its citation in the first interpretation. Thus, the last interpretation points back to the first, while also advancing beyond it.

But now comes the surprise, or in literary terms peripeteia: although heaven and earth were Moses' choices for witnesses against Israel, they were *not* God's. In contrast to Deut. 4:26 or 30:19 (as well as 31:28), Deut. 31:19 is cited to the effect that God intended the *song* itself to be His witness against Israel.[91] To this end Moses was instructed to teach the song to Israel, establishing it "in their mouths." By their internalized learning of the song, Israel would always have it available to them as a witness, reminding them, over and over again, both of their obligations to the terms of the covenant and of God's commitment to them as His chosen people.[92] In contrast to the preceding twelve interpretations where we may have assumed that Moses in summoning heaven and earth as witnesses was acting on God's behalf, this interpretation stresses that God and Moses made different choices of witnesses.

Confronted unexpectedly with two choices of witnesses, the editorial voice of the commentary, sounding like a perplexed student of the text, requests clarification: whose witnesses take precedence (especially in the event that they do not concur in their testimonies), Moses' or God's? In response, Deut. 31:19 is adduced to the effect that the song (God's witness) and not heaven and earth (Moses' witnesses) is the preeminent witness.[93] It should be stressed that this interpretation is occasioned by an ambiguity in the relation of the song, with its call to heaven and earth, to its narrative context, with its statement that God intended the song itself to serve as witness.[94] It is indeed curious that our commentary has waited until its final interpretation to attend to and resolve this ambiguity in the song's favor. With hindsight we may now see that this move was in part prepared for in the first interpretation with its historical depreciation and eschatological removal of heaven and earth as principal witnesses. Yet the eleven intervening interpretations in which heaven and earth alone are attended to as covenantal witnesses may have caused us to forget that depreciation and removal, or to regard it as something of the past and future but not the present. In any case, the choice here by God of the song itself as the privileged witness could not have been anticipated by us from the preceding interpretations.

The commentary continues (B2) by asking implicitly: if it was God's intent that the song itself be His witness against Israel, why did Moses prefer heaven and earth instead? Confronting the certainty of his own death, Moses feared that when he as lawgiver would be gone, Israel would be able to disclaim ever having agreed to the terms of the covenant. In this the midrash simply echoes the introductory words of Deut. 31:27-29: "Well I know how defiant and stiff-necked you are: even now, while I am still alive in your midst, you have been defiant toward the Lord; how much more, then, when I am dead!" Facing his own mortality, Moses turns to nature, summoning two seemingly immortal, eternal witnesses, who would always be able to refute Israel's denial of covenantal responsibility.

Here, as in the middle eleven interpretations, we learn of the logic of Moses' choice of heaven and earth as witnesses. Yet here the dimension of human pathos is so striking that we might again wonder why this explanation was left until last. The contrast between this interpretation and the very first one is even more striking. Here Moses explicitly presumes the permanency of heaven and earth as witness (presumed as well in several of the middle interpretations, but only implicitly), whereas the first interpretation concluded with their eventual removal; they would *not* continue as Israel's witnesses forever. Perhaps implied here is another contrast between Moses' and God's perspectives: from Moses' mortal perspective, especially as he confronts the certainty of his death, heaven and earth, like nature in general, appear as immutable and uncompromisable witnesses, whereas from God's eternal perspective nature can both be compromised through its participation in humanity's idolatrous worship and be divinely transformed in service of His will.[95]

Nonetheless, Moses' choice has the advantage of comprising two witnesses, as specified here three times (but not before) and as required by rabbinic law.[96] As if in response, God asserts, speaking in the first person, that in addition to the song he will be a witness. Whereas Moses chooses heaven above and earth below to witness against Israel, God Himself witnesses from above and the song from below. All that is left is for the commentary to ask whence we know that God is called a witness, to which it responds with three biblical citations to that effect. The symmetry between Moses' twofold choice of witnesses and God's twofold choice of witnesses is complete, even as the song is privileged over heaven and earth.[97] But although heaven and earth are deprivileged they are not removed, as the beginning of our commentary said they would be in the future. Nor is God portrayed here in future forgiving and consoling dialogue with Israel, as he was at the end of the first interpretation. The final three scriptural citations portray God as a future judge and witness *against* Israel for its misdeeds. Israel may be comforted that God remains present as a witness to His covenant with them, not having totally entrusted them to other witnesses, but this is no guarantee that He will not witness against them when the time of judgment arrives.

With this conclusion it would appear that the persistently presumed legal metaphor has broken down. For how could God, the initiator of the covenant, and the song, in which Moses recorded at God's dictation its history and terms, serve as witness to that covenant? Would it not be better for the witnesses to be disinterested parties?[98] But it may be said that even with heaven and earth as witnesses the legal metaphor eventually breaks down: for are they not, from the rabbinic perspective, God's very creations and subjects?[99] But from Israel's perspective, it is probably better to have God as their witness, from whom they might expect some modicum of mercy (as at the end of the first interpretation), having been chosen by Him to begin with. Intermediary agents such as heaven and earth, by contrast, can be expected only to perform their assigned functions (as in most of the middle interpretations); there is little hope in petitioning them for special consideration. But how can God be accessible to Israel as their witness, if, as is implied in the first interpretation, direct dialogue with Him will be possible only in the eschatological future?

This brings us to the song as witness, the most surprising outcome of the commentary: that which has until now been the object of exegesis becomes the subject of that exegesis. Here should be stated what is not stated explicitly by this midrash, but which may be inferred: the song invoked here as witness is not simply the Song of Moses of Deut.32, but the *whole* of the Torah for which it stands.[100] For the rabbis regularly understood Deut. 32:19 ("write for yourselves this song and teach it to the people of Israel; put it in their mouths, in order that this song may be My witness against the people of Israel") to refer not only to the specific song that follows, but to the Torah as a whole of which it is a précis. This identification of song and Torah is explicitly stated in the Babylonian Talmud (*Sanh.* 21b): "Said Raba (ca. 330 *C.E.*): Even though a person's ancestors have passed on to him a Torah scroll, it is a positive obligation for him to copy one for himself, as it is said, 'Therefore, write for yourselves this song' (Deut. 31:19)." This identification derives, once again, from an ambiguity in the relation of the scriptural Song of Moses to its narrative context. Whereas in 31:19-22 God instructs Moses to write down the song as a witness against Israel, in 31:24-29 Moses is said to write down "the words of this *tôrâ* on a scroll (*sēper*) to its very end." Moses then instructs the Levites to "take this scroll of the *tôrâ* and place it beside the Ark of the Covenant of the Lord your God, and let it remain there as a witness (*ʿēd*) against you." However modern biblical critics may understand the juxtaposition of these two passages (and their relation to the preceding *tôrâ* of Deut. 31:9-13 and to the succeeding song of Deut. 32),[101] the rabbis naturally understood them to speak of one and the same thing: the establishing of the song-Torah as a witness against Israel after Moses' death through its regular recitation and study.[102]

Thus, once Moses' song is understood to stand for the Torah as a whole, then the latter is understood to be God's choice as earthly witness. Through this sudden twist, the final interpretation not only points backward, as I have suggested, to the beginning of the commentary but points forward to the succeeding commentary, anticipating the *Sifre*'s interpretation of Deut. 32:2, in which Moses, still introducing his song, says: "May my discourse come down as rain, my speech distill as dew, like showers on young growth, like droplets on the grass" (Deut. 32:2). The *Sifre* begins its commentary on this verse by asserting that "'My discourse' (*liqḥî*) can only mean words of Torah," and proceeds in twenty-one interpretations to treat the metaphors of rain and dew as referring to Torah in general (written and oral), its study, and its sages.[103] Thus, the *Sifre*'s surprising interpretation of Deut. 32:1 as referring to Torah as God's preferred witness to the covenant serves as an introduction to its interpretation of 32:2 as referring not simply to the one-time Song of Moses, but to the for-all-times Torah of Moses. Notwithstanding its internal resistance to moving on, the commentary must eventually advance toward, and in cases such as this may even anticipate, the succession of biblical words to which it is, overall, structurally bound.[104]

Beginning-Middle-End

As I have already suggested but here wish to elaborate, the significance of the song as witness can be fully appreciated only in relation to the beginnning of our commentary. There we noted a temporal gap between Israel's *past* history, portrayed in terms of a sequence of disqualified witnesses, and Israel's *future* judgment, portrayed as a direct dialogical engagement and reconciliation with God. But *present* reality, poised between biblical past and eschatological future, was largely absent in that scheme, except by implication: Israel presently stands, it would appear, *without* effective witnesses to the covenant. The final interpretation would seem to fill this gap: God asserts that the song (Torah) below and He above will continually witness to the covenant, holding Israel accountable for the fulfillment of its terms. If God above cannot in the present be directly engaged, the everpresent song, expressive of His words and will, can. And how is the song to function as witness? By being established in Israel's "mouths" (Deut. 31:19, 21) through their continual recitation and study of it.[105]

Having noted the similarities of language that link the first and last interpretations,[106] even while they are in some discordance with one another, an interesting structural similarity between the two should be noted. In the second half of the first interpretation we are told that in the eschatological future, only *after* God removes heaven and earth (and everything associated with them) as witnesses (B1–5), He and Israel will be fully reconciled (B6).[107] In the final interpretation, it is only after the song is established and then priveleged as witness, that God announces that He too will serve as witness to Israel's behavior. This delay, lengthened by the insertion here and not previously of Moses' personal explanation for his choice of witnesses, is rhetorically significant not only in providing the necessary two witnesses, but also, and perhaps more significantly, in suggesting that God can serve effectively as Israel's witness only if the song is first established as witness in their "mouths." If in the first interpretation eschatological reconciliation with God is predicated on the removal of heaven and earth as witnesses, in the final interpretation God's presence as witness is predicated on the establishment and privileging of the song as witness. Thus, although the ending repeats something of the language, theme, and structure of the beginning, it does so with an important difference: God is accessible to Israel *already* in the present, but only through the witness of the song; His unmediated dialogical presence *remains* deferred.[108] The contrast between God's seeming historical absence and the presence of the song *within* Israel, as expressed I have argued in the overall structure of the *Sifre*'s commentary to Deut. 32:1, reflects well the biblical rationale for the establishing of the song as witness in Deut. 31:16–21, especially verses 17–20 (NJV):

> Then [when they enter the land and have violated the covenant] My anger will flare up against them, and I will abandon them and hide My countenance from them. They shall be ready prey; and many evils and troubles shall befall them. And they shall say on that day, 'Surely it is because our God is not in our midst that these evils have befallen us.' Yet I will keep My countenance hidden on that day, because of all the evil they have done in turning to other gods. Therefore, write down this poem and teach it to the people of Israel; put it in their mouths, in order that this poem may be My witness against the people of Israel."

If, as I have argued, there are thematic, linguistic, and structural links between the beginning and end of the commentary, and if the latter fills somewhat the temporal gap opened by the former, what purpose is served by the intervening eleven interpretations of Deut. 32:1, which go about the business of exegesis, in contrast to what precedes and succeeds them, as if heaven and earth alone are effective witnesses to the covenant, and as if God is hardly to be found?[109] This question can be answered in two, not unrelated ways. First, what might be called the *longue durée* of the middle set of interpretations can be understood to correspond, loosely to be sure, to the longue durée between biblical past and eschatological future, between a time when, to begin with, Israel was worthy enough to bear witness against itself and a time when, in the end, Israel will directly engage and be reconciled with God.[110] Second, the sense of deferred hope that is engendered at the end of the first interpretation is heightened by the long and repetitive sequence of interpretations that presume that Israel's covenantal fortunes have, in the meantime, been entrusted to the care of heaven and earth as intermediary divine agents.[111] The denouement of the final interpretation is all the more stunning after what in retrospect might appear to have been a long detour.

But when viewed retrospectively from the end of the commentary, the middle set of interpretation also take on another meaning. They provide a perfect example of what it means for Israel to establish the song in their "mouths": attending closely and repetitively to the language and intratextual associations of a small, and at first sight unproblematic, specimen of that song in its many possibilities of meaning. Let us jump for a moment from the *Sifre*'s explication of Moses' introduction to his song to its explication of Moses' first words to the people immediately after having completed his song:

> "He [Moses] said to them: Take to heart [lit.: set your heart toward] all the words with which I have warned you this day" (Deut. 32:46): A person needs to direct his heart and his eyes and his ears toward the words of Torah. . . . "That you may enjoin them upon your children to keep" (ibid.): He [Moses] said to them: "I would be most grateful if you would maintain [through constant study and review] the Torah after me. Similarly, you should be grateful to your children if they maintain the Torah after you". . . . "For this is not a trifling [= empty] thing for you [but your very life]" (32:47): There is nothing empty in the Torah, which, once you interpret it, is without its reward in this world [age] while the principal remains untouched until the world to come.[112]

Thus, the future promise is underwritten by present complete attention to *all* the words of Torah for their own sakes.[113] If the song is God's choice as witness to the covenant, then such intensive exegetical engagement with the words of that song fulfills Israel's central covenantal responsibility in, what Frank Kermode calls, the *time-between*.[114] The seeming return to the hope instilled at the end of the first interpretation—to be free of heaven and earth as witness and to be reunited with God—however, is much less than a full return. Israel will never be free of witnesses, but will always carry one of those witnesses *within* themselves, constantly reminding them of their covenantal obligations and the divine *judgment* that awaits them if they fail in those obligations. If, to begin with, Israel was once worthy to witness directly against itself, now it might once again do so, but only to the extent that it maintains the Torah as witness "within their mouths." Israel's covenantal relationship with God is presently mediated not so much by "nature" without as by the song within. Although Israel's hope for direct dialogue with God remains deferred, in the time-between we know what we did not know before: that Israel is not so much suspended between heaven and earth as between God and his song, with God being accessible to Israel in the here-and-now principally through their performative internalization of that song through the multivocal dialogue of its recitation and study.[115]

Countertexts

Before concluding my discussion of the *Sifre*'s commentary to Deut. 32:1, and before returning to the issues that I set forth in this chapter's introduction, I wish to present three texts of very different types as counterpoints to the text of the *Sifre*. Each is strikingly similar to a part of the *Sifre*'s commentary to Deut. 31:1 yet significantly different in its overall thrust. I hope by juxtaposing these texts to highlight our commentary's distinctive features, both of polyphony and of plot.

Fragmentary Targum

The first countertext is from within the rabbinic literary orbit but from a different genre, that of targum, the ancient Aramaic "translation" of Scripture:[116]

> [A] "Give ear" (Deut. 32:1): When the fixed time arrived for the prophet Moses to depart from the midst of the world, he said: "What thing can I establish as witness against this people that does not taste death? I shall establish as witnesses against them heaven and earth, which do not taste death in this world.[117]
>
> [B] However, they [too] will finally perish in the world to come, as [Scripture] explicitly says, "Lift up your eyes to the heavens and gaze upon the earth below; for the heavens will dissipate like smoke, and the earth will wear out like a garment" (Isa. 51:6). However, "I [God] shall in the future create new heavens and a new earth" (Isa. 65:17).
>
> [C1] The prophet Isaiah, when he prophesied in the assembly of Israel, since he was far from heaven and close to earth, assigned "hearing" to the heavens and "listening" to the earth, as [Scripture] explicitly says: "Hear O heavens, and listen O earth, for the *memra* of the Lord has spoken" (Isa. 1:2).
>
> [C2] The prophet Moses, when he prophesied in the assembly of Israel, since he was far from the earth and close to heaven, assigned "listening" to the heavens and "hearing" to the earth, as it [Scripture] explicitly says: "Listen, O heavens and I shall speak; and let [the earth] hear the words of my mouth."

Section A of the targum is similar in its explanation of Moses' choice of heaven and earth to the second part of the thirteenth (final) interpretation (B2) of the *Sifre*. In both, Moses facing his mortality, wishes to have immortal witnesses who will always be around to testify to Israel's acceptance of the laws of the Torah. Likewise, section B of the targum is similar to the second part of the first interpretation (B1) of the *Sifre*. In both, heaven and earth, as they now exist, will not continue into the time of final judgment, when God will create a new heaven and a new earth. But despite these similarities, the ways in which these two traditions have been shaped and combined in this targum and in our commentary are very different. In the targum they are *directly* juxtaposed in *chronological* sequence: Moses chose heaven and earth because they would not taste death "in *this* world," but "in the world to come" they *will* taste death. But the relation of these two statements to each other is not at all clear. When in the world to come will heaven and earth expire, before the day of judgment or after?[118] Will they bear witness against Israel beforehand or not? Nor are we told why they will terminate. The citation of Isa. 1:56 (not found in the *Sifre*) suggests that heaven and earth will die a "natural death," whereupon God will replace them (Isa. 65:17).

In the *Sifre*, by contrast, the parallels to these two contrasting traditions appear in *reverse* order and with a substantial *gap* of eleven interpretations between them. In the *Sifre*'s first interpretation we are told that *before* Israel's final judgment *God Himself* would "remove" (*ma⁽ăbîr*) heaven and earth. God takes this action in response to Israel's request that heaven and earth *not* testify against her.

Whereas in the targum we learn at the outset that Moses chose heaven and earth as witnesses and why, in the midrash only after twelve interpretations of the call to heaven and earth do we learn that this was Moses's choice, and, almost as an afterthought, "we" ask and are told why. The explicit notice of Moses' choices of witness only comes in the *Sifre*'s commentary at the end, when we learn that God had intended a different witness altogether, that of the song itself (and God). Thus, the pathos of Moses' choice of heaven and earth as related by the *Sifre*'s commentary is very much more poignant than it is in the targum's "translation." Thus, even though sections A and B of the targum are akin (however related) to their parallels at the beginning and end (but in reverse order) of the *Sifre* commentary, their significant differences of detail and placement in the latter tell a very different story.

Section B of the targum, in twice citing the prophet Isaiah on heaven and earth, leads to section C, where Isaiah again mentions heaven and earth, now addressing them directly. Sections C1 and C2 as a pair should sound familiar from the *Sifre*, where they appear in the middle section of the commentary as the ninth interpretation. Once again, however, their order is reversed in the two contexts. In the targum, first Isaiah's call to heaven to hear and to earth to listen (= "give ear") is explained and cited, then Moses' call to heaven to listen and to earth to hear is explained and cited. By this ordering the targum is able to conclude with its translation of the actual words of Deut. 32:1 (which its audience, however we may conceive of it, presumably awaited).[119]

The same tradition is employed in the *Sifre*'s commentary as the first of *three* examples of how Isaiah in his call to heaven and earth supported (*sāmak*) Moses' choice of language for the same purpose. Put differently, the verse from Isaiah is intertextually read to confirm the commentary's three explications of Moses' choice of language in Deuteronomy and, in the third case, to solve a problem raised by that explication. It therefore befits the commentary's rhetoric to invoke Isaiah *after* each explication of

Moses' language. Whereas in the targum the interpretation of Isaiah's words and that of Moses' are simply juxtaposed, in the *Sifre* they are more consciously interrelated, as part of a larger construction of correspondences.

Let us now look at the targumic combination as a whole. The first pair (AB) is joined according to a thematic intertextual association: Moses' choice of heaven and earth (Deut. 32:1) and their eventual dissipation and replacement (Isa. 51:6; 65:17). The second pair (CD) is joined according to a linguistic intertextual association: the similar but significantly different language used by Moses (Deut. 32;1) and Isaiah (Isa. 1:2) in addressing heaven and earth. However, when these two pairs are joined they together form something of a circle: Moses' choice of heaven and earth leads to Isaiah's notice of their eventual passage and replacement, which leads to Isaiah's address elsewhere of heaven and earth in language which brings us back to Moses' address of heaven and earth, which is literally cited at the very end but in Aramaic. The circular progression depends on several associative links, but they are not difficult to discern. However, the approximate return to the lemma also facitlitates a progression to the next verse in the scriptural sequence and to its "translation."

As we have seen, the *Sifre*'s commentary is also somewhat circular, beginning and ending with the deprivileging of heaven and earth as witnesses and in the final interpretation filling a gap opened in the first. But what most characterizes the complex relation of the commentary's beginning to its end is the large space (or duration) that separates and is suspended between them. Put differently, the *Sifre*'s commentary not only reverses the order of what in the targum are A and B but suspends between them eleven interpretations, only one of which corresponds to the targum's C and D (again reversed).[120] If the line that connects A and B to C and D of the targum is fairly direct, pulling us right along, there does not appear to be any such direct line running from the commentary's first interpretation (= B), through to its tenth interpretation (=D + C), and on to its final, thirteenth interpretation (= A).[121] It is in the generic nature (and function) of commentary, unlike that of translation (even paraphrastic translation), that it can afford to delay longer, exploring the local midrashic sights and sounds, before needing to progress in its return to its scriptural base. In our commentary, I have argued, this delay heightens the sense of deferral (and perhaps for a while loss) of hope in the eventual removal of heaven and earth (nature) as witnesses and the eventual direct reconciliatory dialogue of Israel with God. When we finally reach the textual end we realize that such hope must remain deferred to the final temporal end. But now we learn that Israel has another witness, one that is internally accessible to it in the seemingly perpetual present: the song itself, which Israel maintains as witness through its dialogical engagement with the multiple possibilities of its interpretation. This, we retrospectively realize, is the significance of the extended textual middle of our commentary.

1 Enoch

The following text bears striking resemblance to the sixth interpretation of the *Sifre* commentary to Deut. 32:1.[122] It is from a work of very different genre and provenance, from what is sometimes called the *Book of the Watchers* of the (First or Ethiopic) *Book of Enoch*. Scholars date it to the second-third centuries B.C.E., although its circulation and influence continued for a good while thereafter. The Enochic corpus purports to transmit to a pious elite secret wisdom about the cosmos and history, from beginning to end. This wisdom was acquired by the antediluvian Enoch when he was "taken" by God (Gen. 5:24). The following quote is from *1 Enoch* 2:1–5:7:[123]

> [A] Contemplate[124] all the events in heaven, how the lights in heaven do not change their courses, how each rises and sets in order, each at its proper time, and they do not transgress their law.
> [B] Consider the earth, and understand from the work which is done upon it, from the beginning to the end, that no work of God changes as it becomes manifest. Consider the summer and the winter, how the whole earth is full of water, and clouds and dew and rain rest upon it. . . . And understand in respect of everything and perceive how He who lives forever made all these things for you; and (how) his works (are) before him in each succeeding year, and all his works serve him and do not change, but as God has decreed, so everything is done. And consider how the seas and rivers together complete their tasks.
> [C] But you have not persevered, nor observed the law of the Lord.[125] But you have transgressed, and have spoken proud and hard words with your unclean mouth against his majesty. You hard of heart! You will not have peace! And because of this you will curse your days, and the years of your life you will destroy. And the eternal curse will increase, and you will not receive mercy. . . . For the chosen there will be light and joy and peace, and they will inherit the earth. But for you, the impious, there will be a curse.[126]

First, some striking similarities are to be noted between this passage and the sixth interpretation of the *Sifre*'s commentary. Both texts implore Israel to attend *visually* to nature,[127] calling attention first to heaven (A) and then to earth (B). Both passages urge attention to the seas, presumably as part of the earth. Both passages emphasize the orderliness of nature, stressing the daily rising and setting of the heavenly lights, and the fact that nature does not change its ways in deviation from God's decrees. Both also state that nature, although subservient to God, was created for the sake of humanity.

Of course, numerous details are present in one but not in the other, for example, the commentary's attention to the animals and the sea's boundaries and the apocalypse's interest in the orderliness of the seasons and rain cycles. But more significant is the difference in rhetorical style between the two. Unlike the apocalypse, the commentary raises a series of rhetorical questions (eight) and cites verses from Scripture (five) in response to those questions. If in both passages nature is portrayed as having personality, as choosing to obey God, then its animation is even more striking in the commentary where the elements of nature themselves speak (four times).[128] In both of these ways the commentary may be said to be more dialogical—drawing together a variety of "voices" that in turn draw the student of the text into engagement with its discourse.

But the most striking difference between these two passages (not unrelated to the other differences just mentioned) can be seen if we compare section C of each, these being reflective of the two very different literary settings within which the two passages are set. In the context of *1 Enoch*, where we find a series of revelations that claim to disclose an imminent, catastrophic judgment, the "impious" are addressed in the second person, from the self-justifying perspective of the sectarian "chosen": observe the regularity with which God's creation adheres to its appointed ways, for thereby you will recognize that you, unlike us, have been doomed to perdition for changing your ways in relation to God's immutable commands. The tone is clearly one of condemnation. The *Sifre* passage, by contrast, in commenting on Moses' farewell speech to the people of Israel, addresses, in principle at least, Israel as a *whole* in the second person: observe the regularity with which God's creation adheres to its appointed ways, for thereby you will recognize how much more you have to gain by not changing your ways in relation to God's immutable commands. The commentary, through its rhetorical questions and a fortiori argument (evoking concern for "your children"), reveals its exhortative rather than self-justifying rhetoric, calling on Israel to obey God's laws, rather than condemning those who have not. Notwithstanding earlier notes of pessimism, the *Sifre*'s commentary asserts at least the possibility of Israel learning from nature (via Scripture) to act meaningfully *within* history.[129]

2 Baruch

The final and most striking countertext is from the late-first century pseudepigraphic apocalypse *2 Baruch*. Its author, most likely writing in Palestine following the destruction of the Second Temple in 70 *C.E.*, expects Israel's final redemption to be close at hand, and urges whole-hearted fulfillment of the commandments of the Torah as its requirement.

In the context of the present passage, Baruch—who in Scripture is the prophet Jeremiah's secretary, but in the apocalypse is a prophetic figure in his own right—having witnessed the destruction of the (First) Temple, laments before God the sufferings of the righteous and the prospering of the wicked. Moses, he says, brought the light of the lamp of "the law" (*nāmûsāʾ*)[130] to Israel only to find that "many whom he illumined took from the darkness of Adam and did not rejoice in the light of the lamp" (18:2). God responds to Baruch as follows (19:1-4):[131]

> [1] That is why [Moses] appointed a covenant for them at that time and said, "Behold I have put before you life and death" (Deut. 30:19), and he called heaven and earth to witness against them (31:28). [2] For he knew that his time was short, but that heaven and earth would last forever. [3] But they sinned and trespassed after his death, even though they knew that they had the Law [= Torah] to reprove them, and the light which nothing could deceive,[132] and the celestial spheres, which witness, and Me. And I judge everything that exists. [4] You, therefore, should not worry yourself about them, nor distress yourself over these things which have been. For it is now the end of time that should be considered.... and not the beginning.

We begin with a familiar motif: Moses, in confronting the certainty of his imminent death and suspecting that many in Israel would thereafter renounce the Torah, calls heaven and earth, which he believes "would last forever," to witness to Israel's covenantal responsibilities and conduct. This is very similar to the final interpretation of the *Sifre*'s commentary and the opening of the *Fragmentary Targum*'s "translation."[133] But where the apocalypse is most significantly like the *Sifre*'s commentary is in its assertion that not only did the Israelites have heaven and earth, which Moses chose, to witness against them, but they also had, and knew they had, the Torah and God Himself to remind and to reprove them.[134] Even though these were of no effect in changing Israel's behavior and forestalling punishment, Israel cannot claim that it did not know what was expected of it. But herein is also where the apocalypse most significantly differs from the *Sifre*'s commentary, for the latter, at least in its outer frame, stresses that, although heaven and earth (like the rest of nature) may have been historically of little avail as witnesses (first interpretation), God and His song (= Torah) remain as effective covenantal witnesses (final interpretation). Whereas the apocalypse speaks of a single, united group of four witesses, the commentary speaks of two groups of two, and rhetorically counterposes the two groups against each other so as to privilege one: Moses' choice of heaven and earth as witnesses must take second palce to God's choice of the Torah and Himself. *2 Baruch* knows nothing of such a distinction or ordering.

This critical difference between the two texts needs to be understood in relation to two other differences, which define important aspects of the difference between apocalypse and midrashic commentary more generally: dialogical and temporal, to which I now turn.

As noted earlier, the *Sifre*'s commentary to Deut. 32:1 is framed by divine-human dialogues. In the second half of the first interpretation, God is portrayed in direct dialogue with the whole congregation of Israel at the time of future judgment. In the middle eleven interpretations God is virtually absent as a speaking or acting presence.[135] Only in the final interpretation is He once again portrayed in direct speech (apart from scriptural citations), emphatically stating, "The song will witness against them from below and *I* from above." God's voice comes, as it were, out of nowhere, entering suddenly into the give and take, questioning and answering, of the commentary. But also note that although the anonymously questioning voice of the commentary has been present throughout,[136] it is precisely here that it assumes a more assertive and collective character, in its crucial interjection, "*We* do not know whose testimony prevails, that of God or that of Moses?" Thus, although an indirect dialogue between Israel and God may be said implicitly to pervade the commentary as a whole, it surfaces in explicit and heightened fashion only in the final interpretation. But this, to reiterate, is still far less that the kind of direct, unmediated dialogue between Israel and God that the opening interpretation imagines for the eschatological future. The commentary as a whole, thus, may be said to point forward to two dialogical destinations, one revealed at its beginning, the other not fully revealed until its end. The first is a consolatory destination of direct and intimate dialogue with God, projected outside of history and beyond present reach. The second is a more dangerous destination of mediated dialogue with God through the present study, interpretation, and performance of the song (Torah) under God's judgemental gaze.[137] I say dangerous because with the song as internalized witness within and against Israel, it can no longer claim never to have received it; neither can Israel expect that at some future time the song will be removed by God at its request. This latter destination unlike the former is presently attainable, we come to learn retroactively, within the text of scriptural commentary itself, especially in its protracted middle—in the longue durée of the time-between.

Yet the text of *2 Baruch* is also fashioned as a dialogue: not one between the congregation of Israel *as a whole* and God nor one that involves the questioning and answering explication of a biblical text, but one between the solitary prophet and God. Baruch, having witnessed the destruction of the Temple and the exile and suffering of the righteous few, of whom he is one, is told by God that he will be "preserved until the consummation of the times" to serve as a witness against the wicked. Although Baruch is to witness against the wicked, we gain the clear impression that the questions he addresses to God and the answers he receives in return are intended to strengthen the sectarian self-justification of the righteous few who would read this text and apply it to themselves in the aftermath of the destruction of the Second Temple. Having been shown "the course of the times and what is to be after these things," Baruch questions God about what appears to him to be the senseless suffering of the righteous. Why, he asks, if the world was created according to divine plan for their sakes, does it appear that "the world which was made because of us remains, but we, for whom it was made disappear." God responds that a new world will shortly come into being for the sake of the righteous, wherein they will no longer suffer. Thus, like the text from *1 Enoch*, what is to be learned—there from nature, here from recent history—concerns not the redemption of Israel as a *whole* but the condemnation of the wicked (both Israelite and non-Israelite) and the vindication of the righteous few, whom Baruch represents in his dialogue with God and for whom the apocalypse that bears his name was presumably intended. It was for their sake that the meaning of the present moment in relation to the rapidly approaching consummation of history was "revealed," and not for the sake of Israel as a whole, most of whom are understood to be doomed already and irreversibly to perdition.

The dialogue between God and Baruch next turns to a comparison between Moses and Adam, the former having done more good in his fewer years than the latter, explains God. In this context Baruch evokes the seeming futility of Moses' efforts to bring the light of the Torah to the people, who preferred "Adam's darkness." Now God must explain why Moses chose heaven and earth as witnesses, which the people ingored as they did the Torah and God Himself, thereby making their future punishment inevitable. Growing impatient with Baruch's continued harping upon the fate of the righteous and the wicked in the distant and recent past, God says: "You, therefore, should no worry yourself about them, nor distress yourself over these things which have been. For it is now the end of time that should be considered. . . and not the beginning" (19:4–5). For the apocalyptic author and audience the present is like a narrow ridge separating the scriptural past on one side from the eschatological future on the other. The former is attended to and interpreted, but usually not directly, only so far as is necessary to anticipate and prepare for the latter, which is felt to press urgently upon the present. With God and the other witnesses in place, Baruch need not concern himself with the past misfortunes of the righteous or prosperity of the wicked, as all of this will very shortly be rectified. The message to the righteous elite is simply to stay their course and await their imminent vindication, for the present in which they languish will be of very *short* duration; they like Baruch should divert their gaze from past and present to "the end of time."

In the *Sifre*'s commentary the present is also suspended between biblical past and eschatological future (both sketched in the first interpretation), but whereas in the apocalypse the present is virtually eclipsed, in the *Sifre*'s commentary it looms large, I have argued, in the textual middle of scriptural study as a religious practice in its own right. The rabbinic authors and audience of the *Sifre*'s commentary undoubtedly confronted the discordances of biblical past, historical present, and eschatological future no less than did those of *2 Baruch*. But whereas in the latter God urges the prophet to transcend the first two through attention to the third, in the former the student of the text is drawn to attend to the words of Torah, wherein the past, present, and future can be found dialectically to coexist.[138] Put differently, from the perspective of the apocalypse the messianic future is pressingly imminent, whereas from the perspective of the midrashic commentary it is presently immanent, if only as a foretasete, in the engaged study and concomitant practice of the words of Torah, even while as a temporal horizon it remains distinct and distant.[139] This difference is most evident when we contrast the attitude of *2 Baruch* to the past, present, and future as expressed in God's words to the prophet in 19:4–5, with that of the *Sifre* as expressed in its very last comment on the Song of Moses as a whole. Addressing the anonymous student of its text, the *Sifre* concludes: "You should say, Great is [such] a song which has within it (*šeyyēš bô*) present, which has within it past, and which has within it the future still to come—which has within it this world [= age] and which has within it the world to come."[140]

Conclusions

Before returning to the questions raised in the introduction to this chapter, I would like to address, in light of the countertexts just examined, the place of nature within the *Sifre*'s commentary to Deut. 32:1. Both of the apocalyptic texts just considered stress nature's central role as witness to the covenant.[141] Because the wicked in their violation of God's laws ignore the example of nature, they are doomed to the covenantal curses. Because the righteous in their observances of God's laws mirror the regularity of nature, they are destined to enjoy the covennntal blessings. The apocalyptic authors, facing what they considered to be world history's imminent consummation, may be said to be like Moses confronting his imminent death: from both perspectives heaven and earth are viewed as eternal forces that surmount and transcend the vagaries of history, whether individual or collective. Even while marking historical time, they stand outside it. Individuals and societies frustrated by their inability to make sense of the course of history and feeling impotent to make a mark upon it, might turn to nature as an alternative arena for redemptive action and self-confirmation. This tendency led, in some circles of Second Temple Jewish society, to what Michael Stone calls the *remythologization* of nature: "heaven and earth" are no longer simply elements of creation that passively fulfill God's ongoing design for the sustenance of the world and its human inhabitants, but are the lead actors in the metadrama of the end of time, from whom humans take their cues.[142]

In light of this, the *Sifre*'s commentary to Deut. 32:1 is striking both for the way in which its first and last interpretations deprivilege heaven and earth and, conversely it would seem, for the way in which heaven and earth are given key covenantal roles in the middle eleven interpretations. But even so, the beginning and ending of the commentary must be differentiated. Although in the first interpretation heaven and earth are portrayed as having been historically compromised and eschatologically removed, in the final interpretation they are neither. Rather, they continue as Moses' choices, bearing witness to the covenant and against Israel, even if in the end we learn that their testimony is secondary in authority to that of God and the song (Torah). Although tempting, it would be wrong, it seems to me, to dispose of the protracted middle section of the commentary with the two instrumentatlist (and hence somewhat reductive) explanations for its presence that I have already offered and still wish to affirm: as a perfect example of the importance of exegetically engaging the textural song of Torah for its own sake, and as a literary device for delaying and hence heightening the rhetorical force of the dramatic peripeteia of the commentary's conclusion.

Heaven and earth (including, as the first interpretation specifies, the nations), representing the created world within which Israel must survive and make sense of its life, are too much of a presence in the commentary to be easily dismissed or eclipsed. Scripture too often assigns to the elements of nature, as to the events of history, the role of rewarding and punishing Israel for that role to be denied. As the first two interpretations suggest, so long as Israel can no longer bear witness against itself it is inescapably under the watchful eye of heaven and earth as divine intermediaries, however compromised those intermediaries may have become. The idea that the natural world, in its orderly compliance with the laws and limits set for it by God, could serve as a reminder to Israel of the necessity of living life in accord with God's will and as an instrument in enforcing that will, is no more foreign to rabbinic literature than it is to its antecedents in postbiblical Israelite wisdom and apocalyptic literature.[143] Ideally at least, a life lived according to Torah *was* a life lived in harmony with the elements of nature, God's handiworks and servants. Like peoples of other cultures, ancient Jews believed that human life was lived under the gaze and to the beat of the heavenly and earthly natural phenomena, with which their economy and security was so interconnected. Nature was always there, whether for inspiration or for an audience, even while its dangers were a constant source of anxiety.[144]

Such undeniable anxiety before nature is variously expressed in most of the middle interpretations of our commentary. Heaven and earth are inescapable and unfeeling recorders of human deeds, rewarding and punishing Israel on God's behalf, and bearing witness against Israel at judgment time (notwithstanding the first interpretation). But even though the elements of nature act as God's intermediaries in administering the covenant, as soon as Israel seeks to worship God by way of their mediation, that worship becomes an act of idolatry, a cardinal violation of the terms of their covenant with God and a compromise of the integrity of their witnesses, upon whom after all they remain dependent.[145] Still, nature is the arena in which the righteous display their supernatural powers and bring blessing to themselves and to the world. For Israel to find its way within this complex and seemingly contradictory web of interrelations with nature was no simple matter.

It is in these terms, it seems to me, that our text's fashioning of something like plot in the midst of polyphony, of commentary from tradition, should be viewed. Moses' scriptural call to heaven and earth evokes a multitude of interpretations that give expression to a variety of ways that Israel's relation to nature in history could be experienced and interpreted. This complexity could not be reduced to a single interpretation or narrative retelling, either of Scripture or Israel's relation to the natural world, including the nations. But the commentary could, with its beginning and ending interpretations, place these multiple possibilities within two organizing, and we might say sense-making, frameworks, one temporal the other spatial, although this distinction should not be pressed too hard. The first interpretation establishes a temporal framework: Israel's ambivalent relationship to heaven and earth in the present is suspended between a past when, to begin with, Israel was innocent enough not to need nature's witness at all (and, presumably, like the righteous of the eighth interpretation, to have dominion over creation), and a future when heaven and earth will be removed as witnesses to faciliate Israel's full and direct reconciliation with God. In the "time-between," however, there is no escaping Israel's ambivalent and anxious involvement with "heaven and earth" as witnesses, however much Israel might fantasize otherwise.

The final interpretation, somewhat prepared for by the commentary's beginning yet in striking contrast to it, establishes an unexpected spatial framework: Israel's relationship to heaven and earth remains but is now enveloped by its relationship to the song (Torah) below and God above. This framework, I wish to stress, does not replace that of the first interpretation but retrospectively refigures it by filling in the temporal gap of its middle. That refigured middle is also the textual middle of the commentary, which now expresses not only Israel's anxious and complex relationship to nature, but also, from the retrospective hindsight of the commentary's ending, Israel's exegetical engagement with and dialogical internalization of the song itself as God's preferred covenantal witness. Even as the latter is privileged, the former cannot be denied. Unlike the authors of the apocalypses, the creators of our text redirect our attention back from the end to the middle, both textual and temporal, wherein Israel can ambivalently relate to nature—including the nations, which we may understand to figure for history as well—through their multivalent study of the song, by which pruposeful practice they can already experience God's presence, albeit in the present indirectly.[146]

In arguing that the *Sifre*'s thirteen interpretations (some of which themselves contain multiple interpretations) of Deut. 32:1 have been editorially configured, I do not wish to argue for their coherence or concordance in any simple sense. Each discrete interpretation can stand quite well on its own—as implied in the linking phrase, *another interpretation*. Nonetheless, such interpretations have been combined and juxtaposed in such a way as to encourage and enable the student of the text to make some sense of them in relation to one another.[147] The ordering of these interpretations in the progressive text of commentary significantly effects the dynamics of such sense-making activity, as the student moves through that commentary in simultaneously linear and circular ways. The contertext of the *Fragmentary Targum* demonstrates one other way, with strikingly different consequences, that the same traditional building blocks could have been and were combined and engaged. Similarly, although the larger conglomerates that I have labeled *beginning, middle,* and *end* may have once stood independent of each other, it is clear that as presently constructed within the continuity of commentary, their mix of structural concordance and thematic discordance both beckon and facilitate their dialogical interpretation.[148]

All of this, and more, suggests the sufficient presence of ordering relations (both linear and dialectical) between the parts (small and large) of the commentary to qualify its being viewed as more than a random conjunction of exegetical assertions. This is not to say that the place of every part can or needs to be explained as the conscious choice of the text's creators.[149] It is sufficient to say that there is enough ordering within the structure of the text to set the work of dialogical commentary on its course. This course, however, requires for its advancement the active participation of students of the text as they work their way through the multiplicity of sometimes discordant interpretatons as these have been selected and arranged for them in the received text of progressive commentary.[150] The heterogeneity of our verse's multiple interpretations (like that of Israel's experience of nature and history) has been editorially configured to some extent, without being eclipsed.

This configured character of the commentary slowly leads the student of the text forward through the variety of interpretations toward its end (whence it will begin anew by attending to the next phrase in the scriptural sequence), but not without relishing for a while the multiple interpretations of its middle, which even when transfigured through the retrospection of its end, is never quite assimilated to that end or stripped of its heterogeneity. For if what I have termed *polyphony* in commentary recalls and re-enacts Israel's past experience of direct engagement with God's word at Sinai, characterized, as it is elsewhere in the *Sifre*, by the synchronic multiplicity of divine voices and their human interpretations,[151] then what I have loosely termed *plot* in the diachronic ordering of those voices points forward in time, however many its delays and reversals may be, to the continually deferred hope for Israel's reconciliation with God through direct dialogue.[152] At the end of the commentary to Deut. 32:1, however, we learn that the hoped for historical end is still far away: first Israel will have to be divinely judged for its adherence to the song that in the time-between it must constantly recite and reinterpret. The student of the redacted text of commenatary, struggling to make sense of its polyphony while moved along slowly by its plot, tastes something both of originary revelation and of final redemption in the very midst fo text and time, both of which linearly progress even as they continually and complexly turn back upon themselves.

Afterword

A fundamental argument of the preceding chapters has been the need to comment upon rabbinic texts not simply with an eye to uncovering what lies *behind* them—whether hermeneutically, traditionally, or historically— but to appreciate what lies *before* them in their pedagogic transforming of Scripture, tradition, and history to engage and empower rhetorically the society of sages and their disciples. Similary, I shall choose here not to repeat reductively what I have already concluded, but to look forward more expansively to the implications of those conclusions for work yet to be done.

The *Sifre* to Deuteronomy itself stresses the identification of rabbinic teaching in all its variety—exegetical, legal, and narrative—with "words of Torah," and of the attentive study of such "words of Torah," scriptural as well as rabbinic, with divine worship or labor. Thus, I have argued, the rabbinic engagement with Torah as covenantal "song" is to be found as much in rabbinic texts of scriptural interpretation as in the intended study and interpretation of those rabbinic texts themselves. Even as such twofold study informs and must lead to religious practice, it is in and of itself, the *Sifre* claims, a performative religious experience of divine presence and redemptive expectation. The rabbinic Torah is not so much a univocal text to be monologically read as a multivocal song to be dialogically, and hence socially, performed. But if the *Sifre* claims this not simply for itself but for rabbinic "words of Torah" in their differentiated aggregate, then might not other types of rabbinic texts, notwithstanding their major differences in rhetorical practice and historical context, yield to a similar sort of inward and outward looking commentary, one that seeks textual meaning in the complex interplay of the centripetal and centrifugal forces respectively of linguistic-literary signification and social-cultural practice?

Because I have chosen in this book to comment upon discrete texts of the *Sifre* whose subject is itself Torah and its reception or study, most have been nonlegal (or narrative) in character, even though a good number of legal texts have also been considered (especially in Chapter 3, but in the others as well). These were generally drawn from the nonlegal frame of the *Sifre*'s commentary, which like the narrative and poetic frame of the Book of Deuteronomy, bracket, but in roughly equal measure, its legal core. My next step will be to sharpen my focus even more on the texts of that legal core, asking whether they, too, should be engaged in the dialogical complexity and performative *work* of their discursive rhetoric and not simply for the legal norms, hermeneutics, or justifications they are conventionally thought monologically to *contain*.

Might the same approach be applied not only to other texts of legal and nonlegal scriptural commentary (or midrash), but also to the pedagogic discourse of the mainly nonexegetical legal digest of the Mishnah, and in turn to its own dialogical commentaries of the two Talmuds? For these, no less than the midrashic texts here explored, exhibit the dialectic of tradition and transformation that provided the religious energy of rabbinic Judaism from its inception through its successive heirs. This is simply to hope that the preceding will prove to be a modest contribution toward and model for a much larger cultural history of rabbinic Judaism and beyond, which by necessity will have to be a collective scholarly commentary itself.

Abbreviations

The following list contains all nonstandard abbreviations used except those for the names of biblical books (including the Apocrypha). For the latter I have adopted the abbreviations used in the *Journal of Biblical Literature (JBL* [1988]: 584), which should be easiliy recognizable.

ʿAbod. Zar.	*ʿAboda Zara*
ʾAbot R. Nat.	*ʾAbot de Rabbi Natan*
Adv. Haer.	Irenaeus, *Adversus haereses*
Ag. Ap.	Josephus, *Against Apion*
ALGHJ	Arbeiten zur Literatur und Geschichte des hellenistischen Judentums
ANRW	*Aufstieg und Niedergang der römischen Welt*
Ant.	Josephus, *Antiquitates Judaicae*
Apoc. Bar.	*Apocalypse of Baruch*
Apol.	Jerome, *Apologia contra Rufinum*
ʿArak.	*ʿArakin*
b.	*Babylonian Talmud,* followed by name of tractate
BASOR	*Bulletin of the American Schools of Oriental Research*
Ber.	*Berakot*
BJS	Brown Judaic Studies
B. Meṣ.	*Baba Meṣiʿa*
B. Qam.	*Baba Qamma*
Cant. Rab.	*Canticles Rabbah*
CBQ	*Catholic Biblical Quarterly*
CBQMS	Catholic Biblical Quarterly Monograph Series
CD	Cairo Geniza text of the Damascus Document
Cher.	Philo, *De cherubim*
Cont.	Philo, *De vita contemplativa*

CRINT	Compendia rerum iudaicarum ad novum testamentum
CSCO	Corpus scriptorum christianorum orientalium
De Or.	Cicero, *De oratore*
Dec.	Philo, *De decalogo*
Deut. Rab.	*Deuteronomy Rabbah*
DJD	Discoveries in the Judean Desert
ʿEd.	*ʿEduyyot*
EncJud.	*Encyclopaedia Judaica* (1971)
ʿErub.	*ʿErubin*
Exod. Rab	*Exodus Rabbah*
F	Page reference in L. Finkelstein's edition of the *Sifre*
Frg. Tg.	*Fragmentary Targum*
GCS	Griechischen christlichen Schriftsteller
Gen. Rab.	*Genesis Rabbah*
Giṭ.	*Giṭṭin*
Ḥag.	*Ḥagiga*
Hilk.	*Hilkot*
Hist. Eccl.	Eusebius, *Historia ecclesiastica*
Homil. in Exod.	Origen, *Homiliae in Exodum*
Hor.	*Horayot*
HTR	*Harvard Theological Review*
HUCA	*Hebrew Union College Annual*
J. W.	Josephus, *Jewish War*
JBL	*Journal of Biblical Literature*
JJS	*Journal of Jewish Studies*
JQR	*Jewish Quarterly Review*
Jub.	*Jubilees*
Ketub.	*Ketubot*
Lam. Rab.	*Lamentations Rabbah*
LCL	Loeb Classical Library
Leg.	Philo, *De legatione ad Gaium*
Leg. All.	Philo, *Legum allegoriarum*
Lev. Rab.	*Leviticus Rabbah*
LXX	Septuagint
m.	*Mishnah,* followed by name of tractate
Meg.	*Megilla*
Mek.	*Mekilta*
Midr. Pss.	*Midraš Tehillim (Psalms)*
Midr. Sam.	*Midraš Samuel*

Midr. Tan.	*Midraš Tanna'im*
Mig.	Philo, *De migratione Abrahami*
Mos.	Philo, *De vita Mosis*
Mo'ed Qaṭ	*Mo'ed Qatan*
Ned.	*Nedarim*
NJV	New Jewish (Publication Society) Version
Num. Rab.	*Numbers Rabbah*
Od.	Homer, *Odyssea*
Ohol.	*Oholot*
Op.	Philo, *De opificio mundi*
OTP	*The Old Testament Pseudepigrapha* (ed. Charlesworth)
p.	*Palestinian Talmud,* followed by name of tractate
PAAJR	*Proceedings of the American Academy for Jewish Research*
Pesaḥ.	*Pesaḥim*
Pesiq. R.	*Pesiqta Rabbati*
Pesiq. Rab Kah.	*Pesiqta de Rab Kahana*
PG	*Patrologia graeca,* ed. J. Migne
Pirqe R. El.	*Pirqe de Rabbi Eliezer*
PO	Patrologia orientalis
Praep. evang.	Eusebius, *Praeparatio evangelica*
Pss. Sol.	*Psalms of Solomon*
Q	Qumran sigla:
1QDM (= 1Q22)	*Dibre Mosheh* from Qumran Cave 1
1QpHab	*Pešer on Habakkuk* from Qumran Cave 1
1QS	*Serek hyyaḥad (Rule of the Community, Manual of Discipline)* from Qumran Cave 1
1QSa	Appendix A *(Rule of the Congregation)* to 1QS
1Q34bis	Liturgical Prayers from Qumran Cave 1
4Q159	Ordinances from Qumran Cave 4
4QEna	First copy of Aramaic fragments of Enoch from Qumran Cave 4
4QEnc	Third copy of Aramaic fragments of Enoch from Qumran Cave 4
4QFlor	*Florilegium* from Qumran Cave 4
4QpIsad	Fourth copy of *Pešer on Isaiah* from Qumran Cave 4
4QTest	*Testimonia* text from Qumran Cave 4
11QTemp	*Temple Scroll* from Qumran Cave 11

Qidd.	*Qiddušin*
Qoh. Rab.	*Qohelet Rabbah*
Quis Her.	Philo, *Quis rerum divinarum heres sit*
Quod. Omn. Prob.	Philo, *Quod omnis probus liber sit*
R.	Rabbi
RAC	*Reallexikon für Antike und Christentum*
RB	*Revue Biblique*
RevQ	*Revue de Qumran*
Roš. Haš.	*Roš Haššana*
RSV	Revised Standard Version
Ruth Rab.	*Ruth Rabbah*
S. ᶜOlam Rab.	*Seder ᶜOlam Rabbah*
Šabb.	*Šabbat*
Sanh.	*Sanhedrin*
SBLMS	Society of Biblical Literature Monograph Series
Schol. in Cant.	Origen, *Scholia in Canticum conticorum*
Šebu.	*Šebuᶜot*
Sed. ʾEl. Rab.	*Seder ʾEliahu Rabba*
Sed. ʾEl. Zuṭ.	*Seder ʾEliahu Zuṭaʾ*
Šeqal.	*Šeqalim*
SJLA	Studies in Judaism in Late Antiquity
Somn.	Philo, *De somniis*
Spec. Leg.	Philo, *De specialibus legibus*
Sukk.	*Sukka*
Sib. Or.	*Sibylline Oracles*
t.	*Tosephta,* followed by name of tractate
T. Moses	*Testament of Moses*
T. Naph.	*Testament of Naphtali*
Tanḥ.	*Tanḥumaʾ*
Taᶜan.	*Taᶜanit*
TDNT	*Theological Dictionary of the New Testament*
Tem.	*Temura*
Tg.	*Targum*
Tg. Ket.	*Targum of the Writings*
Tg. Neb.	*Targum of the Prophets*
Tg. Neof.	*Targum Neofiti*
Tg. Onq.	*Targum Onqelos*
Tg. Ps.-Jon.	*Targum Pseudo-Jonathan*
TRE	*Theologische Realenzyklopädie*
VC	*Vigiliae christianae*
Virt.	Philo, *De virtutibus*

Vit. Ad.	*Vitae Adae et Evae*
VT	*Vetus Testamentum*
ZAW	*Zeitschrift für die alttestamentliche Wissenschaft*
Zebaḥ.	*Zebaḥim*
ZNW	*Zeitschrift für die neutestamentliche Wissenschaft*
Zuṭ.	*Zuṭaʾ*

Notes

1. Introduction: The Turn to Commentary

1. On the occurence of the expressions *siprê* and *siprê dĕbê rab*, meaning in Aramaic respectively "books" and "books of the school," in the Babylonian Talmud and subsequent rabbinic literature, and their relation ot *our Sifre*, see my earlier study, "Sifre Deuteronomy 26 (ad Deut. 3:23): How Conscious the Composition?" *HUCA* 54 (1983): 297-98. The plural terms *siprê* and *siprê dĕbê rab* have come to refer to *two* collections of rabbinic commentary, one to the biblical Book of Numbers and one to the Book of Deuteronomy, which, while customarily copied, printed, and commented upon together, are two distinct, but not unrelated, collections. Because the present study attends only to *Sifre Deuteronomy*, the shorter title *Sifre* will be employed to refer to it alone.

2. In this regard, readers may wish to compare my approach with that of Jacob Neusner, *Sifre to Deuteronomy: An Introduction to the Rhetorical, Logical, and Topical Program*, BJS 124 (Atlanta: Scholars Press, 1987). Neusner tends to discount the commentary aspects of the *Sifre*'s composition in favor of what he considers tobe its "propositional" character. For my views of Neusner's reductive treatment of rabbinic midrash collections as coherent wholes, see my review essay, "Interpreting Midrash 1: Midrash and the History of Judaism," *Prooftexts* 7 (1987): 179–94. The rationale for my choice of *Sifre* texts upon which to focus will be spelled out later.

3. *Webster's Ninth New Collegiate Dictionary*, p. 264. Compare Roland Barthes's characterization of commentary as "the gradual analysis of a single text." *S/Z*, trans. Richard Miller (New York: Hill and Wang, 1974), p. 12.

4. For this term see Geza Vermes, *Scripture and Tradition in Judaism*, rev. ed. (Leiden: E. J. Brill, 1973), pp. 228-29. For an excellent discussion, see Philip S. Alexander, "Retelling the Old Testament," in *It is Written: Scripture Citing Scripture. Essays in Honor of Barnabas Lindars,* ed. D. A. Carson and H. G. M. Williamson (Cambridge: Cambridge University Press, 1988), pp. 99-121. Alexander defines this rubric so as to include only extended narrative retellings, whereas I would include legal retellings as well. For examples, see the following note.

5. A work such as *Jubilees* in its narrative section retells the biblical story, whereas in its legal section (49–50) it both retells and reorganizes (by topical association) biblical laws. The same may be said of Josephus' *Jewish Antiquities*. For other examples of these categories, see my discussion in

"Sifre Deuteronomy 26," pp. 253-55 with notes; and my review essay, "Interpreting Midrash 2: Midrash and Its Literary Contexts," *Prooftexts* 7 (1987): 288.

6. Because the relation of such texts to what we call Scripture is not stated, it is not clear whether they were intended to supplement or supplant the biblical texts upon which they appear to be exegetically based. This is a discussion, e.g., the relation of the Qumran *Temple Scroll* to the Torah, into which we cannot enter here. But note in particular the *Book of Jubilees* (e.g., 1:1-6; 2:1) which claims to have been dictated to Moses at Mt. Sinai during the same forty days when he was receiving the Torah (the "book of the first law" of *Jub.* 6:22) so as to supplement it. Compare the twofold Sinaitic revelation referred to in *4 Ezra* 14:4-6, 23-26, 44-47: twenty-four public books for everyone (what we call Scripture) and seventy secret books for the wise and worthy alone (what we call Pseudepigrapha).

7. Note, for example, the reports of Jesus' preaching at the synagogues at Nazareth (Luke 4:16-28) and Capernaum (John 6:59), and Paul's at Antioch of Pisidia (Acts 13:16-41). Similarly, see Stephen's speech in Acts 7, delivered before the "council." Curiously, the only evidence for orally delivered, continuous commentary in the synagogues comes from Philo of Alexandria. In his *Hypothetica* (cited by Eusebius in *Praep. evang.* 8.8.12-13), he states: "But some priest who is present or one of the elders reads the holy laws to them and expounds them point by point till about the late afternoon, when they depart having gained both expert knowledge of the holy laws and considerable advance in piety" (translation from LCL, 9:433). This indeed sounds like a verse-by-verse commentary, reading and explaining or paraphrasing each textual unit (presumably short) in turn. Philo may be referring to the same custom, but is less explicit, in describing the Essenes in their synagogues (*Quod. Omn. Prob.* 82): "Then one takes the books and reads aloud and another of especial proficiency comes forward and expounds what is not understood. For most of their philosophical study takes the form of allegory, and in this they emulate the tradition of the past" (LCL, 9:58-59). Here it would appear that the explication is not of every verse. Similarly, according to *Somn.* 2.127, only the "obscure points" are expounded. Even more unclear (continuous commentary or select homilies?) is *Spec. Leg.* 2.62: "while one of special experience rises and sets forth what is the best and sure to be profitable and will make the whole of life grow to something better" (LCL, 7:347). A similarly discursive homily may be described by Philo in *Cont.* 75-78, with respect to the Therapeutae. For the synagogues as places of learning, especially on the Sabbath, see also *Mos.* 2.215-16, *Leg.* 156, 157, 312. Philo may be speaking in these different passages of three different practices: continuous commentary, explanations of difficult words or passages, and homilies on selected passages or motifs. He presumably is describing the practices with which he was familiar in the Alexandrian synagogues; we should not presume that the same held true in Palestine (or elsewhere), especially as we have no similar evidence from there. This preponderance of evidence from Philo will become even more significant when we consider that

his extensive biblical commentaries, constituting somewhat less than half of his oeuvre (see note 10), are the closest and most extensive antecedents to later rabbinic commentaries such as the *Sifre*, notwithstanding their significant differences. However, also note that only about half of Philo's treatises take the commentary form; many of his homilies on biblical themes (e.g., *On the Creation*) or persons (e.g., *On Abraham*) are extended exegetical essays. With regard to the relative lack of Palestinian evidence for the practice of scriptural commentary per se, Josephus' statement (*Ag. Ap.* 2.17 §175) that the Jews assembled once a week "to listen to the Law and to obtain a thorough and accurate knowledge of it," it seems to me, is wholly ambiguous in this regard. So is *Ant.* 16.2.4 §43 and the New Testament references to scriptural reading in the synagogues on the Sabbath: Luke 4:16-21; Acts 13:13-16, 27; 15:21. On the similar lack of evidence for public *targum* (Aramaic translation) of Scripture in the synagogues in *prerabbinic* times (which could be understood as a sort of responsive proto-commentary), see my forthcoming book, *Targum and Torah: Early Rabbinic Views of Scriptural Translation in a Multilingual Setting.*

8. A similar distinction is drawn in the study of Hellenistic Greek literature between running commentaries (*hypomnēmata*) to a text and treatises (*syggramata*) on a topic. A further distinction is drawn between commentaries and exegeses (*exēgeisthai*), the latter being discrete interpretations of particular passages, which could be included either in commentaries or treatises. See the literature cited in note 24 in relation to Philo, for whose writings these distinctions are especially important. For an early Christian attempt to distinguish between commentary and preaching (the former explains words, whereas the latter reflects upon them, prolixity being more appropriate to the latter) see Theodore of Mopsuestia (ca. 350-428) (who rejected the methods of Alexandrian allegorical commentary) in the introduction to his *Commentary on John* (ed. J. M. Vosté, CSCO 3 [1940]).

9. Compare Philo's *Life of Moses*, which follows not the scriptural order but a biographical order, even though it is deeply exegetical. In the case of the Gospels, it may also be noted that Matthew, Luke, and John interpret the earlier story of Mark not by "commenting" upon it, but by rewriting, or what Frank Kermode (*The Genesis of Secrecy: On the Interpretation of Narrative* [Cambridge: Harvard University Press, 1979], p. 81) calls *augmenting* it.

10. Thus, of the thirty-six works included in the Loeb Classical Edition, twenty are commentaries (including the *Questions and Answers on Genesis* and *on Exodus* and the eighteen treatises that make up the *Allegorical Commentary*). But these vary greatly to the extent that they are structured in relation to the biblical text.

11. There are fragments of *pěšārîm* to Micah, Zephaniah, Isaiah, and Hosea. For the texts, translations, notes, and overall discussion, see Maurya P. Horgan, *Pesharim: Qumran Interpretation of Biblical Books*, CBQMS 8 (Washington, DC: Catholic Biblical Association of America, 1979). Given the fact that the sectarian Dead Sea Scrolls stress biblical interpretation as a source of the continually revealed Torah rules by which the community lives and is defined

(e.g., 1QS 6.6–8; 8.12–16; CD 6.2–11; 13.2–7; 20.6–7), it is interesting that we have among the scrolls no texts of *continuous* commentary to the legal sections of Scripture. For a comprehensive discussion of the use and interpretation of Scripture in the Dead Sea Scrolls in its many genres, see Michael Fishbane, "Use, Authority and Interpretation of Mikra at Qumran," in *Mikra: Text, Translation, Reading and Interpretation of the Hebrew Bible in Ancient Judaism and Early Christianity,* ed. Martin Jan Mulder, CRINT 2.1 (Assen/Maastricht: Van Gorcum and Philadelphia: Fortress, 1988), pp. 339-77.

12. 1QpHab 7.1-5. Here and in what follows, the translation of *pěšārîm* are from M. Horgan, *Pesharim.* Compare 1QpHab 2:8-10: "the priest, into [whose heart] God put [understanding] to interpret (*lipšôr*) all the words of his servants the prophets by [whose] hand God enumerated all that is going to come upon his people and up[on] his congregation."

13. It should be noted that *pěšer* terminology and interpretation can be found in noncommentary contexts as well, as in CD 4.14-15 and 4QF1 1.14, 19, but this is not our concern here. For the distinction between "continuous pesher" and "thematic pesher," only the former being commentaries in the sense employed here, see M. Horgan, *Pesharim,* p. 3. Similarly, note the atomistic commentaries to Num. 21:18 in CD 6.3-11; Amos 5:26-27 and Num. 24:17 in CD 7.9-8.2; and Ezek. 44:15 in CD 3.20-4.5. However, these do not employ the term *pěšer,* but rather demonstrative pronouns to link the parts of the verse with its signification. On the use of such demonstrative linking terminology, see note 16.

14. Assuming the Teacher of Righteousness was a historical figure, whatever his identity, there is no way to tell whether he in fact composed the *pěšārîm,* or whether they—actually, the interpretations that they contain—have been pseudepigraphically ascribed to him. The extant *pěšārîm* exist in single copies dating from the late first century B.C.E., even though they are thought to refer to events and persons (including the Teacher, as we shall next see) of the mid-second century B.C.E. How much older these commentaries are than the time of their extant copies is a matter of debate and probably speculation.

15. The clearest biblical models would be the portrayals of inspired interpretation by Joseph and Daniel. For more detailed discussion, see in particular Michael Fishbane, "The Qumran Pesher and Traits of Ancient Hermeneutics," in *Proceedings of the Sixth World Congress of Jewish Studies,* vol. 1 (Jerusalem: World Union of Jewish Studies, 1977), pp. 97-114; Lou H. Silberman, "Unriddling the Riddle: A Study in the Structure and Language of the Habakkuk Pesher (1QpHab)," *RevQ* 3 (1961): 323-64; M. Horgan, *Pesharim,* pp. 252-59 (with further bibliography). For a list of the more common hermeneutical methods employed by the *pěšārîm,* most of which involve manipulation of details of language in the lemma (e.g., word-play, substitution of synonyms, etc.), as is common in dream and oracle decoding, see M. Horgan, *Pesharim,* pp. 244-47, where examples are provided.

16. Here again, the declarative linking terminology between lemma and what it signifies can be compared to that employed in the interpretation of dreams,

visions, and oracles. On such usage in Jewish and Christian apocalyptic genres, see Martha Himmelfarb, *Tours of Hell: An Apocalyptic Form in Jewish and Christian Literature* (Philadelphia: University of Pennsylvania Press, 1983), pp. 45-67. Michael Fishbane (*Biblical Interpretation in Ancient Israel* [Oxford: Clarendon Press, 1985], pp. 44-55) uses the term *deictic* for such terminology (e.g., *zeh*) when used by scribal glossators to Scripture. I will use this term later to denote declarative language that points from scriptural words to their succinctly decoded meanings: "this is," "this means," "this teaches." This sort of procedure of direct correspondence also characterizes most ancient Near Eastern commentaries, on which see J. Krecher, "Kommentare," in *Reallexikon der Assyriologie und vorderasiatischen Archaeologie* 6, nos. 3-4 (1981): 188-91.

17. That the sect's self-understanding was connected to their obligatory, collective practice of scriptural study (especially of the prophetic writings) can be seen in the following passage (1QS 8.13-16): " They shall separate themselves fromt the settlement of the men of iniquity and shall go into the wilderness to prepare there the true way, as it is written, 'In the wilderness prepare a way. . . make level in the desert a highway for our God' (Isa. 40:3). This refers to the study (*midrāš*) of Torah [that] He commanded through Moses, that they should do according to all that has been revealed from time to time and according to what the prophets revealed by His holy spirit." For the importance of study activity, which sometimes borders on liturgy, see also 1QS 6.6-8; 1QSa 1.6-8; CD 3.12-16; 6:2-5.

18. Compare the *Damascus Document* (CD 1.1-2.2) that begins with a narrative rendition of the sect's proto-history: God's raising of the sect and the Teacher of Righteousness and His rejection of the rest of Israel. The passage draws heavily upon scriptural language, mainly prophetic, without explicitly citing any scriptural verses. Here we might compare the citation of the Prophets in the Gospel of Matthew, which similarly understands recent history as the fulfillment of prophetic utterances: "All this took place to fulfill what the Lord had spoken by the prophet" (1:22); "Then was fulfilled what was spoken by the prophet Jeremiah"(2:17); etc. In these, story takes precedence over Scripture as an organizing principle, even while heavily dependent upon it.

19. At most, the *pěšārîm* may refer back to the preceding lemma or anticipate the following lemma. For examples see Horgan, *Pesharim*, pp. 245-46 note 70.

20. For examples, see in particular, CD 7.9-8.2; 4QFlorilegium; and 4QTestionia.

21. For discussions of multiple interpretations in the *pěšārîm*, with examples, see Bilha Nitzan, *Pesher Habakkuk: A Scroll from the Wilderness of Judaea (1QpHab)* (Jerusalem: Bialik Institute, 1986), pp. 46-51, 70, 95-97, 166-67 [Hebrew]; Herbert Basser, "Pesher Hadavar: The Truth of the Matter," *RevQ* 13 (1988): 389-406. However, the examples there given are ones in which a *single* interpretation of a lemma may depend on multiple (usually two) meanings or readings of one of the words of that lemma for its parts. These are not multiple interpretations in the sense of explicitly *alternative* interpretations, such as are found with so much more frequency, as we shall soon see, in

the commentaries of Philo and the early rabbinic midrashic collections.

22. For a discussion of the extent to which this comparison has been overdrawn, see M. Horgan, *Pesharim*, pp. 250-52 (with bibliography in the notes). See also David Stern, "Midrash and Indeterminacy," *Critical Inquiry* 15 (1988): 142-43.

23. Philo's *Allegorical Commentary* covers in detail about a third of the Book of Genisis (Chapters 1-17), whereas his *Questions and Answers* cover large parts of Genesis and Exodus. Whether more once existed, whether Philo had intended to complete more but never did, or whether he considered only these parts of the Pentateuch to suit, for his purposes, the allegorical commentary format, is impossible to know.

24. This is not the place to consider in any detail such antecedent and contemporary commentaries to the Greek literary "canon," with which we may presume Philo to have been familiar. These commentaries were of two types. The first were those produced by the Alexandrian "grammarians," centered in the Museum and Library. Unfortunately, the actual forms of such commentaries are impossible to reconstruct because they are preserved only as excerpted and reworked fragments in later collections of textual scholia. It appears, however, that the purpose of such commentaries, unlike those of Philo, was to establish "correct" texts, elucidate their language, and explicate their more obscure details, all to justify and strengthen their place as "fitting" constituents of the hellenic canon. For introductions to this Alexandrean tradition of philological and text-critical commentary, see Rudolf Pfeiffer, *History of Classical Scholarship from the Beginnings to the End of the Hellenistic Age* (Oxford: Clarendon, 1968), pp. 221-233, 275-76; Leonard Whibley, ed., *A Companion to Greek Studies* 4th ed. (Cambridge: Cambridge University Press, 1931), §§136, 201, 202; John White, ed., *The Scolia on the Aves of Aristophanes* (Boston and London: Ginn and Co., 1914), pp. ix-lvi. Closer to Philo's style and purpose of commentary, and presumably more influential, were the dialectical and allegorical commentaries produced by the philosophic movements (e.g., Stoic and Middle Platonic). Once again, extant examples of these are very limited. Such commentaries, it appears, sought to locate the particular ideas of the author's "school" in what were considered the originary texts of hellenic culture (e.g., Homer) or in the works of his philosophical forebears (e.g., Plato, Chrysippus) by uncovering in them, through a dialogical sequence of "questions and solutions," an allegorical "second sense." Two commonly cited examples are the Stoic (Pseudo-) Heraclitus' *Homeric Allegories* (first century C.E.; see Héraclite, *Allégories d'Homère*, ed. and trans. Félix Buffière [Paris: Société d'édition "Les belles lettres," 1962]) and an anonymous commentary to Plato's Theaetetus (H. Diels and W. Schubart, *Anonymer Kommentar zu Platons Theaetet (Papyrus 9782)* [Berlin: 1905]). For English translations of extracts of the last, which is roughly contemporaneous with Philo and shares many structural characteristics, including multiple interpretations, see David T. Runia, "Further Observations on the Structure of Philo's Allegorical Treatises,"*VC* 41 (1987): 131-133. Also noteworthy is Porphyry's commentary to Homer's description

of the cave of the nymphs (*Od.* 13.102-112) in his *De antro nympharum*, but this is not, strictly speaking, a running commentary. For discussion of such philosophical commentaries in relation to Philo, see Runia, ibid., pp. 114-117; idem, *Philo of Alexandria and the Timaeus of Plato* (Leiden: E. J. Brill, 1986), pp. 502-505; John Dillon, "The Formal Structure of Philo's Allegorical Exegesis," in David Winston and John Dillon, *Two Treatises of Philo of Alexandria: A Commentary on De Gigantibus and Quod Deus Sit Immutabilis,* BJS 25 (Chico, Calif.: Scholars Press, 1983), pp. 77-87; Heinrich Dörrie, "Zur Methodik antiker Exegese," *ZNW* 65 (1974): 121-38; Thomas H. Tobin, *The Creation of Man: Philo and the History of Interpretation,* CBQMS 14 (Washington, D.C.: Catholic Biblical Association, 1983), pp. 174-75. See also Pierre Hadot, "Théologie, exégese, révélation, écriture, dans la philosophie Grecque," in *Les règles de l'interpretation,* ed. Michel Tardieu (Paris: Cerf, 1987), pp. 13-34. Both types of commentary, philological and philosophical, are generally presumed to have served internally directed pedagogic purposes, that is, the training (in a broad sense) of disciples. On the possible oral, pedagogical backdrop to philosophical commentaries to Plato, see Pierre Boyancé, "Études philoniennes," *Revue des* Études *Grecques* 76 (1983): 80-81, who cites in particular, Cicero, *De or.* 1.47. For useful discussion of Greek philological and philosophical commentary as possible Alexandrian backdrops to the commentaries of Philo, who in any case *adapted* the forms and methods of non-Jewish commentary, especially philosophical, to his own purposes of scriptural interpretation, see John David Dawson, "Ancient Alexandrian Interpretation of Scripture" (Ph.D. dissertation, Yale University, 1988), pp. 11-67. It should also be noted that although Philo was preceded by several important Jewish writers in Alexandria, and although he speaks of having inherited Jewish traditions of interpretation (without naming his authorities), we have no evidence that his antecedents wrote running biblical commentaries per se that he might have taken as models. The only possible exception is Aristobulus (second century B.C.E.), who, according to Church Fathers (Clement of Alexandria and Eusebius) who cite his work, produced a work on the Pentateuch. However, from the cited fragments of Aristobulus it is not clear that his biblical exegesis took the form of a running commentary, more likely having been a paraphrastic retelling. On Aristobulus, see Nicolaus Walter, *Der Thorausleger Aristobulos: Untersuchungen zu seinen Fragmenten und zu pseudepigraphischen Resten der jüdisch hellenistischen Literatur* (Berlin: Akademie-Verlag, 1964). A recurring question in Philonic Scholarship is to what extent Philo should be viewed in relation to a much longer and broader context of Alexandrian Jewish scriptural study and interpretation. For the view that Philo followed and heavily drew upon a long chain of antecedent Alexandrian Jewish exegesis, see Thomas H. Tobin, *The Creation of Man: Philo and the History of Interpretation.* For and overview of the question of Philo's exegetical relation to his Alexandrean setting, both Jewish and non-Jewish, see Burton L. Mack, "Philo Judaeus and Exegetical Traditions in Alexandria," *ANRW* II 21, no. 1 (1984), pp. 227-71. See also note 29.

25. On the method of *quaestio et solutio*, or *aporiai kai luseis*, see Heinrich Dörrie, "Erotapokriseis A (Nichtchristlich)," *RAC* 6 (1966): 342-347. Often cited for comparison is Porphyry's question and answer commentaries to Homer, which some have suggested served pedagogic purposes. See Hermann Ludwig Schrader, ed., *Porphyril Quaestionum Homericarum ad Iliadem Pertinentium Religuias* (Leipzig: B. G. Teubner, 1890-92). On Philo's use of this form, see Peder Borgen and Roald Skarsten, "Quaestiones et Solutiones: Some Observations on the Form of Philo's Exegegsis," *Studia Philonica* 4 (1976-77): 1-15. On the question and answer form as the "mother-cell" of Philo's allegorical commentaries, see Valentin Nikiprowetzky, "L'Exégèse de Philon d'Alexandrie dans le *De Gigantibus* et le *Quod Deus sit Immutabilis*," in David Winston and John Dillon, *Two Treatises of Philo of Alexandris*, pp. 5-75. The emerging consensus is that Philo's *Questions and Answers* were an earlier, more concise form of commentary, which were subsequently "fleshed-out" in the fuller *Allegorical Commentary*. Eusebius (*Hist. Eccl.* 2.18.1) understands Philo first to have written the "Allegories of the Sacred law" (*Leg. All.* 1-3), then the "Problems and Solutions in Genesis and in Exodus," and finally other allegorical treatises. It is often said (see David T. Runia, "The Structure of Philo's Allegorical Treatises: A Review of Two Recent Studies and Some Additional Comments," *VC* 38 [1984]: 230; idem, "Further Observations on the Structure of Philo's Allegorical Treatises,"*VC* 41 [1987]: 107, 112) that the question and answer format derives from the manner of biblical explication in the synagogues of Philo's time, but, so far as I can tell, there is no evidence for this. See above, notes 7 and 42. Philo's heavy use of dialogical rhetoric probably represents Platonic influence. Note that two of his nonexegetical treatises (*On Providence* and *Alexander*, or *Whether Animals Have Reason*) are in dialogue form.

26. This is especially true in the early (so-called tannaitic) commentaries to legal Scriptures, in which this dialogical device plays a more formulaic role than in the nonlegal commentaries, where its use is frequent but less regularized. On the relation of early rabbinic scriptural commentary to the non-Jewish Greco-Roman forms of commentary, especially philosophical, which it is likely to have *adapted* to its own ideology and social purposes, see note 43.

27. This structural aspect of Philo's commentaries is especially stressed in the two articles by David Runia, cited in note 25.

28. On the *pĕšārîm* in this regard, see notes 19 and 20. The comparison to early rabbinic commentary needs to be qualified somewhat. The earlier rabbinic commentaries (such as the *Sifre*) cite other verses of Scripture more frequently than does Philo, but they do not usually digress as far as does Philo in interpreting them. Whereas Philo draws his secondary verses from the Pentateuch alone, the early rabbinic commentaries draw theirs as well from the Prophets and Writings with fairly equal frequency.

29. An example will be given later. For another good example, see *Cher.* 21-30. Note *Mos.* 1.4 (LCL 6.278-79), where in introducing his telling of the life of Moses, Philo makes the following remarkable statement: "[I will] tell the story of Moses as I have learned it, both from the sacred books, the wonderful

monuments of his wisdom which he has left behind him, and from some of the elders of the nation (*tou ethnous presbyteroi*); for I always interwove what I was told with what I read, and thus believed myself to have a closer knowledge than others of his life's history." It has always been a crux of Philonic scholarship to identify the unnamed authorities whose interpretations he so frequently cites. See David M. Hay, "Philo's references to Other Allegorists," *Studia Philonica* 6 (1979-80): 41-75; Thomas H. Tobin, *The Creation of Man; Philo and the History of Interpretation;* and note 24 (end). It is possible of course that in at least some instances Philo invents these anonymous authorities so as to put into their mouths interpretations that are simply foils to his own. For this view see John Dillon, "The Formal Structure of Philo's Allegorical Exegesis," pp. 83-84; idem, *The Middle Platonistis: A Study of Platonism, 80 B.C.-A.D. 200* (London: Duckworth, 1977), p. 143; with which compare David T. Runia, *Philo of Alexandria and the Timaeus of Plato,* p. 505. Cf. Jerome's advice to scriptural commentators, cited in note 66.

30. David T. Runia ("The Structure of Philo's Allegorical Teatises," pp. 237-38) stresses Philo's exegetical "modesty" with regard to the open and provisional quality of his proffered interpretations, sometimes qualifying them with "perhaps" (*mēpote*). But Philo is not adverse to claiming for his "highest" interpretations divine inspiration, even as he is uncertain whether his words can properly express them. See *Cher.* 27. On the relation of Philo's multiple readings of Scripture to the Stoic views of language that underlie his exegetical practices, see John David Dawson, "Ancient Alexandrian Interpretation of Scripture," pp. 40-53.

31. For a similar contrast see David Stern, "Midrash and Indeterminacy," pp. 143-44. Because Philo's privileging of the allegorical over the literal levels of meaning is not as absolute as among his Stoic and Middle Platonic antecedents and contemporaries (see Thomas H. Tobin, *The Creation of Man,* pp. 154-72), and because his ranking of multiple nonliteral interpretation is not as pronounced or consistent as in later Christian allegorical exegesis (beginning already with Origen, on whom see note 43), the structural similarities between Philo and the early rabbinic commentaries are historically more significant, notwithstanding their equally significant hermeneutical differences, it seems to me, than Stern allows. On Philo's practice of adducing multiple, ungraded "literal" senses, see Jean Pépin, "Remarques sur la théorie de l'exégèse allégorique chez Philon," in *Philon d'Alexandrie,* ed. Roger Arnaldez et al., Colloques nationaux du Centre national de la Recherche Scientifique (Paris: Éditions du Centre National de la Recherche Scientifique, 1967), pp. 155-61. On Philo's transitional place between Greek philosophical allegorization and the later more temporally progressive (and hence hierarchical) allegorization of Christian Church Fathers, see Pépin, *Mythe et allégorie: les origenes grecques et les contestations judéo-chrétiennes,* rev. ed. (Paris: Études Augustinennes, 1976), pp. 231-42; Jon Whitman, *Allegory: The Dynamics of an Ancient and Meideval Technique* (Cambridge: Harvard University Press, 1987), pp. 58-68.

32. It has the additional advantage of having a parallel in Philo's *Questions and*

Answers on Genesis 3.11. Although Philo provides there essentially the same interpretation as in his *Allegorical Commentary*, he arrives at his conclusion more directly and immediately without citing another verse, without dwelling as long on the problematic nature of the first literal meaning of the lemma, and without enchaining a series of interpretations.

33. Philo continues here in the same vein.
34. *Quis Her.* 277-83 (LCL, 4:424-29). Philo's imagery and language, especially with respect to the four physical elements and the ethereal fifth, are familiar from non-Jewish Greek sources (especially Plato and Aristotle), as indicated in the notes to the Loeb edition, p. 575.
35. The expression is from David T. Runia, "The Structure of Philo's Allegorical Treatises," p. 237.
36. Philo proceeds immediately to the phrase "nourished with peace," again moving from literal-physical understanding of peace to allegorical-spiritual one, from worldly peace to the peace of the soul. Compare Philo's treatment of Gen. 1:26 in *Op.* 69-70, where the soul journeys through the physical elements to the heavenly ether. Then, just as the soul is about to gaze upon God, it is blinded, and Philo suddenly redirects our attention to the literalness of the lemma.
37. An important issue of debate among Philonic scholars is the extent to which Philo has structured the experience of overall spiritual progression, through the fashioning of overarching literary and thematic cohesions, into the larger units of his commentary (a chapter, treatise, or series of treatises), and not only in the sub-units of discrete lemmata and their interpretations. See especially, J. Cazeaux, *La Trame et la chaîne: ou les structures litté*raires et l'exégèse dans cinq des traités de Philon d'Alexandrie, ALGHJ 15 (Leiden: E. J. Brill, 1983); Burton Mack, "Argumentation in Philo's *De Sacrificiis*," forthcoming in a volume on *De Sacrificiis* in *Studies in Hellenistic Judaism.* For well-balanced discussion of this issue, see David T. Runia, "The Structure of Philo's Allegorical Treatises"; idem, "Further Observations on the Structure of Philo's Allegorical Treatises."
38. *Mig.* 89 (LCL, 4:182-83).
39. For a similar assessment of Philo's view of the validity of Scripture's literal level of meaning, even as it provides the opportunity and necessary to move beyond it to the allegorical level, see Thomas H. Tobin, *The Creation of Man: Philo and the History of Interpretation*, pp. 154-61, 178. For a different, more negative view of Philo's regard for the letter of Scripture and observance, see David Winston, "Two Types of Mosaic Prophecy According to Philo," in *Society of Biblical literature 1988 Seminar Papers*, ed. David J. Lull (Atlanta: Scholars Press, 1988), p. 454. Compare my treatment of Philo's negative view of those who would flee society to achieve spiritual perfection: "Ascetical Aspects of Ancient Judaism," in *Jewish Spirituality from the Bible through the Middle Ages*, ed. Arthur Green, vol. 13 of *World Spirituality* (New York: Crossroad Publishing, 1986), pp. 263-66.
40. For a discussion of this language of textual imprint in Philo, see John David Dawson, "Ancient Alexandrian Interpretation of Scripture," pp. 160-65.

41. See above, notes 24 and 25.

42. I have intentionally kept my discussion of Philo's commentaries on the literary level. To what extent these commentaries in their present structures reflect the methods of Jewish teaching and preaching of Scripture in Alexandrian oral settings (especially the synagogue), whether by Philo or by others, is vexedly unclear. On this question contrast the views of Harry Austryn Wolfson, *Philo: Foundations of Religious Philosophy in Judaism, Christianity, and Islam,* 2 vols. (Cambridge: Harvard University Press, 1947), vol. 1, pp. 95-96; Valentin Nikiprowetzky, *Le commentaire de l'Écriture chez Philon d'Alexandrie,* ALGHJ 11 (Leiden: E. J. Brill, 1977), pp. 170-80; Thomas H. Tobin, *The Creation of Man: Philo and the History of Interpretation,* pp. 172-76; and note 25 (end). The old question of whether Philo is primarily a Jew in Greek garb or the reverse is simplistic in its framing of the issue, and in any case irrelevant here. The fact is that Philo chose to effect his ambitious sociocultural translation through commentaries to Scripture and *not* to the writings of Plato (etc.), however much he knew and was influenced by the latter.

43. Space does not permit here a detailed comparison of earliest rabbinic commentary with that practiced, in the same general Greco-Roman milieu, by pagan philologists and philosophers and by Christian Church Fathers. Regarding the former, most comparative studies have focused on specific parallels of exegetical method or terminology, especially with those of the Alexandrian grammarians, and not on the larger *structures* of commentary that are my concern here and that find more suggestive parallels, mutatis mutandis, in the Stoic and Middle Platonic philosophical commentators. See David Daube, "Rabbinic Methods of Interpretation and Hellenistic Rhetoric," *HUCA* 22 (1949): 239-65; idem, "Alexandrian Methods of Interpretation and the Rabbis," *Festschrift H. Lewald* (Basel: Helbring & Lichtenholm, 1953), pp. 27-44; Saul Lieberman, *Hellenism in Jewish Palestine,* 2d ed. (New York: Jewish Theological Seminary of America, 1962), pp. 47-82; E. E. Hallewy, "Biblical Midrash and Homeric Exegesis," *Tarbiz* 31 (1961): 157-69 [Hebrew]. The last draws some attention to the common employment of question and answers as a structure of commentary. Unfortunately, however, the number of *extant* running commentaries from Greco-Roman pagan philosophers is very limited, as noted in note 24, making systematic comparison difficult. The earliest known Christian practitioner of scriptural commentary (as distinct from exegesis more generally) is the Gnostic Heracleon (fl. ca. 145-180), whose commentary to the Gospel of John is cited by Origen, but is not extant in running form. See A. E. Brooke, *The Fragments of Heracleon* (Cambridge: Cambridge University Press, 1891); Elaine H. Pagels, *The Johannine Gospel in Gnostic Exegesis: Heracleon's Commentary on John* (Nashville: Abingdon Press, 1973). It is perhaps not coincidental that the earliest Christians whose scriptural commentaries are actually known to us, Hippolytus of Rome (ca. 170—ca.236) and Origen (185–253) (Clement's biblical commentaries being entirely lost), were trained in Alexandria. Both wrote close in time to the composition of the *Sifre,* with

Origen having lived in proximity to Palestinian rabbinic sages in Caesarea at the time he composed many of his commentaries. Hippolytus' commentaries to Daniel and the Song of Songs survive, but they tend to be a series of expository sermons, in the case of Daniel on select scriptural passages, rather than a running commentary. He is reported to have written many more scriptural commentaries, but they are lost or extant only in fragments. His concise commentary to the Blessing of Moses (Deut. 33) will be cited in the next chapter. The best overview of Hippolytus, especially on the exegetical materials, is still that of Marcel Richard, in *Dictionnaire de spiritualité, ascétique et mystique, doctrine et histoire* 7.1 (1968): 531-71. More recently, see Miroslav Marcovich, "Hippolyt von Rom," *TRE* 15 (1986): 381-87. For Hippolytus as a biblical commentator, see David Satran, "Hippolytus of Rome: The Origins of Christian Biblical Commentary," Chapter 4 of *Nebuchadnezzar Dethroned: The Interpretation of Daniel 4 in Early Jewish and Christian Literature*, Harvard Semitic Monographs (Atlanta: Scholars Press, 1991). It may be said that commentary writing as a powerful expression of Christian theology and self-understanding begins only with Origen, who wrote homilies, scholia, and commentaries on virtually every book of Scripture, although much has been lost and much of what remains is preserved only in later translations. Most significant, for our purposes, is his allegorical commentary to Song of Songs, his only extant continuous commentary to the Hebrew Bible, preserved in four books. Origen's brief comments to Deut. 33:1-3 will be cited in the next chapter. Of particular relevance to this study is the recent book by Karen Jo Torjesen, *Hermeneutical Procedure and Theological Method in Origen's Exegesis*, Patristische Texte und Studien 28 (Berlin: De Gruyter, 1986). Torjesen demonstrates that Origen's employment of the commentary form to enchain interpretations, both in the multiple levels of meaning adduced for a given lemma (from literal to spiritual in three to five steps) and in the commentary's progression from lemma to lemma, are integrally connected to the structure of his Christian logos theology of Scripture. Furthermore, the structured movement of the commentary (both micro and macro), in its repeated progression from letter to spirit, and of the reader (or "hearer") step by step through the interpretations of the commentary, performatively effects a parallel journey of the soul of the reader from purification from sin, to the acquisition of knowledge, to redemption through spiritual perfection. This step-by-step transformation is the result of the reader's progressively having become one with Christ as logos incarnate in Scripture. Although Torjesen does not discuss the commentary models that Origen might have *adapted* to his own sociotheological program, a comparison of her findings with recent discussion of the structures of Philo's commentaries (see above, notes 24, 25, and 37) would prove, it seems to me, very fruitful.

44. It is often stated, on no evidence except the presumption that exegesis evolves from simple to complex, that these two types of interpretations can be chronologically separated, the deictic representing an earlier stratum, the dialogical a later one. On the present literary level, the two types of exegesis

are so integrally connected that their separation into chronologically discernible (literary) strata would be impossible. See Reuben Hammer's introduction to *Sifre: A Tannaitic Commentary on the Book of Deuteronomy* (New Haven: Yale University Press, 1986), p. 4. with notes. I wish to stress that my distinction between deictic and dialogical should not be drawn too sharply, for as I have argued earlier in relation to the *pĕšārîm*, even commentaries that are deictic, to the extent that they structurally differentiate between the lemma and its interpretation, may be said to be dialogical, in that they draw their readers into the shuttle between the two. The difference is simply that in raising the dialogical aspect of all commentary to a more explicit level, what I have termed *dialogical commentary* draws its audience into a more dynamic and open-ended participation in the work of interpretation.

45. See above, notes 26, 28, and 31.

46. I have adapted the heuristic distinction between the constative and performative aspects from Jerome J. McGann, *Social Values and Poetic Acts: The Historical Judgment of Literary Work* (Cambridge: Harvard University Press, 1988), esp. pp. 19-31; and Stanley Fish, *Doing What Comes Naturally: Change, Rhetoric, and the Practice of Theory in Literary and Legal Studies* (Durham: Duke University Press, 1989), pp. 57-67; both of whom refer back to John Searle, "The Logical Status of Fictional Disclosure," in *Expression and Meaning: Studies in the Theory of Speech Acts* (Cambridge: Cambridge University Press, 1979), pp. 58-75; and ultimately to J. L. Austin, *How to Do Things with Words*, 2d ed. (Cambridge: Harvard University Press, 1975). Thus, McGann (p. viii) states: "We need to do more than explain what our texts are saying (or what we think they are saying); we need to understand *what they are doing in saying what they say*." Compare Fredric Jameson's distinction (*The Political Unconscious: Narrative as a Socially Symbolic Act* [Ithaca: Cornell University Press, 1981], p. 108) between what a text "means" and how it "works." Similarly, George Steiner (*After Babel: Aspects of Language and Translation* [Oxford: Oxford University Press, 1985]), p. 82, paraphrasing Humboldt, states: "Language does not convey a preestablished or separately extant content, as a cable conveys telegraphic messages. The content is created in and through the dynamics of statement." The same may be said, I am arguing, of the communicative dynamics of commentary.

47. Thus, the commentary's bridge between Scripture and the present of its sociohistorical context may be conceived of as bearing two-way traffic between the two. See in this regard my comments in "Interpreting Midrash 2," pp. 295-96. Compare Peter Brook's statement ("The Idea of a Psychoanalytic Literary Criticism," *Critical Inquiry* 13 [1987]: 343); "Meaning...is not simply in the text nor wholly the fabrication of a reader (or a community of readers) but comes into being in the dialogical struggle and collaboration of the two, in the activation of textual possibilities in the process of reading." Such "dialogical" notions of textual interpretation are propounded especially by followers of Mikhail Bakhtin, Hans-Georg Gadamer, and certain psychoanalytical approaches to the study of literature. For Bakhtin, see "Discourse

and the Novel," trans. Caryl Emerson and Michael Holquist, in *The Dialogic Imagination*, ed. Michael Holquist (Austin: University of Texas Press, 1981), pp. 259-422. Among his interpreters, see especially Tzvetan Todorov, *Mikhail Bakhtin: The Dialogical Principle*, trans. Wlad Godzich (Minneapolis: University of Minnesota Press, 1984): Katerina Clark and Michael Holquist, *Mikhail Bakhtin* (Cambridge: Harvard University Press, 1984), esp. pp. 9-15, 347-50. Gadamer's chief work in this regard is *Truth and Method*, trans, from the German (*Wahrheit und Method* [Tübingen, 1960]) by G. Barden and J. Cumming (New York: Crossroad Publishing, 1986), to which useful guides are Joel C. Weinsheimer, *Gadamer's Hermeneutics: A Reading of Truth and Method (New Haven: Yale University Press, 1985); and Georgia Warnke, Hermeneutics, Tradition and Reason* (Stanford: Stanford University Press, 1987). For a concise, useful survey of approaches to the dialogics of interpretation from psychoanalytical perspectives (mainly derivative of Freud and Lacan), see Terry Eagleton, *Literary Theory: An Introduction* (Minneapolis: University of Minnesota Press, 1983), pp. 151-93, with a bibliography on pp. 228-29, as well as the essay by Peter Brooks cited earlier. For a fuller treatement see Meredith Anne Skura, *The Literary Use of the Psychoanalytic Process* (New Haven: Yale University Press, 1981). The only attempt, of which I am aware, of applying a psychotherapeutical model of dialogue to midrash is that of Mordechai Rotenberg, *Re-biographing and Deviance; Psychotherapeutic Narrativism and the Midrash* (New York: Praeger Publishers, 1987). For a dialogical view of the relation of a text's rhetoric to its reception by its readers, see Paul Ricoeur, "The World of the Text and the World of the Reader," Chapter 7 of *Time and Narrative*, vol. 3, trans. Kathleen Blamey and David Pellauer (Chicago: University of Chicago Press, 1988), pp. 157-179. Ricoeur builds on Wolfgang Iser, *The Act of Reading: A Theory of Aesthetic Response* (Baltimore: Johns Hopkins University Press, 1979); but even more so on Hans Robert Jauss, *Toward an Aesthetic of Reception,* trans. Timothy Bahti (Minneapolis: University of Minnesota Press, 1982). For the idea that the text's meaning is constructed or enacted in the communicative "working space" between text and reader, see Roger Chartier, *Cultural History: Between Practices and Representations* (Ithaca: Cornell University Press, 1988), pp. 12-14.

48. Neither of these, in reality, is a pure type but is so characterized here to pose heuristically two opposite poles in relation to which I wish to position my own dialogical model. For exemplifications, see my two review essays, "Interpreting Midrash," referred to in notes 2 and 5.

49. See, for example, Jonah Fraenkel, "Hermeneutical Questions in the Study of the Aggadic Narrative," *Tarbiz* 47 (1977-78): 139-172 [Hebrew]: the "historical" text expresses a reality outside itself, whereas the "literary" text (e.g., aggadic tales) expresses itself alone, having no connection to anything outside itself.

50. Despite his qualifications (that rabbinic literature is interested in the broad scheme of history but not in its present particulars), Yosef Hayin Yerushalmi (*Zakhor: Jewish History and Jewish Memory* [Seattle: University of Wash-

ington Press, 1982], pp. 16-26) may be cited as a recent example of this attitude. For convenient entrances to the larger discussion of the possibilities of historical pursuit following the loss of hermeneutical innocence, see David Simpson, "Literary Criticism and the Return to 'History'," *Critical Inquiry* 14 (1988): 721-47; John E. Toews, "Intellectual History after the Linguistic Turn: The Autonomy of Meaning and the Irreducibility of Experience," *American Historical Review* 92 (1987): 879-907; Hayden White, "The Question of Narrative in Contemporary Historical Theory," *History and Theory* 23 (1984): 1-33. For further bibliography, see Chapter 2, note 11.

51. I have in mind here Michel Foucault's challenge, "to restore to discourse its character as an event," in "The Discourse on Language," in *The Archaeology of Knowledge,* trans. A. M. Sheridan Smith (New York: Pantheon Books, 1972), p. 229.

52. This issue will concern us in different ways in each of the following chapters and will be the particular focus of attention in Chapter 4. For a very rough estimate of the frequency of such multiple interpretations, in both the legal and nonlegal sections of the *Sifre,* see Chapter 4, note 1.

53. This is not to deny that these commentaries may incorporate traditions of interpretation from different times and circumstances, editorially combined, even if in several stages, by some unknown redactor(s) to form a running commentary to their prophetic texts. Rather it is to stress that the structural manner of their organization is commensurate with the claim made by and for them that they were prophetically authored, whether directly or indirectly, by the Teacher of Righteousness. See note 14.

54. See note 29.

55. See especially §313 (F355.9-13), to be discussed in Chapter 2, and the texts cited and discussed in Chapter 3, especially §351 (F408.14-17). The oral Torah is nonetheless said to have been revealed at Sinai and even perceived, at least in part, by those standing there.

56. This is a provisional dating; final judgment will have to await my sequel to this book, which will treat in greater detail the relation of the *Sifre*'s legal commentary to the rules of the Mishnah and Tosephta, and to the legal explications of the same in the two Talmuds. At this point, my dating of the *Sifre* is based on the cumulative evidence of four sorts: (1) Its language (as represented by our most dependable manuscript, MS Vatican 32) is clearly that of Mishnaic Hebrew. See Moshe Bar-Asher, "A Preliminary Study of Mishnaic Hebrew as Reflected in Codex Vatican 32 of Sifre Bemidbar," *Te'uda* 3 (1983): 139-164. Based on considerations of its language, the Academy of the Hebrew Language's Historical Dictionary of the Hebrew Language project dates the *Sifre* to a period approximately forty to fifty years after the completion of the Mishnah (ca. 220 C.E.) (2) The sages to whom the *Sifre*'s interpretations are attributed are all of the tannaitic period, the latest being R. Bannaia (ca. 230), suggesting redaction a generation later. (3) Where close parallels exist they are frequently with other so-called tannaitic midrashim (notwithstanding the different ways in which common traditions have been shaped and incorporated). (4) The repeated emphasis on the

appointment of rabbinic sages to positions of judical and administrative authority, it being the prerogative of the Patriarch alone to make such appointments, and the implied acknowledgment of some rabbinic resistance to such centralied appointment authority, fits well within a mid-third century context, especially one close to the patriarchal "house," perhaps among the students of Rabbi Judah the Patriarch. This last point will be argued more fully in Chapter 3. On the question of dating, see my earlier stydy, "Sifre Deuteronomy 26 (ad Deut. 3:23): How Conscious the Composition?" *HUCA* 54 (1983): 297-98; with which may be compared Hammer, *Sifre*, pp. 7-8, and the literature cited there in the notes.

57. Even though the Babylonian Talmud (*b. Sanh.* 86a) later attributes to R. Joḥanan (ca. 250 C.E.) the view that the anonymous legal teachings of the *Sifre* are to be ascribed to R.Simeon (bar Yoḥai, ca. 150), and that they are all predicated on the teachings of R. Akiba (ca. 125), it is not certain whether this refers to our *Sifre* and whether it is not simply an ex post facto ascription. I simply stress here that such an overall attribution is not found within the *Sifre* itself. I shall return to this question in the sequel to this study (see below, note 75).

58. For an attempt to describe the *Sifre* according to a *limited* number of formal structures and correlate those structures with the *Sifre's* topical "program," see Jacob Neusner, *Sifre to Deuteronomy: An Introduction to the Rhetorical, Logical, and Topical Program.* For the view that there is a relation between the anonymity of the narrator and the plural of the "modern" text, see Roland Barthes, *S/Z*, pp. 41, 151. By Barthes's definitions, the *Sifre* hovers somewhere between the "classic" attributed text and the "modern" unattributed one. Compare also Paul Ricoeur's distinction (*Time and Narrative*, vol. 3, pp. 163-64) between the "reliable narrator" and the "unreliable narrator" of modern literature, the latter requiring a "new type of reader: a reader who responds." For the term *mastercode* (or *metanarrative*), compare Fredric Jameson's statement (*The Political Unconscious*, p. 10), "Interpretation is here construed as an essentially allegorical act, which consists in reading a given text in terms of a particular interpretive master code" (similarly, ibid., p. 58). For a "postmodern" critique of the totalizing effects of such metanarratives or codes, and a celebration of the heterogeneity of "petits recits" that they seek to repress, see the writings of Jean-François Lyotard, especially *The Postmodern Condition: A Report on Knowledge*, trans. Geoff Bennington and Brian Massumi (Minneapolis: University of Minnesota Press, 1984); and *Instructions païennes* (Paris: Éditions Galilée, 1977).

59. Compare the more general statement by Frederick Jameson (*The Political Unconscious*, p. 9): "We never really confront a text immediately, in all its freshness as a thing-in-itself. Rather, texts come before us as the always-already-read; we apprehend them through sedimented layers of previous interpretations, or—if the text is brand-new—through the sedimented reading habits and categories developed by those inherited interpretive traditions." Jameson calls for a method of interpretation that he terms *metacommentary,* "according to which our object of study is less the text itself

than the interpretations through which we confront and appropriate it" (ibid., p. 10). In these terms, all rabbinic commentary can be said to be metacommentary, but one in which the layers of tradition, however much sedimented, are never sedentary. As Hans-Georg Gadamer (*Truth and Method*, p. 419) describes the "event" of interpretation: "In as much as the tradition is newly expressed in language, something comes into being that had not existed before and that exists from now on." For the interrelation of transmission and transformation of tradition more generally and in social terms, see John Vansina, *Oral Tradition: A Study in Historical Methodology* (Chicago: University of Chicago, 1961); and Edward Shils, *Tradition* (Chicago: University of Chicago, 1981).

60. See especially Chapter 3. Although the *Sifre*'s commentary in its quality of multiple interpretations is closer to Philo than to *pēšer*, in its primary social orientation it is closer to *pēšer*, than to Philo. If Philo's commentaries seem preoccupied with the transformative journey of the individual soul (which is not to deny the social face of Philo's commentaries), then the Dead Sea *pēšārîm* and the *Sifre*'s commentary are preoccupied with the self-understanding of an elect audience (the sectaries for the former, Israel and the class of rabbinic sages for the latter), and the collective transformation they expect as a consequence of their interpretive and performative engagement with Scripture.

61. See §48 (F109.1-11). This text and similar ones, including those referred to in the following notes, will be treated in greater detail in Chapter 3.

62. See especially § 306 (F336.15-337.3).

63. See for example, §13 (F22.1-5); §34 (F60.8-14).

64. For the first image see §48 (F110.8-12), to be treated in Chapters 3, with which compare §306 (F338.9-13). For the second image see §48 (F110.3-5), again, to be treated in Chapter 3. The image of the digging of wells is employed in the Damascus Document (CD 3.12-16; 6.3-5) to signify the sect's communal study of Torah as a way of revealing God's hidden will, whereas those who have rejected their inspired interpretations are said to have "forsaken the well of living waters" (CD 19.34).

65. For this image of Torah study, compared to the gathering of waters so as later to be able to disperse them in small quantities, see §306 (F336.10-14) and §306 (F338,14-339.3). Similarly, the multiplicity of types of rabbinic Torah discourse (like the multiplicity of types of sages) are all one, which like the rain fructify by dividing into tiny droplets. See §306 (F339.6-14), to be treated in Chapter 3.

66. §48 (F109.13-110.3), to be treated in Chapter 3. Compare *b. Hag.* 3b, where the student confronted with contradictory rabbinic rulings is told to "make your ear like a hopper and acquire a discerning heart." In other words, gather in *all* of rabbinic opinions, even when contradictory, and then apply yourself to understand each and every one and to differentiate between them. On this passage, see most recently David Stern, "Midrash and Indeterminacy," *Critical Inquiry* 15 (1988): 138-41. In the parallel in *t. Hag.* 7:12 it is said: "Make your heart like chambers within chambers and bring into it [that is,

into its innermost parts] both the words of the house of Shammai and the words of the house of Hillel." Compare the task that Jerome (342-420) sets for the commentator, who should "repeat the opinions of the many, and say, 'Some explain this passage in this way, others interpret it in that: these try to support their sense and understanding of it by these proofs and by this reasoning'; so that the judicious reader, when he has persued the different explanations and familiarized himself with many that he can either approve or disapprove, may judge which is the best, and, like a good banker, reject the money from a spurious mint." *Apol.* 1.16, as cited by H. F. D. Sparks, "Jerome as Biblical Scholar," in *The Cambridge History of the Bible*, vol. 1, *From the Beginning to Jerome*, ed. P. R. Ackroyd and C. F. Evans (Cambridge, Mass.: Cambridge University Press, 1970). p. 536.

67. I have adapted the term *circulatory system* from Stephen Greenblatt, "Capitalist Culture and the Circulatory System," in *The Aims of Representation: Subject/Text/History,* ed. Murray Krieger (New York: Columbia University Press, 1987), pp. 157-73, My view of the circulatory interrelation of textual formation and reception may be compared to Paul Ricoeur's dialectic of a text's configuration by its author and refiguration by its readers, in *Time and Narrative*, vol. 3, esp. pp. 157-79. The expression *illocutionary force* is adapted from the vocabulary of speech-act-theory, on which see note 38. The relationship between the practice of commentary and the empowerment of the class of sages in third century Palestine, a time of significant rabbinic expansion and solidification, is explored in greater detail in Chapter 3.

68. On the configuration of the heterogeneity of tradition in relation to that of Israel's past, as well as to that of its relation to the nations, see Chapter 2; in relation to the solidification of the society of the sages, see Chapter 3; in relation to time more generally and to nature, see Chapter 4. For the relation of the heterogeneity of literature to that of its sociohistorical context, see in particular the writings of Mikhail Bakhtin and Jean-François Lyotard, a convenient access to which, in terms of this interrelation, can be obtained through David Carroll, "Narrative, Heterogeneity, and the Question of the Political: Bakhtin and Lyotard," in *The Aims of Representation*, pp. 69-106.

69. This picture presumes a place for the creation, preservation, and use of *written* texts of "Oral Torah" in the content of oral teaching and study. The common assumption that the dictum, "Written teachings are not to be recited from memory; oral teachings are not to be recited from writing" (*b. Giṭ.* 60b), prohibits all use (and hence the existence) of written texts of rabbinic teaching needs to be seriously questioned. Certainly, rabbinic literature knows of such texts of rabbinic teaching and does not object to their use, at least as aids, in study. The problem arises when such texts are *publicly* taught or recited from writing, thereby blurring the distinction between them and Scripture. On this question in relation to the rabbinic countenance of texts of targum, which could not, however, be read from publicly in the synagogue, see my forthcoming book, *Targum and Torah.* For the existence of written aids in the study of the rabbinic oral Torah, see Saul Lieberman, *Hellenism in Jewish Palestine*, pp. 87-88. For recent discussions of the fluid intermixing of written and oral

cultures more generally, see Jack Goody, *The Interface between the Written and the Oral* (Cambridge: Cambridge University Press, 1987); and Ruth Finnegan, *Literacy and Orality: Studies in the Technology of Communication* (Oxford: Blackwell, 1988). Finnegan stresses the performative dimensions of the social enactment of texts, and the orality that therefore suffuses such literarity. For the same issue in relation to ancient Greek poetry, as an orally and publicly enacted literature that collaboratively engages its audience, see Bruno Gentili, *Poetry and Its Public in Ancient Greece: From Homer to the Fifth Century*, trans. A. Thomas Cole (Baltimore: Johns Hopkins University Press, 1988); and Jesper Svenbro, *Phrasikleia: Anthropologie de la lecture en Grèce ancienne*, (Paris: Editions La Découverte, 1988). For another attempt to relate written to oral in the transmission of midrashic tradition, see Avigdor Shinan, "Siprût hāʾaggādâ bên higgûd ʿal peh ûmĕsôret kĕtûbâ," in *Meḥqĕrê yĕrûšālayim bĕpôlqlôr yĕhûdî* 1 (Jerusalem: Magnes Press, 1981): 44-60. My "circulatory" understanding of the textuality of the *Sifre* (and by implication rabbinic literature more generally), requires a rethinking of how we conceive of the "authority," "canonicity," and "integrity" of such texts as "books" in their ancient social setting. See my earlier remarks, in relation to the work of Jacob Neusner, in "Interpreting Midrash 1: Midrash and the History of Judaism," *Prooftexts* 7 (1987): 185-86. I will deal with this issue in greater depth in relation to my treatment of the *Sifre*'s legal commentary in the sequel to this book (see note 75). For the reuse of traditions of early rabbinic ("tannaitic") scriptural commentaries by the redactors of the Talmuds in their dialogical commentary to the Mishnah, see E. Z. Melamed, *Halachic Midrashim of the Tannaim in the Babylonian Talmud* [Hebrew], 2d. ed. (Jerusalem: Magnes Press, 1988); idem, *Pirqê mābôʾ lesiprût hattalmûd* (Jerusalem, 1973), pp. 258-70, 275-94; and Martin S. Jaffee, trans. with and intro., *The Talmud of Babylonia: An American Translation. XXXVI Tractate Horayot*, BJS 90 (Atlanta: Scholars Press, 1987), pp. 30-34.

70. My purpose in approaching the text of commentary in this way is not so much to get behind the extant text to recover the earlier history of its sources, which in most cases is an impossibility, as to understand the character of the text as it exists as an editorially configured composite, which character in turn affects the nature of its reception (my second perspective, to be discussed next). For a fuller description and justification of this method, see my previous study, "Sifre Deuteronomy 26 (ad Deut. 3:23): How Conscious the Composition?" *HUCA* 54 (1983): 245-57. The question of the extent to which these editorial practices unite the text of the *Sifre* as a whole, especially its legal core and narrative frame, and differentiate it from other commentary collections of similar vintage, will be treated in the sequel to this book. See note 75. For previous scholarship on this question see my aforementioned study, pp. 252, 296-98; as well as Abraham Goldberg, "The School of Rabbi Akiba and the School of Rabbi Ishmael in Sifre Deuteronomy Pericopes 1-54" [Hebrew], *Teʿuda* 3 (1983): 9-16.

71. Here I am reminded of Jorge Luis Borges's metaphor for the impossibility of any exact act of translation, that of Pierre Menard's initial thought of

becoming Cervantes so as to be able to translate his *Don Quixote*. See "Pierre Menard, Author of Quixote," in *Labyrinthes: Selected Stories and Other Writings*, ed. Donald A Yates and James E. Irby (New York: New Directions, 1962), p. 40.

72. For a fuller discussion, framed in realation to the historical study of earlier political discourse, see J. G. A. Pockock, *Politics, Language, and Time: Essays on Political Thought and History* (New York: Athenean, 1971), pp. 23-33. Even as I have earlier referred to a single document or major section thereof as constituting a "network" of interassociative significations and representations, I here use similar language to denote the more extensive cultural matrices of meaning with which such a text, both in its creation and in its reception, is historically *and* hermeneutically interconnected. A similar idea is conveyed by Hans Robert Jauss (*Toward Aesthetic of Reception*) in his view of the dialectical interaction of a text's "horizon of expectations" with that of its historically locatable reading community. This is very similar to Hans-Georg Gadamer's view, as articulated in his *Truth and Method*, of the dialogical nature of a text's interpretation by its traditionally prejudiced receivers. Compare as well, James Boyd White, *When Words Lose their Meaning: Constitutions and Reconstitutions of Language, Character, and Community* (Chicago: University of Chicago Press, 1984), esp. pp. 8–10. By contrast, structuralists and post-structuralists often conceive of the weblike quality of texts as being textually *self-contained*. Thus, Roland Barthes variously speaks of a text as a "weaving of voices" or "codes" (*S/Z*, pp. 20-21), as a "musical score" (pp. 28-30), as a "telephone network gone haywire" (p. 132), and as an "interwoven...lace" or "braid" (p. 160). For the image of a text as a "woven fabric," the lines of whose representational figures extend beyond themselves in seemingly countless intertwinings, but still *within* the textual fabric, see J. Hillis Miller, "The Figure in the Carpet," *Poetics Today* 1, no. 3 (1980): 107-18. Miller begins his discussion of Henry James's story of the same title by citing Tolstoy's image of "the labyrinth of linkages" (p. 107).

73. Even as I look beyond an immediate passage, first to other passages in the *Sifre* and only then to rabbinic literature more broadly, to inform my understanding of it, I resist both changing its text (as determined by the best manuscript readings) and interpreting it out of its most immediate discursive context so as to bring it into harmony with its parallels. Thus, I am in pursuit of a middle ground between those who advocate reading each rabbinic document autonomously of the others as a coherent unity and those who advocate reading all rabbinic texts together as an undifferentiated whole.

74. It will be seen that I frequently cite the interpretations of the *Sifre*'s own traditional commentators (twelfth through nineteenth centuries). They have been welcome companions whose interpretations, even when they differ from my own, have sensitized me to how much the *Sifre*'s text both calls for interpretation and is continually open to diverse and even discordant interpretations. The manuscripts and editions wherein these commentators can be found are listed in the bibliography at the end of this book. For a further discussion of the traditional commentaries to the *Sifre*, see Menahem

Kahana, "Commentaries to the Sifre Which Are Concealed in Manuscripts" [Hebrew], in *Seper Zikkaron to Rab Yiṣḥaq Nissim*, ed. Meir Banehu (Jerusalem: Yad Harab Nissim, 1985), vol. 2, pp. 95-118.

75. In a sequel study, provisionally titled, *Rabbinic Law and Biblical Commentary: Legal Discourse in the Midrash Sifre to Deuteronomy*, I shall similarly treat a selection of the *Sifre's* commentaries to legal portions of Deuteronomy. There, in conclusion, I will be able to make broader statements about the collection as a whole and its place within the larger setting of ancient rabbinic culture, but not as a substitute for critically engaging the diverse practices of its local parts.

76. *S/Z*, pp. 11-13. As will be seen, unlike Barthes I have not designed my commentary so as to encompass the text of the *Sifre* according to a prescribed set of ahistorical "codes." For such an attempt, see note 58. Nor do I believe that the *Sifre's* own commentary to Scripture can be so structurally reduced and hermenteutically self-contained. Rather, Barthes's overall justification of the medium of nontotalizing, "step-by-step" commentary of a single "classic" text strikes me as an apt characterization of the practice of the *Sifre's* own commentary to Deuteronomy, and, mutatis mutandis and more modestly, of my own historically critical commentary to sections of the *Sifre*.

2. Re-Presenting Revelation

1. I employ the word *re-present* to mean "to present again or anew" (*Webster's Ninth New Collegiate Dictionary*, p. 1000). This is simply to stress the aspect of creative renewal and transformation, in contrast to simple mimesis, that characterizes commentary's refigurative relation, often subtle, to the texts and traditions with which it works. See also note 10.

2. Also to be considered will be the *Sifre's* commentary to Deut. 32:10. Other parts of the *Sifre* that make briefer reference to the event of revelation will be cited in the notes.

3. The Hebrew literally reads "peoples" (*ʿammîm*) even though it is often rendered by ancient and modern translators as "people," taken to refer to the people of Israel in particular. This is in part because the following expression *kol qĕdōšāyw* (here translated, "their hallowed") has a singular pronominal suffix, presumably meaning "the sanctified of the people." See note 119. This ambiguity and its consequences for the commentary will be discussed later.

4. The translation, with slight modification, is from *The Torah: The Five Books of Moses*, 2d ed. (Philadelphia: Jewish Publication Society of America, 1962), pp. 389-90. The *Sifre's* commentary on the next verse (33:5) will be treated in Chapter 3. Although verse 5 is usually viewed as the concluding verse of the preface to Moses' blessing, the *Sifre's* commentary, as we shall soon see, considers that verse to begin a new section of Moses's "prayer," verses 2-4 constituting an introductory praise of God, followed by Moses petition on Israel's behalf, beginning with verse 5. On the "Blessing of Moses" in general, besides the standard scholarly commentaries, see F. M. Cross and D. N.

Freedman, "The Blessing of Moses," *JBL* 67 (1948): 191-201; T. H. Gaster, "An Ancient Eulogy on Israel," *JBL* 66 (1947): 53-62; I. L. Seeligmann, "A Psalm from Pre-Regal Times," *VT* 14 (1964): 75-92. On 33:2-5 in particular, and the acute difficulties of its translation and interpretation, see P. D. Miller, "A Critical note on Deut. 33:3a *HTR* 57 (1964): 241-43; J. T. Milik, "Deux documents inédits du désert de Judah," *Biblica* 38 (1957): 245-54; B. Margulis, "Gen. 49:10/Deut. 33:2-3," *VT* 19 (1969): 202-210.

5. Of course, many other verses are also woven into the commentary, but these are the ones that are understood to allude directly to the event of revelation itself.

6. At this point in my argument it makes no difference whether we posit a single commentary maker or a series of them, each revising or supplementing the work of his predecessors. On the mediated nature of all interpretation, see Chapter 1, note 59.

7. *I assume that the two Mekiltas* (conventionally associated with the "schools" of R. Ishmael and of R. Simeon bar Yoḥai), notwithstanding their differences from one another and from *Sifre Deuteronomy*, originate from much the same sociohistorical context of third century Palestine. Although Ben Zion Wacholder ("The Date of the Mekilta De-Rabbi Ishmael," *HUCA* 39 [1968]: 117-144) has argued for a significantly later date for the *Mekilta*, his arguments if valid would apply equally to the *Sifre*. However, for a trenchant critique of Wacholder's arguments, see Manahem Kahana, in *Tarbiz* 55 (1986): 515-20. After completing this chapter I received an article by Menahem Kahana ("*Dappîm min hammĕkîltāʾ lidbārîm pārāšôt haʾăzînû wĕzōʾt habbĕrākà,*" *Tarbiz* 57.2 [1988]: 165-201) in which he publishes a fragment of a midrashic commentary that he identifies as the largely lost *Mekilta* to Deuteronomy, which parallels a significant portion of the *Sifre*'s commentary here discussed. As noted later (notes 122, 148, and 227), Kahana's comparisons of that commentary with ours confirms the conclusions that I draw from comparisons with the *Mekilta* to Exodus and other early rabbinic sources. So far as I can tell, the manifold rabbinic traditions relating to the revelation of the Torah at Sinai have not received the critical attention that they deserve, especially considering the centrality of rabbinic conceptions of revelation to rabbinic self-understandings. Where this theme has been the focus of scholarly attention, its localized literacy crystalizations have too often been assimilated to one another in the work of synthetic summarization. The most complete collection of such rabbinic texts, excised and recombined according to the order of the account in the Book of Exodus, is that of S. Y. Agnon, *ʾAttem Rĕʾîtem*, vol. 1 (the only volume completed), *Pārāšat Mattan Tôrâ* (Jerusalem: Schocken Books, 1959). The revelation of the Torah and its related motifs find their fullest scholarly discussion, albeit in a homiletical rather than historical-critical vein, in Abraham Joshua Heschel, *Theology of Ancient Judaism*, 2 vols. (London and New York: Soncino, 1962-65) [Hebrew]. See also Benjamin Oppenheimer, *Maʿămād Har Sînay: Hannĕbûʾâ Ûbĕḥîrat Yiśrāʾel Bĕpôlmôs Ḥazal,*" *Molad* 8 (31), nos. 39-40 (249-50) (1980): 91-110; and Joseph Heinemann, *ʾAggādôt wĕtôlĕdôtêhen* (Jerusalem: Keter,

1974), pp. 117-29. On the theme of Torah more generally in rabbinic literature, see Jacob Neusner, *Torah: From Scroll to Symbol in Formative Judaism*, Part Three of *The Foundations of Judaism: Method, Teleogy, Doctrine* (Philadelphia: Fortress Press, 1985).

8. Under the rubric of "time" I include as well present circumstances. Under this rubric may also be considered the repeated allusions to future-messianic time, which may be regarded as extensions of present-time perspectives (e.g., present suffering pointing toward future-messianic vindication). Issues of temporality, both textual and historical, in the discursive mode of commentary will be addressed more fully in Chapter 4.

9. For Josephus' exegetical retelling of the event of revelation as a continuous narrative, see *Ant.* 3.5.1-8 §§75-101. For other noncommentary narrations, but not as continuous as that of Josephus, see also Pseudo-Philo, *Biblical Antiquities* 11-13; *Dec.* 32-49; *S. ʿOlam Rab.* 5(end)-6; *Pirqe R. El.* 41.

10. These terms are adapted from the writings of Jean-François Lyotard, who opposes them to the repressive "grands récits" or "maître-récits" of more totalizing forms of discourse. See, for example, *Instructions païennes* (Paris: Éditions 1977), pp. 17-19, 23, 31, 32, 34-5, 39, 41; *The Postmodern Condition: A Report on Knowledge*, trans. Geoff Bennington and Brian Massumi (Minneapolis: University of Minnesota Press, 1984), pp. 15, 34, 60, 65-66; *Le Différend* (Paris: Minuit, 1983), p. 228. Whereas the text of Scripture upon which our commentary is based was presumably encountered as a continuous narrative apart from its exegetical atomization, notwithstanding the rough seams that tell of its own editorial formation from fragmentary sources, it is not self-evident that what I have here called *tradition* and *time* can similarly be conceived of as having been encountered as continuous narratives apart from to their fragmentation and re-presentation in discursive contexts such as that of commentary. We simply have no continuous early rabbinic narrations of revelation, or for that matter of rabbinic history, nor evidence that any ever existed. But it should be noted that prior to the advent of printing, Scripture itself would have been encountered primarily as it was *heard* in the synagogue or school, where it would have been engaged not as a continuous narrative but as a broken one, divided into verses that were accompanied by responsive translation or explication. On this see my forthcoming nomograph, *Targum and Torah: Early Rabbinic Views of Scriptural Translation in a Multilingual Setting.* For the expression "network" to denote the interassociative nature of our commentary's significations and representations, see Chapter 1, note 72.

11. The question of the representational dimensions of literary (and historical) texts is one that has been discussed extensively by literary (and increasingly historical) critics and theoreticians. From my introductory comments here it should be evident that I am in disagreement with both of two opposite and equally reductive positions: one that views such texts as representing aspects of the world outside themselves in simply mimetic ways, and the other that views such texts as self-enclosed, self-disclosing "worlds" of historically unbounded signification. A full bibliography on this debate would be an

impossibility here. For the post-structuralist critique of referentiality, the reader might begin with Michael Riffaterre, *Semiotics of Poetry* (Bloomington: Indiana University Press, 1978). Among more recent attempts to join the post-structuralist critique of the representational employment of discourse with the necessity to functionally situate such discourse in sociohistorical context, I have found the following helpful: Stephen J. Greenberg, ed., *Allegory and Representation: Selected Papers from the English Institute 1979-80* (Baltimore and London: Johns Hopkins University Press, 1981); Fredric Jameson, *The Political Unconscious: Narrative as a Socially Symbolic Act* (Ithaca: Cornell University Press, 1981): David Carroll, *The Subject in Question: The Language of Theory and the Strategies of Fiction* (Chicago: University of Chicago Press, 1982), esp. Chapter 4, "Representation or the End(s) of History: Dialectics and Fiction"; Murray Krieger, ed., *The Aims of Representation: Subject/Text/History* (New York: Columbia University Press, 1987); Jerome J. McGann, *Social Values and Poetic Acts* (Cambridge: Harvard University Press, 1988), esp. Chapter 6, "The Scandal of Referentality"; Roger Chartier, *Cultural History: Between Practices and Representations* (Ithaca: Cornell University Press, 1988); Hans Kellner, "Narrativity in History: Post-Structuralism and Since," in *The Representation of Historical Events*, Beiheft 26 of *History and Theory* (1988): 1-29; Lynn Hunt, ed., *The New Cultural History* (Berkeley: University of California Press, 1989); and the works of Dominick LaCapra: *Rethinking Intellectual History: Texts, Contexts, Language* (Ithaca: Cornell University Press, 1983); *History and Criticism* (Ithaca: Cornell University Press, 1985); *History, Politics, and the Novel* (Ithaca: Cornell University Press, 1987). See also, in addition to my more general comments in Chapter 1, my introduction to Chapter 3. For the expression *world of representations* (rather than any simple representation of the world), see Roger Chartier, *Cultural History*, pp. 11, 14.

12. This is the reading (*middayyānô*) in Geniza fragment TS C2 211, as well as in *Yalquṭ Šimʿoni* and *Midraš Ḥakamim*. MS Berlin has "from his direction" (*mimmanhîgô*) MS London and the Editio Princeps have *mrʾyny*, which makes no sense.

13. Finkelstein, following MS Berlin and *Midraš Ḥakamim* has "early prophets," but the other textual witnesses have "early sages." *Midraš Haggadol* has "sages and prophets." Cf. *b. Meg.* 17b, where the establishment of the eighteen benedictions is alternatively identified with the rabbinic sages at Yabneh and with the 120 elders, who included prophets, presumably of the Great Assembly. On the basis of the reading "early prophets," Finkelstein (*New Light from the Prophets* [London: Valentine Mitchell, 1969], pp. 37-45) argues that the *Sifre's* version of the service goes back to preexilic times.

14. F394.4-395.6. The order and wording of the eighteen benedictions as here presented does not agree with that of the liturgy as we know it. For discussion see S. Schechter, *JQR* 10 (1898): 655-57; and L. Finkelstein, *New Light from the Prophets*, pp. 37-45. Note that MS London has "holy and awesome is your name," whereas MS Berlin reverses the order of "who releases the bound" and "who heals the sick." Cf. *Midraš Haggadol* ad loc.; as well as *b. Meg.* 17b.

15. See Saul Lieberman, "Roman Legal Institutions," *JQR* 35 (1944/45):27.
16. Compare the *Sifre*'s comparison and contrast of Moses' and David's petitions to God concerning their personal sins in §26 (F36.1-39.2), treated by me in detail in "Sifre Deuteronomy 26 (ad Deut. 3:23): How Conscious the Composition?" *HUCA* 54 (1983): 245-301. Note that in the present passage David's prayer follows a slightly different pattern than Moses': praise of God—*praise* (rather than needs) of Israel—praise of God. The pattern is roughly maintained but has to be adjusted to the available biblical proof texts. This is "rectified" in *Yalquṭ Šimʿoni* Kgs. 192; ibid. Pss. 888; and *Midraš Haggadol* ad Deut. 33:2; where David is said to have petitioned for Israel's needs.
17. For other rabbinic traditions concerning the establishment and arrangement of the Eighteen Benedictions, either at Yabneh or by the elders of the Great Assembly, see *b. Meg.* 17b and *b. Ber.* 28b.
18. Cf. *b. Ber.* 32a, where R. Simlai similarly interprets Moses' prayer of Deut. 3:23-25 as a model for prayer: praise of God followed by personal petition.
19. Seir is the same as the land of Edom (see Gen. 32:4; Judg. 5:4), which is rabbinically understood to signify Rome (and later Christendom). Presumably Latin is intended here, but Greek could also be included.
20. According to Gen. 21:21, Paran is the dwelling place of Ishmael, from whom the Arabs are descended.
21. F395.10-13. The word for "came" (*ʾātâ*) is an Aramaism.
22. F395.7-9. In Finkelstein's edition the order of what is here B and C is reversed, following *Midraš hagadol* and *Midraš Ḥakamim*. In MS London and other textual witnesses the order is as I have presented it. Otherwise, in following MS London I have departed only slightly from Finkelstein's text. In C, MS London omits from "When the Holy One . . . revealed Himself" through "The Lord came from Sinai," but this is presumably a case of scribal homoioteleuton.
23. Thus, S. R. Driver (*A Critical and Exegetical Commentary on Deuteronomy,* ICC, 3d ed. [Edinburgh: T. and T. Clark, 1901], p. 390) states: "It is not said that Jehovah came *to* Sinai, but that He came *from* it; hence the verse cannot relate to the delivery of the law, when Jehovah 'Came down *upon* Sinai' (Ex. 19 18.20), but describes, under grand poetic imagery, how from spots bordering on the wilderness of the wanderings, Jehovah had displayed Himself gloriously to His people, assisting them with His presence, and guiding them on their journey to Canaan." For a somewhat different understanding, see Peter C. Craigie, *The Book of Deuteronomy* (London: Hodder and Stoughton, 1976), pp. 392-94. Compare Hippolytus of Rome's commentary, *Bénédictions de Moise* (PO 27:1-2, ed. and trans. from Armenian and Georgian by M. Brière et al. [1954], p. 128): "En disant ceci le Prophète remet sous les yeux le secours qui vint effectivement au peuple de la part de Dieu dans les guerres des nations étrangères, menées par Séhon, roi d'Hésébon, et par Og, roi de Basan, guerres dans lesquelles il (Iahvé) leur apparut avec des Anges pour les sauver de leurs ennemis, épargnant ainsi (à) son peuple (la défaite)."

24. See *b. Sanh.* 88b; *Midr. Pss.* 92:3; and *Exod. Rab.* 5:9; 28:6. Elsewhere the heteroglossia of revelation is described as a multiplicity of *voices: Mek. Yitro* 9; *Pesiq. Rab Kah.* 12:25; *Yalquṭ Šimʿoni* Pss. 709 and 843 (*Yelammedenu*).

25. The understanding that the seventy languages were intended each for a different nation is expressed only in the significantly later formulation of *Exod. Rab.* 5:9. Although the *Sifre* commentary will soon describe God's efforts to give the Torah first to the other nations, there is no reason to assume (as does Joseph Heinemann, *ʾAggādôt wĕtôlēdōtêhen*, p. 119) that this is the reason that it is said to have been revealed in four languages. For a fuller discussion of the rabbinically conceived multilinguistic nature of the revelation of the Torah to Israel (and its subsequent interpretation), see my forthcoming monograph, *Targum and Torah*.

26. Compare *Exod. Rab.* 5:9, where it is said that God's voice encircled the world. When Israel heard God's voice coming from the south, they went in that direction seeking Him. Then, when it came from the north, they sought God there. The same happens for east, west, above (heaven) and below (earth). The people thus confused could not tell from which direction God was coming.

27. Such as Meribath-Kadesh of Deut. 32:51.

28. The ancient versions (the Septuagint, Vulgate, Peshiṭta, and all of the *targumim*) translate as though the Hebrew were *wĕʾittô* ("and with Him," as we find in the Samaritan Pentateuch) instead of *wĕʾātâ*, understanding the verse to mean that God was accompanied by "myriads from Kadesh" (Septuagint) or "holy myriads" (all the others). That Kodesh is not a place name (e.g., Kadesh) is argued by Origen, *Selecta in Deut.* (Migne, *PG*, 12:817A). For the *Sifre's* interpretation of this phrase to refer to God's angelic entourage, even though it earlier recognized *wĕʾātâ* as an Aramaism (presemably meaning "and he came"), see later, sections I and J.

29. Such specification is supplied in the later reworkings of the tradition in *Midraš Haggadol* and *Midraš Leqaḥ Ṭob* ad Deut. 33:2: Sinai = North, Seir = East, Paran = South, Rebeboth-Kadesh = West (*rûaḥ maʿărābît*, perhaps a word play). But note how these find the fourth direction within the lemma itself, without resort to Hab. 3:3, where Teman would have to be interpreted as South. If the later versions may be said to be hermeneutically (in a narrow sense) preferable, relying entirely on the lemma, the *Sifre's* may be said to be rhetorically more engaging as I shall argue. The *Sifre's* interpretation of the lemma is also found in §314 (F356.13-15), but in a shortened form.

30. The dual idea of God's word encompassing and manifoldly engaging Israel at the time of revelation will find expression as well in §343 K and §313 C-E, all to be commented upon later.

31. The phrase between the two prooftexts is found in MS London, the Editio Princeps and Geniza fragment TS C2 211, but not in MS Berlin and *Midraš Ḥakamim* followed by Finkelstein. The same if true for other differences between my translation and Finkelstein's text in what follows.

32. Once again I follow the better textual witnesses: MS London, Geniza fragments TS C2 211, *Yalquṭ Šimʿoni*, and the Editio Princeps. Finkelstein, following MS Berlin and *Midraš Ḥakamim*, has: "Not only did they not obey

[what they heard at Sinai], but they were not even able to obey the seven commandments. . .When the Holy One, blessed be He, saw this, He gave them [= the seven commandments] to Israel." However, in other texts it is the property of the nations that is given to Israel when the former fail to uphold th seven Noahide commandments. See note 142. In what follows, I similarly follow the better witnesses.

33. One letek equals fifteen se'ahs. According to *m. B. Meṣ.* 6.5, a letek is a normal load for a donkey.

34. According to MS Berlin and *Midraš Ḥakamim*, followed by Finkelstein, after the descendants of Noah cast off the seven commandments, "Israel came and received them."

35. F395.14-397.2.

36. Compare Tosaphot to *b. B. Qam.* 38a, where it is said that Mt. Paran refers to a part, or side, of Mt. Sinai, where God offered the Torah to the descendants of Ishmael. Thus, God's coming to Israel *from* Sinai is taken to mean that God came to Israel only after having offered the Torah to the other nations. For another explanation of "from Sinai," see *Mek. Baḥodeš* 3 (ed. Lauterbach, vol. 2, pp. 218-19), cited in note 179.

37. Cf. *Tgs. Ps.-Jonathan, Fragmentary* (MSS V, N, L, P), and *Neofiti*, in which God goes first to the descendants of Esau, then to those of Ishmael, and finally, with the myriads of holy angels, to Israel. Clearly, the *targum* is more constrained by the order of the biblical verse than is the midrashic commentary. But compare §311 (F352.5-8), where it is said simply that when God gave the Torah to Israel He first observed the nations and, determining that they were not worthy to receive the Torah, gave it to Israel. As we shall see in comparison with its early parallels, the *Sifre* is alone in stressing that God, having failed with the descendants of Esau and the others, tried all the other nations before coming to Israel.

38. For other parallels, none of which duplicates the specific combination and shaping of the traditions in the *Sifre*, see the following: *Lev. Rab.* 13:2 (ed. Margoliot, pp. 272-76); *Pesiq. Rab Kah. Haḥodeš Hazzeh* 5 (ed. Mandelbaum, 1:81-82); *Pesiq. R.* 21 (ed. Friedmann, col. 99b); *b. 'Abod. Zar.* 2a-b; *b. B. Qam.* 38a; *Exod. Rab.* 27:9; *Num. Rab.* 14:10; *Tanḥ. Běrākâ* 4; *Tanḥ. Běrākâ* (ed. Buber) 3; *Pirqe R. El.* 41; *Midraš 'ăśeret Haddibběrôt* (in *Bet ha-Midrash*, ed. A Jellinek, 1:68); *Yalquṭ Šim'oni* Pss. 887. For the nations having rejected the seven Noahide commandments, see also *Sifre* §322 (F372.6), and for the nations not having been worthy to receive the Torah, see §311 (F352.5-7).

39. *Mekilta deR. Ishmael Baḥodeš* 5 (ed. Lauterbach, 2:234-36).

40. In other words, God never intended for them to receive the Torah. As the *Mekilta* implies in its choice of a *mashal*, this is because the nations would not have been able to fulfill it. Compare teh *Mekilta*'s subsequent statement (ed. Lauterbach, 2:236) that the Torah was given in the wilderness rather than in the land of Israel so that the nations should not have the opportunity to say, "It is only because the Torah was given in their land that we did not accept it." Nevertheless, the *Mekilta* concludes (ibid., 2:237) by saying that the Torah,

like wilderness, fire, and water, is "free to all inhabitants of the world." Compare the *Sifre*'s statement (§345, to be discussed later), that once the Torah was betrothed to Israel, it became like a married woman to the nations of the world.

41. These two somewhat conflicting views of the Noahide laws—that their authority derives from devine fiat or from human acceptance—are found elsewhere in rabbinic sources. For early formulations of the seven Noahide laws, see t. ʿ*Abod. Zar.* 8:4 and *b. Sanh.* 56a. For the most recent discussion, see David Novak, *The Image of the Non-Jew in Judaism: An Historical and Constructive Study of the Noahide Laws* (New York: E. Mellen, 1983). For a briefer description, see Saul Berman, "Noachide Laws," *EncJud* 12 (1971): 1189-91.

42. The traditional commentators to the *Sifre* note the following incongruity between the *mashal* and its *nimshal*: unlike the two loads borne by the dog and donkey in the *mashal*, the seven Noahide commandments are already included in the 613 commandments of the Torah that Israel accepted at Mt. Siani. How then can Israel be said to bear an additional burden as a result of the nations' failure to bear the seven Noahide commandments? Various solutions have been proposed. For example, David Pardo argues that having rejected the obligatory status of the Noahide commandments, the nations are not entitled to the rewards for fulfilling them, and these rewards accrue to Israel in addition to the rewards that Israel has earned through its own obedience to the Torah. But the converse of that argument would also hold, as the commentary *Toledot* ʾ*Adam* suggests: Having rejected the Noahide commandments the nations are no longer culpable for their violation, and Israel now receives the punishments for the nations' violations of those laws. These commentaries, in trying to make sense of an incongruity in the *Sifre*'s commentary, find more there than its text warrants. I would prefer to leave that incongruity stand, and understand the commentary to say that Israel is justified in its self-understanding as God's chosen recipient of His Torah by the moral failure of the nations, but also bears a greater moral burden as a consequence. Some have argued that this protest against the nations of the world who have rejected God's law is an anti-Christian polemic. I will return to the question of the identity of the "nations of the world" in the concluding section to this chapter, where see especially notes 225 and 226. Incidentally, it should be stressed that our commmentary does not so much credit Israel with having fulfilled the commandments as with having accepted, and continuing to accept, them. Israel may also include murderers, adulterers, and robbers, but it knows that such behavior does not accord with the covenantal obligations it bears.

43. What follows comes next in MS London, Geniza fragment TS C2 211, the Editio Pinceps, and *Yalquṭ Šimʿoni*. Only MS Berlin and *Midraš Ḥakamim* have the order followed by Finkelstein, in which the following section comes after what I have labeled *F*. Much the same tradition as follows is found in the *Mekilta de R. Ishmael Baḥodeš* 5 (ed. Lauterbach, 2:234-35), where it is placed

before the tradition of God's having offered the Torah to the different nations, and with some other important differences that will be noted later.

44. F397.16-398.4.

45. In the parallel in the *Mekilta*, Ps. 29:3 is connected to the lemma there, "I am the Lord your God" (Exod. 20:2), in which the tetragram also figures prominently.

46. This citation, which in the mouths of the nations constitutes the climax to this section of the commentary, is absent in the parallel in the *Mekilta*, referred to in note 43. In most other parallels, the blessing is also absent: *Mek. Baḥodes* 1 (ed. Lauterbach, vol. 2, p. 198); *Mek. Amalek* 3 (ed. Lauterbach, 2:62-63). However, in *b. Zebaḥ.* 116a the nations bless Israel as here. Compare Pseudo—Philo, *Biblical Antiquities* 11:5 (trans. M. R. James, p. 107): "And behold the mountains burned with fire and the earth shook and the hills were removed and the mountains overthrown: the depths boiled, and all the habitable places were shaken: and the heavens were folded up and the clouds drew up water."

47. In the *Mekilta* parallel, in which the present tradition *precedes* that of the offering of the Torah to the nations, this problem is not as accute. But the rhetorical force of the present arrangement, ending with the nations' blessing of Israel, it seems to me, is stronger here and leads well into the next interpretation (F).

48. F397.3-8.

49. For the identification of Seir with Esau with Rome, see note 19. Notice that according to the previous interpretation, God went at the time of revelation from the descendants of Esau to those of Ammon and Moab to those Ishmael, before coming to Israel. Yet the lemma ("God shone upon them from Seir") is now taken to suggest the direct progression from Seir to Israel. That the commentary speaks of successive political dominions seems clear to me from the final sentence. For the same interpretation, see the commentary *Zeraʿ ʾAbraham.*

50. This would have been particularly the case in the years of Roman political anarchy between the reigns of Alexander Severus (221-35) and Diocletian (284-305), precisely the period during which the *Sifre* is likely to have been edited. On the impact of Roman political instability on Jewish life and attitudes in Palestine, see E. Mary Smallwood, *The Jews under Roman Rule from Pompey to Diocletian: A Study in Political Relations*, SJLA 20 (Leiden: E. J. Brill, 1981), pp. 526-33). Note especially Smallwood's statement (p. 527): "Jewish fortunes had now reached their nadir, and salvation must surely be within sight." Similarly, see Michael Avi-Yonah, *The Jews under Roman and Byzantine Rule: A Political History of Palestine from the Bar Kochba war to the Arab Conquest* (Jerusalem: Magnes, 1984), pp. 89-136. Note especially Avi-Yonah's citation (pp. 128-32) of midrashic statements attributed to mid-third century Palestinian sages, to the effect that Roma (Esau/Edom), like the beasts of Dan. 7, would soon fall, to be followed immediately by Israel's redemption. See also Hammer, *Sifre*, p. 506 note 13: "Such a statement would

seem appropriate to the period of Persian incursions against Rome and to the time prior to Christianity's ascent, i.e., during the third century." But note that much the same tradition of *direct* succession from Esau to Jacob, representing respectively the present and future ages, is expressed in the late first century apocalyptic text *4 Ezra* 6:7-10.

51. See in particular, Gerson D. Cohen, "Esau as Symbol in Early Medieval Thought," in *Jewish Medieval and Renaissance Studies*, ed. A, Altmann (Cambridge: Harvard University Press, 1967), pp. 19-48. Jacob Neusner (*Judaism and Scripture: The Evidence of Leviticus Rabbah* [Chicago: University of Chicago Press, 1986]; *Judaism and Christianity in the Age of Constantine: History, Messiah, Israel, and the Initial Confrontation* [Chicago: University of Chicago, 1987]) has made much of this motif of brotherly enmity in *Leviticus Rabbah* and *Genesis Rabbah* as referring necessarily to the ascension of Christianity after Constantine's "conversion" in the early fourth century. But such a precise identification, it seems to me, is unwarranted given the fact that the motif occurs several times in *Sifre Deuteronomy* (§2 [F10.6], §41 [F85.7], §322 [F371.15], §356 [F424.15]), which most likely derives in its redacted form from the mid-third century. On the dating of the *Sifre* as a collection, see above Chapter 1, note 56. That Constantine's conversion had such a great and sudden impact in the early fourth century, causing a formative crisis in Jewish self-understanding, may also be questioned from Christian sources, as Robert Wilken argues in *John Chrysostom and the Jews: Rhetoric and Reality in the Late Fourth Century* (Berkely: University of California Press, 1983), pp. 128-29.

52. The words *another interpretation* are found in MS London, Geniza fragment TS C2 211, *Yalquṭ Šimʿoni*, and the Editio Princeps, but not in MS Berlin, *Midraš Ḥakamim*, and *Midraš Haggadol*.

53. This translates Finkelstein's text, *pirkēs ʾet ʿaṣmô*, which follows *Yalquṭ Šimʿoni*. However, MSS London and Berlin, Geniza fragment TS C2 211, and the Editio Princeps (misrepresented in Finkelstein's apparatus), as well as *Midraš Ḥakamim and Midraš Haggadol*, have *pirsēm ʾet ʿaṣmô* ("he made himself known, displayed himself"). The two words, *pirkēs* and *pirsēm* could easily have been scribally confused with one another. The former is a Greek loan word (usually connected with *perkazō*, meaning "to darken one's face"), meaning to change one's physical appearance so as to appear more attractive. On the difficulties of the Greek etymology, see Eliezer Ben Yehuda, *A Complete Dictionary of Ancient and Modern Hebrew*, vol. 10 (Jerusalem, 1944), col. 5187. The latter also derives from Greek, although less directly, perhaps from *parrēsia*, denoting "open speech." However, see Ben Yehuda, *Dictionary*, vol. 10, col. 5206. The former is less well established in early rabbinic usage (and therefore may more likely to have been confused by copyists), appearing in only one other "tannaitic" source. In *m. B. Meṣ.* 4:12 it is said that a seller cannot change the appearance of an item he wishes to sell, whether that be a person (slave), an animal, or a utensil, so as to make it seem more valuable. The problem with the reading *pirsēm ʾet ʿaṣmô* is that it does

not fit as well with the accompanying image of the son having cut his hair, presumably again so as to make himself more attractive and worthy of his father's gift. Interestingly, traditional commentators to the *Sifre*, even when their text had *pirsēm ʾet ʿaṣmô*, refer to *Yalqut Šimʿoni*'s *pirkēs ʾet ʿaṣmô* for its proper understanding. See also David Hoffmann's correction of *pirsēm* to *pirkēs* in his edition of *Midraš Tannaʾim* (Berlin: H. Itzkowski, 1908-9), p. 210. In either case, the sense is that the son must do something to demonstrate publicly that he, in contrast to his brothers, is worthy of his father's favor.

54. F397.8-15.
55. On the unworthy children of Abraham and Isaac compared to the wholly worthy children of Jacob, see §31 (F49.8-53.9) and §312 (F353.3-354.8), where the language is very similar. Thus, it is likely that the tradition of the *nimshal* circulated independently of the *mashal* to which it is here joined, or as I shall argue, somewhat uncomfortably juxtaposed.
56. The idea of the son physically, and somewhat deceptively (see note 53) altering his appearance so as to receive his father's gift, may be related to Gen. 27, where Jacob wears Esau's clothing and makes his skin apear hairy so as to receive his father Isaac's blessing. In the *mashal*, we find the reverse, however, with the son cutting his hair (*šaʿar*, perhaps a play on Seir = Esau) to appear worthy.
57. Compare the formulations of §343 J3, where Israel is said to tell the nations that they have no share (*ḥēleq*) in God, and §345 C, where it is said that the Torah, "an inheritance of the congregation of Jacob" (Deut. 33:4), is like another person's wife to the nations. Both of these will be treated later. Compare also §311 (F352.5-7), cited in note 120. But contrast these traditions with *Mek. Baḥodeš* (ed. Lauterbach, 2:198), where it is said that the Torah was given in the open, public space of the wilderness, so that the nations should not think, as they might had it been given in the Land of Israel, that they have no share (*ḥēleq*) in it.
58. Joseph is understood to refer to Israel in Egypt, even though God's enthronement on the cherubim could not have been experienced until the tabernacle with its holy ark was constructed in the wilderness.
59. F.398.5-9. I have translated *hôpîaʿ* of Ps. 50:1 as an imperative form (as in 80:2 and 94:1) in accordance with the midrashic sense, even though it is usually understood in this verse to be perfect in form, describing a completed action. I have searched in vain for other early rabbinic interpretations of this verse as referring to the messianic future, even though Zion in general often has messianic associations. Perhaps the word *miklal* (here translated "perfect"), might be taken to mean "complete" in a temporal sense. For a later messianic interpretation of the whole of Ps. 50, see the commentary of David Qimḥi (Radaq) to Psalms ad loc. Our passage is cited, with only minor variants, in *Menorat Ha-Maor* (ed. H. G. Enelow, vol. 3, p. 331). But in a different version, the third appearance is said to be in relation to the final judgment of Edom, and the fourth appearance in relation to Gog and Magog. See *Midraš Haggadol* and *Midraš Leqaḥ Ṭob* ad loc.; and *Midraš Šelošah Weʾarbaʿah* 33

(in *Batei Midrashot*, ed. Shlomo Aharon Wertheimer, vol. 2, pp. 49-50).
60. See Wayne Sibley Towner, *The Rabbinic Enumeration of Scriptural Examples* (Leiden: E. J. Brill, 1973).
61. The verb *hôpîaʿ* appears as well in Job 37:15. The other notable self-disclosure of God to Israel, according to rabbinic tradition, occurred at the Sea of Reeds, but there the verb *hŏpîʿa*, the lexical cement of the present interpretation, is not employed.
62. F398.10-13. The passage is cited, with minor variants, in *Menorat Ha-Maor* (ed. H. G. Enelow, vol. 3, p. 331).
63. See note 28.
64. According to *Pesiq. Rab Kah. Baḥodeš* 22 (ed. Mandelbaum, p. 220), God brought with Him to Sinai only the best of His angels, a sort of elite body guard. This is implied as well in the next interpretation of the *Sifre*. For a different interpretation see David Pardo ad loc., who says that God displayed only a part of his splendor as any more would have been too much for the people to behold.
65. Note in this connection that *Midraš Haggadol* has "king of flesh and blood," as in the following interpretation.
66. For the intermediary function of the angels at revelation, see *Cant. Rab.* vol. 1, p. 2, referred to in note 198. For this idea in the New Testament, most likely dependent on the Septuagint's version of Deut. 33:2-3 (on which see notes 28 and 89), see Acts 7:38, 53; Gal. 3:19; Heb. 2:2. This idea is also taken for granted in later patristic exegesis. For an early rabbinic view of the angels' role in *assisting* the Israelites in receiving revelation, see note 200. See also Judah Goldin, "Not by Means of an Angel and Not by Means of a Messenger," in *Essays in Memory of Erwin Ramsdell Goodenough*, ed. Jacob Neusner (Leiden: E. J. Brill, 1968), pp. 412-24; Ephraim E. Urbach, *The Sages: Their Concepts and Beliefs*, trans. Israel Abrahams, 2 vols. (Jerusalem: Magnes, 1979), vol. 1, pp. 146-50.
67. Finkelstein (following MS Berlin) has *pĕlātyāʾ* (Greek: *plateia*), meaning an open street or place. The better supported reading (MS London, Geniza fragments TS C2 211, *Yalquṭ Šimʿoni*, and the Editio Princeps) is *pammîlyāʾ* (Latin: *familia*), meaning the royal entourage or "family." This is also the reading in *Menorat Ha-Maor* (ed. H. G. Enlow, vol. 3, p. 331), which cites the *Sifre* by name. *Midraš Haggadol* has *pallātîn* (Greek: *palation*), meaning "palace." Parallels listed in the following note have other variants, such as *qampôn* (Latin: *campus*), meaning a public court or field. In *Mek. Šîrtāʾ* 3, the king enters a *mĕdînâ* ("province," or "large city"), surrounded by guards and soldiers, from whom he cannot be distinguished. In the present context, in which the king's royal entourage is being compared to God's divine, angelic entourage, the term *pammîlyāʾ* is particularly apt because it is also used to refer to the household on high.
68. There are many variants among the witnesses to the text here. I have followed MS London, but have been unable to make sense of *qmṣyn* (presumably *qĕmāṣîn*), which in Geniza fragment TS C2 211 appears as *qbwṣyn* (presumably *qĕbûṣin*), and in the Editio Princeps and later parallels (*Pesiq.*

Rab Kah. Baḥodeš 22 [ed. Mandelbaum, p. 220]; *Yalquṭ Šimᶜoni* Exod. 286; *Yalquṭ Šimᶜoni* Pss. 796; *Menorat Ha-Maor* [vol. 3, p. 332]) as *qwwṣym* (presumably *qĕwŭṣîm*, on which see later in this note). *Pesiq. Rab. Kah. Zōʾt Habbĕrākâ* (ed. Mandelbaum, p. 449) and *Yalquṭ Šimᶜoni* Deut. 951 have *gûṣîm* ("short") togehter with *ʾărûkîm* ("tall"). MS Berlin *Midraš Haggadol*, and *Midraš Ḥakamim* have *mĕšûbbaḥîm* ("praiseworthy"). The word is omitted entirely in the text utilized by R. Yedaiah Happenini, and in an oriental manuscript known to the marginal glossator of the edition of the *Sifre* printed with the commentary *Zeraᶜ ʾAbraham* (Radzivil: 1820), as it is in the parallel in *Tanḥ. Bĕrākâ* 5. I favor *qĕwûṣîm*, understanding it to refer to men with curly locks, a sign of beauty, most likely under the influence of Cant. 5:2, 11. Thus, in *Deut. Rab.* (ed. Lieberman, p. 15), it is said that God appeared to the Israelite infants in Egypt and again at the Sea as a young man who was *qāwûs nāʾeh šēʾēn kĕyôṣēʾ bô* ("with beautiful hair unlike any other"). (ibid., n. Lieberman10) suggests that the text should read *qābûṣ nāʾeh ûmĕšûbbaḥ*, as is found in a *Yelammedenu* midrash (in *Bet Ha-Midrasch*, ed. A. Jellinek, vol. 6, p. 85), but I see no need for this. See also Buber's note (p. 108a, note 155) in his edition of *Pesiqta de Rab Kahana*. For a similar use of this term, see *t. Nazir* 4:7 and parallels, about a young man with beautiful curly hair who becomes a Nazirite. See as well Marcus Jastrow, *A Dictionary of the Targumim, the Talmud Babli and Jerushalmi, and the Midrashic Literature*, 2 vols. (New York: Choreb, 1926), cols. 1325a, 1356b; but see also ibid., col. 1325a for the meaning "undersized," from which I assume the variant *qûṣîm* derives. The forms *qbwṣym* and *qmṣyn* can be seen as subsequent scribal transmutations, with the latter deriving from the former. See also *Aruch Completum*, ed. A. Kohut, s. v. *qwwṣ* (vol. 7, pp. 73-74).

69. *Midraš Haggadol* has, "he is recognized (*nîkkār*) as an ensign amidst the myriads holy." The same is found in *Midraš Leqaḥ Ṭob*. The verb *to recognize* will recur in the next two sections.

70. The word *ᶜălāmôt* is read as *ᶜal māwet/mût* ("upon death"), as in Ps. 48:15, or *ᶜad māwet* ("unto death"). The latter is explicitly stated in the parallel in *Mek. Širtāʾ* 3, whereas the former is supplied in the citation of our passage in *Menorat Ha-Maor* (vol. 3, p. 332). Compare *Cant. Rab.* 1:3 end (1:23 in S. Dunski's edition), where it is said that Aquilas translated the word as *ʾattānasyāʾ* (= Greek *athanasia* ["immortality"], as if the Hebrew were *ʾal māwet*. In fact, Aquilas's translation is of *ᶜal-mût* in Ps. 48(47):15 (see *Origenis Hexaplorum*, ed. F. Field, vol. 2 [Oxford: Clarendon Press, 1875], p. 169), as noted in *p. Moᶜed Qaṭ*. 3:7 (83b). The citation in *Menorat Ha-Maor* provides the sense of what precedes as follows: "What is the nature of your God that you are killed and slain for him, and you [still] love him."

71. The expression is *hitᶜārĕbû ᶜimmānû* in most and the better witnesses. For this expression, see Ps. 106:35: "They mingled themselves with the nations and learned their ways." The nations invite Israel to be absorbed into them, thereby losing their distinctive identity for which they will no longer have to suffer.

72. I understand *nʾmr* in what precedes to be *nōʾmar*, an imperfect active form,

rather than *ne'ĕmar*, a perfect passive form ("it has been told"). Hammer (p. 355) prefers the latter, translating, "You have been told only a fraction of His praise, yet you think that you know Him!" Similarly, Genezia fragment TS C2 211 and the citation in *Menorat Ha-Maor* (vol. 3, p. 332), have, "You have been told. . *and* you [still] do not know him." Compare *Mek. Šîrtā'* 3 (ed. Lauterbach, vol. 2, p. 26), where Israel says to the nations: "Have you any notion of Him? Let us tell (*n'mr*) you a little bit of His Glory." For this translation, see Judah Goldin, *The Song at the Sea: Being a Commentary in Two Parts* (New Haven: Yale University Press, 1971), p. 116. Goldin translates the parallel in *Mek. deR. Simeon bar Yohai* (ed. Epstein-Melamed, p. 79), which is similar to the previously cited Geniza fragment and citation of the *Sifre* in *Menorat Ha-Maor*, but without the critical *and,* as follows: "Let us tell you a little bit of His glory; you have no notion of Him." Unlike these parallels, in the *Sifre*'s version of the tradition Israel wishes the nations to have some notion, if only partial, of their lover. I understand the abbreviated citation of Cant. 5:10-16 to constitute their partial praise of Him.

73. For a similar expression, see Zech. 8:23.

74. For this expression, see Josh. 22:25, 27.

75. F398.14-399.10.

76. The same word play is found in *Mek. Širta* 1 (ed. Lauterbach, vol. 2, pp. 10-11): *Cant. Rab.* 5:10 (5:6 in Dunski's edition); *Pesiq. Rab Kah. Bahōdeš* 22 (ed. Mandelbaum, p. 220); ibid. *Zō't Habbĕrākâ* (ed. Mandelbaum, p. 449); *b. Hag.* 16a.

77. This same tradition, with some variations, including a *mashal* similar to the *Sifre*'s, but in relation to the crossing of the sea (the king's escort now being a military one), is also found in *Mek. Šîrtā'* 3 (ed. Lauterbach, vol. 2, pp. 24-27) and *Mek. deR. Simeon bar Yohai* (ed. Epstein-Melamed, p. 78). See the notes of Judah Goldin, *The Song at the Sea,* p. 85.

78. But see notes 71, 73, and 74.

79. Given the seemingly important place of the Song of Songs in Jewish-Christian dispute at the time that the *Sifre* was compiled (mid-third century), it is possible that the "nations of the world" in the present context refer specifically to the Church. On this question, see Ephraim E. Urbach, "The Homilectical Interpretations of the Sages and the Expositions of Origen on Canticles, and Jewish-Christian Disputation," in *Scripta Hierosolymitana* 22 (1971): 247-75; Reuven Kimelman, "Rabbi Yohanan and Origen on the Song of Songs: A Third-Century Jewish-Christian disputation, " *HTR* 73 (1980): 567-95. However, neither of these treats our passage or the interpretation of Cant. 5:10-16 in the context of Jewish-Christian disputation. Although early Christian exegetes interpret the details of Cant. 5:10-16 with regard to Jesus (see especially, Origen, *Scholia in Cantica Cantic.* [Migne, *PG* 17:373-76]), I find nothing in their interpretations that would require viewing our text specifically as an anti-Christian response. Urbach ("The Homiletical Interpretations," pp. 250-51) mentions our passage, with its mention of Israel's dying for God, as alluding to the martyrology of R. Akiba (it is elsewhere attributed to R. Akiba; see note 81). For other attempts at historically locating the

dialoge, see Gedaliah Alon, *Tôlĕdôt Hayyĕhûdîm Bĕ'ereṣ Yiśrā'ēl Bitqûpat Hammišnâ Wĕhattalmûd* (Tel Aviv: Hakibutz Hameuchad, 1967-70), vol. 1, p. 327, note 25; I. Baer, "Israel, the Christian Church, and the Roman Empire from the Days of Septimus Severus to the 'Edict of Toleration' of 313 C.E.," *Zion* 21 (1956): 3. I will return in the conclusion to this chapter to the question of a possible anti-Christian polemic. On the importance of the dialogical nature of Song of Songs for its history of interpretation, see Gerson D. Cohen, "The Song of Songs and the Jewish Religious Mentality," *The Samuel Friedland Lectures, 1960-66* (New York: Jewish Theological Seminary of America, 1966), p. 14, citing *Cant. Rab.* 1:11 (ad Cant. 1:1). Cf. Origen, *Commentary on Song of Songs* 1.1.

80. For both of these views see *Cant. Rab.* 1:2 (2:12 in Dunski's edition). For the association of Cant. 5:13 with the giving of the Torah at Sinai, see *Pesiq R.* 20 (ed. Buber, cols. 94b-95a.)

81. The closest parallel is found in *Mek. Šîrtā'* 3 (ed. Lauterbach, vol. 2, pp. 25-27) and *Mek. deR. Simeon bar Yoḥai* ad Exod. 15:2 (ed. Epstein Melamed, p.79), in relation to Israel's physical vision of God at the time of the splitting of the Red Sea. There too the dialogue follows a tradition of Israel having immediately recognized God among His heavenly escort, brought in commentary to Exod. 15:2 ("This is my God"), but unrelated to Israel's recognition of God at Sinai. But in the two *Mekiltas*, the juxtaposition of Israel's recognition of God at the Sea with their dialogue with the nations is much less proximate than it is in the *Sifre*. In the *Mekiltas*, after the interpretation of "This is my God," we find three interpretations, each attributed to a different tannaitic sage, of the words "and I will glorify Him" prior to the dialogue of Israel with the nations, there attributed to R. Akiba. This in turn is followed by another interpretation of the same verse (Exod. 15:2), attributed to the sages in general, which understands it to refer to Israel's escorting of God to the Temple. For notes to the *Mekilta* parallel, see Goldin, *Song at the Sea*, pp. 112-119. For a fuller discussion of the *Mekilta* parallel, see Daniel Boyarin, "'Language Inscribed by History on the Bodies of Living Beings': Midrash and Martyrdom," in *Representations* 25 (Winter 1989): 139-51. Boyarin interprets the "time" of the dialogue between Israel and the nations to be eschatalogical, but I am not convinced of this, at least not as the tradition reads in its setting in the *Sifre*. Isolated parts of the dialogue appear in *Cant. Rab.* 5:9 (5:5 in Dunski's edition), *Agadath Shir Hashirim* (ed. Schechter, p. 39), and *Midraš Šir Hašširim* (ed. Grünhut, 39b-40b) as commentary to Cant. 5:9; and in *Cant. Rab.* 7:1 (7:2 in Dunski's edition) as commentary to Cant. 7:1.

82. In J3, a related term (*nā'wâ*) is used for God's beauty as described by Israel.

83. The link between these two biblical phrases is explicitly made in *Cant. Rab.* 5:10 (5:6 in Dunski's edition). They are also associated in *b. Ḥag.* 16a. It is difficult to believe that a rabbinic student of the *Sifre* would not have this association come to mind, especially as the commentary in citing Cant. 5:10-16 explicitly states that what follows is an abbreviated rendition.

84. On *qĕwûṣîm* in section J1, see note 68. Compare also section G, where the

king's son (the descendants of Jacob) cuts his hair so as to be worthy of the king's special favor. The other two descriptions of the king's entourage, "beautiful" and "mighty," as previously noted, are here applied by the nations to Israel. Note that in *Cant. Rab.* 5:11-16 (5:7-6:4 in Dunski's edition) the various physical descriptions of the male lover (God) are interpreted as metaphors, mainly for the Torah, its study, and rabbinic sages. Thus, his head is the Torah, the black curly hair is either the letters on the ruled lines or the crowns on the letters, each of which needs to be interpreted. Alternatively, the black curly hair is the disciples of the sages, the Sanhedrin, etc. For similar interpretations of the physical attributes of the male lover as signifying the written and oral Torahs and their study and performance by the righteous and the sages, see *Tg. Ket.* Cant. 5:10-16. Given the *present* context of the commentary, can we assume that Israel is understood to describe to the nations not so much parts of God's mystical body (as these verses were interpreted in Shiur Koma traditions), as the Torah by which His will and presence is apprehended by those who apply themselves to its study? For this interpretation, see David Pardo ad loc. Compare §41 (F86.14-87.7), where the "eyes" of Cant. 7:5 are interpreted to signify the rabbinic elders who are appointed over the community. For the importance of Cant. 5:10-16 in Shiur Koma traditions of mystical speculation, and the view that our tradition as it is related to Israel's visionary experience at the sea in the two *Mekiltas* (see note 81) is an expression of such speculation, see Gershom Scholem, *Jewish Gnosticism, Merkabah Mysticism and Talmudic Tradition*, 2d ed. (New York: Jewish Theological Seminary of American, 1965), pp. 36-42 with notes on pp. 129-31, and Appendix D by Saul Lieberman, pp. 118-26, esp. p. 123 [Hebrew]. For a link between the exposition of Cant. 5:13 and a mystical interpretation of revelation at Sinai, see note 80.

85. Compare especially the parallels in *Mek. deR. Ishmael Širta*ʾ 1 and 3 (ed. Lauterbach, vol. 2, pp. 10, 24-25, 26-27); *Cant. Rab.* 5:9; 7:1.

86. The Hebrew is *haddîbbûr* or *haddîbbēr*, the latter being better attested here, referring to the hypostatized divine utterance, particularly of each of the ten commandments.

87. "His voice" is missing in MS London, but is present in all other witnesses.

88. F399.11-15.

89. There is a masoretic note to this effect. The Vulgate has "in his right hand was a fiery law." *Tg. Onqelos* translates: "His right hand from out of the fire wrote the Torah (ʾôrāyĕtāʾ) and gave it to us." Similarly, the other *targumim* state that God stretched His hand forth from the fire so as to give the Torah to Israel. The Septuagint translates, "on [or from] his right hand were angels with Him," which is impossible to reconcile with the MT, and is probably influenced by its understanding of the preceding verse (on which, see note 28). Similarly, the Peshitta translates, "and with Him were myriads of angels from [= by] His right hand," omitting the problematic word or words entirely. For various scholarly efforts to understand the word ʾēšdāt, usually through emendation, see S. R. Driver, *Deuteronomy*, pp. 390-93.

90. For twelve by twelve miles defining the dimensions of the Israelite camp, see

§357 (F428.1-2); *p. Giṭ.* 1:2 (43c); Rashi ad *b. Šabb.* 88b; and Louis Ginzberg, *Legends of the Jews*, 7 vols. (Philadelphia: Jewish Publication Society of America, 1913-38), vol. 6, pp. 38, note 210, 82-83, note 445. See also *Tg. Ps.-Jon.* Exod. 20:2.

91. For God's self-disclosure described in terms of light and fire, see also Hab. 3:3-6 and Ps. 50:2-3. Josephus in his paraphrase of the story of revelation recounts (*Ant.* 3.5.2§81)as follows: "As for the Hebrews, the sight that they saw and the din that struck their ears solely disquieted them." Philo (*Dec.* 32-49) expounds at length on the interrelation of voice to fire in divine revelation and its human reception, and notes the paradox of a voice becoming visible (*Mos.* 2.213; cf. *Mig.* 46-47). On Philo's view of revelatory communication at Sinai, see David Winston, "Two Types of Mosaic Prophecy According to Philo," in *Society of Biblical Literature 1988 Seminar Papers*, ed. David J. Lull (Atlanta: Scholars Press, 1988), pp. 448-52. Compare the different views attributed to R. Ishmael and R. Akiba on the relation of the audible to the visible aspect revelation in *Mek. Baḥodeš* 9 (ed. Lauterbach, vol. 2, p. 226), with our text being closer to R. Akiba's view. See also notes 187 and 198. For a close parallel to our text, attributed to R. Simeon b. Yoḥai in disagreement with "the sages," see *Cant. Rab.* 1:2 (1:13 in Dunski's edition). There it is said that the size of the Israelite camp was eighteen by eighteen miles. Note that in a subsequent interpretation there, attributed to R. Ḥelbo, it is upon inscribing the tablets that the voice reverberates throughout the world. For the fiery divine commandments encircling Israel see also *Frg. Tg.* (MS P) Exod. 20:2. However, according to *Tgs. Neofiti* and *Ps.-Jonathan*, Israel watched as each fiery commandment went up to heaven and back before carving out its words on the tablets. This may be related to the aforementioned interpretation attributed to R. Ḥelbo in *Cant. Rab.* 1:2, according to which the divine speech carved out the commandments on the tablets of its own accord, and not as a tool in God's hand.

92. For this tradition see §313 (F355.12-13) and §344 (F401.15-402.1), both of which will be treated later. For fuller depictions, including the calculation that each Israelite had to walk 240 miles (24 miles for each of ten commandments) in one day, see *Mek. Baḥodeš* 2 and 9 (ed. Lauterbach, vol. 2, pp. 202, 269); *t. ʿArak.* 1:10; *b. Šabb.* 88b; *Midr. Pss.* 68:7 (ed. Buber. p. 159a); *Pirqe R. El.* 41; *Midraš ʿăśeret Haddibbĕrôt* (in *Bet ha-Midrasch*, ed. A. Jellinek, vol. 1, p. 69). See also L. Ginzberg, *Legends of the Jews*, vol. 6, p. 38, note 210. The idea that God at revelation addressed each Israelite individually and equally is already developed by Philo, *Dec.* 36-43. For a different rabbinic metaphor for God's self-disclosure to each Israelite individually, see *Pesiq. Rab Kah. Baḥodeš Haššĕlîšî* 25 (ed. Mandelbaum, vol. 1, pp. 223-24) and parallels.

93. Hammer (p. 355) translates, "Just as fire lives forever (*ḥayyîm lĕʿôlām*), so do the words of Torah live forever." This is unlikely since "fire" is throughout this section treated as a singular noun, wheras *ḥayyîm* as a verb would require a plural subject. For Torah bringing life to the world, see Chapter 3, note 34.

94. MS London adds "immediately" (*miyyād*) . For other variants compare the

text published by Menahem Kahana as the *Mekilta to Deuteronomy* (see note 7), p. 194: "Just as with fire, whoever uses it is warmed by it . . . so too, whoever is occupied with words of Torah has life; whoever departs from words of Torah has no life." The same is found in *Midraš Haggadol.*

95. I follow MS London which is very similar to the Editio Princeps, but there are many variants to the text in other witnesses. Somewhat fuller, but essentially the same, is the version of *Yalquṭ Šimʿoni* (with slight variants in the text of the *Sifre* commented upon by R. Yedaiah Happenini): "Just as fire leaves a mark upon the body of whoever uses it, so too with words of Torah, people who labor with it are recognizable among other people. So too the disciples of the sages . . . " Finkelstein follows MS Berlin, which is virtually identical to *Midraš Ḥakamim* and the citation in *Menorat Ha-Maor* (ed. Enelow, vol. 3, p. 333), and similar to Geniza fragments TS C2 211 and TS C6 113 (not available to Finkelstein), representing a yet fuller version that splits this comparison into two: "Just as fire leaves a mark upon the body of whoever uses it, so too words of Torah leave a mark on the body of whoever uses it. Just as with fire whoever labors with it is recognizable among other people, so too the disciples of the sages . . . " It is not clear in this longer version what is meant by the mark left on the bodies of those who "use" the Torah. See note 110. *Midraš Haggadol* and *Midraš Leqaḥ Ṭob* have a similar tradition before them but *interpret* this "mark" negatively as a punishment of those who "use" the Torah for personal gain. The same now appears in the text published by Menahem Kahana as the *Mekilta to Deuteronomy* (p. 194). But in the preceding comparison (Torah like fire is used in this world and the next world) "using" Torah appears to be understood positively. For the negative view of "using" the Torah, see §48 (F114.3-6), discussed in Chapter 3, and see note 217 there for other references in early rabbinic literature.

96. Some witnesses reverse the order of "speech" and "walking": the Editio Princeps, MS Berlin, *Midraš Ḥakamim, Midraš Haggadol* (walking, dress, speech), the manuscript published by Menahem Kahana as *Mekilta to Deuteronomy,* and the text cited by R. Yedaiah Hapenini in his commentary. The better witnesses, including Geniza fragments TS C2 211 and TS C6 113, have the order as I have translated it. Dress (*ʿaṭîpatān*) may refer to distinguishing cloaks, such as those worn by philosophers.

97. F399.16-400.6. The citation in *Menorat Ha-Maor* (ed. Enelow, vol. 3, p. 333) omits M. MS London alone omits "had the law not" (*ʾilmālēʾ dāt*) presumably a scribal error of homoioteleuton. The text at the very end is *laʿamôl bāh* according to the better witnesses: MS London, *Yalquṭ Šimʿoni* (MS Oxford and the Salonica printing), Geniza fragment TS C2 211, the Editio Princeps, and the text cited by R. Suleiman in his commentary. Finkelstein fails to record these in his critical apparatus. He follows the reading *lăʿamôd bāh* ("to withstand it") found in MS Berlin, Geniza fragment TS C6 113, *Midraš Haggadol* (and now the text published by Menahem Kahana as *Mekilta to Deuteronomy*), and *Midraš Ḥakamim.* This reading is likely to have been influenced by the parallel in *b. Beṣa* 25b: "Were it not that the Torah was given to Israel, no nation or language would be able to stand before [withstand]

them." According to this tradition, the Torah's law by disciplining Israel, restrained their zeal vis-à-vis the nations. There is no reason, however, to "correct" the *Sifre*'s text according to this tradition as some (e.g., Meir Friedmann in his commentary to his edition of the *Sifre* [Vienna, 1864], and David Hoffmann in a note to his edition of *Midraš Tannaʾim*) have suggested. By retaining *laʿămôl* (on text-critical grounds), M intersects with L4 and L6, where the same verb is used. For this verb used for the study of Torah, see *m. ʾAbot* 1:14: "Know before whom you labor (*ʿāmēl*), which in *b. Ber.* 28b, with reference to prayer becomes "know before whom you stand."

98. On the expression "words of Torah" referring in the *Sifre*, as elsewhere in rabbinic literature, both to the written Torah and to rabbinic teachings, see Chapter 3, note 219.

99. Compare Philo, *Dec.* 49 (trans. F. H. Colson; LCL vol. 7, pp. 30-31), commenting on Exodus 19: "Since it is the nature of fire both to give light and to burn, those who resolve to be obedient to the divine utterances will live for ever as in unclouded light with the laws themselves as stars illuminating their souls, while all who are rebellious will continue to be burnt, aye and burnt to ashes, by their inward lusts, which like a flame will ravage the whole life of those in whom they dwell." Thus, the Torah gives light to those who obey it and burns those who reject it. Here again, the comparison with fire does not produce easily the conclusion derived from it. The incongruity of the *Sifre*'s comparison of Torah to scorching fire ("the *mashal* does not suit the *nimshal*") has been noted by several traditional commentators: David Pardo and *Zeraʿ ʾAbraham* ad loc, and *Zayit Raʿanan* ad *Yalquṭ Šimʿoni*. Compare §306 (F338.4-8): "R. Banaya says: If you perform [= study] words of Torah for their own sakes, words of Torah are life to you . . . but if you do not perform words of Torah for their own sakes, they kill you."

100. *Mek. Baḥodes* 4 (ed. Lauterbach, vol. 2, pp. 220-21). Compare *m. ʾAbot*, 1:10, in the name of R. Eliezer ben Hyrcanus: "Warm yourself by the light of the sages, but beware their burning coals lest you get burned . . . for all of their words are like coals of fire."

101. Elsewhere (*Baḥodeš* 5 [ed. Lauterbach, vol. 2, p. 237]), the *Mekilta* knows how to compare the two positively. Note as well that *Mekilta deR. Simeon bar Yoḥai* ad Exod. 19:8 (ed. Epstein-Melamed, pp. 143-44) presents an expanded list of such positive comparisons, including the one under discussion, but in the simpler, more direct form: "Just as with fire, one who gets [too] close to it is burned, [whereas] one who gets [too] far from it is chilled, so too with words of Torah, one who gets [too] close to it is burned, [whereas] one who gets [too] far from it is chilled."

102. Some have suggested (re)reading the *Sifre* text in this way: "Just as with fire, one who is near it is *warmed.*" See Friedmann's note to his edition of the text, David Pardo ad loc., the commentary *Brît ʾAbraham* to *Yalquṭ Šimʿoni* and the reworkings of *Midraš Leqaḥ Ṭob*, and *Midraš Haggadol* (and now the text published by Menahem Kahana as *Mekilta to Deuteronomy*, p. 194). The last two may reflect a play between *ḥām lô* with respect to fire and *yēš lô ḥayyîm* with respect to Torah.

103. See in particular *Mek. Baḥodeš* 4 (ed. Lauterbach, vol. 2, p. 224) and 9 (ed. Lauterbach, vol. 2, pp. 275-76). See also the view attributed to R. Jose in a *barayta'* in *b. Sukk.* 5a and the discussion that follows it: Moses went up and God came down, but a distance always separated them. For the idea that the people at Sinai beheld God's *word,* see notes 91, 187, and 198.

104. See for example *Pesiq. Rab. Kay.* 12:10 (ed. Mandelbaum, p. 212 bottom), as well as the later rabbinic sources discussed by David J. Halperin, *The Faces of the Chariot* (next note). But the *Mekilta* too, in the context of its commentary to the Song at the Sea (e.g., *Širta'* 3 and 4 [ed. Lauterbach, vol. 2, pp. 24, 30-31]), has no problem asserting that God physically revealed Himself to Israel at the Sea.

105. See David J. Halperin, *The Merkabah in Rabbinic Literature* (New Haven: American Oriental Society, 1980), pp. 55-59, 128-33, 140; idem, *The Faces of the Chariot: Early Jewish Responses to Ezekiel's Vision* (Tübingen: J. C. B. Mohr [Paul Siebeck], 1988), pp. 262-358: Ithamar Gruenwald, *Apocalyptic and Merkavah Mysticism* (Leiden: E. J. Brill, 1980), pp. 37-38, 128-30. When read during the normal course of the lectionary cycle, Exod. 19-20 would have been accompanied by Isa. 6, another mystical vision of heaven. Compare §49 (F114.14-115.5), discussed in Chapter 3, where study of Torah among the sages appears as the equivalent of, and perhaps implicitly as an alternative to, heavenly ascent.

106. *T. Ḥag.* 2:6. See also *p. Ḥag.* 2:1 (77a); and *'Abot R. Nat.* 28 (ed. Schechter, p. 43b), where the relation of the *mashal* to its context is problematic.

107. Compare the fate of Ben Zoma, who is reported to have been destroyed by intensive study of the account of Creation. See *t. Ḥag.* 2:6; *Gen. Rab.* 2:4. The image of a narrow path with dangers on either side is also found in *4 Ezra* 7:6-8, where a steep path passes through a narrow gate leading from the present world to the future world, with fire on one side and deep water on the other. Cf. Matt. 7:13-14.

108. Most traditional commentators recognize that the present comparison relates to exposition of the Merkabah, even though the present context deals with the revelation of the Torah as a whole. See the commentaries cited at the end of note 99.

109. On the problematic positive employment of the verb *to use* with respect to Torah, see note 95 end. For the motif of Torah study as a source of life, see §11 (F86.7-8;) §46 (F104.5-10); §48 (F108.6-9); § 306 (F338.4-8). On the words of Torah as an elixir of life, see §45 (F103.3). On words of Torah living forever, see also §306 (F336.1-4). On the future-worldly rewards of Torah study, see §41 (F87.8-10); §48 (F113.15-17); §336 (F385.12-13). See also later, §344 C2, with note 158.

110. See note 94, for textual variants in which those who use or labor in the Torah are also said to be "marked" in their bodies. The parallel in *Mek. de R. Simeon bar Yoḥai* ad Exod. 19:18 (ed. Melamed-Epstein, pp. 143-144) simplifies the comparison by not mentioning physical marks at all: "Just as with fire, persons who labor with it are recognizable among others, so too the disciples of the sages are recognizable by their speech, by their manner of walking, and

by their dress in the market." For an attempt to understand how the disciples of the sages might be physically marked, see David Pardo's commentary: Just as the faces of those who work with fire are reddened, so too a person's wisdom lights up his face.

111. Although he does not cite our text, Maimonides (*Mišneh Torah, Hilk. De'ot* 5:7-9), in describing how a disciple of the sages should behave, especially in the market, focuses on his speech, manner of walk, and dress (in that order). For a similar example of metaphoric slippage from "words of Torah" to "disciples of the sages," see §306 (F339.6-14), to be discussed in a subscetion of Chapter 3. The figure and class of the rabbinic sage and his relation to Israel more broadly is the subject of Chapter 3.

112. See note 84, where I demonstrated that the verses from Cant. 5:10-16 by which Israel hoped for the nations to recognize its lover are elsewhere taken as referring not only to the Torah but to the rabbinic sages in their study of it. Thus, God's praises are revealed in the praises of Torah and its sages.

113. I take *dāt* in its simplest sense as "law," although it may also denote "reason" or "logic." Other commentators have understood the "fire" of Torah to be its inner, secret meanings, which are clothed in simple language (*pěšāt*). See David Pardo ad loc., and the commentaries *Zayit Ra'anan* and *Brit 'Abrahan* to *Yalquṭ Šim'oni*, the former cited approvingly by the *Zera' 'Abraham* commentary to the *Sifre*. This distinction, however, is a later retrojection. For *dāt* here as law, observance of commandments, worldly obligations, etc., see the commentaries of *Toledot 'Adam* and *'Ohale Yehuda*. R. Suleiman comments that the Torah contains within itself the heavenly edict to study Torah without getting burned by it. For the twofold nature of Torah, comprising law (*halakah*) and narrative (*aggadah*), see §48 (F113.7-8), treated in Chapter 3, as well as note 96 there.

114. For a discussion, see S. D. Driver, *Deuteronomy*, pp. 393-94, as well as the bibliography cited in note 4.

115. The text of the *Sifre* that I translate follows MS London, adjusted at times in accord with Geniza fragments, and therefore varies slightly from that of Finkelstein.

116. This is the reading in MS London, the Editio Princeps, and *Yalquṭ Šim'oni*. The expression "stand over Israel" is missing in the other witnesses, including Genza fragment TS C6 113. The text published by Menahem Kahana as the *Mekilta to Deuteronomy* (p. 196) has in place of *parnāsîm*, *gědôlîm* ("great ones"), a term also used for rabbinic appointments in §12 (F23.3-4). This term will be used by the *Sifre* in its second interpretation of the lemma (B2).

117. MS London has *bězûyîn*, which literally means "treaded upon." The Editio Princeps has *šěbûyîm*, meaning "taken captive." Geniza fragment TS C2 211 has *bězûzîn*, meaning "despoiled."

118. F400.8-14.

119. Thus, the Septuagint has *his people*. Similarly, the Peshiṭta has *people* in the singular. This is probably influenced both by the broader context, where God's love of the nations has no place, and by the use of the third person singular pronominal suffix in the next clause. But note *Tg. Onqelos* translates

peoples as "tribes" (of Israel), as is the interpretation of Rashi, Ibn Ezra, and *Midraš Leqaḥ Ṭob*. See Driver, *Deuteronomy*, p. 393.

120. Compare §311 (F352.5-7): "Another interpretation: 'When the Most High gave to the nations (*gôyîm*) their inheritance' (Deut. 32:8): When the Holy One blessed be He, gave the Torah to Israel, he stood, looked out, and observed, as it is said, 'He stood, shook [= measured] the earth, saw, and made to tremble [= dismissed] the nations' (Hab. 3:6). But there was no nation among all the nations that was worthy to receive the Torah except for Israel. 'He set the borders of the peoples (*'ammîm*)' (Deut. 32:8)." It would appear that *gôyîm* in the lemma is understood to be Israel, even as they are contrasted with the nations, the *gôyîm* of Hab. 3:6. For *gôyîm* as Israel, see Rashi ad Isa. 42:6. Compare the parallel in *Midraš Haggadol*, where Deut. 32:8 is interpretted to mean that God had intended to give the Torah to the nations. Herbert W. Basser (*Midrashic Interpretations of the Song of Moses* [New York: Peter Lang, 1984], p. 126 note E3) refers to Justin Martyr, *Dialogue with Trypho* 131, who takes Deut. 33:8 to mean "that the Gentiles are heirs to God's promises together with Israel."

121. Similarly, *Tgs. Ps.-Jon., Frg.* (MSS V, N, L), and *Neof.* ad loc. say that God offered the Torah only to the descendents of Esau and Ishmael so as to demonstrate His love for His people Israel. David Pardo in his commentary to the *Sifre*, stating that the plain sense of *'ammîm* is the plural *peoples,* relates the present passage to that above in which God offered the Torah to the other nations, thereby showing His love for them too.

122. Contrast this with the text published by Menahem Kahana as the *Mekilta to Deuteronomy* (p. 198, lines 43-44): "Another interpretation: 'Lover, indeed, of the people(s)': This teaches that with the very same love that the Holy One, blessed be He, loved Israel he loved the nations of the world." The Sifre passage may also be compared with §97 (F159.1): "Each and every one [of Israel] was dearer to the Holy One, blessed be He, than all the nations of the world." Compare also *Mek. Širta'* 3 (ed. Lauterbach, vol. 2, p. 23): "Another interpretation of 'my strength' (Exod. 15:2): You are the helper and supported of all the inhabitants of the world, but mine above all!"

123. See in particular Chapter 3, and notes 114-119 there.

124. For the association of Moses and David as *parnāsîm*, see §26 (F36.2 and 38.9), on which see my study, "Sifre Deuteronomy 26 (ad Deut. 3:23)," pp. 245-301. Moses and David were also associated, also in chronological order, in §343 A2-3, discussed earlier.

125. For a different understanding, see *Tg Ongelos*, where *hallowed* are understood to signify the people of Israel as a whole, and *under your hands* is understood to refer to God's redeeming of them, by His might, from Egypt. Similarly, *Tg. Ps.-Jon.* understands *hallowed* to refer to all of Israel. However, *Tgs. Frg.* (MSS V, N, L) and *Neof.* understand *hallowed* to refer to the angels. So far as I can tell, the *Sifre* is the only early source to take *hallowed* here to refer to Israel's (rabbinic) leaders. Note, however, *Deut. Rab.* (ed. Lieberman, p. 130), where the next clause ("They follow in your footsteps") is taken to refer to the "desciples of the sages." The *Sifre*'s interpretation fits its overall attention to

the central place of the sage, as well as rabbinic leadership appointments, within Israel, as will become more evident in the next chapter. See also note 150.

126. The phrase *tukkû lĕraglekā* has been variously understood by both traditional and critical commentators because the first word is an inexplicable hapax legomenon. Some suggested possibilities have been: "they reclined by your feet," "they followed by your feet," "they were struck by your feet," and "they were under your feet." See Driver, *Deuteronomy*, pp. 393-94. The *targumim* take the expression to refer to Israel's being lead under or after the clouds of glory in their journey through the wilderness. See also note 152.

127. Note §97 (F158.17) according to MS Vatican: "'Israel for his own treasure' (Ps. 135:4). 'And to Him shall you cleave'(Deut. 13:5). Even though he brings upon you sufferings, 'And to Him shall you cleave.' And so too it says, 'And they follow in your footsteps': Even though they are smitten for the sake of your Torah, they do not budge." The same interpretation of Deut. 13:5 and 33:3 is found in §32 (F57.6) according to MS Vatican. This would seem to support the first alternative. However, in the present context such an interpretation would leave the interpretation of the next clause (A4) suspended, whereas I understand the latter to provide the apotasis to the present interpretation. The text published by Menahem Kahana (see note 7) as the *Mekilta to Deuteronomy* (pp. 196.22, 198.41) makes this connection explicit. See Kahana's detailed discussion of this point, p. 170.

128. For the interrelation of Israel's sufferings, their possission of the Torah, their dearness to God, and the envy of the nations, see the following: §32 (F57.1-4): "Rabbi Simeon bar Johai says: Dear (*hăbîbîm*) are sufferings, for three precious gifts were given to Israel which the nations of the world desire for themselves, and they were only given to them at the price of suffering, and these are they: Torah, the Land of Israel, and the world to come." §32 (F56.13): "Dear are sufferings, for the name of the Lord rests on one to whom sufferings come." §311 (F351.16-17): "Should you ask why sufferings have come, it is because of the dearness (*hibbātām*) of Israel [to God]." It has been suggested that such positive views of Israel's sufferings are responses to the historical circumstances at the time of the Bar Kochba rebellion and its aftermath, especially as they are often attributed to R. Akiba and his students, who are said to have suffered particularly at the hands of the Romans. See Hammer's note (*Sifre*, p. 506, note 1) to our text. See also Reuben Hammer, "A Rabbinic Response to the Post Bar Kochba Era: Sifre Ha'azinu," *PAAJR* 52 (1985): 37-53; M. D. Herr, "Persecution and Martyrdom in Hadrianic Days," in *Scripta Hierosolymitana* 23 (1972): 85-125. It would be a mistake, however, to reductively view such traditions simply as reflections of or responses to a particular set of events, without also considering how they function rhetorically within the larger (and later) discursive contexts in which are presently set. The cluster of motifs that revolve around the theme of Israel's sufferings and their theological significance would have continued to resonate powerfully and to receive literary expression and re-expression in subsequent periods, and retroactively to be associated with the names of R.

Akiba and his disciples, even when martyrdom and religous persecution per se
were no longer actually experieced by Jews. See in this regard, Saul
Lieberman, "The Martyrs of Caesarea," *Annuaire de l'Institut de Philologie
et d'Histoire Orientales et Slaves* 7 (1939-44): 395-446; idem, "On Persecution
of the Jewish Religion," in *Salo Wittmayer Baron Jubilee Volume*, ed. Saul
Lieberman, 3 vols. (Jerusalem: American Academy for Jewish Research,
1975), vol. 3, pp. 213-45 [Hebrew]. Compare my treatment above of §343 J. I
shall return to this question in the conclusion to this chapter.

129. MS London, Geniza fragment TS C2 211, the Editio Princeps, *Yalquṭ
Šimʿoni* and *Menorat Ha-Maor* (ed. Enelow, vol. 3, p. 333) all have *gērîm*, as
does the citation of the *Sifre* in Tosaphot ad *b. B. Qam.* 38a. Only MS Berlin
and *Midraš Ḥakamim* have *yĕhûdîm* ("Jews"), followed by Finkelstein.
Midraš Haggadol and the text published by M. Kahana as the *Mekilta to
Deuteronomy* (p. 198) have, "go and learn the Torah of the Jews." Geniza
fragment TS C2 182 leaves out this word altogether. Saul Lieberman
("Achievements and Aspirations of Modern Jewish Scholarship," *PAAJR*
46-47 [*Jubilee Volume*] [1980]: 373 note 14) dismisses this reading without
solid textual support. It may be presumed here, in keeping with the *Sifre*'s
exclusivist attitude toward the nations that we have seen elsewhere (but see
especially later, §345 C, where it is said that for the nations to study the Torah
is comparable to adultery), that the only way for a non-Jew to study rabbinic
Torah would be to convert (or feign conversion). For this explanation, see
Tosaphot ad *b. B. Qam.* 38a.

130. There is a problem here in that Rabban Gamaliel (presumably II) was the
Patriarch at Yabneh and not at Usha. If the story is historically representa-
tional (which cannot be assumed), we would have to change either Usha to
Yabneh, as Finkelstein suggests (*PAARJ* 6 [1934-35]: 216), or Rabban
Gamaliel to Rabban Simeon b. Gamaliel (his son), as does MS Berlin and
Midraš Ḥakamim. For further discussion and references to earlier treatments,
see Hammer's note (*Sifre*, p. 507 note 3), as well as note 137 here.

131. For this formulation, see Chapter 3, note 111. Note that it is the full
curriculum of written and oral (rabbinic) Torah that they study and not
simply the Jewish system of civil law as some (see citations in note 137,
especially the article by Saul Lieberman) have presumed.

132. This is the reading of MS London, although not recorded by Finkelstein in his
critical apparatus. The other witnesses simply have, "the great ones of
Israel. . . in place of Israel," except that *Yalquṭ Šimʿoni* (MS Oxford) has, "in
place of all of Israel." The Hebrew here translated as "seized" is *mitmaškĕnîn*,
a denominative of *maškôn* ("pledge"). On this, see note 150.

133. MS Berlin and *Midraš Ḥakamim* add "and even though they sin." Geniza
fragment TS C6 113 has "even though they sin and anger [You]."

134. Only the Editio Princeps has "your fear." MS London (contrary to
Finkelstein's critical apparatus) has "your Torah" like the other witnesses.

135. F400.15-401.11.

136. On this rule, see note 148.

137. For another story of a Roman official asking Rabban Gamaliel about the dual

(written and oral) Torah of the rabbis, see §351 (F408.12-409.2), on which see Chapter 3 and note 68 there . In §357 (F429.2), a story is told, in language similar to that of the present one, in which the government of the house of Caesar sent two officers to find the burial place of Moses. Those who assume the basic historicity of our story (or the others), must strain to identify (and reconcile) its details with a likely historical set of circumstances. See Moshe David Herr. "The Historical Significance of the Dialogues between Jewish Sages and Roman Dignitaries," in *Scripta Hierosolymitana* 22 (1971), p. 133 with note 45 for other references; Heinrich Graetz, *Geschichte der juden*, vol 4 (Leipzig, 1908), p. 108, who suggests the Romans were sent by the emperor Dimitian (early second century) to obtain information to support his charges against the Jews: Isaak Halevy, *Dorot Hariʾšonim*, 4 vols. (Berlin, 1923), vol. 1e, p. 350; Saul Lieberman, "Achievements and Aspirations," pp. 373-77, who says that the story must antedate the Hadrianic persecutions and must refer to gentile government officials from Syria, who wish to ascertain the nature of Jewish *civil* law as it would be applied in Jewish courts in Syria (cf. note 131). Lieberman's refutation (ibid., p. 373) of Boaz Cohen's suggestion (*Jewish and Roman Law: A Comparative Study*, vol. 1 [New York: Jewish Theological Seminary of America, 1966], p. 25) that the story is "apocryphal," to my mind, is not convincing. Once the story is not taken to be historically representational in any simple way, then its details must be considered in relation to the larger *discursive* context in which the story is now found, as is my practice here. Such stories of meetings between Roman officials and rabbinic leaders are a stock literary device, adapted from wider hellenistic usage, whereby the former serve as confirming foils for rabbinic self-understandings. See also note 130.

138. For example, in §343 (F399.7) the nations are impressed with *nĕʾotô wĕšibḥô* (the pleasing and praiseworthy qualities) of God, whereas here they proclaim how *nāʾeh ûmĕšûbbeḥet* (pleasing and praiseworthy) is the rabbinic Torah. On this language, see also Boaz Cohen, *Jewish and Roman Law*, p. 25.

139. Lieberman ("Achievements and Aspirations," pp. 374, 376-77), reading the story apart from its rhetorical context (see note 137), understands it as being "more favorable to the Romans than to the Jews," and therefore "incomprehensible in the mouth of a rabbi who survived the [Hadrianic] persecutions." I fail to see this. Quite to the contrary, when viewed in the broader discursive setting of the *Sifre*'s commentary, the story places praise of the rabbinic Torah, and thereby of Israel, in the mouths of the Roman officers despite their original intentions to the contrary and despite the fact that one of the rabbinic laws discriminates against them. The story both mocks the Romans and extracts from them what its rabbinic creators would wish to have Israel say about itself. Such a story in its present form could easily have been created and circulated in the third century, whatever the origins of its component parts might have been.

140. On the relative antiquity of the larger section of the Palestinian Talmud of which this passage is a part, see Saul Lieberman, *The Talmud of Caesarea; Jerusalem Tractate Neziqin* (= Supplement to *Tarbiz* II.4) (Jerusalem, 1931)

[Hebrew]. Nonetheless, Lieberman ("Achievements and Aspirations," p. 376) considers the *Sifre*'s version of the story to be still earlier and our "main source."

141. The law as it applies to Israelites distinguishes between the owner of an ox that habitually gores and who has been warned to restrain his animal (*mûʿād*), and the owner whose ox is not known to gore (*tām*). The former pays full damages, whereas the latter only pays half damages. See *b. B. Qam.* 14a.

142. This verse is understood to refer to the time of the revelation of the Torah at Sinai, because earlier (3:3) it is said, "God comes from Teman, the Holy One from Mt. Paran; Selah," which clearly echoes Deut. 33:2. Earlier in the *Sifre*'s commentary (§343 G), Hab. 3:3 was cited as a complement to Deut. 33:2. Hab. 3:6 is also cited in the *Mekilta*'s parallel to §343 H, quoted earlier, in relation to God's offering and the nations' rejection of the Torah. For the same interpretation of Hab. 3:6, plus others, see also *b. B. Qam.* 38a in the name of R. Abbahu. Thus, only after God offered the Torah to the nations and they rejected it, including the seven Noahide commandments (one of which prohibits stealing), did God "loosen" their property to Israel. For this interpretation, see David Pardo's commentary to the *Sifre* here. However, compare §311 (F352.5-7), cited in note 120, where Hab. 3:6 is taken to mean that God gave the Torah to Israel after having measured the nations and having found them unworthy.

143. The verse is similarly interpreted in *b. B. Qam.* 38a, in the name of R. Joḥanan. See the MaHarŠaʿ to *b. B. Qam.* 38a, who notes that Paran refers to Ishmael, and it was the descendants of Ishmael who rejected the Torah because they could not live by the prohibition of robbery (see §343 D4, discussed earlier). Hence, it is argued, it was only fair that their property not be protected by Israelite law.

144. Maimonides, *Mišneh Torah Hil. Nizqe mamon* 8:5, applies this reasoning to the other half of the rule: because the gentiles do not hold a man accountable for damages done by his animals, it is unfair to hold an Israelite responsible for the damages his ox does to the ox of a gentile. For a similar interpretation, see *Šiṭṭah Mequbbeṣet* ad *b. B. Qam.* 38a. On the question of whose laws govern damage claims between a Jew and a Gentile, see also §16 (F26.9-27.2) and *b. B. Qam.* 113a-b, as well as Maimonides' commentary to *m. B. Qam.* 4:3.

145. The most common explanation, found elsewhere, is that the gentile is not included in "his fellow" of Exod. 21:35. See, for example, *b. B. Qam.* 38a, where another account is given of our story. In that account there is no mention at all of the rule regarding the stolen property of a gentile. There the Roman emissaries agree to the "truth' of all of the rabbinic Torah, but object to the inconsistency of the mishnaic rule regarding the goring ox of an Israelite that gores the ox of a gentile: if he is not culpable because the gentile is not "his fellow" (Exod. 21:35), then the gentile owner of an ox that gores the ox of an Israelite should likewise not be culpable. Similarly, David Pardo, in commenting on our *Sifre* passage, says that the gentile is not included in "your fellow" (of Exod. 20:14; Deut. 5:18), but then notes that this logic would also

require not holding the gentile culpable under Jewish law. Because of this inconsistency other commentators use Exod. 21:35 to absolve the Jewish ox owner from culpability, and then turn either to Hab. 3:6 or to Deut. 33:1 to justify stricter treatment of the gentile ox owner. See, for example, the MaHaraM and the MaHaRšaL ad *b. B. Qam.* 38a.

146. See *m. ʿAbod. Zar.* 2:1; *b. ʿAbod. Zar.* 26a.

147. Others interpret this to mean that the Roman emissaries decided not to tell Rome the justifying reasons for this seemingly discriminatory law. But this reading cannot be sustained by the text. See the commentary *Pĕnê Mōšeh* ad loc., as well as Rashi ad *b. B. Qam.* 38a.

148. Similarly, see *Sifra Ḥoba pereq* 22 (21) (ed. Finkelstein, vol. 2, p. 211), where the second occurrence of *ʿămîtô* ("his fellow") in Lev. 5:21 is interpreted to exclude the "other," presumably meaning the gentile (as per Rabbenu Hillel's interpretation ad loc.). Likewise, see *t. ʿAbod. Zar.* 8(9):5; and the *barayta* cited in *b. Sanh.* 57a; which permit the stealing of an Israelite from a gentile but forbid the reverse. But compare *t. B. Qam.* 10:15 (ed. Lieberman, p. 53): "One who steals from a gentile must return [what he stole] to the gentile. The stealing from a gentile is worse than the stealing from an Israelite, and if he has denied by oath [the theft] and then dies, [his inheritors] must return it [to the gentile] because of profanation of the divine name." For a similar view see *Sed. ʾEl. Rab.* 26 (ed. Friedmann, p. 140). For discussion of the tosephtan passage, see Saul Lieberman, *Tosefta Ki-Fschuṭah*, vol. 9 (New York: The Jewish Theological Seminary of America, 1988), pp. 121-22. Note also Lieberman's suggestion that the aforementioned *Sifre* passage refers not to the obligation to return the stolen property to the gentile, but to the obligation to pay an added fifth, as in Maimonides, *Mišneh Torah Hil. Gezelah Waʾabedah* 7:7. But Lieberman fails to consider our *Sifre* passage in this context. Compare also *b. B. Qam.* 113a-b, where the view that it is forbidden to rob a gentile is attributed in a *barayta* to R. Akiba, and where R. Simeon the Pious is said to have distinguished between stolen property of a gentile, which is forbidden under normal circumstances, and lost property of a gentile, which is permitted. But the text also presumes that others permit, at least in principle, the stolen property of a gentile. See also *Midraš Tannaʾim* (ed. Hoffmann, p. 121), as well as Tosaphot ad *b. B. Qam.* 38a. For the later codification of this law, forbidding the stolen property of a gentile, see Maimonides, *Mišneh Torah Hil. Gezelah Waʾabedah* 1:2; *Hil. Genevah* 1:1; *Šulḥan ʿAruk Ḥošen Mišpaṭ* 348.2; 359.1. For the codification of the rule permitting holding onto the lost property of a gentile, except where it will cause the profanation of God's name, see *Mišneh Torah Hil. Gezelah Waʾabedah* 11:3; *Šulḥan ʿAruk Ḥošen Mišpaṭ* 266.1-4. For other sources, see Lieberman, *Tosefta Ki-Fschuṭah*, 9:121. Compare now the text published by M. Kahana (see note 7) as the *Mekilta to Deuteronomy* (p. 196.29-30), in which proof of God's greater love for Israel is demonstrated by the law, "The stolen property of an Israelite is forbidden but the lost object of a gentile is permitted." The same appears in *Midraš Hagadol*. In comparing this version of the tradition to that of the *Sifre*, Kahana (pp. 183-85) argues that the *Sifre*

represents an *earlier* stage in the development of the halakah than does the *Mekilta*, the latter reflecting a more sympathetic view of the gentile in this regard. But this presumes a representational view of rabbinic legal discourse and a linear understanding of its development. There is no reason why both views of stealing from a gentile could not have coexisted in different discursive settings. See note 204.

149. On this detail being an editorial edition to the tradition, see Saul Lieberman, "Achievements and Aspirations," p. 373, note 14. But see note 129 here.

150. See §29 (F46.2-3) and §306 (F341.13) where Moses is both the "sage of sages" and the "great of the greats." See as well §13 (F23.3) where rabbinic appointees are referred to as *gĕdôlîm*. For the use of the verb *mĕmaššĕkēn* in relation to David, also called a *parnās* of Israel, see §26 (F38.2), with my analysis in "Sifre Deuteronomy 26 (ad. Deut. 3:23), pp. 300-301. Compare also *b. Šabb.* 33b, where it is said that the righteous (*ṣaddîqîm*) (the "holy ones" of the next interpretation) are seized in place of their generation.

151. On the language of Ezekiel, with its priestly resonances, see Moshe Greenberg, *Ezekiel 1-20*, AB 22 (Garden City, N.Y.: Doubleday, 1983), pp. 104-106, 118. Compare §13 (F23.7-10), where, through a word play, Deut. 1:13 is interpreted to mean that Israel's (rabbinic) judges bear the guilt of Israel on their "heads," with Ezek. 33:7-9 cited as support. But there the judges are responsible for Israel's guilt to the extent that they do not properly warn Israel of the consequences of their misconduct. See my treatment in Chapter 3, note 149.

152. David Pardo, in his commentary to the *Sifre*, suggests that *tukkû* here is from *tōk*, deceit or oppression, as in Ps. 10:7 and 55:12. This would suggest an understanding of the verse as, "they are sinful at your feet (= in your presence)." But the same play might also lie behind the preceding interpretation of this clause: "they are oppressed at your feet."

153. As *Midraš Haggadol* here paraphrases, "Even when You are filled with anger against Israel, you remember your love of the tribes and treat them mercifully."

154. *With him* is found in MS London, the Editio Princeps, *Yalquṭ Šimʿoni*, Geniza fragments TS C2 211 and TS C2 182. It is not in MS Berlin and *Midraš Ḥakamim* and is omitted by Finkelstein.

155. This phrase is repeated in its entirety only in Geniza fragment TS C2 211, and is omitted in MS London, the Editio Princeps, and in *Yalquṭ Šimʿoni*. MS Berlin and *Midraš Ḥakamim* have simply, "They take upon themselves."

156. F401.12-402.2.

157. Compare Hippolytus of Rome's interpretation of this same clause (PO 27, 1-2 [1954], p. 131): "'Tous les sanctifiés (sont) sous tes mains': Car couverture et abri pour tous, qui peut l'être, sinon le Seigneur qui a étendu ses mains et sanctifié tous ceux qui courent à Lui, comme la poule (fait) pour couvrir ses poussins? (Matt. 23:37)." For *ṣaddîqîm* as a term for a subset of rabbinic sages (although not limited to them), used in conjunction with *parnāsîm*, see §306 (F339.6-14), to be discussed in Chapter 3, note 106 there. Ideally at least, Israel's leaders should be *ṣaddîqîm*, whose righteousness is rabbinically

conceived to be a consequence of their Torah learning. On the rabbinic *ṣaddîq* more generally, see Rudolf Mach, *Der Zaddiq in Talmud und Midrasch* (Leiden: E. J. Brill, 1957).

158. The idea that the souls of the righteous are both taken and kept by God is very common, but nowhere else, so far as I can tell, is it related to Deut. 33:3. Compare §357 (F428.13-15); *Sifre Num.* 40, 139 (ed. Horowitz, pp. 44, 185); *Sifre Zuṭ.* (ed. Horowitz, p. 319); *Mek. Širta'* 9 (ed. Lauterbach, vol. 2, p. 67); *b. Šabb.* 152b; *'Abot R. Nat.* 12 (ed. Schecter, col. 25b); *Tanḥ. Bešallaḥ* 5 (ed. Buber, col. 28b). David Pardo comments that this is another way in which God's love of Israel distinguishes them from the nations, for whereas the pious of the nations have a part in the world to come, their souls are not in the interim bound up with God. For the idea that the righteous after their deaths retire to the Garden of Eden, see §10 (F18.2); §357 (F427.4). For the future rewards of the righteous who suffer in this world, see §53 (F120.12-121.1).

159. For other places in which this tradition is more fully recounted, see note 92. For the identification of present-day Torah study among the desciples of the sages with the war that Moses fought against the angels to receive the Torah at Sinai, see note 200.

160. As noted earlier, this story echoes aspects, including language, of the dialogue between Israel and the nations in §343 J3. In both cases the gentile's intentions are reversed. See note 138.

161. The distinctive place of Israel's leaders, and perhaps even a hint of the suffering by which they are marked, was found in an earlier part of the commentary as well: §343 L6. The idea of eternal life, both of the words of Torah and of those who labor in them, was also expressed earlier: §343 L5.

162. Israel's suffering as God's beloved is reminscent of §343 J3, whereas the return to the original encounter with revelation recalls §343 K. Israel's suffering at the hands of the nations also brings to mind an earlier section (§343 D6-8) in which it is said that Israel bears a heavier burden because of the nations' rejection of the seven Noahide commandments.

163. MS Berlin and *Midraš Ḥakamim*, followed by Finkelstein, have here, "For the ark [of the covenant]."

164. F402.3-5. MS London alone omits from after the first "only for our sakes" until the next, presumably due to a scribal error of homoioteleuton.

165. David Pardo explains that had the text wished to communicate the simple sense of God's commanding Israel, it would have used the direct pronominal object *'otānû* rather than the indirect pronominal object *lānû*.

166. The commentary *Toledot 'Adam* explains that the Temple was not built for the sake of the sacrifices to God, but for the sake of housing the Torah for Israel. This, although sensitive to the text's meaning, goes beyond it. Compare the interpretation of Exod. 31:14 attributed to R. Simeon b. Menasiah in *Mek. Šabbata'* 1 (ed. Lauterbach, vol. 3, p. 198): The Sabbath was given "to/for you" (*lākem*), meaning for your benefit and not vice versa. Compare the *Sifre*'s interpretation of *lākem* ("to you") as "for you" in §135 (F191.9), to be treated in Chapter 3.

167. Geniza fragments TS C2 211, TS C2 182, and TS C6 113 add "for us."

168. Geniza fragment TS C2 182 has "I might conclude that it is an inheritance for the children of kings or the children of elders [alone]," and then proceeds to "Scripture teaches," without asking explicitly about the "children of commoners."

169. MS Berlin, *Midraš Haggadol, Midraš Ḥakamim,* and the Editio Princeps have here "from whence," lacking in MS London, and Geniza fragments TS C2 182, TS C2 211, and TS C6 113.

170. F402.6-8. Deut. 29:10 continues, "your children, your wives, even the stranger (*gēr*) within your camp, from woodchopper to waterdrawer."

171. Israelites are the descendents of Jacob rather than of Moses, and to him they collectively trace their covenantal pedigree. On the significance of Jacob, rather than Abraham or Isaac, as the patriarch to whose descendants the Torah was given, see earlier, §343 G.

172. The connection between the expression "inheritance of the congregation of Jacob" and the question about royalty and commoners is not a smooth one. I take it to derive from the idea of inheritance as suggesting a genealogical link between those who inherit the Torah and Jacob their ancestor. See the next note. Other commentators suggest that the idea of nobility is suggested by the following verse (33:5), "When there was a king in Jeshurun." See, for example, *Zayit Raʿanan* to *Yalquṭ Šimʿoni.* The *Sifre*'s commentary to that verse will be treated in Chapter 3. But there the word *king* is understood to refer to God.

173. Elsewhere in rabbinic literature (e.g., *b. Sanh.* 59a), Deut. 29:9 is cited in support of the idea that the Torah is the inheritance of Israel ("for us") and not of the nations, but this does not seem to me to be the point of the *Sifre*'s commentary here, although it will be in the next comment. For the inclusion of the convert (biblical "stranger"), see Deut. 29:10, cited in note 170. Thus, David Pardo understands "the children of commoners" of our commentary to refer to converts, that is, those who are not *genealogically* descended from the patriarchs. Similarly, Ramban in his commentary to Deut. 33:4 notes that the text does not say that the Torah is an inheritance to the "house of Jacob" or to the "seed of Jacob," but to the "congregation of Jacob," thereby including "all who have been gathered to him" (*kol hanniqhălîm ʿalāyw*), referrring in particular to the converts (*gērîm*). Elsewhere in the *Sifre* (§247 [F276.5-6]) it is stressed that the "congregation of converts" is included in the "congregation of Israel." Still, I think that, if there is here an oblique rabbinic polemic, it is against the priestly claims for a privileged juridical and pedagogical status, the priests having remained the only hereditary privileged class after the cessation of the monarchy. In this regard, note that the phrase *congregation of Jacob* of Deut. 33:4 is elsewhere interpreted in the *Sifre* to denote all of Israel (again citing Deut. 29:9) rather than its genealogical divisions (priests, Levites, Israelites). See §48 (F112.7-11), to be discussed in Chapter 3, with note 192 there. Compare also §41 (F86.4-5), to be discussed in Chapter 3, where it is stated that since all of Israel were commanded at Sinai, even the *qāṭān* (who is linked to the sage) among them may teach Torah that ultimately derives from God. On the tension between priests and sages in the *Sifre* more generally, see Chapter 3. The expression *this day* in Deut. 29:9 may also be understood to

signify the perpetual present of the commentary: now also all of Israel are recipients of the Torah, and not just those who are the biological descendants of the Israelites who originally stood at Mt. Sinai. Such expressions are also interpreted in the *Sifre* in support of rabbinic legal and pedagogic authority (the authorities of "this day"). On this, see Chapter 3, note 196.

174. The lemma is not found here in any of the witnesses, because it was previously quoted and commented upon as part of the second interpretation of "Moses charged us with the Teaching." MS Berlin and *Midraš Ḥakamim,* followed by Finkelstein, have "another interpretation."

175. MS Berlin, *Midraš Ḥakamim,* and Geniza fragment TS C2 211 have here *mĕ'ôrāśâ,* which would represent a less radical permutation of the word *heritage,* but not the correct spelling of *betrothed.* MS Berlin, *Midraš Ḥakamim, Midraš Haggadol,* and Geniza fragment TS C2 182 follow with "this teaches that." For the word-play, see also *b. Ber.* 57a; *Pesaḥ.* 49b; *Sanh.* 59a; in each of which it is employed to make a somewhat different point.

176. F402.8-12.

177. See note 173.

178. For the same interpretation see *b. Ber.* 57a, as well as *Exod. Rab.* 33:7, where Hos. 2:21 is cited for the marriage image. Compare *b. Pesaḥ.* 49b, where Deut. 33:4 is similarly interpreted to mean that a disciple of the sages who engages Torah before an unlearned Israelite (*'am hā'āreṣ*) is like one who has intercourse with his betrothed in front of another man. For the idea that what took place at Sinai was a wedding ceremony, either between God and Israel or between Israel and the Torah, see L. Ginzberg, *Legends of the Jews,* vol. 6, p. 36 note 200. Note in particular *Mek. Baḥodeš* 3 (ed. Lauterbach, vol. 2, pp. 218-19), where the idea that God as bridegroom came *from* Sinai to Israel as bride (rather than the reverse) is exegetically linked by R. Jose to Deut. 33:2 ("The Lord came *from* Sinai"). Just as the metaphor of Israel's being wed to God can be represented by Israel's being wed to the Torah that He gave them, so, too, it can be represented by Israel's being wed to the Sabbath, also given by God as a token of His love. For the latter idea, see Ginzberg, *Legends,* vol. 6, p. 41, note 221. The disputed legal question whether and under what circumstances gentiles can study the Torah is a complex one that I cannot enter into here. See in particular *b. Sanh.* 59a, where the view of R. Joḥanan is similar to that of our commentary, but is opposed by the opinion of R. Meir, cited as a *barayta',* that "a gentile who occupies himself with [= studies] the Torah is like the High Priest, as it is said, '[You shall keep my statutes and my ordinances,] which if a man fulfills he shall live by them' (Lev. 18:5). 'Priests, Levites, and Israelites' is not written here but 'a man.' Thus you learn: Even a gentile who occupies himself with the Torah is like the High Priest." The *gemara* interprets this to refer only to that study relating to the seven Noahide commandments. For various understandings of this passage, some more restrictive and others more liberal regarding gentile study of the Torah (written and oral), see, to begin with, the commentaries to *b. Sanh.* 59a, as well as Maimonides, *Mišneh Torah Hil. Melakim* 10:9. See also note 57.

179. Here and in what follows I translate MS London (which differs only slightly

from *Yalquṭ Šimʿoni* and Geniza fragment TS C2 211). MS Berlin, *Midraš Ḥakamim*, and Geniza fragment TS C2 182, followed by Finkelstein, have in place of the lemma, "Do not read 'betrothed' (*mĕʾôrāsâ*) but 'heritage' (*môrāšâ*)," with MS Berlin and *Midraš Ḥakamim*, followed by Finkelstein, adding, "This teaches that the Torah is an inheritance to Israel." To my knowledge, this would be the only case of a "don't read" interpretation providing the basis, as if it now were Scripture, for another "don't read" interpretation. Only MS Berlin introduces this section with "another interpretation," adopted by Finkelstein.

180. Here *Midraš Haggadol* alone, followed by Finkelstein, adds: "So too a disciple of the sages who has turned away from the words of Torah to attend to other [heretical] matters should not be embarrassed to return to them should he so desire, even after a hundred years, because he can say, 'I am returning to my inheritance.'" This is also found in *Exod. Rab.* 34:7, where C and D are reversed. However, it is unlikely that this was ever part of the text of the *Sifre*. MS Berlin, *Midraš Ḥakamim*, Geniza fragment TS C2 182, and Geniza fragment TS C2 211, followed by Finkelstein, introduce the concluding citation of the lemma with, "therefore it is said."

181. F402.13-18.

182. On a divorced woman being unable to return to her former husband if she has been married in the interim to another, see Deut. 24:4. For this as a metaphor for God's relation with Israel, see Jer. 3:1. See §306 (F330.3-7), to be commented upon in Chapter 4, where the same marriage and divorce metaphor is midrashically applied to Israel's future reconciliation with God. For the idea that separation from words of Torah results necessarily in attachment to idolatry, see §43 (F96.6). Note in this regard the interpolation found in *Midraš Haggadol*, cited in note 180.

183. Compare the tradition, first expressed in *Mek. ʿAmaleq* 4 (ed. Lauterbach, vol. 2, pp. 188-89), that, whereas the Land of Israel, the Temple, and the Davidic monarchy were granted to Israel conditionally (dependent on their conduct), the Torah was given to them unconditionally. Deut. 33:4 is there cited as proof for the last: Torah is an unconditional, inalienable inheritance of the congregation of Jacob.

184. F355.6-7.

185. F355.7-8. The exact meaning of *ṣārôt* ("distress") is unclear here. See Friedmann's suggestion (in a note to his edition of the text) to change the text to *haṣṣadôt* ("desolation"[?]), but there is little text-critical basis for this. For the term *robbers* (*līsṭès* = Greek *lēstēs*) elsewhere in the *Sifre*, see §1 (F6.7), §43 (F101.10), §282 (F298.5), and §343 (F396.8). In each of the first two cases, as often elsewhere in early rabbinic literature, the term appears in a *mashal*, being a figure for lawlessness more generally. It would seem that the commentary's three terms—*distress, marauding troops,* and *robbers*—correspond here to the three difficult terms of the lemma: *tōhû, yĕlēl,* and *yĕšimôn.*

186. F355.8-9.

187. Finkelstein, following *Midraš Haggadol* and *Midraš Ḥakamim*, has "seeing it

and considering it" (*rôʾîm ʾôtô wĕmaśkîlîm bô*). But MS London, MS Oxford, *Yalquṭ Šimʿoni*, and the Editio Princeps all have just *mistakkĕlîm bô* which conveys the sense both of "observing" and of "gaining understanding." This choice of words may be significant because of the use of the verb *histakkēl* elsewhere in relation to mystical visions, where it similarly denotes seeing and knowing. See for example, *m. Ḥag.* 2:1, where the verb is used in a mystical context, but in juxtaposition with the verb *dāraš.* Here the verb is employed as a paraphrase of *yĕbônĕnēhû,* since the root *byn* can convey in biblical wisdom literature both the sense of understanding and the sense of perception with the eyes. For the latter, see Prov. 7:7; Job 9:11; 23:8. The visual sense may also derive from Exod. 20:15: "And all the people saw the [plurality of] voices-thunderings." On this verse rabbinically understood, see note 198.

188. Literally, "how much midrash is in it," and similarly for what follows.

189. F355.9-11.

190. The Hebrew is *nirtāʿîm,* meaning literally, "were [not] shaken." The same word occurs in §344 (F401.15), but there it is said that Israel *were* startled or thrown back (*nirtāʿîm laʾăḥôrêhem*), as in the parallels in *Mek. Baḥodeš* 2 (ed. Lauterbach, vol. 2, p. 202) and 9 (ibid., p. 269). The parallels in *t. ʿArak.* 1:10 and *b. Šabb.* 88b, however, use other verbs. Note how *Midraš Haggadol* solves this difficulty: "Even though they were thrown back twelve miles and returned eleven [?] miles, they were not harmed, neither by. . . ." On the nations being shocked when God shook the whole earth at the time of revelation, see §343 E (and compare §343 F), discussed earlier.

191. This follows MS Oxford, the Editio Princeps, *Yalquṭ Šimʿoni* (MS Oxford): *miqqôl haqqôlôt. Midraš Haggadol* has "by the voice of the thunder" (*miqqôl haqôl*). MS London has the strange formulation, "by the voice of the divine utterance of the thunderings" (*miqqôl haddibbēr haqqôlôt*). Finkelstein follows MS Berlin and *Midraš Ḥakamim*: "by the thunderings" (*min haqqôlôt*). *Yalquṭ Šimʿoni* (Salonika) has simply, "by the voice of the lightnings" (*miqqôl hallappîdîm*).

192. F355.11-13. The phrase *the voice of the lightnings* is found in MS London, MS Oxford, the Editio Princeps, *Yalquṭ Šimʿoni* (MS Oxford), and *Midraš Haggadol.* Finkelstein follows MS Berlin and *Midraš Ḥakamim*: "by the lightnings" (*min hallappîdîm*). For *Yalquṭ Šimʿoni* (Salonica), see the previous note. See also note 198.

193. For discussion, see M. Avi-Yonah, *The Jews under Roman and Byzantine Rule,* pp. 89-136. As always, however, such midrashic references to historical circumstances are general enough to permit their application to circumstances of later times as well.

194. Whereas in Exod. 19:12 God instructs Moses to bound the people, in 19:23, Moses, in repeating God's instruction, speaks of bounding the mountain. This ambiguity may be reflected in the *targumim: Tgs. Fragmentary* (MSS P, L, V, N) and *Ps.-Jonathan* "translate" our verse to mean that God surrounded Israel with the protective clouds of glory, whereas *Tgs. Onqelos* and *Neofiti* speak of God having caused Israel to camp round about the Shekina (divine

presence). *Mekilta de R. Simeon bar Yoḥai* (ed. Epstein-Melamed, p. 141), stresses that God set a boundary around Mt. Sinai on all sides, implying that God gathered the people round about the mountain. It would be difficult to reconcile this image with that of Israel standing opposite God as his divine utterances left his right hand to encompass them (§343 K).

195. See Driver, *Deuteronomy*, p.357; BDB, col. 107.

196. In the other three sets of interpretations of this verse different contexts are suggested, and, hence, different understandings of the word *yĕbônĕnēhû* are suggested, including both the sense of instruction and the sense of God's attending to Israel's needs. Note that the understanding of *yĕbônĕnēhû* as "he instructed him" is already found in the Septuagint (*epaideusen auton*), which does not otherwise construe the verse as referring to the revelation at Sinai. The *targumim* all understand the verb in terms of teaching, using forms of the verbal root ʾlp. In the present interpretation, the *Sifre*'s commentary emphasizes the sense of *bînâ* ("discernment"), rabbinically understood as the ability to penetrate below the surface meanings of a text and learn its extended meanings. For this understanding, see the commentaries of David Pardo and *Zeraʿ ʾAbraham*, as well as *Midraš Leqaḥ Ṭob* to our verse. Compare Chapter 3, note 138.

197. Similar elasticity can be seen in the preceding set of interpretations of this verse (§313 [F354.9-355.5]). There the verse is taken to refer to Abraham, that is, to God accompanying Abraham in his move from Ur of the Chaldees to Canaan, even as the word *yĕbônĕnēhû* is understood to signify Abraham's having made God known to others as the God of heaven and earth.

198. See notes 91 and 187. Consider also the *Mekilta*'s commentary to Exod. 20:15 ("All the people saw the thunderings") (*Baḥodes* 9 [ed. Lauterbach, vol. 2, pp. 266-67]). There the view is attributed to R. Akiba that Israel "saw and heard what could be seen," in other words, they both heard and saw each divine utterance. For the same idea, of God's voice having become visible, see *Pirqe R. El.* 41 (Warsaw, 98a) and *Midr. Samuel* 9:4 (ed. Buber, p. 74), as well the references to Philo in note 91. Subsequently in the *Mekilta*, the view is attributed to R. Judah the Patriarch that "as soon as the divine utterance came forth they interpreted it," citing Deut. 32:10. Compare earlier, §343 B (F395.10-13), where it is said that God revealed the Torah to Israel in multiple languages. For the relation fo multiple languages to multiple interpretations, see notes 24 and 25. That the Torah revealed to Moses at Sinai already contained within it the later unfolding of the oral Torah in all its branches is stated frequently elsewhere in the *Sifre:* §48 (F113.8-9), §58 (F124.11-14), §59 (F125.1-2), §306 (F339.6-14), §313 (F355.9-11), §317 (F359.13-18), §344 (F401.3-4), §351 (F408.15). Here it is stressed that already at Sinai each Israelite could perceive that potential. But contrast the later formulation attributed to R. Joḥanan in *Cant. Rab.* 1:2 (1:12 in Donsky's edition), in which it is said that an angel would take each divine utterance-commandment to each Israelite, *telling* them how many laws were "contained"in each, etc., whereupon the Israelite would accept it. On the intermediary function of the angels at revelation, see note 66.

199. Compare also §343 L, treated earlier, where each divine utterance or command is said to have encircled Israel. For fuller expressions of the idea that Israel was thrust back twelve miles, see notes 92 and 190.

200. See note 190. Note in particular *Mek. Baḥodeš* 9 (ed. Lauterbach, vol. 2, pp. 269-70), where God not only sends His angels to assist Israel as they are thrust back and must return, but helps them Himself. There it is also said, in the name of R. Judah b. El'ai, that God commanded the clouds of glory to sprinkle Israel with water so as to protect them from the scorching heat of revelation. The commentaries of David Pardo, *Zeraˤ ʾAbraham,* and *ʾOhale Yehudah* to the *Sifre* similarly understand God's protection of Israel here to refer to the angels' role in assisting them in receiving the commandments. For Moses' receiving the Torah at Sinai compared to the waging of a war, see §49 (F114.14-115.5), to be discussed in Chapter 3.

201. Even for the latter tradition two versions are given: one that they were startled when struck by the divine utterances (§344 C3), and one that they were not (§313 E).

202. For a fuller discussion and a more extreme example, see Chapter 4, and note 9 there for bibliography.

203. For the "song" of Torah incorporating past, present, and future—this world and the next—see Chapter 4, note 140.

204. The same story presents us with yet another, but not unrelated problem of midrashic re-presentation, that of *halakah* ("law"), which in a sense brings us to the question of the commentary's ability to represent its own *performative* present. For in our version of the story it is assumed that both in Rabban Gameliel's time *and* at the time of the commentary (one to two centuries later) the *halakah* permitted stolen property of a gentile to a Jew, whereas other versions of the same story tell of Rabban Gamaliel's having reversed that law, thereby forbidding stolen property of a gentile to a Jew. Here again, we could explain this discrepancy chronologically (the *Sifre* represents an earlier stage in the development of the law from that represented in other texts) or sociologically (the *Sifre* represents a variant legal norm than that represented in parallel texts). But a third possibility needs also to be considered: just as biblical "text" and historical "event" become plastic in their re-presentation within the fabric of midrashic discourse, so, too, *halakah*. In other words, the stolen property of a gentile could simultaneously have been permitted and forbidden: permitted in legal principle (because of the anomalous status of gentiles and their property in Jewish law) and forbidden in social application (because of the metalegal principle of avoiding "profanation of the divine name" in the eyes of the nations). See note 148. For this view, see Gedaliah Alon, *The Jews in Their Land in the Talmudic Age,* trans. Geshon Levi, vol. 2 (Jerusalem: Magnes, 1984), pp. 554-55 [Hebrew original: 1967, vol. 1, pp. 346-47]; as well as Rashi ad *b. Sanh.* 57a. Once again, our imagined commentary maker would have fashioned a version of the story with a version of the law that suited the rhetorical moment of his commentary. The underexplored question of the relation of *halakah* to rabbinic, and in this case midrashic, discourse is one to which I will return in the sequel to this book. On

the question of the difficulties of employing rabbinic texts such as the *Sifre* to representationally reconstruct the sociohistorical circumstances of the time of the commentary's creation and reception, see Chapter 3.

205. In other words, from the fact that rabbis interpreted scriptural language as they did, it is not self-evident that they viewed language and speech in general as being equally polysemous. For such a view, see Howard Eilberg-Schwartz, "Who's Kidding Whom? A Serious Reading of Rabbinic Word Plays," *JAAR* 55 (1987): 765-88. A comparison of midrashic methods of interpreting Scripture with those employed in the Talmuds for interpreting the Mishnah suggest otherwise, at least in relative terms. Likewise, the fact that the rabbis did not value the writing of history or biography as we conceive of them, favoring rather the episodic re-presentation of events in other discursive media, does not mean that they were antihistorical, sought to escape from history, or denied its reality. For an example of such a view see Chapter 1, note 50. Just because rabbinic stories are not strung together continuously to form narrative history or biography, but rather are scattered about in multiple and variant re-presentations in texts of commentary, does not necessarily mean that their "authors" denied the substance of history any more than they denied the text of Scripture. Rather, rabbinic attitudes to language and time need to be assessed in relation to the specific discursive practices, or "illocutionary acts," in which they function. On this problem more generally, see John R. Searle, "The Logical Status of Fictional Discourse," in *Expressions and Meaning: Studies in the Theory of Speech Acts* (Cambridge: Cambridge University Press, 1979), pp. 58-75. See also Chapter 1, note 50.

206. For Josephus' retelling, and other prerabbinic exempla, see note 90. There is, however, a tendency in later midrashic collections toward greater narrativity. On this, see Yaakov Elbaum, "From Sermon to Story: The Transformation of the Akedah," *Prooftexts* 6 (1966): 97-116. This tendency comes to full expression in *Pirqe de R. Eliezer* (see especially Chapter 41 on Sinai), and similar medieval narrative *"midrashim"*, which, however, no longer take the form of biblical commentary per se. Although I have argued that the fragments of larger traditions are woven into our commentary (e.g., the reference to the Israelites being thrust back twelve miles by each commandment, on which see notes 92 and 190 for reference to other contexts where the presumed tradition is presented more fully), there is no reason to assume that such larger traditions were ever in ancient times strung together as continuous rabbinic narrations of the story of revelation. We only know these traditions in their fractured refiguration as redacted commentary.

207. The one rather anomalous exception is *Seder 'Olam Rabbah*, which is structured as a chronography rather than as a history. For bibliography on the question of rabbinic historiography and biography, see Chapter 3, note 12, as well as Yosef hayim Yerushalmi, *Zakor: Jewish History and Jewish Memory* (Seattle: University of Washington Press, 1981), pp. 16-26.

208. For a fuller statement of the "circulatory" model here presumed, see the end of Chapter 1.

209. For the former, see §343 C, K; §13 C. For the latter, see §343 B, §313 D, as well

as the *Sifre*'s own multiple interpretations of scriptural words and phrases.

210. For the desired unity of Israel, upon which God Himself, as it were, is dependent, see §346 (F403.7-404.4), as well as §96 (F158.1-2).

211. That rabbinic Torah is one and the rabbinic sages are one, notwithstanding the heterogeneity of both, is stated in §306 (F339.6-14), to be discussed in Chapter 3. See also Chapter 3, note 41. My point here is that the multivocality of interpreted Torah is delimited not so much by any constant set of enumerable *principles,* whether hermeneutical or ideological (dogma), as by the evolving *practice* of Torah study as it is textually circumscribed in the redacted collections in which that study finds its literary crystallization and as it is socially circumscribed by the society of sages who transformatively circulate the traditions circumscribed and configured by those collections. Both are understood to embody the revealed will of God. For more on this subject, see Chapter 4.

212. See §343 C, J1, K; §344 A4, B4, C4; §313 C, E.

213. See §343 L4, M; §344 C3 (with which compare §343 K and §313 E). Note also the world-shaking effects of revelation in §343 E, F.

214. See §344 B3.

215. See §343 D1-6 (but cf. §343 E, where the nations appear as outsiders to the whole event of revelation).

216. See §343 G.

217. See §343 J3, but compare §344 B1.

218. See §343 D7, 8. On Israel dying for God's sake, see §343 J3.

219. See §343 J3; §344 A3, C3; §313 A-B. On the possibility of historically locating the referents of such sufferings and self-sacrifice, see notes 42, 50, 51, 79, 128, 193, and 227-28.

220. See §343 G, J3; §345 A, C.

221. See §344 A1, B1, C1. Note in this regard Israel's ambiguous desire to communicate to the nations God's praises (§343 J3) and even perhaps the virtues of its Torah (§344 B1). On the ambiguities in Israel's claims for an exclusive relationship with God and Torah, see notes 57 and 179.

222. This, I have argued, is especially evident in Israel's dialogue with the nations (343 J3) and in the story of the Roman officers who come to study Torah at Rabban Gamaliel's school (§344 B1).

223. See §343 L6. See also §344 C2 for the intimacy with God that the souls of the righteous experience after death.

224. See §344 A2, B2. The theme of Israel's rabbinic leaders is picked up again in the commentary's treatment of the next verse (Deut. 33:5), to be discussed in Chapter 3.

225. See also §344 C2, on the eternal life of the souls of the righteous, who from a rabbinic perspective acquire righteousness through Torah study and practice. See notes 157 and 158.

226. See especially my discussion of §343 D, J3; §343 B1. See also note 230.

227. See notes 79 and 128. Another *possible* candidate would be §343 D6-8, where the *Sifre* (unlike its parallel in the *Mekilta*) stresses that the nations *rejected* the seven Noahide commandments that they had previously *accepted.* Although this may be an allusion to what to the rabbis would be Christianity's

228   From Tradition To Commentary

antinomian turn, it could simply be meant to emphasize the gentiles' moral
unsuitability for divine favor. See note 42. See also my discussion of §345,
where the Torah is said to be betrothed to Israel and like another man's wife to
the nations.

228. For bibliography on possible anti-Christian polemics in early rabbinic
midrash, see Chapter 4, note 35. In considering this possibility here, I checked
(using as my guide, *Biblicia Patristica: Index Citations et Allusions bibliques
dans la Littérature Patristique,* 4 vols. [Paris: Centre National de la Recherche
Scientifique, 1975-87]) the extant Patristic commentaries to the verses
interpreted by the *Sifre* (especially Deut. 32:10; 33;2-4; Hab. 3:3-6; Cant.
5:9-16), but found nothing by which I could identify the *Sifre*'s commentary as
a response to Christian interpretations of the same verses. Most suggestive,
but hardly determinative, is the early Christian interpretation of Hab. 3:3 (see
§343 C and note 142) as referring to Jesus' coming. See, for example, Irenaeus,
Adv. Haer. 3.20.4; 4.33.11; origen, *Schol. in Cant.* (Migne, *PG* 253 B4); idem,
Homil. in Exod. 9.4 (*GCS* 29: 242.13). On the supposed historicist implications of the apparant references to Rome, see notes 50, 51, 79, 128, 130, 137,
and 139. Joseph Heinemann (*'Aggādôt wĕtôlĕdōtehen,* pp. 117-19) argues
that the tradition of the offering of the Torah to the nations was at first
directed against the "hellenistic" nations and only subsequently against
Christianity, but does not make a convincing case.

229. This can be seen in the following tally of the occurrences of forms of the word
'ummâ ("nation") to refer negatively to the gentile nations in *Sifre
Deuteronomy,* according to the biblical lections into which the text of the
Sifre is presently divided: *Dĕbārîm: 1; Wā'ethannan:* 2; *'Ēqeb:* 3; *Rĕ'ēh:* 3;
Šōpĕṭîm: 2; *Kî-tēṣē':* 5; *Kî-tābô':* 0; *Nĕṣābîm:* 3; *Ha'ăzînû:* 37; *Zō't
habbĕrākâ:* 13. Compared to these sixty-nine negative references, I could find
only six neutral references to the "nations" in all of *Sifre Deuteronomy,* and
needless to say, no positive ones. But even more significant is the fact that
approximately 75 percent of the negative references are concentrated in about
25 percent of the text. To give some sense of how *Sifre Deuteronomy*
compares in this regard with the other "tannaitic" midrashic collections, *Sifre
Numbers* contains only eight negative references to the "nations," and the
Sifra only nineteen. Closer to *Sifre Deuteronomy* is the *Mekilta of R. Ishmael*
with forty negative references, of which thirty-five (about 90 percent) are
concentrated in the section *Bĕšallaḥ* and *Yitrô* (about 50 percent of the text),
wherein lie all of the parallels from the *Mekilta* that we have examined.

230. See the similar conclusions reached by Menahem Kahana ("*Dappîm
hammĕkîltā' lidbārîm pārāšôt ha'ăzînû wĕzō't habbĕrākâ,*" *Tarbiz* 57.2
[1988]: 165-201, esp. 180-186 and 200-201) regarding the tendency of the
editor of the *Sifre* (or at least of *Zō't Habbĕrākâ* and *Ha'āzînû*) to rework his
materials with an especially negative slant against the nations. It is significant
that Kahana comes to this conclusion after comparing the *Sifre*'s commenatary to Deut. 33:3-4 with that of what may be a fragment from the
Mekilta to Deuteronomy for the *very same verses.* For examples, see notes
122 and 148.

231. For this terminology, see note 10. Compare how Israel's ambivalent covenantal relationship to nature (including the nations) is expressed through a multiplicity of discrete yet interconnected small narrative interpretations of Deut. 32:1, as discussed in Chapter 4. Note Hans Kellner's paraphrase of N. R. Ankersmit's conception of the relationship of historical narrative to historical past: "If one view of the past prevails, there is *no* view of the past because only a multiple play of perspectives provided by a variety of narrations can enable us to 'see' at all the contours and specificity of each view of the past." In Hans Kellner, "Narrativity in History: Post-Structuralism and Since," p. 21, referring to F. R. Ankersmit, *Narrative Logic: A Semantic Analysis of the Historian's Language* (The Hague: Martinus Nijhoff, 1963), p. 240.

3. The Early Rabbinic Sage and His Torah in the Text of the *Sifre*

1. Although, as will be seen, several terms are employed by the *Sifre*, as by rabbinic literature more generally, for the sage, *ḥakām* is the most frequent and inclusive of them, denoting members of the rabbinic class. On the use of the word *class* for the rabbinic sages, see Lee I. Levine, *The Rabbinic Class in Palestine during the Talmudic Period* (Jerusalem: Yad Izhak be Zvi, 1985), p. 2 [Hebrew]. In such literary contexts the terms *rab* ("master") and *rabbî* ("my master") are used mainly in direct address, as titles preceding a particular sage's name, or when the master-disciple relationship is specifically being referred to. However, in ancient inscriptions it is difficult to discern when the term *rabbî* and its cognates is a conferred title denoting a member of the rabbinic class and when the term is simply honorific, denoting someone deserving of respect. See Hershel Shanks, "Is the Title 'Rabbi' Anachronistic in the Gospels?" *JQR* 53 (1962-63): 337-45; idem, "Origins of the Title 'Rabbi,'" *JQR* 59 (1968-69): 152-57; with responses by S. Zeitlin, in *JQR* 53: 345-49, and *JQR* 59: 158-60; E. Lohse, in *TDNT* 6 (1968): 961-65; Shaye J. D. Cohen, "Epigraphical Rabbis," *JQR* 72 (1981): 1-17.

2. See in particular the following writings of Ephraim E. Urbach: "Class-Status and Leadership in the World of the Palestinian Sages," in *Proceedings of the Israel Academy of Sciences and Humanities* 2, no. 4 (1966): 38-74; "Talmudic Sage: Character and Authority," in *Jewish Society through the Ages*, ed. H. H. Ben-Sasson and S. Ettinger (New York: Schocken, 1969), pp. 116-47; *The Sages: Their Concepts and Beliefs*, trans. Israel Abrahams, 2 vols. (Jerusalem: Magnes, 1979), esp. vol. 1, pp. 564-648. For more critical approaches, which are consequently more limited in focus, see for the Babylonian sages, Jacob Neusner, *A History of the Jews in Babylonia*, 5 vols. (Leiden: E. J. Brill, 1965-70), vol. 4, pp. 279-402; and for the Palestinian sages, Jacob Neusner, "The Quest for Authority," in *Judaism in Society: The Evidence of the Jerushalmi: Toward a Natural History of Religion* (Chicago: University of

Chicago, 1983), pp. 115-97; Levine, *The Rabbinic Class.* On the ancient sage more generally, see John G. Gammie and Leo G. Perdue, eds., *The Sages in Israel and the Ancient Near East* (Winona Lake, Ind.: Eisenbraun's, 1990), in which a greatly reduced version of this chapter appears.

3. Much has been written on this passage. See in particular Elias Bickerman, "La chaine de la tradition Pharisienne," *RB* 59 (1951): 153-65; Moshe D. Herr, "Continuum in the Chain of Torah Transmission," *Zion* 44 (1979): 43-56 [Hebrew].

4. Note the following often-cited saying: "Even that which an advanced disciple will some day teach before his master was already said to Moses at Sinai" (*p. Pe'a* 2.6 [17a]).

5. The issue of the reliability of attributions of sayings to named sages is too complex to enter into here. Suffice it to say that where multiple versions of a tradition are found in different rabbinic texts, the same saying, often with variant wordings, is frequently attributed to different sages, often of the same generation, but often not.

6. For references and a fuller discussion, see my article, "Of Priests, Scribes, and Sages in Second Temple Times," *JBL* (forthcoming).

7. See previous note.

8. This is the argument of M. D. Herr ("Continuum in the Chain of Torah Transmission" [note 3]), who understands the shift of Torah teaching from priests to sages to have taken place in early Hellenistic times, and the "chain of tradition" tradition to have come into being some time in the last century B.C.E. or the first century C.E.

9. The results of such interpretive activity is first collected in *Abot de R. Natan*, the first three chapters of which are a loose commentary to the three sayings attibuted to the men of the Great Assembly. For a sampling of the continuation of such interpretation, see Judah Goldin, ed. and trans., *The Living Talmud: The Wisdom of the Fathers and Its Classical Commentaries* (New Haven: Yale University Press, 1955).

10. The terminology of symptomatic, critical, and transformative, and the conception of their dialogical interplay, is adapted from Dominick LaCapra, *History, Politics, and the Novel* (Ithaca: Cornell University Press, 1987). For a fuller discussion of the interrelation of historical and literary criticisms in the study of rabbinic literature, see Chapter 1 of this book, as well as my two-part review essay, "Interpreting Midrash 1: Midrash and the History of Judaism," *Prooftexts* 7, no. 2 (May 1987): 179-94; "Interpreting Midrash 2: Midrash and its Literary Contexts," *Prooftexts* 7, no. 3 (September 1987): 284-300 (with corrigenda in *Prooftexts* 8, no. 1 [January 1988]: 159-60). For another rabbinic text that similarly transforms the priesthood in terms of the rabbinic self-understanding as Israel's leadership, see Martin S. Jaffee's introduction to his translation of *The Talmud of Babylonia: An American Translation. XXVI. Tractate Horayot,* BJS 90 (Atlanta: Scholars Press, 1987), pp. 8-36.

11. These are the Mishnah and *Tosephta* (although the latter's redaction in the form we have it may be later) and the so-called tannaitic midrashim (*Mekilta of R. Ishmael, Mekilta of R. Simeon bar Yoḥai, Sifra, Sifre Numbers, Sifre*

Zuṭa, Sifre Deuteronomy, fragments of a *Mekilta* to Deuteronomy), and possibly parts of *Seder ʿOlam Rabba. Baraytot* found in the two Talmuds must be individually assessed.

12. On the general problem of the use of highly rhetoricized rabbinic narrative forms for purposes of historical and biographical reconstruction, especially with regard to the figure of the sage, see Henry Fischel, "Story and History: Observations on Greco-Roman Rhetoric and Pharisaism," in *American Oriental Society, Middle West Branch, Semi-Centennial Volume,* ed. Denis Sinor (Bloomington: Indiana University, 1969), pp. 59-88. For a discrete case study, see Robert Goldenberg, "The Depostion of Rabban Gamaliel II: An Examination of the Sources," *JJS* 23 (1972): 167-90; as well as idem, "History and Ideology in Talmudic Narrative," in *Approaches to Ancient Judaism,* vol. 4, *Studies in Liturgy, Exegesis, and Talmudic Narrative,* ed. William Scott Green, BJS 27 (Chico, Calif.: Scholars Press, 1983), pp. 159-71. On the impossibility of using rabbinic sources to write biographies of individual sages, see William Scott Green, "What's in a Name? The Problematic of Rabbinic Biography," in *Approaches to Ancient Judaism: Theory and Practice,* vol. 1 (Missoula, Mont.: Scholars Press, 1978), pp. 77-96; Jacob Neusner, "The Present State of Rabbinic Biography," in *Hommage Georges Vajda: études d'histoire et de pensée juives,* ed. Gérard Nahon & Charles Touati (Louvain: Peeters, 1980), pp. 85-91 (with references to Neusner's earlier writings on this question). This set of problems is not unique to the study of ancient Judaism, as can be seen from M. I. Finley, *Ancient History: Evidence and Models* (New York: Viking Press, 1986), esp. Chapter 2, "The Ancient Historian and His Sources."

13. Jacob Neusner's work on the Mishnah (summarized in *Judaism: The Evidence of the Mishnah* [Chicago: University of Chicago, 1981], esp. 14-22) correlates what is attributed to clusters of sages who lived around the same time (pre-70 C.E., 70-135, and post-135) with the historically unfolding legal and ideational logic of that document. Other, less tightly structured rabbinic documents have not yielded to this kind of analysis. Neusner admits, however, that such a logic may have been retroactively imposed by the redactors of the Mishnah, just as they retroactively imposed their formal preferences. For example, thinking that the sages of Yavneh were preoccupied with certain issues, the redactors might have shaped the traditions they received accordingly. But, even if we accept the logic of Neusner's ideational history, we might ask how much we can learn about a generation of rabbis far anterior to the time of the redaction of the document in which its views are first reported, if all we can identify with that earlier generation are the topics of its discourse disembodied from the unrecoverable discursive practices by which it addressed those topics.

14. Curiously, pertinent archeological and extra-rabbinic evidence picks up again beginning in the third century.

15. For such a picture, see may article, "Of Priests, Scribes, and Sages in Second Temple Times."

16. Depictions of what occurred at Yavneh per se remain, therefore, highly

speculative. For two recent examples, see Shaye J. D. Cohen, "The Significance of Yavneh: Pharisees, Rabbis, and the End of Sectarianism," *HUCA* 55 (1984) 27-53; and Jacob Neusner, "The Formation of Rabbinic Judaism: Yavneh (Jamnia) from A.D. 70-100," *ANRW* II 19, no. 2 (1979): 3-42.

17. See, for example, Shaye J. D. Cohen, "The Significance of Yavneh"; idem, *From the Maccabees to the Mishnah* (Philadelphia: Westminster Press, 1987), p. 218 (with pp. 101-103, 160, 172-73).

18. See "Of Priests, Scribes, and Sages in Second Temple Times."

19. A major exception might have been the early (pre-70) followers of Jesus, but we know too little about them (having to depend again on later, retroactively transformative sources) to say much about their pattern of organization or self-understanding in relation to the Temple and its priesthood. For other possible exceptions, see "Of Priests, Scribes, and Sages in Second Temple Times."

20. For evidence for the continued importance and influence of the priesthood in Palestine long after the destruction of the Temple in 70 C.E., and therefore for its continued impact on rabbinic self-understanding, see the following: Reuven Kimelman, "The Conflict between the Priestly Oligarchy and the Sages in the Talmudic Period," *Zion* 48 (1983): 135-48 [Hebrew]; Stuart S. Miller, *Studies in the History and Translations of Sepphoris,* SJLA 37 (Leiden: E. J. Brill, 1984), pp. 103-132; Dalia Ben-Hayim Trifon, "The Priests After the Destruction of the Second Temple," (Ph.D. diss., Tel-Aviv University, 1985) [Hebrew]: Isaiah Gafni, "'Scepter and Staff': Concerning New Forms of Leadership in the Period of the Talmud in the Land of Israel and Babylonia," in *Kĕhūnnâ ûmĕlûkâ: yaḥasê dāt ûmĕdînâ bĕyiśāᵓēl ûbāᶜammîm,* ed. I. Gafni and G. Motzkin (Jerusalem: Zalman Shazar Center, 1986-87), pp. 79-91 [Hebrew]; David Goodblatt, "*Yĕhûdĕ ᵓereṣ-yiśrāᵓēl baššānîm 70-132,*" in *Hāhîsṭôryâ šel ᶜam yiśrāᵓēl: yĕhûdâ wĕrômâ—mĕrîdôt hayyĕhûdîm,* ed. Uriel Rappaport (Jerusalem: Alexander Peli, 1983-84), pp. 162-165. Note as well the prominence of "Eleazar the Priest" on the rebel coins from the Bar Kokhba caves sixty-five years after the destruction of the Temple. This Eleazar, whatever his identity, was presumably the religious leader of the revolt, second only to Bar Kokhba the "Prince." For details see Leo Mildenberg, "The Eleazar Coins of the Bar Kochba Rebellion," *Historia Judaica* 11 (1949): 77-108. Archeological evidence, in the form of synagogue inscriptions, also indicates that those of priestly descent continued to keep records of (and perhaps to commemorate) their weeks of service (*mišmārôt*) in the Temple for centuries after its destruction. See Joseph Naveh, *On Stone and Mosaic; The Aramaic and Hebrew Inscriptions from Ancient Synagogues* (Jerusalem: Israel Exploration Society, 1978), nos. 51 (Caesarea), 52 (Ashkalon), 56 (near Gazza), 106 (Yemen) [Hebrew]; and Ephraim E. Urbach, in *Tarbiz* 42 (1972-73): 304-309. Note also the prominently inscribed "Samoe (?), priest and *sophodidaskalos* (teacher of wisdom)" in the synagogue at Sardis (5th century C.E.). See *BASOR* 187 (October 1967): 23 (fig. 48), 29, 38.

21. See especially Deut. 17:8-13, 18; 19:7; 21:5; 24:8; 27:9-10; 31:9-11; 25-26; 33:10.
22. For the biblical elders as successors to Joshua, see Josh. 24:31 and Judg. 2:7.
23. Herbert W. Basser (*JBL* 107 [1988]: 152-53) suggests that *šěnôt* is understood to mean "perversions" (*šěnût*): each generation has people whose deviant behavior is like that of the early rebellious generations. However, it is also possible that the word is understood to suggest that the later generations are different from the earlier ones in that the later ones are not so entirely wicked. It is this difference that needs to be discerned (*bînû*). The text could also be understood to mean that each and every generation is judged according to its own deeds, but it seems to me that the point of the comment is as I have translated it and explain it below. Finkelstein, following MS Berlin and *Midraš Ḥakamim,* does not include here the people of the generation of the Dispersion, which is found in the other witnesses, including MS London.
24. The phrase *generation and generations* is interpreted as three generations, with *generation* figured as one and *generations* as two, the minimum plural. On the three generations preceding the "days of the Messiah," see §318 (F363.3).
25. §310 (F350.10-351.11). In some details I have differed with Finkelstein's text, preferring the readings of better witnesses.
26. The theme of the three rebellious generations recurs in the next unit (§311). On this sequence of generations in the *Sifre* see as well §43 (F92.17-94.7); §307 (F344.13-14); §318 (F361.4-10). On the rabbinic exegetical portrayal of a chain of early rebellious generations and its historiographic implications for rabbinic self-understanding, see my *Enosh and His Generation: Pre-Israelite Hero and History in Postbiblical Interpretation* (Chico, Calif.: Scholars Press, 1984), esp. pp. 216-25, 226-27, 231-34.
27. Num. 11:17 stresses that the elders receive the same prophetic spirit as Moses. The association of the seventy biblical elders with the Sanhedrin, which in turn represents, if only ideally, the central locus of rabbinic teaching and judicial authority, is common. For similar uses of Num. 11:16 to associate the rabbinic sages with the seventy biblical elders, see §§41 (F86.4-12) and 346 (F403.1-6), both of which will be treated later.
28. This works two ways: rabbinic sages are referred to as *elders,* and scriptural elders are rabbinized. For the first, see: §41 (F86.14-87.1); §48 (F112.8); §106 (F166.2); §269 (F289.9); §189 (F308.11); §346 (F403.4). For the second, see: §41 (F86.10); §47 (F106.1); §205 (F241.4-6); §210 (F243.16-244.1); §218 (F251.9-10). Note that *Midraš Haggadol,* in reformulating our text, substitutes *sages* (*ḥakāmîm*) for *elders,* making explicit, as it often does, what it finds implicit in its source. For an early rabbinic text in which the connection between the rabbinic sages and the anonymous lay elders of Moses' time is drawn more explicitly, see *m. Roš. Haš.* 2:9, and its elaboration in *t. Roš. Haš.* 1:18 and *b. Roš. Haš.* 25b. Moses is referred to both as an *elder* and a *sage* or *master,* whose students' students are the rabbinic sages. For the former, see §12 (F21.6), which may be a later addition. For the latter two, see

§26 (F39.1); §29 (F46.2); §29 (F48.15); §305 (F327.6); §306 (F341.13). According to §355 (F418.11-14), in the future Moses will lead each group of Torah scholars as it enters the world to come.

29. The association of elders with prophets, in that order, is also found in §313 (F356.8-9): "'He encompassed him (*yĕsōbĕbenhû*)' (Deut. 32:10): with elders. 'He cared for him (*yĕbônĕnēhû*)' with prophets." We may have here two word plays, the first connecting *yĕsōbĕbenhû* with *sāb* ("elder") and the second reversing the consonants *ybn* to yield *nby* ("prophet"). *Midraš Haggadol* has *prophets* for the first interpretation and *sages* for the second. For the association of prophets with elders, see also §41 (F86.14-87.2), to be discussed later, esp. in note 47. Note as well the parallels between Jer. 18:18 and Ezek. 7:26, the former having *ḥākām* where the latter has *zĕkēnîm*. The *Targum to the Prophets* renders both with *ḥakkîm* (Aramaic for *ḥākām*).

30. For rabbinic sources that state the "men of the Great Assembly" included both prophets and elders, see *b. Meg.* 17b; *p. Ber.* 1.5; 2.4; *Ruth Rab.* 4.4.

31. For a critical edition of the text, see Chaim J. Milikowshy, ed. and trans., "Seder Olam: A Rabbinic Chronology" (Ph.D. diss., Yale University, 1981), pp. 439-40. The final sentence of the passage is found in MSS Milan and Parma, but not in the majority of witnesses, and therefore appears to be an explanatory gloss, based on the "notarikon" of *zqn* as *zeh qānâ (ḥokmâ)* ("this one has acquired wisdom"). But even without this gloss, elder and sages are equated in the juxtaposition of Deut. 32:7 and Prov. 22:17. For a comparison of the prophet with the elder, stating that the words of the elders (sages) need to be followed more scrupulously than those of the prophets, see *p. Ber.* 1.7 (3b).

32. Compare §49 (F114.14-115.4), to be treated later, where it is said that direct human contact with and recognition of God is impossible, but if one attaches oneself to the society of the sages and their disciples, it is the equivalent of having ascended to heaven to receive the Torah.

33. Here, and in what follows, I render with a rhetorical question according to MS Vatican (and the better witnesses), which varies slightly from the text of Finkelstein, who follows *Midraš Haggadol*, and less consistently *Yalquṭ Shimʿoni* and MS Berlin. The alternative would be to render, "One who learns from a [single] sage is not like one who learns from [the collectivity of] sages," and similarly later, which would be difficult to reconcile with the opening interpretaion (A). The connection between single sage and plural sages, constituting the transition from Deut. 11:13 and its interpretation to Eccl. 12:11 and its, is not clear here. It probably derives from the fact that the two verses preceding Eccl. 12:11 speak of the teachings of Kohelet, the single *ḥākām*: learning from such a sage is like learning "the words of the sages."

34. This is the reading (*ḥayyîm labbĕʿālîm*) in MSS Vatican and Casanata, and similarly in *Midraš Haggadol (ḥayyîm libʿālehā)*, wereas most witnesses have the morphologically similar "life to the world" (*ḥayyîm lāʿôlām*).

35. §41 (F86.4-13).

36. Cf. *m. ʾAbot* 4:1: "Ben Zoma says: Who is wise (*ḥākām*)?: One who learns from every person, as it is said, 'From all my teachers I have gained

understanding' (Ps. 119:99, as here construed)." For other expressions of an "egalitarian" Torah ethic, see notes 37, 102, and 192. Compare in particular §345 (F402.6-8), treated in Chapter Two. There the verse "Moses commanded us the Torah" (Deut. 33:4) is interpreted to mean that the Torah is the possession of all of Israel, and in conjunction with another verse, "You stand this day, all of you" (Deut. 29:9), is taken to mean that the Torah is an inheritance of "commoners" (*běnê qěṭānîm*) no less than "nobility." Compare Philo, *Dec.* 36-43, who similarly interprets the multiplicity of divine voices addressed to *all* of Israel at Mt. Sinai to signify an egalitarian Torah ethic. See also Chapter 2, note 92. On the possibility of all of Israel in later times being, in a sense, prophetically inspired in their behavior, see *t. Pesaḥ.* 4:14 and parallels.

37. For this interpretation see *Mattenot Kehunnah* to *Num. Rab.* 14:4. Compare §48 (F112.7-13), to be treated later, where "you (plural) shall surely obey (*šāmōr tišmĕrûn*) in Deut. 11:22, also in relation to God's commandments, is interpreted to mean "all are equal with respect to Torah." See note 192.

38. On this slippage between Moses and God, see S. R. Driver, *A Critical and Exegetical Commentary on Deuteronomy*, ICC, 3d ed. (Edinburgh: T. and T. Clark, 1901), pp. 99, 130; Judah Goldin, "Not by Means of an Angel and Not by Means of a Messenger," in *Religions in Antiquity: Essays in Memory of Edwin Ramsdell Goodenough,* ed. Jacob Neusner (Leiden: E. J. Brill, 1968), pp. 423-24. Several ancient versions (the Samaritan Pentateuch, some versions of the LXX, and the Vulgate) have in 11:14, "He will grant." The same is found in a *mezuzah* text from Qumran (see *DJD* 3:161).

39. For similar exegeses elsewhere in the *Sifre,* see note 196.

40. It is unclear whether Sanhedrin here refers to an authoritative, national institution in rabbinic times or to the Sanhedrin of Second Temple times. For the view that such a body was no longer a reality in Palestine by the third century C.E., see Lee I. Levine, "Was There a 'Sanhedrin' in the Land of Israel in the Period of the Talmud?" in *The Rabbinic Class in Palestine during the Talmudic Period,* pp. 47-52 [Hebrew].

41. The earliest parallel, in *t. Soṭa* 7:9-12 (and *b. Ḥag.* 3a-b with slight variants), contains the explication of Eccl. 12:11 without that of Deut. 11:13 and sets it in an entirely different narrative frame. There the emphasis is not on the sage as a link between Israel and God, but on the claim that, despite the multivocality of contradictory rabbinic teachings and rulings, they all derive from a single lawgiver and God. Note that these parallels do not interpret Eccl. 12:11 in relation to the Sanhedrin, nor do they connect their interpretation of that verse with the Shema (Deut. 6:4), whereas the *Sifre* passage passes over the scriptural words *well-planted nails* in its atomistic decoding of Eccl. 12:11. For other parallels in later collections, which do not emphasize as much as does the *Sifre* the role of the sage, see: *p. Sanh.* 10 (28a); *Qoh. Rab.* 12:11; *Num. Rab.* 14:4; *'Abot R. Nat.* A 18 (ed. Schechter, pp. 67-68); *Pesq. R.* 3 (7b); *Tanḥ. Beḥuqqotay* 15.

42. This is Hammer's paraphrase (p. 411, note 19) of Finkelstein's note ad loc.

43. We have here a word play, in which *Bat-rabbim* is understood either as *bêt rabbîm*, the house of study in which decisions are determined by the majority

(*rabbîm*) or *bêt rabbānîm,* the house of rabbinic masters.

44. This expression (*'āśâ tôrâ*) can mean both the study of the Torah and the fulfillment of its commandments. See Shraga Abramson, in *Leshonenu* 19 (1954): 61-65. Abramson (p. 63) gives our passage as an example of the latter meaning, but I see no reason to exclude the former.

45. §41 (F86.14-87.7).

46. Similarly, *Cant. Rab.* 1:15 and 7:5 have: "'Eyes': These are the Sanhedrin, which are the eyes of the community." *Nose* (or face) of Cant. 7:5c is not specifically interpreted by the *Sifre.* Presumably, it is the face of Israel as a whole, oriented, by virtue of its rabbinic *eyes,* toward Damascus, here messianically understood. *Lebanon,* elsewhere taken to signify the Temple, is not a focus of interpretive attention here. Compare §1 (F7.13-14); *Cant. Rab.* 7:4 (5).

47. See §346 (F403.4-6), to be discussed later in this chapter and §13 (F23.7-10), also discussed later in the chapter. For the association of prophets and elders, see notes 29-31.

48. The Hebrew here reads literally "and the magistrate," but verse 12 has "or the magistrate."

49. The translation is from *The Torah: The Five Books of Moses,* 2d ed. (Philadelphia: Jewish Publication Society of America, 1962), p. 357. See also, *Notes on the New Translation of the Torah,* ed. Harry M. Orlinsky (Philadelphia: Jewish Publication Society of America, 1970), p. 251. For an example of such a referral to a central tribunal, see Deut. 19:16-18.

50. S. R. Driver, *A Critical and Exegetical Commentary on Deuteronomy,* p. 207. See as well his comments on Deut. 16:18 (ibid., p. 200). For the combination of priests and laity on the courts of the Dead Sea Scrolls, and for the scrolls' attribution of primary judicial authority to the priests, see 1QS 5.1-3; 8.1; 9.7; CD 10.4-6; 11QTemp 57.11-15; 61.7-9; 4Q159 frg. 2-4 lines 3-4; 4QIsa[d] frg. 1, lines 2-4. See also note 63 here.

51. The parallel *barayta'* in *b. Sanh.* 87a adn *p. Sanh.* 18.4 (30a) has *mûplā' šebbĕbêt dîn,* a *mûplā'* who sits on a court. The parallel is found in the context of a discussion of the mishnaic "elder that rebels against the decision of the court" (*m. Sanh.* 11:2), that is, an elder who differs in his legal opinion from his colleagues and continues to teach contrary to their consensus. He may appeal to a higher court to decide between him and them, but if he does not submit to the verdict of the higher court he is culpable of capital punishment (*m. Sanh.* 11:1). The point here, it seems to me, is that such an appeal process (soon to be spelled out) and penalty applies only in the case of a senior authority, one in a position to teach and influence others. According to *m. Hor.* 1:4, *Sifra Ḥoba' parašah* 4:4 (ed. Finkelstein, vol. 2, pp. 141-42), *t. Hor.* 1:2, and a *barayta* in *p. Hor.* 1:4 (46a) (the last two in the view of Rabbi Judah the Patriarch), only a court with a *mûplā'* sitting on it is culpable for its erroneous teachings. According to *t. Sanh.* 7:1, a text similar to our own, the expert of each court accompanies the petitioner to the next higher court. Thus it is also possible, it we read our passage in terms of these others, to understand *mûplā'* in our text to refer not to the status of the petitioner but to

the requirement that the courts to which he comes seeking a legal ruling have at least one such senior sage on them, an officer according to some, who then accompaiies him in seeking the ruling of the next highest court. Louis Finkelstein ("A Difficult Baraita and the Light It Sheds on the History of the Sanhedrin," *PAAJR* 46-7 [1979-80]: 97-109 [Hebrew]; idem, *ʿOd ʿal muplaʾ šebbebet din*, in *Studies in Rabbinic Literature, Bible, and Jewish History* [in honor of E. Z. Melamed], ed. Y. D. Gilat, Ch. Levine, and Z. M. Rabinowitz [Ramat Gan: Bar-Ilan University, 1982], pp. 75-79), understanding our passage as an accurate representation of the Second Temple Sanhedrin, takes the term *muplaʾ* to refer to a Pharisaic legal authority who sat on and advised that otherwise priestly high court. According to this view, the priestly high court required the presence of such a sage for it to be a valid high court from which Torah emanated. For other discussions that try to determine the meaning of the term *muplaʾ*, see P. R. Weiss, "The Office of the Mufla," *JJS* 1 (1949): 172-77; Chanoch Albeck, ed., *Šišša sidre mišna, Seder neziqqin* (Jerusalem and Tel-Aviv: Bialik Institute and Dvir. 1959), pp. 503-505; Hugo Mantel, *Studies in the History of the Sanhedrin* (Cambridge: Harvard University Press, 1961), pp. 135-39; Zvi Aryeh Steinfeld, "The Mufla of the Court," *Sinai* 82 (1978): 24-40 [Hebrew]. Clearly the word *muplaʾ* in our passage is connected to the biblical *yippāleʾ* by a word play. For similar plays see *b. Ber.* 4a and *Tem.* 2b.

52. In the parallel in *b. Sanh.* 87a, the word is *yôʿēṣ* (an expert advisor), where a prooftext (Nah. 1:11) connecting *yôʿēṣ* with *mimmek* is cited. It is possible that a word play (as in the previous exegesis) is involved, reading the lemma's *mimmekā* ("for you") as *mûmḥeh* (someone with specialized expertise). Tosaphot to *b. Sanh.* 87a define *muplaʾ* as *mûmḥeh. M. Hor.* 1:4, *Sifra Ḥobaʾ parašah* 4:4 (ed. Finkelstein, vol. 2, pp. 141-42), and *p. Hor.* 1:4 (46a) (see preceding note) connect *muplaʾ* with the biblical *ʿēdā* of Lev. 4:13 and Num. 15:24, interpreted to refer to those who are qualified to testify through their teaching.

53. §152 (F205.8-206.1). For explanations of how each category of law derives from the words of the lemma see Rashi ad *b. Sanh.* 87a. Thus, *matters* are "words," by which such dedications to the Temple are made; leprosy is rabbinically understood as a punishment for the "dispute" of "evil gossip"; and *gates* is connected with agricultural poor offerings on the basis of Deut. 14:28-29; 26:12. The last exegesis is missing in the parallel in *p. Sanh.* 18.4 (30a).

54. So as not to be misunderstood, I should stress that the shift is not absolute but relative.

55. What follows (through the citation of Deut. 17:10) is paralleled in (or drawn from) *m. Sanh.* 11:2, where it relates to the trial of an "elder that rebels against the decision of the court." See note 51. In the parallel *baraytaʾ* in *b. Sanh.* 87a, what follows is stated in interpretation of the seemingly redundant expression "and you shall ascend" of Deut. 17:8.

56. The verse continues: "observing scrupulously all their instructions to you (*kĕkōl ʾăšer yôrûkā*)," thereby identifying the "place" as a source of teaching

(*tôrâ*), an identification not found in Deut. 17:8. Note that in *t. Sanh.* 7:1 (and *Hag.* 2:9), which does not quote Deut. 17:10, we find *halakah* in place of Torah. Whereas our *Sifre* text identifies the court's teaching as Torah, the Temple Scroll (11QTemp 56.3-4), in rephrasing the same biblical passage, stresses that the court's teaching is "from the *book* of the Torah."

57. §152 (F206.1-9).
58. On the Temple being the highest place in the world, see also §352 (F410.17-18), citing Deut. 17:8, but compare the variants. On the Land of Israel being the highest land, see also §23 (F33.15-17) and §37 (F73.7-13). The parallel in *b. Sanh.* 87a supplies a separate verse, Jer. 23:7, to prove that the Land of Israel is higher than the other lands. Note also Tosaphot there, who imply that what is meant here is not literal height but figurative height.
59. The separation is indicated in MS Vatican and the Editio Princeps by the division into two units (*pisqā'ôt*): §§152 and 153. The latter comments upon what, in the masoretic text, is a new verse.
60. §153 (F206.10-207.3).
61. Cf. §155 (F208.1). For *šōpēt* as a lay judge (as in Deut. 19.17), see S. R. Driver, *A Critical and Exegetical Commentary on Deuteronomy*, p. 208. Cf. the interpretations of Philo and Josephus, cited in note 63; Maimonides, *Hilk. Sanh.* 2:2.
62. For similar citations of Eccl. 7:10 to justify rabbinic judicial authority (inherited from the anonymous biblical elders), see *b. Roš. Haš.* 25b and *t. Roš. Haš.* 1:18 (ed. Lieberman, pp. 311-12), both in conjunction with Deut. 17:9, but without reference to a judge who was once related to one of the litigants but is not any longer; and *Sifre Deut.* §190 (F230.6-9), which is identical to our passage. For other examples of the *Sifre*'s exegetical legitimizing of the *present* rabbinic leadership, see note 196.
63. Hammer (p. 190) translates the final interpretation as follows: "(By telling you), 'These are the details of the judgment.'" The word *these* (*'ēlû*), is not part of what the court would say but, as previously, the deictic terminology that connects the lemma with its interpretation. My interpretation rests on the small but significant changes of the definite noun (*hammišpāṭ*) of the lemma to the indefinite noun (*mišpāṭ*) of its midrashic signfication and the replacement of dēbar ("utterance" or "matter") with diqdûqê ("details"). The Temple Scroll (11QTemp 56.1-2) interestingly separates *haddābār* and *hammišpaṭ* as two distinct communications, perhaps as teaching and ruling. Some further details may be noted: The separation of levitical priests into priests and Levites can also be seen in 11QTemp 56.07, according to Yadin's reconstruction; 11QTemp 61.8-9 to Deut. 19:17; CD 3.21-4 citing Ezeq. 44:15 (as per *Vulgate* and *Pešiṭta*); Josephus, *Ant.* 4.8.14 §218; *Tg. Neof.* and *Pešiṭta* Deut. 17:9; and versions to 2 Chr. 5:5; 30:27. Similarly, the understanding of "and to the magistrate" as "*or* to the magistrate" (cf. Deut. 17:12, to which *Sifre Deut.* §155 [F208.1] provides the same interpretation) appears in the Temple Scroll (11QTemp 56.1, with Yadin's note ad loc.). Philo (*Spec. Leg.* 4.36 §§188-92) understands the single magistrate to be the High Priest, whereas Josephus (*Ant.* 4.8.14 §218) substitutes *gerousia* (council of elders) and the Temple Scroll (11QTemp 56.1), most likely influenced by Deut. 19:17, has (according to Yadin's reconstruction) "magistrates.". In the

next unit of the *Sifre* (§154 [F207.4-5]), the high court in Jerusalem (pre-70 C.E.) is distinguished from the court and rabbinic teachings at Yavneh with regard to capital punishment, which is said to be within the authority of the former but not the latter (cf. §144 [F198.3-4]). The same distinction is made in *m. Sanh.* 11.4 and *p. Hor.* 1.1 (45d). On the judge not being related to the litigants, see the parallel in *b. San.* 28b in relation to *m. Sanh.* 3:4.

64. The Samaritan Pentateuch has *twrwtyk* (presumably, *tôrôtêkā*, "your Torahs"), as is suggested by the *Peshiṭta* and *Targum Ps.-Jonathan.*

65. §351 (F408.12-409.2).

66. Compare §208 ad Deut. 21:5 (F243.7-10, except that at the end of line 7 and the beginning of line 8 *ribbîm* and *něgā'îm* should be reversed according to the manuscripts). There, *nega'* is interpreted as referring to bodily plague-spots to be examined by a priest, whereas *rîb* is interpreted as referring to conflicts to be adjudicated by a (presumably nonpriestly) court of three. For a similar interpretation see *Sifra Tazri'a Parašat Nega'im* 1 (ed. Weiss, col. 60b). Although the biblical word *nega'* in the contexts of Deut. 17:8 and 21:5 seems clearly to denote a form of physical injury committed by one person to another, its more common usage in the Hebrew Bible is to denote a form of plague (as in Deut. 24:8), and it is in this latter sense that the word in those two verses is interpreted by the *Sifre* despite their contexts. For the priests' role in inspecting and ruling on such plagues when they are bodily, see Lev. 13-14 but compare *Sifra* op. cit.

67. See note 64. For a similar interpretation of Lev. 26:46, see *Sifra Behuqqotay pereq* 8:12 (ed. Weiss, col. 112c).

68. For an attempt to identify Agnitus, see Moshe D. Herr, "The Historical Significance of the Dialogues between Jewish Sages and Roman Dignitaries," in *Studies in Aggadah and Folk-Literature*, ed. Joseph Heinemann and Dov Noy, vol. 22 of *Scripta Hierosolymitana* (Jerusalem: Magnes, 1971), pp. 128-32. The same question is posed to Hillel and Shammai in *Abot R. Nat.* A 15; B 29; *b. Šabb.* 31a (by a prospective convert). In Chapter 2, I dealt with the difficulties of lifting such stories from their present commentary contexts as simple historical representations.

69. Compare §344 (F401.2-6), treated in Chapter 2, where Rome sends two officials to learn the nature of the *Jews'* Torah. They come to Rabban Gamaliel at Usha, where they study Scripture and the branches of the rabbinic oral Torah curriculum (*midraš, halakot*, and *haggadot*).

70. The commentary continues by exegetically specifying the types of incense and burnt offerings referred to as part of the priests' duties in the continuation of the lemma.

71. For *talmûd tôrâ* as the paramount positive religious obligation, see *m. Pe'a* 1:1, with which compare §336 (F385.12-386.11). §44 (F103.2) refers explicitly to *talmûd tôrâ* as one of the commandments (*miṣwôt*).

72. Alternatively, *'ăbôdâ* here may mean physical labor. See Hammer, p. 85, and p. 411, note 25. But in view of what follows, where study and "service at the altar" are said to be expressed by the same word, I have understood the present question to refer to sacrificial worship. See the following note.

73. For the same interpretation of these seemingly redundant expressions in Gen.

2:15, see *Tgs. Neofiti, Fragmentary* (MSS P, V, N, L). and *Ps.-Jonathan* ad loc. The underlying assumption here could be either that before Adam sinned there was no need for sacrificial worship, but only for study and the fulfillment of the seven Noahite commandments that, according to rabbinic traditions, were already incumbent upon Adam and Eve or that before Adam sinned, there was no need for physical labor to maintain the Garden. Most of the traditional *Sifre* commentaries I consulted (Rabbenu Hillel, David Pardo, *Zera‛ ʾAbraham, ʾOhalê Yehuda*) favor the former, but others (*‛Emeq Hanneṣib, Toledot ʾAdam*) favor the latter, as do I. Rabbinic texts evidence contrasting views regarding the questions whether Adam physically worked and whether he offered sacrifices while in the Garden of Eden. See *Gen. Rab.* 16:5 (ed. Theodor-Albeck, p. 149), with Theodor's comments ad loc; *ʾAbot R. Nat.* A 11 and B 21 (ed. Schechter, pp. 44-45); *Pirqe R. El.* 12; Louis Ginzberg, *Legends of the Jews,* vol. 5 (Philadelphia: Jewish Publication Society of America, 1953), p. 92, note 54.

74. §41 (F87.11-88.13). My division of E follows MS Vatican, which places the sign for the end of the *pisqaʾ* at the end of the first sentence. For the second sentence ("If you have performed...") as a separate thought, see §49 (F115.5), to be treated later in this chapter.

75. This could either be the first (ca. 70 C.E.) or second (ca. 140 C.E.) sage of this name.

76. It should be noted that this interpretation is absent in MS Vatican and the related MS Casanata, but that omission is most likely due to a scribal error of homoioteleuton. Some traditional commentators (Rabbenu Hillel, David Pardo, and R. Suleiman), attempting to harmonize R. Eliezer ben Jacob's interpretation with the earlier preferences for study and prayer, suggest that just as a priest should serve at the alter with an undivided heart (complete attention and proper intention), so, too, a person should have an undivided heart in study and prayer. In §32 (F55.2) the same interpretation is offered of the phrase "with all your heart" in Deut. 6:5.

77. The traditional commentators to the *Sifre* struggle with this problem. Some suggest that the rewards of Deut. 11:14-15 may be earned by righteous individuals as well as by the people as a whole. See *ʾOhalê Yehuda, Zera‛ ʾAbraham*, and Nahmanides ad Deut. 11:13. Others suggest that Deut. 6:5 is understood to refer to both private and public acceptance of death rather than transgression of commandments. See *Toledot ‛Adam* with reference to R. Joḥanan's view in *b. Sanh.* 74a. *Sifre Deut.* §32 contains several interpretations that take Deut. 6:5 to refer to giving one's life in observance of the commandments.

78. Deut. 6:4 is the *Shema‛* credo, which treated as liturgy in §31 (F53.9-10) and §34 (F62.6-63.2). The subsequent verse (6:6: "These instructions... shall be upon your [sing.] heart") is understood to suggest the private prayer of the individual in *b. Ber.* 15a-b. But Deut. 6:5-7 is also taken to refer to aspects of study and teaching in §33 (F59.4-9) and §34 (F60.8-13, 61.5-62.5).

79. *Private* (or individual) and *public* (or communal) is a common distinction in rabbinic discussion of prayer. It should be noted that the distinction between

"individual" and "public' as differentiating Deut. 6:5 from 11:13 may have meant something else if and when this interpretation circulated independently of the present commentary, but that once read in its present context its reference to prayer is suggested. Note that in Rashi's commentary to Deut. 11:13 he gives the interpretation of *serving Him* only as meaning "prayer" (excluding study), followed immediately by the distinction between individual and public.

80. Alternatively, *serving Him* still refers to study, whereas the following *with all your heart and with all your soul* is taken to refer to performance. On the complementary relation between study and performance, see §48 R, to be discussed later, and note 208. An earlier section of §41 (F84.16-86.3) deals explicitly with the issue of the relation of study to performance in commenting on Deut. 5:1: "'Hear, O Israel, the laws and rules that I proclaim to you this day! Study them and observe them faithfully!': This teaches that performance is dependent upon study, but study is not dependent on performance." Later the commentary states that when the rabbis of R. Akiba's generation debated, "Which is greater, study or performance?" they all (except R. Tarfon) agreed: "Study is greater because it leads to performance." §41 begins (F84.7-15) by asserting that the obligation to study Scripture's commandments obtains regardless of the obligation to perform them.

81. The overall structure of the passage may be represented as follows: A-B-C-B'-A', with A being study and A' being the combination study and practice, B being prayer and B' being the combination private and public prayer, and C being Temple worship. Compare ʾAbot R. Nat. A 4, which begins by asserting the superiority of Torah study over Temple worship and the replacement of the latter by the former, then, in seeming contradiction, affirms that the world depends on the maintainance of the Temple service for the blessing of rain, and concludes by asserting that acts of loving kindness have replaced the Temple service. For a discussion of other midrashic texts that "act" as though the Temple were standing, see Marc Bregman, "Past and Present in Midrashic Literature," p. 54. Compare as well §152 (F206.1-9), treated earlier.

82. The first verb, *šāmaʿtā*, presumably alludes to the verbal construction *šāmōʿa tišmĕʿū* with which Deut. 11:13 begins.

83. It should be stressed that in Second Temple times the temple sacrifices and rituals, especially during the fall festive of Sukkot (Tabernacles), were considered to be efficacious as petitions for propitious rainfall during winter months.

84. For study as a collective religious practice among the Dead Sea sectaries, see 1QS 6.6-8; 8.12-16; CD 6.2-11; and my discussion in, "Of Priests, Scribes and Sages in Second Temple Times."

85. MSS Vatican, London, and Berlin, and *Yalquṭ Šimʿoni* (Salonika) have *dôrĕšê haggādôt* (or *ʾaggādôt*). However, the Editio Princeps, *Midraš Haggadol,* and *Yalquṭ Šimʿoni* (MS Oxford) have instead, *dôrĕšê rĕšûmôt* ("expounders of traces"). Strictly on text-critical grounds, the former is the superior reading, even if the latter is the more difficult. On the latter, see most recently Daniel Boyarin, "On the Identification of the *Dorshei Reshumot*: A

Lexicographical Study," *Beer-Sheva* 3 (1988): 23-35.

86. §49 (F114.14-115.5).

87. §343 (F399-11-400.6), treated in Chapter 2, likens *words of Torah* to fire: one who gets too close to them gets burned, and were it not for the laws contained in the Torah, a person would be unable to withstand its fire. The sage is likened to one who works with fire, able to get closer to it than others without getting burned, yet being distinguishable from others because of the mark that it leaves on him.

88. Note the close parallel in §33 (F59.4-8), where the following comment on Deut. 6:6 is ascribed to Rabbi Judah the Patriarch: "I do not know how one can love (variant: serve and love) God...Place these words [of Torah] on your heart, for by so doing you will come to know the one who spoke and the world came into being and cling to His ways." Here too, study of Torah brings a person as close as possible to love of and attachment to God. For the importance of *social* attachment (*dibbûq*) to the rabbinic sages or "fellows" and their disciples, see the following rabbinic passages, which cite Deut. 11:22 and/or Deut. 10:20: *b. Ketub.* 111b; *Pesiq. R.* 11 (ed. Friedmann, col. 42a); *Tanḥ Maṭṭot* 1; *Sed. ʾEl. Zut.* 17 (ed. Friedmann, p. 18); Maimonides, *Mišneh Torah, Hilk. Deʿot* 6:2. While some of these passages specifically stress marrying one's daughter to a rabbinic disciple and providing him with material support, this sense should not be projected onto our passage. Note how Maimonides combines this tradition, especially as it appears in *b. Ketub.* 111b, with the *Sifre's* emphasis on attachment to God through joining the sages in study.

89. I understand the verb *nṭlth* as *nĕṭaltāh*, with a third person singular feminine suffix referring to Torah. Alternatively, the feminine suffix could refer to the preceding "fire," except that the use of Ps. 68:19 makes Torah the more likely referent (as is understood by the *Sifre's* traditional commentators; see especially David Pardo ad loc.). Ps. 68:19 is frequently interpreted in rabbinic literature to refer to Moses' ascension to heaven to receive the Torah, and to the opposition he encountered there from the angels. See *b. Šabb.* 88b-89a; *ʾAbot R. Nat.* A 2 (ed. Schechter, p. 10), with Schechter's note ad loc.; *Pesiq. R.* 20 (ed. Buber, col 98a); *Exod. Rab.* 28.1; 30.5; 33.2; *Ruth Rab.* 2.3; *Pirqe R. El.* 46; *Midraš Haggadol* ad Exod. 19:20 (ed. Margulies, pp. 395-96); *Tg. Ket. Ps.* 68:19. For discussion of the interpretation of this verse in relation to claims for Moses' having ascended to heaven, see David J. Halperin, *The Faces of the Chariot: Early Jewish Responses to Ezekiel's Vision* (Tübingen: J. C. B. Mohr [Paul Siebeck], 1988), pp. 302-305, 310-311; 316-17, 419-20. The metaphoric slippage from fire to Torah is not surprising, given the *Sifre's* own description of Torah as a burning fire in §343 (F399.16-400.6). The idea that Moses' status as the ideal teacher derives, at least in part, from the suffering he endured in receiving the Torah is expressed elsewhere in the *Sifre*: §14 (F23.11-14); §306 (F337.10-338.1). On Moses' successors' acquiring Torah through suffering, see the last reference and §32 (F57.4-6).

90. See Chapter 2, notes 92, 159, and 200.

91. For Moses as the intellectual progenitor of the sages, see note 28. For the

equation of the study of Torah with the receiving of Torah at Sinai, see §58 (F124.12-14), to be quoted shortly and note 95.

92. On *haggadot* as a distinct branch of the rabbinic curriculum of Torah studies, see §48 (F113.8-9); §306 (F339.8, 14); §317 (F359.17) (where *halakot* are said to be the "body" of the Torah and *aggadot* is said to attract a person's "heart" like wine); §344 (F401.4). Compare *t. Soṭa* 7:21; *Mek. Wayyassaʿ* 1 (ed. Lauterbach, 2:95). For the sages divided into groups according to their specialized areas of knowledge (Scripture, Mishnah, Talmud), see §355 (F418.12-13).

93. Compare §323 (F372.12-14): "Had Israel scrutinized the words of Torah that I gave them, no nation or kingdom would have ruled over them."

94. This is argued by Martha Himmelfarb in a book in progress, provisionally titled, *Apocalyptic Ascent and the Heavenly Temple*, parts of which she was kind enough to let me read.

95. §58 (F124.12-14).

96. Although sometimes referred to as *midraš halakah* ("legal midrash"), approximately four-sevenths of *Sifre Deuteronomy*'s commentary is nonlegal. Its mix of legal and narrative exposition follows, more or less, the contents of the Book of Deuteronomy, with a legal core surrounded by a narrative frame. But in three places the *Sifre* commentary explicitly emphasizes the importance of combining legal and nonlegal studies: §§48 (F113.7-8), 317 (F359.16-18), 343 (F400.6), the first and last of which will be treated later, the second of which is cited in note 92.

97. §135 (F191.8-18).

98. In *b. Pesaḥ.* 68b the same interpretation is presented as a dispute between R. Eliezer and R. Joshua, with R. Eliezer arguing that the festival day should either be entirely for study or entirely for eating and drinking, and R. Joshua arguing for a part of the day for each.

99. Hammer (p. 177) translates *sixth day* (*šiššî*) as "six days," referring to the preceding six days. But this surely is wrong because the first day is also a holy day (Exod. 12:16; Lev. 23:7-8; Num. 28:18, 25). Presumably the sixth day represents the intermediary days as a group, it being the one that adjoins and hence is most in need of definition with respect to the following seventh day of assembly.

100. The connecting *and* in the lemma is probably understood to equate the six days with the seventh, whereas the definite article of *the seventh day* distinguishes it from them.

101. Compare *Mek. Pisḥaʾ* 9 (ed. Lauterbach, vol. 1, pp. 68-70), where it is argued that work is prohibited on the intermediary days as on the first and last days, with no distinction between them. *Sifra ʾEmor* 12.4-8 (ed. Weiss, col. 102b) is similar to our *Sifre* passage in distinguishing between the level of work disallowed on the first and last days and on the intermediate days. In *b. Ḥag* 18a the text of the *Mekilta* is combined with that of the *Sifre*.

102. For other examples in the *Sifre* of sages having the authority to assign legal measures (*šiʿûr*) to biblical laws, see §135 (F191); §143 (F196); §222 (F255); §283 (F300). For the tension between an "elitist" Torah ethos and an

"egalitarian" one, see notes 37 and 192.

103. This is the reading in MS London, as well as in MS Oxford and *Yalquṭ Šimʿoni*. Finkelstein, following the MS Berlin, has *talmûd*, whereas the Editio Princeps and *Midraš Ḥakamim* have neither.

104. Following MSS London and Oxford, and *Yalquṭ Šimʿoni*.

105. Again, I am following MS London. Other witnesses, followed by Finkelstein, add *red*.

106. This is the reading in MS London, which has *rabbānê* (not *libnê* as in Finkelstein's apparatus) *tôrâ ḥakāmîm* according to my copy. MS Oxford and *Yalquṭ Šimʿoni* have only slight variations on this. Finkelstein follows, as he often does, MS Berlin and *Midraš Ḥakamim*. I understand the text to describe three types or qualities of Torah sages.

107. The prophet Elijah sent his servant seven times to look for signs of rain until on the seventh try he spotted a small cloud in the distance. The rain storm then came suddenly.

108. This is the reading in MSS London and Oxford, the Editio Princeps, and *Yalquṭ Šimʿoni*. Finkelstein, following *Midraš Ḥakamim*, has *midrāš, haggādôt,* and *hălākôt*.

109. §306 (F339.6-14).

110. For a detailed examination of the *Sifre*'s commentary to the scriptural introduction to Song of Moses, with its interpretation of that song as representing Torah as a whole, see Chapter 4.

111. For other references to such a curriculum, see note 92, plus §58 (F124.11-14), §59 (F125.1-2), §161 (F212.1-4), §313 (F355.9-11); as well as *Sifra Šemini paraša* 1:9 (for the proper text and its interpretation, see my forthcoming book, *Targum and Torah: Early Rabbinic Views of Scriptural Translation in a Multilingual Setting*. On these divisions, see Louis Finkelstein, "Midrash, Halakhah and Aggadot," in *Yitzhak R. Baer Jubilee Volume on the Occasion of His Seventieth Birthday*, ed. S. W. Baron et al. (Jerusalem: Historical Society of Israel, 1960), pp. 28-47 [Hebrew]. Other rabbinic passages stress the interdependency of these branches of study and the ideal of becoming a master of all of them. See note 96. For further references and discussion, see Judah Goldin, "The Freedom and Restraint of Haggadah," in *Midrash and Literature,* ed. Geoffrey H. Hartman and Sanford Budick (New Haven: Yale University, 1986), pp. 57-59.

112. For other water metaphors employed by the *Sifre* to describe the learning and teaching of the sage, see §41 (F87.2-3), treated earlier; §48 (F110.8-12) and §48 (F110.3-5), to be treated later; as well as §306 (F336.10-14), §306 (F338.9-13), and §306 (F338.14-339.3).

113. This structural pattern is not as evident in Finkelstein's eclectic text as in MS London that I have followed in my translation. See notes 103, 105, and 106.

114. For Joshua as *parnās*, see §334 (F384.9), where it is said that he remained righteous (that is, humble) despite his appointment. For David and Moses as *parněsîm*, see §26 (F36.2, 38.9) and §344 (F400.10). Note that all of these are nonpriestly leaders of Israel who in other texts are regarded as rabbinic

antecedents. For Hillel, Joḥanan ben Zakkai, and Akiba as *parnĕsîm* (after Moses), see §357 (F429.6-14).

115. For the Jewish use of the term *parnās* for a communal leader or administrator, see P. Benoit et al., *Grottes de Murabba'at,* vol. 2 of *DJD* (Oxford: Oxford University, 1961), pp. 156-57 (Mur 42); and Y. Yadin, "Expedition D," *IEJ* 12 (1962): 249-50 (Mur 44). On the *parnās* see Martin Goodman, *State and Society in Roman Galilee, A.D. 132-212* (Totowa, N.J.: Rowman and Allanheld, 1983), pp. 121-26; Lee I. Levine, "The Sages as *Parnesim,*" in *The Rabbinic Class in Palestine During the Talmudic Period,* pp. 109-112 [Hebrew]; G. McLean Harper, Jr., "Village Administration in the Roman Province of Syria," *Yale Classical Studies* 1 (1928): 102-68, esp. pp. 127-28. The *parnās* fills roles similar to those of the Qumran *mĕbaqqēr.* On the latter, see my "Of Priests, Scribes, and Sages in Second Temple Times." It may be said that the rabbinic sages sought to combine leadership roles that at Qumran (and elsewhere in Second Temple sources) were divided between priests and Levites.

116. §157 (F209.6-7), §162 (F212.13-213.2). In §334 (F384.6-14), Joshua's appointment as *parnās* is associated with Joseph's and David's appointments as kings.

117. §162 (F212.13-213.2). Compare §305 (F324.8-15). See *b. Giṭ.* 60a, where R. Isaac Nappaḥa (ca. 300 C.E.) states that after a priest and a Levite have been called to the Torah the following order obtains: disciples of sages who have been appointed *parnĕsîm* over the public, disciples of sages who are worthy of being appointed *parnĕsîm* over the public, disciples of sages whose fathers were appointed *parnĕsîm* over the public, heads of the synagogues, and finally, any man. On hereditary rabbinic positions and authority, see Gedalyahu Alon, *Jew, Judaism and the Classical World: Studies in Jewish History in the Times of the Second Temple and Talmud,* trans. Israel Abrahams (Jerusalem: Magnes, 1977), pp. 436-57; Moshe Beer, "The Sons of Moses in Rabbinic Lore," *Bar-Ilan University Yearbook of Judaic Studies and the Humanities* 13 (1976): 149-57 [Hebrew], summarized in idem, "The Hereditary Principle in Jewish Leadership," *Immanuel* 10 (Spring, 1980): 57—61. On the tension between such hereditary inheriting of rabbinic positions of authority and the ideal of the sage as one who merits his position solely on the basis of his learning and deeds, and for an explanation of why this phenomenon developed in Palestine but not Babylonia, see as well Isaiah Gafni, "'Scepter and Staff': Concerning New Forms of Leadership in the Period of the Talmud in the Land of Israel and Babylonia," pp. 84-91 [Hebrew].

118. Compare *b. Šabb.* 114a: "R. Joḥanan (ca. 250 C.E.) said: Who is a disciple of the sages (worthy of) being appointed *parnās* over the public? One who when asked about any matter of *halakah* is able to respond, even regarding the tractate Kalla."

119. For patriarchal appointments as a way of providing financial support for disciples, see *b. Hor.* 10a. For more extensive discussion, see Lee I. Levine, "The Jewish Patriarch (Nasi) in Third Century Palestine," in *ANRW* II.19,

246 *From Tradition To Commentary*

no. 2: 660-61; idem, *The Rabbinic Class in Palestine during the Talmud Period,* pp. 13, 18-19, 25, 46 [Hebrew]; Ephraim E. Urbach, "Class-Status and Leadership in the World of the Palestinian Sages," *Proceedings of the Israel Academy of Sciences and Humanities* 2, no. 4 (1966): 170; Gedaliah Alon, *Tôlĕdôt Hayyĕdhûdîm Bĕʾereṣ Yiśrāʾēl Bitqûpat Hammišnâ Wĕhattalmûd* (Tel Aviv: Hakibutz Hameuchad, 1967-70), vol. 2, pp. 140-42 (abbreviated in the English translation of the same, *The Jews in Their Land in the Talmudic Age,* trans. Gershon Levi, vol. 2 [Jerusalem: Magnes, 1984], pp. 719-20).

120. The Hebrew phrase is *môšîb zĕqēnîm bîšîbâ.* For *yĕšîbâ* as court, and for the understanding of the phrase to mean appointing someone a sage or judge, see David M. Goodblatt, *Rabbinic Instruction in Sasanian Babylonia* (Leiden: E. J. Brill, 1975), pp. 65-67, where our text and others, plus earlier secondary literature, are cited. Compare Shalom Albeck, *Law Courts in Talmudic Times* (Ramat-Gan: Bar-Ilan University Press, 1980), pp. 84-99 [Hebrew]. For other occasions of this usage in the *Sifre,* see §13 (F22.8-11), §16 (F26.2-3), §48 (F113.16), §321 (F370.5). In the first two of these the context clearly suggests appointment as judges. Compare §41 (F87.1).

121. §346 (F403.1-6). A similar use of Num. 11:16 was encountered in §41 (F86.9-10), treated earlier.

122. The theme of Israel's unity below conferring unity on God above continues in the succeeding section of the commentary (F403.7-404.4), also found in §96 (F158.1-2).

123. The conventional midrashic pattern is for the cited verse to provide the association of two terms, thereby facilitating a similar association in the lemma, where only the first term is found. On this pattern in the *Sifre,* see Saul Lieberman, *Hellenism in Jewish Palestine,* 2d ed. (New York: Jewish Theological Seminary of America, 1962), pp. 49-51; Isaac Boaz Gottlieb, "Language Understanding in Sifre Deuteronomy: A Study of Language Consciousness in Rabbinic Exegesis" (Ph.D. diss., New York University, 1972), pp. 9-35.

124. Thus, the new Jewish Publication Society translation has, "Take all the ringleaders."

125. This is already stated clearly in *Sifre Num.* §131 (ed. Horovitz, p. 172), which paraphrases Num. 25:4 as follows: "[God] said to [Moses]: 'Appoint the heads of the people to be judges, so they will hang the sinners before the sun.'" Similarly, see *p. Sanh.* 10.2 (28d); *b. Sanh.* 35a; *Tanḥ. Balaq* 19; *Tanḥ. Balaq* 28 (ed. Buber, p. 148); *Num. Rab.* 20.23; *Frg. Tg., Tg. Ps.-Jon., Tg. Onq.* (implicitly), and Rashi ad Num. 25:4.

126. See §310 (F350.10-351.11); §41 (F86.4-12), treated earlier, and notes 28, 29, and 30. In §355 (F418.11-14) the phrase *heads of the people* is interpreted to refer to Moses' standing at the head of the divisions of scholars. For other examples of the association of the Patriarch with Moses, see note 144.

127. Cf. Exod. 18:13-26, where Moses shares his authority with a lay leadership at Jethro's recommendation, and Num. 11:16-25, where he does so at God's command.

128. This ambiguity within the verse as the basis for the *Sifre*'s commentary is noted by David Pardo ad loc.

129. §13 (F21.8-9).
130. By contrast, Josephus (*Ant.* 3.4.1 §§71-72) portrays the people as having to *approve* these appointments. However, when Josephus himself is in a position to make such appointments in the Galilee he does not seek local advice or approval (*J. W.* 2.20.5 §§570-71). See Louis Ginzberg, *Legends of the Jews,* vol 6, p. 28, note 164. For another exegetical tack, note that the Damascus Document (CD 6.2-3) stresses *God's* having "raised up" the sect's "wise" and "discerning" leadership, thereby stressing their prophetic status, as if to compensate for the Book of Deuteronomy's seeming removal of God altogether from the judicial process (in contrast to Exod. 18:13-26).
131. For the association of Exod. 1:10 with *ʿēṣâ,* see b. *Soṭa* 11a; *Exod. Rab.* 1:9.
132. §13 (F21.10-11). Determining both the correct text and its interpretation here is difficult. I adopt the reading found in MSS Vatican and Berlin (*wĕtîqîm kĕsîpîm*), which in a slightly varied form (*wĕtîqîm kĕsûpîm*) appears in MSS London and Oxford, the Editio Princeps, and *Yalquṭ Šimʿoni.* The second word, when understood to be a passive participle of the root *ksp,* has been thought by some to mean "bright," "precious," or "pure" (*Zayit Raʿanan* to *Yalquṭ Šimʿoni;* Rabbenu Hillel, *Toledot ʾAdam,* and Friedmann ad loc.; Marcus Jastrow, *Dictionary,* col. 655a), and by others to mean "humble" (David Pardo, and *Zeraʿ ʾAbraham* ad loc.). It is more likely that the text originally read *pĕsîpîm,* as in *Sifre Num.* 92 (ed. Horovitz, p. 92, but note the critical apparatus), in relation to Moses' appointment of the seventy elders in Num. 11:16. This would be a variation of *pĕsippās,* found in similar contexts in *Sifre Zuṭaʾ* Num. 11:16 (ed. Horovitz, p. 271) and Num. 27:16 (ed. Horovitz, p. 320), where it denotes a cut or polished stone (Greek, *psēphos*). This word has been understood to connote either a many-sided scholar who has mastered all kinds of learning (*ʾAbot R. Nat* A 28 [ed. Schechter, p. 86]; B 46 [ed. Schechter, p. 129]; J. N. Epstein, *Tarbiz* 8 [1936-37]: 378), or a judge who renders decisive judgments (see *Lam. Rab.* 2.1 [ed. Buber, pp. 98-99, with note 36]; and Horovitz's note to *Sifre Zuṭaʾ* Num. 11:16). For the multifaceted nature of rabbinic learning, see §48 (F113.5-11), to be treated later. Finkelstein's expanded reading translated by Hammer (p. 37) and followed by Neusner (1:44) as, "men that are as multifaceted as a mosaic, that is to say, men who are trustworthy and suitable," is that of *Midraš Haggadol* alone. Note that in the three parallels in *Sifre Num.* and *Zuṭaʾ,* in addition to requiring that each appointee be *pĕsippās* it is stated that he should be a "master of wisdom" (*baʿal ḥokmâ*), in other words, a sage. Our text omits that requirement at this point so that it may dialectically emerge in the commentary's continuation.
133. For the name Arios, presumably a nonrabbi if not a non-Jew, see *t. B. Meṣ.* 3:11 (ed. Lieberman, p. 74), according to MS Erfurt. Moshe D. Herr ("The Historical Significance of the Dialogues between Jewish Sages and Roman Dignitaries," p. 149) considers Arios to have been a convert, but the evidence is too slim to allow any such identification.
134. §13 (F22.1-5). On variants to this text, and on the superiority of the present reading based on MS Vatican, see Finkelstein's notes, and Saul Lieberman, in *Kiryat Sefer* 14 (1937-38): 325-26. Hammer (p. 37) translates the last

expression of the passage (*yôšēb wětôheh*) as, "he is at a loss," and Neusner (1:44) translates, "daydreams." Finkelstein in his notes to this passage suggests that it means that the poor money changer is embarassed that no one comes to him. I understand it to mean that without customers, the poor money changer sits idly without purpose.

135. The two terms *ḥākām* and *nābôn* are frequently juxtaposed. See, for example, Deut. 4:6 and 1 Kings 3:12, and Gen. 41:31, 39, where they appear in reverse order. See also §304 (F323.8). The Passover Haggadah (ed. Goldschmidt, p. 117) has: "Even if all of us were wise (*ḥăkāmîm*), all of us discerning (*nĕbônîm*), all of us elders (*zĕqēnîm*), all of us knowing (*yôdĕ῾îm*) in the Torah." These are simply the three terms of Deut. 1:13 with the addition of *elders,* which is not found in the Sephardic versions of the Passover Haggadah and is probably a later gloss (see Goldschmidt's note ad loc.).

136. For other occurences of the expression *qiyyēm tôrâ* meaning to maintain Torah (that is, to fix it in one's mind) through its repetition and memorization, see §48 (F111.17-112.6) and §335 (F385.6, 8, 9), both of which will be treated later. the same verb when used with reference to a specific commandment (*miṣwâ*) can refer to the practical fulfillment of that commandment, but in some cases, as in §336 (F386.4), the distinction between these two meanings can become blurred.

137. For nonsages approaching sages with questions that necessitate their fluency in Torah teachings, see §34 (F60.8-9), cited in note 156.

138. For other understandings of this contrast, see Finkelstein's and Lieberman's notes to this passage (in note 134), where reference is made to *b. Hor.* 14a; *p. Hor.* 3.7 (48c); *b.* ῾*Erub.* 100b; *b. Ḥag.* 14a; and ʾ*Abot R. Nat.* 29. These scholars assume that the contrast here between *ḥākām* and *nābôn* is the same as between *sînay* ("Sinai": one who is an erudite collector and arranger of laws and traditions), and ῾*ôqēr hārîm* ("uprooter of mountains": one who is deft at cutting through difficult legal questions) elsewhere. Other texts (see earlier) contrast the *ḥākām,* who masters what has been taught to him, with the (superior) *nābôn,* who on his own searches out deeper meanings. For other understandings of our text, see V. Aptowitzer in *Tarbiz* 3 (1932): 462-3; and S. Ch. Kook, ibid., pp. 466-67. Compare §41 (F84.7-15), where the obligations to study Scripture's commands is said to be independent of the present obligation to perform them.

139. In Exod. 18:21 four different criteria, moral rather than intellectual, are suggested by Jethro. According to §15 (F24.7-8), Moses could find only men with three of the seven qualities suggested to him by Jethro. For further discussion, see Finkelstein's note ad loc.

140. For *ḥākām* as a term for the sect's laity overall, see 1QSa 2.16; CD 6.3; 1QH 1.35. In 1QSa 1.28, however, we find the combination *ḥăkāmîm, nĕbōnîm,* and *yĕdū῾îm* from Deut. 1:13 used to refer, perhaps messianically, to the community members in general. Although neither term, *ḥākām* or *nābôn,* appears frequently in the Dead Sea Scrolls, other forms of the root *byn* appear about four times as often as forms of the root *ḥkm.* See Karl Georg Kuhn, *Kondordanz zu den Qumrantexten* (Göttingen: Vandenhoeck and Ruprecht,

1960), pp. 31-32, 72. By contrast, in *Sifre* to Deuteronomy forms of the root *ḥkm* occur almost five times as often as those of *byn*. See Biniamin Kosovsky, *Otzar Leshon Hatanna'im: Thesaurus "Sifrei" Concordantiae Verborum*, vol. 2 (Jerusalem: Jewish Theological Seminary of America, 1972), pp. 457-58, 801-803. In the Dead Sea Scrolls the verb *hēbîn* is commonly used to denote the prophetic enlightenment of the community by its *priestly* leaders and by God. For the former, see 1QS 3.13 (*maśkîl*); 6.15 (*pāqîd*); 1QSa 1:5 (men of the messianic council); CD 13.2 (priest), 5 (*mēbaqqēr*), 8 (*mēbaqqēr*); 14.7 (priest). For the latter, see, 1QS 4.22; CD 1.10. For the function of the *mēbaqqēr* at Qumran, see my article, "Of Priests, Scribes, and Sages." For the *maśkîl*, see Carol A. Newsom, "The Sage in the Literature of Qumran: The Function of the *Maskil*," in John G. Gammie and Leo G. Perdue, eds., *The Sage in Israel and the Ancient Near East*. As in the *Sifre*, the Damascus Document passage understands the "wise" and "discerning" as fulfilling their juridical functions (seeking and applying God's will) through their activity of Torah study and interpretation, metaphorically represented in CD 6.3-9 as the digging or opening of wells.

141. See Chaim Rabin, ed. and trans., *The Zadokite Documents*, 2d ed. (Oxford: Clarendon Press, 1958), p. 21 (note to CD 6.2).

142. This translation of the lemma accords with modern translations (e.g., RSV and NJV) and ancient versions (e.g., LXX and *Tg. Ps.-Jonanthan*) that understand the third attribute (*yĕdū'îm*) in relation to the two that precede it and not in specific relation to the following phrase, *from* (or *for*) *your tribes*, which governs all three. That *yĕdū'îm* is a third and separate attribute may be inferred from Deut. 1:15, as the *Sifre* (§15 [F24.7-8]) itself understands it. In the present context, as we shall soon see, the *Sifre* understands *yĕdū'îm* in relation to what follows it differently.

143. §13 (F22.6-11). For discussion and parallels, see S. Lieberman, in *Kiryat Sefer* 14 (1937-38): 331-32.

144. The parallel in *Sifre Num.* 92 (ed. Horovitz, p. 93), in commenting on Num. 11:16, makes a similar point to that of our commentary, but without making reference to the patriarch and without directly suggesting local opposition to patriarchal appointments: "'Whom *you* know to be elders of the people' (Num. 11:16): You [Moses] should know if they are chosen before Me. 'That they be elders of the *people*' (ibid.): This teaches that a person is not seated on a court below unless he is [suited to be] seated on a court above. [No sooner is he seated than] the people praise him saying, 'So-and-so is proper and pious and suitable to be a sage.'" On problematic nature of this text (and hence the awkwardness of my translation) and the possibility of its containing an eclipsed twofold interpretation, see Horovitz's note ad loc. The same is stated even more clearly and forcefully in *Sifre Zuṭa'* on Num. 11:16 (ed. Horovitz, p. 271), where allusion is made to the patriarch: "Every elder upon whom the head of the generation [= the patriarch] bestows honor is approved [by God] from heaven, and the people respond [to such appointments] saying, 'So-and-so is proper and pious and suitable to be named a sage,'" In these parallels, unlike our commentary, the people instantly recognize the qualifications of

the appointees and thereby confirm their appointment. The fact that our commentary seems more concerned with the people's limited role in and possible opposition to such appointments need not reflect a different historical setting or attitude to it, but may be occasioned simply by the biblical text with which our commentary is engaged. In Deut. 1:13 the relation between the people's roles and Moses' role in making such appointments is most ambiguously expressed. The association of Moses with Rabban Gamaliel, again with regard to judicial appointments, is made in §16 (F26.1-8) (see note 152). Note also the association of Moses with Judah the Patriarch in §335 (F385.5-11), to be discussed later in the chapter. The association of Moses with the patriarch and his authority of judicial appointment was also made in §346 (F403.1-6), discussed earlier (see note 126).

145. For this tension between the sages being of, but distinct from (and superior to), the people, see notes 37, 102, and 192.
146. §13 (F23.1-4).
147. Local resentment to such appointments in fact may be hinted at in the preceding interpretation (E). For internal rabbinic questioning of the qualifications of patriarchal judicial appointments, see *Sanh.* 7b, where Resh Laqish (ca. 250) is reported to have said, with reference to Deut. 16:18-21, "Whoever appoints an unworthy judge over the public is like one who plants an [idolatrous] Asherah within Israel." For contrasting discussions and references to other rabbinic passages that evidence resistance to patriarchal appointments, see Saul Lieberman, *Siphre Zutta* (New York: Jewish Theological Seminary, 1968), pp. 87-88; Gedalyahu Alon, *Jews, Judaism and the Classical World*, pp. 414-16; as well as Lee I. Levine, "The Jewish Patriarch (Nasi) in Third Century Palestine" (see note 119), p. 665. The claim that oversight for all judicial and administrative appointments should rest with the rabbinic Patriarch may be subtly suggested as well in §144 (F197.1-198.3). There, in exegetically describing a system of national and local magistrates and officers, a statement attributed to R. Judah (bar Ilai) is inserted: "And from whence do we infer that *one* is to be appointed over all of them? Scripture teaches, 'Officers you shall appoint for you (sing.)' (Deut. 16:18)." The singular *for you* is understood to refer to Moses, as if to say that the magistrates and officers are to serve under him (and under his sucessor, the patriarch). The same statement is found in *b. Sanh.* 16b, but there it is placed after the discussion of the appointment of local *courts*. As a result, the commentators (e.g., Rashi) to the talmudic text understand R. Judah's statement to refer to the establishment of a single high court (the Sanhedrin). But the Tosaphot, in commenting on the talmudic text, note that in its *Sifre* parallel, where the (redacted) order is different, the reference must be to the *patriarch*.
148. The text in square brackets is only found in MS Berlin and *Midraš Ḥakamim* and the text of Rabbenu Hillel's commentary. It is not found in MS Vatican and other early witnesses. If this text is a later insertion it simply makes explicit the word play that is certainly implicit in the interpretation.

149. §13 (F23.5–10). If the prophet does not warn the wicked man that God will soon take his life for his evil ways, then the prophet is culpable for his death. If the prophet does warn the wicked man to change his ways and he does not, then the wicked man dies but the prophet bears no responsibility for his death.

150. That the leaders referred to here are judges can be inferred from preceding commentary as well as from what follows immediately (H). For Israel's welfare being dependent on the appointment of its (rabbinical) judges, see §144 (F200.3-4): "'[Justice, justice shall you pursue,] that you may live and inherit the land' (Deut. 16:20): This teaches that the appointment of judges is sufficient to restore Israel to life, to settle them on their land, and to prevent their being felled by the sword." This presumes, of course, that such appointments are properly (that is, rabbinically) qualified.

151. The association of appointed elders, prophets, and sages is also made in §41 (F86.14-87.7), treated earlier.

152. According to §15 (F24.3-25.2), Moses had both to cajole the judges into serving by stressing the honor of leading the children of Abraham, Isaac, and Jacob, and to impress upon Israel the honor due to the judges as leaders in all manners of life: commerce, negotiation, and entering and leaving. On the last pair, compare the similar role of the Levites and the overseer (*mĕbaqqēr*) in the Dead Sea Scrolls, for which see my "Of Priests, Scribes, and Sages in Second Temple Times." Similarly, §16 (F26.1-8) emphasizes that the appointment of sages to public office (again drawing an analogy between Moses and the patriarch) represented a *change* to which some sages had not yet grown accustomed. They needed to be reminded: "In the past you were independent, but now you are servants of the community." A different version of the story appears in *b. Hor.* 10a-b.

153. The section of text that follows within square brackets is not found in the better textual witness (MSS Vatican and London, *Yalquṭ Šimʿoni* and the Editio Princeps), but is found in MS Berlin, *Midraš Haggadol,* and *Midraš Ḥakamim.* Omitting it, however, would be problematic because the rhetorical formula "Why is this said? Because it is said . . . " is conventionally followed by a verse other than the lemma.

154. §48 (F107.13-108.5).

155. This rhetorical strategy, of drawing a positive analogy between Torah and something from common experience (usually a part of nature), only to find that if the analogy is pushed too far it becomes negative and requires another analogy to correct it, is employed elsewhere in the *Sifre:* §306 (F336.1-4); and §48 (F111.5-6, 12-13), to be discussed later.

156. These motifs will be further amplified in the remainder of the larger unit (§48), and are frequently expressed elsewhere in the *Sifre*'s commentary. Note especially the long series of interpretations of the metaphors of rain and dew for Torah teaching in §306 (F335.12-341.8), of which the following (F336.15-337.3) are particularly pertinent to our discussion: "'Like showers on young grasses' (Deut. 32:2): Just as these showers descend upon the grasses and suffuse them, thereby preventing them from becoming wormy, so one should

pore over words of Torah in order not to forget them. And similarly R. Jacob the son of R. Ḥanilai said to Rabbi [Judah the Patriarch]: 'Come and let us pore over some laws so that they not become rusty.' 'Like raindrops on young herbs'(ibid.): Just as these raindrops descend upon the herbs and cleanse and enlarge [by repeatedly striking them], so too one should enlarge words of Torah by reviewing them two, three, and four times." For another expression of the internalization of Torah through its repeated study, see §34 (F60.8-13): "'Impress [these teachings] upon your children' (Deut. 6:7): They should be so well honed within your mouth that when someone inquires of you concerning a teaching you will not hesitate but will answer him immediately. Similarly, it says, 'Say to wisdom, "You are my sister," and call understanding a kinswoman'(Prov. 7:4), and it says, 'Bind them on your fingers; write them on the tablet or your mind (heart)' (Prov. 7:3)." The expression *your children* of the lemma is subsequently interpreted to mean "your disciples," suggesting that the setting for these interpretations is intrarabbinic. For a similar use of Job 28:17, comparing Torah to gold and glass, see *ʾAbot R. Nat* 24 (ed. Schechter, p. 78), where it is attributed to R. Elisha b. Abuyah; *b. Ḥag.* 15a; and other parallels.

157. A Roman *as*, worth about a twenty-fourth of a *denar*.

158. §48 (F108.6-9). For a slightly variant parallel, see *ʾAbot R. Nat.* 23 (ed. Schechter, p. 78), where no mention is made of the bird being safeguarded for the king's son. I will comment on this detail later.

159. The immediate antecedent to this verse is a statement of Israel's privilege, among the nations, at having received the ordinances of the Torah.

160. Deut. 32:47 may be verbally linked to 4:9 by the similarity of their respective words *rēq* ("empty") and *raq* ("only"), which are identical when unvocalized. They may also be linked by their common reference to "your life." The same interpretation of Deut. 32:47 is given near the end of this unit (section Q). Presumed by these interpretations is the fuller exposition of §336 (F385.12-386.5), where Deut. 32:47 is interpreted to mean that every part of Scripture, even the seemingly prosaic, requires interpretation for which there is reward both in this world (age) and the next. There a specific example is given. Cf. *Gen. Rab.* 1:14 (ed. Theodor-Albeck, p. 12), where it is said that if you find anything in Scripture to be empty of meaning is it only empty because of your inability to interpret it, that is, it is empty only with respect to you.

161. §48 (F108.9-109.2).

162. For this interpretation, see David Pardo's commentary. Cf. *b. ʿErub.* 54b for a similar use of Prov. 12:11. For a different interpretation, see *Zeraʿ ʾAbraham* and Hammer (p. 417 note 7), who take the text to be referring to the kind of student who puts off until tomorrow what he should learn today. This interpretation is difficult to sustain from the text of the *Sifre* as we have it. For the idea of learning a little at a time, but absorbing it well as a basis for further learning, see §79 (F145.1-3): "'Be careful to heed (*šĕmōr wĕšāmaʿtā*)' (Deut. 12:28): If you learn (*šāmaʿtā*) a little [at a time], in the end you will learn a lot. If you preserve (*šāmartā*) a little [at a time], in the end you will learn a lot. If you preserve what you have learned, in the end you will preserve what you

have not [yet] learned. If you preserve what you already have, in the end you will learn for future [keeping]. If a person merits to learn Torah he merits for himself and for his succeeding generations until the end of all generations." Although Finkelstein argues that this passage originates as a marginal gloss to the *Sifre*, it is included in the better manuscripts, including MS Vatican. Similarly, §306 (F339.3-5) stresses the need to begin one's Torah studies with a manageable amount; once this is mastered the rest follows more easily. See also sections D and N that follow.

163. For a similar use of the agricultureal metaphor of sowing and harvesting in relation to study and constant review, see *b. Sanh.* 99a (end); *t. Ohol.* 16:8; *t. Para* 4:7: "Whoever studies but does not labor (var.: review) is like one who sows but does not harvest. Whoever studies and forgets what he has studied is like a woman who gives birth and buries." Elsewhere, our commentary acknowledges that the ideal of constant Torah study is confounded by the reality of having to plough and harvest to make a living (itself a positive Torah obligation, according to at least one view). See §42 (F90.12-17).

164. The preceding section of text is problematic. I have followed MS Vatican, with the words most recently in square brackets taken from MS London, *Yalquṭ Šimᶜoni,* and the Editio Princeps. Finkelstein adopts the smoother text of the MS Berlin, *Midraš Haggadol,* and *Midraš Ḥakamim.* There the sense is that by virtue of having acquired a field or vineyard one is called *man* (that is, a person of substance), but by not working that field or vineyard, one is additionally called *lazy* or *lacking sense.*

165. MS Vatican here has *wisdom (ḥokmâ)* for "sages" (*ḥakāmîm*).

166. §48 (F109.2-11).

167. Compare the story in *b B. Meṣ.* 59b, in which R. Eliezer b. Hyrcanus is banned from the society of sages for ruling contrary to the majority in declaring an object "clean" rather than "unclean." There the issue is not so much the substance of his ruling but his refusal, despite his learning, to engage the other sages on their own discursive terms of argumentation. There too God is said to support the sages' punishment of R. Eliezer for the sake of maintaining social order. Compare as well the Damascus Document's characterization of the Qumran sect's opponents, who reject their laws, as those who remove or break the boundary: CD 1.16; 5.20; 19.15-16; 20:25.

168. These first four sections find parallel but variant expression in *ʾAbot R. Nat. A* 24 (ed. Schechter, p. 78), where they are also combined but in a different order (A, C, D, B) and as the teachings of R. Elisha ben Abuya. For other parallels to the individual sections, see Finkelstein's notes.

169. §48 (F109.12-13). The text here is problematic. I have followed MS Vatican, which differs only slightly from MS London, *Yalquṭ Šimᶜoni,* and the Editio Princeps. Finkelstein's text follows MS Berlin and *Midraš Haggadol,* combining as one statement what is here divided as commentary on the two halves of the verse. The two parts are combined later in section J. David Pardo in his commentary to the *Sifre* suggests emending the first part of this text (by the omission of the word *lōʾ*) to read: "This refers to a disciple who at first learns everything." Thus, the disciple who learns everything at once at the

beginning loses his appetite for more, whereas the one who learns little by little always hungers for more.

170. We observed a similar metaphorical slippage in §306 (F339.6-14), where rain showers refer first to words of Torah and then to Torah sages. Similarly see *Abot R. Nat.* 24 (ed. Schechter, 78), where the gold and glass of Job 28:17 are first interpreted as metaphors for words of Torah and then for those who labor in them.

171. The word for honeycomb (*nōpet*) can also mean sieve (*nāpâ* in some witnesses).

172. §48 (F109.13-110.3).

173. For the motif of sages rendering contradictory legal judgments, see later (Q), §48 (F112.14-113.4). For the disciple of the sages compared to a sieve, see *m. ʾAbot* 5:15; *ʾAbot R. Nat.* A 40, B 45 (ed. Schechter, p. 127). Cf. *b. Ḥag.* 3a-b, where a student, overwhelmed by the contradictory views expressed in the house of study exclaims: "How can I learn Torah in such a setting?" He is told: "Make your ear like a hopper and acquire a discerning heart so as to learn from those who declare unclean and from those who declare clean," etc. With all of these metaphors, the incommensurate Torah teachings enter into, or pass through, the desciple, who having gathered them together within himself needs to apply his mind to them so as to understand and distinguish between them. For other parallels, see Chapter 1, note 66.

174. §48 (F110.3-5).

175. For the metaphor of a sponge applied to the disciple of the sages, see *m. ʾAbot* 5:15; *ʾAbot R. Nat.* A 40, B 45 (ed. Schechter, p. 127).

176. §48 (F110.5-8).

177. The scriptural *bôrekā* ("your cistern") is construed as *bĕʿîrkā* ("in your city").

178. Compare §34 (F61.15-62): "'You shall [continuously] speak of them' (Deut. 6:6): Make them you principal and not incidental concern, by having your worldly affairs (*maśśaʾ ûmattān*) concerned with them and by not mixing other kinds of teachings (*dĕbārîm ʾăḥērîm*) with them, as someone we know does. You should not say, 'I have learned the wisdom of Israel, now I will go and learn the wisdom of the nations.' Hence Scripture says, 'to walk in them' (Lev. 18:4), and not to be free of them."

179. Cf. *ʾAbot R. Nat.* A 8, where the student is urged to study all branches of the rabbinic Torah curriculum with a single teacher: "Thus that person remains in one place and is filled with good and blessing."

180. I follow MS Vatican which differs somewhat from Finkelstein's text, especially in having "cistern" (*bôr*) rather than "well" (*bĕʾēr*) in the interpretation. This preference is shared by J. N. Epstein in *Tarbiz* 8 (1936-37): 388. The difference between these two—the cistern as a sealed container and the well as a pervious collector of water—is crucial to my interpretation. The language here is almost identical with that of section E. See note 169.

181. §48 (F110.8-12).

182. For this understanding see the commentary of David Pardo. A similar comparison, between a sealed cistern and the more natural ditches and caves, is made in §306 (F338.9-13). For the cistern metaphor, see also *m. ʾAbot* 2:8.

For the use of the well metaphor for Torah and its communal study in the Dead Sea Scrolls, see Chapter 1, note 64.

183. §48 (F110.12-111.16).

184. For this rhetorical strategy, see note 155.

185. The parallels in *Yalquṭ Hammakiri* Isa. 55:1 and *Yalquṭ Šimʿoni* Isa. 480 do not make the transition from oil back to honey. For parallel texts that compare Torah to water, wine, and oil, see Finkelstein's notes. For the combination Torah, wine, and heart, see note 92.

186. For this use of the verb *qiyyēm* with Torah, see note 136.

187. Finkelstein follows a reading from *Midraš Haggadol* (but found only in one manuscript) that has "Scroll of Pottery (*ḥarîsîm*)." All other early witnesses have Scroll of the Pious (*ḥasidim*). See J. N. Epstein in *Tarbiz* 8 (1936-37): 378.

188. §48 (F111.17-112.6). I have followed MS Vatican, which differs somewhat from Finkelstein's text.

189. See in particular sections C and D, with notes 160 and 162. For similar interpretations, also employing Deut. 8:19, see *Mek. Wayassaʾ* 1 (ed. Lauterbach, vol. 2, p. 95), with Lauterbach's note ad loc.; *Mek. Baḥodeš* 2 (ed. Lauterbach, vol. 2, p. 203); *Mek. R. Simeon bar Yoḥai* 15:26 (ed. Epstein-Melamed, p. 105).

190. The text is difficult here. I have followed the sense of *Yalquṭ Šimʿoni*.

191. §48 (F112.7-13).

192. For other expressions of an "egalitarian" Torah ethic, see notes 37 and 102, as well as the following: §161 (F212.5): "The commoner is equal to the king with regard to words of Torah"; §345 to Deut 33:4 (F402.6-8), discussed in Chapter 2: the Torah is an inheritance to royalty and commoners alike. For similar exegeses, see *Sifra ʾAḥarê Mot* 13.13 (ed. Weiss, col. 86b) and *b. Sanh.* 59a, both of which emphasize the inclusion of the non-Israelite (who is not a priest, Levite, or Israelite); and *Midr. Pss.* 1.18 (ed. Buber, 9b), which emphasizes the inclusion of the convert (who is not genealogically a priest, Levite, or Israelite). For the rabbis as a recognizable class within Israel, see §343 (F400.5-6), discussed in Chapter 2. For hereditary rabbinic positions of leadership, see §162 (F212.13-213.1), and note 117.

193. On Ezra as priestly scribe, see my "Of Priests, Scribes, and Sages in Second Temple Times." For Ezra's having rewritten the destroyed, and hence abandoned, Scriptures, see *4 Ezra* 14:21-26. Cf. b. *Sukk.* 20a.

194. For reports of R. Akiba's editorial activity, see *ʾAbot R. Nat.* A 18 (ed. Schrechter, p. 67); *p. Šeqal.* 5.1 (col. 48c), as understood by Saul Lieberman, *Hellenism in Jewish Palestine*, pp. 90-91.

195. Hammer, following Finkelstein, who in turn follows Rabbenu Hillel, harmonizes sections O and P by stating: "The sense seems to be that those who were of common origin did indeed save the Torah." See also C. Albeck, "Introduction to the Tractate ʿEduyyot," in *Šiššâ Sidrê Mišnâ, Sēder Nēzîqîn* (Jerusalem: Bialik Institute, 1959), p. 276, note 3. However, Ezra the priestly scribe was not of "common origin" and Shaphan's authority derived, presumably, from royal appointment. Thus, R. Akiba stands out in relation

to the two other scribes even as he is associated with them.

196. For such phrases interpreted to legitimate rabbinic teaching and judicial authority, compare the *Sifre's* interpretation of "in charge *at that time*" (Deut. 17:9) in conjunction with Eccl. 7:10 (§153 [F206.13], with note 62), as well as the *Sifre's* interpretation of the phrase "that I have set before you *this day*" (Deut. 32:11) (§58[F124.12-14]). See also the *Sifre's* interpretation of "that I command you *this day*" (Deut. 11:13) (§41 [F86.4-12]), "that I command you *this day*" (Deut. 6:6) (§33 [F59.9-10], cited in Chapter 4, note 7), and "You stand *this day*" (Deut. 29:9) (§345 [F402.8], discussed in Chapter 2). On the rabbinic understanding of such phrases as referring to the commentary's own present, see Marc Bregman, "Past and Present in Midrashic Literature." *Hebrew Annual Review* 2 (1978): 47; Isaak Heinemann, *Darke ha'aggada*, 3rd ed. (Jerusalem: Magnes Press, 1970), pp. 43, 164.

197. This is the text best supported by the extant manuscripts (including MS Vatican) and the text upon which Rabbenu Hillel's commentary is based. Finkelstein, in his not ad loc., considers it to be "certainly a scribal error" (as do earlier commentators), and suggests "correcting" it in accord with the parallels in the Tosephta and Talmud (cited in note 199). Hammer (p. 417, note 15) adopts Finkelstein's view. I see neither a need nor a justification for this. For further discussion, see note 199.

198. §48 (F112.14-113.14).

199. For the disciple's activity of gathering and sorting the contradictory teachings of sages as words of Torah, see above, section F and n. 173. For the linking of this activity to the fear that Torah teaching will in the future be lost if it is not preserved, see *t. ʿEd.* 1:1 and the parallel to our text in a *barayta* in *b. Šabb.* 138b. The latter text continues with a fuller, more dialectical version of what we find in the *Sifre*. There, Amos 8:12 is interpreted with reference to a woman who in the *future* will have to wander between synagogues and houses of study in search of a ruling on the purity status of a loaf of bread. The *Sifre* text in its brevity is more ambiguous, and it would be a mistake (see note 197) to assume that it should be read in light of the talmudic text, because their literary and rhetorical contexts (and perhaps purposes) are different. In the *Sifre* it is not clear who it is that goes from city to city in search of rulings (sages or nonsages?). Unlike the talmudic parallel, the activity is described as *permitted* by the sages in the present, rather than projected into the future as a sign of what will happen when Torah is forgotten in Israel.

200. The expression *kol hammiṣwâ* is understood to contain three levels or layers of meaning, corresponding to the three stages in which the expression is built up: the indefinite noun *miṣwâ* alone, the same noun with the addition of the definite article, and the definite noun with the addition of the inclusive particle *kol*.

201. On these three as the tripartite curriculum of oral Torah (*mišnâ*) studies, see notes 92 and 111.

202. §48 (F113.5-11).

203. The very same interpretation of Deut. 32:47, identically expressed, was previously included in the commentary in §48 section B. See note 160.

204. On the well-rounded scholar, see note 131. On the tension between legal and nonlegal studies, see note 96. Cf. *b. Soṭa* 40a, where people flock to the teacher of non-legal teachings. On this tension, see Judah Goldin, "The Freedom and Restraint of Haggadah" (note 111 here).

205. Becoming a disciple of the sages meant acquiring, in the person of one's master, a new father, with potentially negative consequences to the disciple's relationship to his real father. Although ideally a disciple's father should rejoice in his son's learning, other emotions at loosing one's son to the influence of another may have been more common. This is most pointedly expressed in the hagiographic story of R. Eliezer ben Hyrcanus' leaving his father's home, against the latter's will, to study Torah with R. Joḥanan ben Zakkai in Jerusalem. The father travels to Jerusalem to disinherit his son but upon hearing him expound Torah to the praises of the sages is so filled with pride that he reinstates (and more) him. See *ʾAbot R. Nat.* A 6 (ed. Schechter, pp. 30-31), B 13 (ed. Schechter, pp. 30-33), and parallels. For a statement that the honor due one's master takes precedence over that due one's father, see *m. B. Meṣ.* 2:11. On the rabbinic master as "father," see §34 (F61.10-14). For other texts in which the master-disciple relationship is equated with that of father-son, see §182 (F224.11), §305 (F327.6), §335 (F385.7-9).

206. For another example of God's benefiting from the activity of sages, see §346 (F403.1-6), treated earlier, and note 122.

207. §48 (F113.12-15).

208. On the question of the relation of study (*talmûd*) to action (*maʿăśeh*) see §41 (F84.7-9; 84.16-86.3), where the two are stressed, but the former is given priority over the latter. See note 80. This is in contrast to *ʾAbot* 3:9, 17, where it is said that it is better for one's deeds to exceed one's wisdom, than vice versa. For other *Sifre* passages that connect study with practice as complements, see §29 (F48.7), §41 (F88.11), §161 (F212.3).

209. The Hebrew here is *bišbîl šeʾēšeb bîšîbâ*. On this expression, see note 120.

210. §48 (F113.15-114.2).

211. Compare the almost identical interpretation in §41 (F87.8-10): "'Loving the Lord your God' (Deut. 11:13): Lest you should say, 'I am studying Torah in order that I become rich, in order that I be called *Rabbi,* in order that I receive a reward in the world to come,' Scripture teaches, 'Loving the Lord your God.' Everything that you do you should do out of love." A close parallel to both is found in a *baraytaʿ* in *b. Ned.* 62a. Cf. the saying attributed to Antiochus of Soko in *m. ʾAbot* 1:3: "Be not like slaves that minister to the master for the sake of receiving a bounty, but be like slaves that minister to the master not for the sake of receiving a bounty."

212. See §§153, 306, 346, and 13, treated earlier, as well as notes 114-120 and 149-152.

213. We know of two sages with this name, the first flourishing around 100 C.E., the second around 150.

214. See Dan. 5:2-3, where King Belshazzar uses temple vessels for drinking at a ribald banquet.

215. The words *this world and the world to come* are found in MSS Vatican and

London, *Yalquṭ Šimʿoni,* and the Editio Princeps. Finkelstein's text has just *the world,* following MS Berlin, *Midraš Haggadol,* and *Midraš Ḥakamim.* On the world having been created with Torah, see the sources listed in Finkelstein's notes ad loc. On the Torah having been created before the world, see §37 (F70.5-6).

216. §48 (F114.3-6).

217. On *using* Torah for worldly gain, see *m. ʾAbot* 1:13; 4:5; *ʾAbot R. Nat.* B27 (ed. Schechter, p. 56); and the close parallel in *b. Neb.* 62a. For other parallels to this text and its theme, some of which may understand *using* Torah in a theurgic sense, see Finkelstein's notes ad loc., and Gershom G. Scholem, *Jewish Gnosticism, Merkavah, Mysticism, and Talmudic Tradition,* 2d ed. (New York: Jewish Theological Seminary of America, 1965), p. 54, note 36, pp. 80-81. For a positive sense of the expression *using* (being preoccupied with) Torah, see §343 (F400.2-4).

218. §335 (F384.15-385.4).

219. The expression *words of Torah* (*dibrè tôrâ*) is sometimes employed to refer to the written Torah as distinguished from the oral rabbinic Torah (*dibre sōpĕrîm*): §115 (F174.9), §154 (F207.6-7); *m. Sanh.* 11:3. Elsewhere, as here, it means either Torah teaching as a whole (scriptural and rabbinic), or its rabbinic component in particular: §41 (F86.6-8), §48 (F110.1-3), §306 (F339.8).

220. Although *t. Ḥag.* 1:9 has the same areas of law suspended by a hair, *p. Ḥag.* 1.7(8)(76c-d) suggests that rabbinic purity laws also have little scriptural basis upon which to rest.

221. On the Levites as gatekeepers, see 1 Chr. 23:4 and Philo, *Spec. Leg.* 1.156. For the Levites occupying a medial position between the priests and the laity in the Dead Sea Scrolls, and for a striking parallel in which the rabbinic sage is similarly positioned, see my "Of Priests Scribes, and Sages in Second Temple Times."

222. As we saw in our examination of §48, the *Sifre* commentary understands the verb *šmr* in such contexts to signify the repeated study and review of words of Torah, leading to their being maintained (*qiyyûm*) in the memories of their students.

223. For alternative names, which do not make chronological sense, see Finkelstein's critical apparatus.

224. The text is problematic here. I have followed MS London while trying to make the translation read smoothly.

225. §335 (F385.5-11).

226. See especially §34 (F61.5-10): "'Impress them upon your children' (Deut. 6:7): These are your disciples."

227. See especially §48 (F109.12-13) and §48 (F110.8-12), both treated earlier.

228. Compare the frustration of R. Eliezer b. Hyrcanus at his deathbed: "Woe unto me! For my two arms that are like two Torah scrolls depart from the world!... I carried away from my teachers no more than does a man who dips his finger in the sea; and I gave away to my disciples no more than a paintbrush takes from the tube." *ʾAbot R. Nat.* 25 (ed. Schechter, p. 81)

(trans. J. Goldin, p. 109) and parallels. There R. Akiba mourns the loss of his teacher as a father (citing 2 Kings 2:12).

4. Polyphony and Plot: Torah as Song as Covenantal Witness

1. Using the frequency of the phrase *dābar ᵓaḥēr* ("another interpretation") as a very rough index for the frequency of alternative interpretations in a midrashic commentary, I calculate that they occur, on an average, 2.54 times more frequently in aggadic sections of *Sifre* Deuteronomy than in halakic sections of equal length. This is based on a total count of 237 occurrences of *dābar ᵓaḥēr* in the *Sifre*, 183 of which are in aggadic sections and 54 of which are in halakic sections, with the commentary as a whole containing 57 percent aggadic text and 43 percent halakic text. On the multivocality of Scripture being a matter not just of its narrative interpretation but also of its legal interpretation, see end of note 4.

2. *B. Sanh.* 34a. Parallels can be found in *b. Šabb.* 88b; *p. Ned.* 3:2 (37d); *p. Šebu.* 3:9 (10) (34d); *Mek. Baḥodeš* 7 (ed. Lauterbach, 2:252); *Midr. Pss.* 92:3 (p. 403); *Exod. Rab.* 5:9; 28:6.

3. It is the nature of God's "might" that His single utterance can yield several meanings, and that several of His utterances cannot reduce (as if redundantly) to a single meaning.

4. Medieval commenatators to *b. Sanh.* 34a and *Šabb.* 88b (see Tosaphot to both passages and Rashi to the latter) note the discrepancy between the biblical verse in which the *rock* is shattered by the powerful blow of the hammer, and the rabbinic interpretation in which the *hammer* itself releases fragments upon hitting the rock. Although it would be more "natural" to think of the hammer, representing the act of interpretation, as causing sparks to fly from the rock, representing God's word in Scripture (see Rashi to *b. Šabb.* 88b; Jacob Levy, *Wörteruch über die Talmudim und Midraschim*, rev. L. Goldschmidt, 4 vols. [Berlin: B. Harz, 1924], vol. 3, p. 390, col. 1, s.v. *nîṣôṣ*; and most recently, David Stern, "Midrash and Indeterminacy," *Critical Inquiry* 15 [1988]: 135-36), this is *not* what the talmudic texts say, in part because the prooftext from Jeremiah compares God's word to the *hammer*. However, the talmudic interpretation reworks Jeremiah's metaphor no less radically. Now the hammer does not shatter (*yĕpōṣēṣ*) the rock as in Jeremiah, but itself emits numerous, tiny sparks (*nîṣôṣot*, presumably a word play), understood to be the fire of Jeremiah's preceding metaphor, upon striking the rock. In this image, multiple sparks are emitted without either the rock's or the hammer's being perceptively diminished; divine speech (in Scripture) divides while remaining one, and can do so over and over again. This is still not quite the same as Rabbenu Tam's substitution of the metaphor of a hard sapphire being hit by a hammer on an anvil (taken from *Cant. Rab.* 5:14 and parallels), where the hammer itself shatters (presumably into pieces), the anvil splits, but

the sapphire remains intact (cited in the Tosaphot referred to earlier). Note how the problem of the talmudic passage is "solved" in *Midr. Pss.* 42:3 (ed. Buber, col. 202a) by *splitting* the metaphor itself in two: "The divine utterance issued and divided into seven voices, and from seven voices into seventy languages. R. Joshua says: This is like a man who strikes an anvil [with a hammer], and sparks fly off in every direction. R. Jose b. Ḥanina says: This is like a man who strikes a rock with a hammer, and small pieces of rock (*ṣĕrôrôt*) fly off in every direction . . The Holy One, blessed be He, would issue an utterance from His mouth and it would divide into several lights." My point here is that the multivocality of divine speech (at Sinai and in Scripture) is not so much the *product* of human interpretation (of an otherwise univocal expression) as its *anticipation*. It is rabbinically conceived as being as much an aspect of divine revelation as of its human reception, as the two are conjoined in interpretation. It should be noted that the Talmud cites this tradition concerning the multivocality of Scripture in relation to legal exegesis. See above, note 1.

5. This is similar to the *Sifre*'s view (§343 [F395.7-13], discussed in Chapter 2) that God approached Sinai from four directions, revealing the Torah in four languages. The idea of seventy languages (the same number as the number of nations), like that of four directions, suggests the comprehensiveness (not infinitude) of meaning encompassed by revelation. See Chapter 2, notes 24 and 25.

6. §313 (F355.9-11), cited in whole and discussed in Chapter 2. Note as well, *Mek. Baḥodeš* 9 (ed. Lauterbach, vol. 2, pp. 266-67): 'Rabbi [Judah the Patriarch] says: This is to proclaim the excellence of the Israelites. For when they all stood before Mt. Sinai to receive the Torah they interpreted (*mĕparrĕšîm*) the divine utterance as soon as they heard it. . . As soon as the word came forth they interpreted it." The same text previously explains the plural lightnings and thunderings of revelation (Exod. 20:18) in terms of God's intent that each Israelite perceive revelation according to his or her specific capacity. For a fuller explication, see *Pesiq. Rab Kah. Baḥodeš Haššeliši* 25 (ed. Mandelbaum, vol. 1, pp. 223-24).

7. §58 (F124.11-14). For another expression of the idea that Torah should be regarded as freshly received, see §33 (F59.9-10): "'Which I command you *this day*'(Deut. 6:6): Let [these words] not be like an old edict to which no one pays any regard, but like a new edict to which everyone rushes to read." For a similar thought, see *b. Ber.* 63b: "The Torah is as dear to those who study it every day as it was on the day that it was given from Mt. Sinai." For similar interpretations of *this day,* see Chapter 3, note 196.

8. §49 (F114.14-115.5). For a fuller discussion of this passage, see Chapter 3.

9. This is not the place to enter into a full discussion of the celebration of midrash's "infinite" indeterminacy by some post-structuralist literary critics. See my brief remarks in "Interpreting Midrash 2: Midrash and Its Literary Contexts," *Prooftexts* 7 (1987): 293-94. On this question in literary theory more generally, see, for example, David Hoy, "Jacques Derrida," in *The Return of the Grand Theory in the Human Sciences,* ed. Quentin Skinner

(Cambridge: Cambridge University Press, 1985), pp. 43-64. For a sensitive historian's approach to the multiplicity but not undecidability of meaning in texts from the past, see J. G. A. Pockock, *Politics, Language, and Time: Essays on Political Thought and History* (New York: Atheneum, Publishers, 1971), pp. 23-33. For a fuller discussion of the relationship of midrashic multiplicity of meaning to literary theories of indeterminacy, see William Scott Green, "Romancing the Tome: Rabbinic Hermeneutics and the Theory of Literature," *Semeia* 40 (1987): 147-68; David Stern, "Midrash and Indeterminacy," *Critical Inquiry* 15 (Autumn 1988): 132-61.

10. Similarly, Jerome McGann (*Social Values and Poetic Acts: The Historical Judgment of Literary Work* [Cambridge: Harvard University Press, 1988], p. 212), in describing what he calls *nonnarrative* types of texts, states: "While the text is clearly a progressive text, its movement is not governed by a narrativized totality." For other types of such "nonnarrative" texts, see ibid., pp. 132-51. Note that, here and in the following discussion, in describing the progressive nature of scriptural commentary, I have adapted terms that derive from the analysis of narrative fiction. Because the commentary of the *Sifre* is not a continuous narrative, but a succession and interweaving of "petits récits" (as I argue in Chapter 2), and because its "authors" would not, we may assume, have been receptive to the designation of their work as one of "fiction," some might think my adaption of such terminology here to be illigitimate. Increasingly, however, scholars of other types of nonnarrative and nonfictional discourse have found the application of terms of narrative analysis to be useful, even as they need to be adapted when transferred to different discursive media. For discussion and references see Shlomith Rimmon-Kenan, *Narrative Fiction: Contemporary Poetics* (London: Methuen, 1983), p. 130-32, to which may be added Jerome McGann's discussion cited earlier, and Fredric Jameson, "On Interpretation: Literature as a Socially Symbolic Act," in *The Political Unconscious: Narrative as a Socially Symbolic Act* (Ithaca: Cornell University Press, 1981), pp. 17-102.

11. The pair prospection-retrospection (or protention-retention) is adapted from Husserl by David Carr in *Time, Narrative, and History* (Bloomington: Indiana University Press, 1986), summarized in idem, "Narrative and the Real World: An Argument for Continuity," *History and Theory* 25 (1986), 117-31. Peter Brooks (*Reading for the Plot: Design and Intention in Narrative* [New York: Alfred A Knopf, 1984], p, 28) discusses the dialogical interplay of anticipation and retrospection in a similar way. See also Roman Ingarden, *The Literary Work of Art: An Investigation on the Borderlines of Ontology, Logic and the Theory of Literature*, trans. George G. Grabowicz (Evanston: Northwestern University Press, 1973); idem, *The Cognition of the Literary Work of Art*, trans. Ruth Ann Crowley and Kenneth R. Olson (Evanston: Northwestern University Press, 1973). The same dynamic may be said to have operated in the way in which a series of interpretations would have been encountered and understood in a preliterary or social context, say in the rabbinic house of study, where a variety of interpretations might have been heard in succession. One difference, however, is that the student of a *text* of

commentary may return to an earlier interpretation to review or reconsider it in light of a later one. In any case, as we know very little about the social manner of study within early rabbinic circles, and as the present study focuses on an extant written commentary, my remarks will pertain to the literary rather than preliterary encountering of such a multiplicity of interpretations.

12. For example, see my treatment of §310 (F350.10-351.11) in Chapter 3 in which the first of two sets of juxtaposed interpretations of a dissected verse moves from biblical beginnings to the present, whereas the second moves from the present to the messianic future, but in such a way as to allude to the intermediary place of the present as filled in by the text's students. Similarly, it is not uncommon for the last interpretation of a series to point to the messianic future, even as the exact route between here and there remains unspecified. For previously treated examples in the *Sifre*, see §41 (F86.4-87.7); and the very end of §48 (F114.3-6). See also §313 (F354.9-356.10), a part of which was treated in Chapter 2, where four sets of interpretations of Deut. 32:10, each taking the verse to refer to a different period in Israel's sacred history, are arranged in chronological order: Abraham, the giving of the Torah at Sinai, the wandering in the Wilderness, the messianic future. Clearly such chronological arrangements of discrete, alternative interpretations are by design, whatever their intent. I should caution that I am not arguing that such chronological ordering is the principal rhetorical logic in the ordering of interpretations in the *Sifre*, but only one that is well evidenced. In later, more homiletical midrashic commentaries (e.g., *Leviticus Rabbah*), where a messianic consolation is often placed as the final interpretation of a series, this logic is more common, and hence comes to be expected, whether to rhetorical advantage or disadvantage.

13. Thus in §48 (F112.7-13), cited and discussed in Chapter 3 we find the sequence Shaphan, Ezera, and R. Akiba. Similarly, in §343 (F394.4-396.6), cited and discussed in Chapter 2, we find the sequence Moses, David, Solomon, and the "early sages." Consider as well §357 (F429.6-14), where we encounter the sequence Moses, Hillel, Yoḥanan ben Zakkai, and R. Akiba, as well as a fuller chronological sequence of pairs extending from Rebecca to R. Akiba. In each of these, the fact that a chronological sequence of biblical leaders continues with the sages or their immediate antecedents serves to establish a continuum stretching from the biblical past into the rabbinic present. Note also the chronological progression from Egypt to the days of the Messiah in §343 (F398.5-9), treated in Chapter 2, and the chronological progression from the generation of the Flood to the days of the Messiah in §318 (F361.4-362.14).

14. There is an extensive literature on such issues of time in narrative. For two good introductions to this literature, see Shlomith Rimmon-Kenan, *Narrative Fiction: Contemporary Poetics*, esp. pp. 43-58, 89-91, 117-29; Wallace Martin, *Recent Theories of Narrative* (Ithaca: Cornell University Press, 1986), esp. pp. 85-90, 123-26, 187-90. In addition to other works specifically cited in the preceeding and following notes, I have benefitted from David Carroll, "The Times of History and the Order of Discourse," Chapter 5 of *The Subject in Question: The Languages of Theory and the Strategies of Fiction*

(Chicago: University of Chicago Press, 1982), pp. 119-39; Seymour Chatman, *Story and Discourse: Narrative Structure in Fiction and Film* (Ithaca: Cornell University Press, 1978), pp. 43-95; Jonathan Culler, "Story and Discourse in the Analysis of Narrative," in *The Prusuit of Signs: Semiotics, Literature, Deconstructionism* (Ithaca: Cornell University Press, 1981), pp. 169-87; Gérard Genette, *Narrative Discourse: An Essay in Method*, trans. J. E. Lewin (Ithaca: Cornell University Press, 1980), pp. 86-112; idem, *Narrative Discourse Revisited*, trans. Jane E. Lewin (Ithaca: Cornell University Press, 1988), pp. 21-37; A. A. Mendèlow, *Time and the Novel* (New York: Humanities Press, 1965); Menakhem Perry, "Literary Dynamics: How the Order of a Text Creates its Meanings," *Poetics Today* 1, no. 1 (1979-80): 35—64, 311-361; idem and Meir Sternberg, "The King through Ironic Eyes: The Narrator's Devices in the Biblical Story of David and Bathsheba and Two Excursuses on the Theory of the Narrative Text," *Hasifrut* 1 (1966): 263-92 [Hebrew]; Meir Sternberg, *Expositional Modes and Temporal Order in Fiction* (Baltimore: Johns Hopkins University Press, 1978); idem, *The Poetics of Biblical Narrative: Ideological Literature and the Drama of Reading* (Bloomington: Indiana University Press, 1985). On textual gapping and their filling, see in particular the works by Menakhem Perry and Meir Sternberg just cited. For Roland Barthes on the retarding and releasing of narrative progression, see *S/Z*, trans. Richard Miller (New York: Hill and Wang, 1974), pp. 75-76, 84-85, 187-88, 209-210. The question of time in rabbinic literature has not received the attention that it deserves. For two different approaches, see Marc Bregman, "Past and Present in Midrashic Literature," *Hebrew Annual Review* 2 (1978): 45-59; and Jonah Fraenkel, "Time and Its Shaping in Aggadic Narrative" [Hebrew], in *Studies in Aggadah, Targum and Jewish Liturgy in Memory of Joseph Heinemann* (Jerusalem: Magnes Press and Hebrew Union College Press, 1981), pp. 133-62.

15. Thus, Paul Ricoeur (*Time and Narrative*, vol. 1 [Chicago: University of Chicago Press, 1984], pp. 52-87) uses the sequence prefiguration, figuration, refiguration to denote such an interplay in the life of an individual or society. However, Ricoeur argues that such a temporalization of life is imposed upon it by our narratives. For a critique of Ricoeur's position, arguing that the process of temporal prospection and retrospection is inherent in our individual and collective experiences of time even prior to our narrativizations of those experiences, see David Carr's review of Ricoeur in *History and Theory* 23 (1984): 357-70, as well as his own more extensive treatment of the problem in *Time, Narrative, and History*. For an excellent survey of recent literature on the question of the relation of historical temporality to that of history, see Hayden White, "The Question of Narrative in Contemporary Historical Theory." *History and Theory* 23 (1984): 1-33, reprinted in idem, *The Content of the Form: Narrative Discourse and Historical Representation* (Baltimore: Johns Hopkins University Press, 1987).

16. Frank Kermode, *The Sense of an Ending* (Oxford: Oxford University Press, 1967), pp. 35-36. Although I adapt below some of Kermode's terminology, I should stress that my argument will be that it is precisely in the discordancies

of beginning, middle, and end of the *Sifre* text to be examined that the "fiction" of its explanatory structure intersects the discordancies of collectively lived time. But note Kermode's own reconsiderations, in "Endings, Continued," in *Languages of the Unsayable: The Play of Negativity in Literature and Literary Theory,* ed. Sanford Budick and Wolfgang Iser (New York: Columbia University Press, 1989), pp. 71-94.

17. Peter Brooks, *Reading for the Plot,* p. 19. It is this sense of plot that I am here employing, rather thatn that of the underlying, essentialized story line of a narrative.

18. Compare Reinhard Koselleck's discussion (*Futures Past: The Semantics of Historical Time,* trans. Keith Tribe [Cambridge: MIT Press, 1985], pp. 267-88) of the dynamic interplay of a culture's "horizon of expectations" and its "space of experience" across the gap that separates the two. See also in this regard Hans Robert Jauss, *Toward an Aesthetic of Reception,* trans. Timothy Bahti (Minneapolis: University of Minnesota Press, 1982). For the dialectic of continuity (or sedimentation) and disruption in text and time, in relation to the work of Michel Foucault (especially *The Archeology of Knowledge,* trans. A. M. Sheridan Smith [New York: Pantheon Books, 1972]), see Paul Ricoeur, *Time and Narrative,* vol. 3, trans. Kathleen Blamey and David Pellauer (Chicago: University of Chicago Press, 1988), pp. 216-19. Frederick Jameson (*The Political Unconscious,* p. 81) speaks of a text's transformative drawing of the "Real" of its social and political context into its discursive texture.

19. Compare Jerome McGann's phrase *disciplined discontinuities* (*Social Values and Poetic Acts,* p. ix) to describe the poetic text in its capacity to engage its readers.

20. This is one of the largest collections of multiple interpretations to a single verse in the *Sifre* to Deuteronomy. For another example, see §48, presented and analyzed in Chapter 3. I would not wish to make too much of the number thirteen, since some of the interpretations could be divided or subdivided differently.

21. This it would appear is the intent of the song as expressed by its introduction in Deut. 31:16-22.

22. The many critical issues of the Song's date, composition, filiations, and awkward placement at the end of the Book of Deuteronomy need not detain us here. Some will be alluded to later (notes 28 and 101) as they bear on the *Sifre*'s commentary. For critical discussions of the Song of Moses see the standard scholarly commentaries to Deuteronomy, as well as the following: J. R. Boston, "The Wisdom Influence upon the Song of Moses," *JBL* 87 (1968): 198-202; W. L. Moran, "Some Remarks on the Song of Moses," *Biblica* 43 (1962): 317-27; Patrick W. Skehan, "The Structure of the Song of Moses in Deuteronomy (Deut. 32:1-43)," *CBQ* 13 (1951): 153-63; Dov Rappel, "*Širat 'Ha'ăzînû',*" *Beth Mikra* 12, no. 3 (31) (1966-67): 3-26; 13, no. 1 (32) (1967-68): 14-23; 13, no. 2 (33) (1967-68): 28-47 [Hebrew]. For a discussion of the later literary echoes of the song, see Harold Fisch, "The Song of Moses: Pastoral Reverse," Chapter 5 of *Poetry with a Purpose: Biblical Poetics and Interpretation* (Bloomington: Indiana University Press, 1988), pp. 55-79.

Because the Song of Moses is something of a summary of Israel's sacred history, it appears to have been important in the liturgical-lectionary cycle in Second Temple and rabbinic times. Note, for example, the fragments found at Qumran (Patrick W. Skehan, "A Fragment of the 'Song of Moses' [Deut. 32] from Qumran," *BASOR* 136 [1954]: 12-15). According to *b. Roš. Haš.* 31a, when the Temple stood, the *musaph* offering for the Sabbath was accompanied by the reading of sections of Deut. 32.

23. The expression (*hēʿîd bě-*) is drawn from Deut. 4:26; 30:19; and 31:28; in all of which heaven and earth are called by Moses to witness against Israel. Deut. 32:1 does not itself use the language of witnessing. This expression is repeated with respect to each of the twelve witnesses that follow. Even though the nature of each witness is somewhat different, I will retain the same translation to convey the lexical and structural repetitiveness of the Hebrew.

24. Once again, the same language is repeated with respect to each of the twelve witnesses (with a slight variation in the case of Judah). Even though the nature of each corruption is somewhat different, I will retain the same translation to convey the semantic and structural repetitiveness of the Hebrew. In each case, Israel commits sinful acts in some relation to its covenantal witnesses, therby involving them in the corruption. The implications of this will be discussed later.

25. Because Jerusalem straddled the territories of Benjamin and Judah, "inhabitants of Jerusalem" is taken to refer to the Tribe of Benjamin. However, the next verse cited, concerning the corruption of Judah, makes no mention of Benjamin (although it continues with, "an abomination is committed in Israel and in Jerusalem"), which is therefore dropped in the corruption clause according to the better textual witnesses (including MS Vatican). On whether the Temple was in the territory of Benjamin or of Judah, or divided between the two, see §352 (F411.1-16).

26. On text-critical grounds I favor the reading *šimkā* ("your name"), which is found in MSS Vatican, Oxford, and London, *Yalquṭ Šimʿoni* (MS Oxford), the Editio Princeps, and a Geniza fragment (Ox. Heb. c10, not recorded by Finkelstein in his edition). Finkelstein prefers the reading *šěmî* ("my name"), found in *Midraš Ḥakamim, Midraš Haggadol,* MS Berlin (in the text itself and not in a gloss as Finkelstein records it), and in *Yalquṭ Šimʿoni* (Salonika ed.). Reuven Hammer (*Sifre: The Tannaitic Commentary on the Book of Deuteronomy* [New Haven: Yale University Press, 1986], p. 299) and Herbert W. Basser (*Midrashic Interpretations of the Song of Moses* [New York: Peter Lang, 1984], p. 31) follow Finkelstein, but see their notes. Jacob Neusner's translation (*Sifre to Deuteronomy: An Analytical Translation*, vol. 2 [Atlanta: Scholars Press, 1987], p. 299), "my name endures on account of my Baal worship," has little textual basis. For an explanation, see below, note 33.

27. §306 (F328.1-330.7).

28. For additional biblical examples of such invoking of heaven, earth, and other elements of nature, see Isa. 1:2; Ps. 50:4; Mic. 1:2; 6:1; Isa. 34:1. S. R. Driver (*A Critical and Exegetical Commentary on Deuteronomy*, ICC, 3d ed. [Edinburgh: T. and T. Clark, 1901], pp. 348-49) wishes to distinguish the call to

heaven and earth here from the earlier occurrences. Here, argues Driver, Moses simply wishes heaven and earth to lend solemnity to his song by being present as an audience. Compare Philo's interpretation of the Song of Moses in *Virt.* 11.72-75: Moses sings a song principally of praise and thanksgiving, convoking "a divine assemblage of the elements of all existence and the chiefest parts of the universe, earth and heaven" as an audience of mortals and angels for his musical performance. The mortals ("earth") in the audience were to learn from him "thankfulness of heart," whereas the angels ("heaven") were to determine "whether the song had any discordant note." However, Pseudo-Philo (*Biblical Antiquities* 19:4) understands heaven and earth in the song to serve as witnesses, conflating Deut. 4:26 and 30:19 with 32:1: "Howbeit, this day I call heaven and earth to witness against you, for the heaven shall hear this and the earth shall take it in with her ears" (trans. M. R. James, pp. 127-28). The same is expressed in *Biblical Antiquities* 32:9. For the Song of Moses as an example of the prophetic *rîb* ("lawsuit") pattern, see Herbert B. Huffmon, "The Covenant Lawsuit in the Prophets," *JBL* 78 (1959): 285-95; G. E. Wright, "The Lawsuit of God: A Form-Critical Study of Deuteronomy 32," in *Israel's Prophetic Heritage: Essays in Honor of James Muilenburg,* ed. Bernhard W. Anderson and Walter Harrelson (New York: Harper and Bros., 1962), pp. 26-67; R. B. Y. Scott, "The Literary Structure of Isaiah's Oracles," in *Studies in Old Testament Prophecy,* ed. H. H. Rowley (Edinburgh: T. & T. Clark, 1950), p. 179. For other ancient sources that stress the witnessing role of heavenly bodies, see Louis Ginzberg, *Legends of the Jews,* 7 vols. (Philadelphia: Jewish Publication Society of America, 1913-38), vol. 5, p. 38, note 105.

29. Compare the roles of witnesses, according to the mishnaic law of capital punishment, in warning the accused before committing the crime, in testifying against him in court, and in carrying out the court's verdict. See *m. Sanh.* 5-6 (especially 6:4), and note 45. In the *Sifre's* commentary, legal and didactic functions are combined, as can be seen in the first interpretation, where didactic functions predominate in A1-13 and legal functions predominate B1-6.

30. For the idea that *heaven and earth* stands for all of creation, see Philo's interpretation, cited in note 28.

31. The order may be explained partly as follows. Roads and nations follow heaven and earth because the prooftext for the earth's witnessing (Jer. 6:19) is adjacent to those for roads and nations (Jer. 6:16, 18). Mountains would then be a continuation of earth, or as places of idolatry associated with the nations. Next come the animate creatures, in a stock order that reverses that of creation, moving from higher to lower forms of life, to conclude with the ant. As a suitable prooftext cannot be found for the birds, they are included in A10 with the wild animals. Although the progression as a whole appears to be chronological, with Israel at first witnessing against itself and in the end (present) not even being able to learn from the ant, the order of the intermediary stages is determined not so much by chronology as by other principles of ordering and association. For later versions of our text, which

attempt to improve upon the logic of its order here, see *Midraš Haggadol*, and *Mishnah of R. Eliezer* (ed. Enelow), pp. 60-61. Note in particular that these place the nations after the inanimate parts of nature and immediately before the animals, whereas the *Sifre* places the nations among the inanimate parts of nature.

32. On valleys being the sites of Israel's idolatrous practices, see Jer. 7:31-32; 32:35. There is a certain discordancy between this (B2) and the preceding (B1) units. If the old earth has been replaced with a new one, why is Israel still disturbed by the high places where she performed idolatry? We simply have here two ways in which God eliminates Israel's former witnesses, one by removing them entirely and the other by transforming them.

33. For the text, see note 28. For the rabbinic view of idolatry as the human application of God's name to His creations, see my book, *Enosh and His Generation: Pre-Israelite Hero and History in Postbiblical Interpretation* (Chico, Calif.: Scolars Press, 1984), esp. 111-131. See also Basser's note ad loc. (p. 31).

34. David Kimḥi (RaDaQ), in commenting on Hos. 2:19, interprets the second half of the verse as referring to the *nations* who will no longer invoke the idols by (God's) name. On the expression *běnê bayit* (members of one's household) as non-Israelite servants (who would have picked up some of the speaking habits of their masters), see Judah Goldin, "The First Pair (Yose ben Yoezer and Yose ben Yohanan) or the Home of a Pharisee," *AJS Review* 5 (1980): 41-62. In other contexts, the expression could refer to one's wife. For examples, see Michael Sokoloff in *Maarav* 1 (1978-79): 82.

35. The commentary presumes the biblical law of Deut. 24:3-4, that a man cannot take his former wife if she has, in the meantime, been married to another man. With Jeremiah it asks, How can God violate His own law? This section has been understood by others as an anti-Christian polemic, putting into Israel's mouth the Christian claim that the former covenant with Israel had been abrogated, only for that claim to be rejected by God. See Basser ad loc. (pp. 31-33). On anti-Christian polemics in midrashic commentary, see Reuven Kimelman, "Rabbi Yohanan and Origen on the Songs of Songs: A Third-Century Jewish-Christian Disputation," *Harvard Theological Review* 73 (1980): 567-95; Ephraim E. Urbach, "The Response of the People of Ninveh and the Jewish-Christian Dispute," *Tarbiz* 20 (1949): 118-122 [Hebrew]; idem, "The Homiletical Interpretations of the Sages and the Expositions of Origen on Canticles, and the Jewish-Christian Disputation," *Scripta Hierosolymitana* 22 (1971): 247-75; Norman J. Cohen, "Analysis of an Exegetical Tradition in the *Mekilta de-Rabbi Ishmael*: The Meaning of ʾ*Amanah* in the Second and Third Centuries," *AJS Review* 9, no. 1 (1984): 1-25; Lou H. Silberman, "Challenge and Response: Pesiqta Derab Kahana, Chapter 26 As an Oblique Reply to Christian Claims," *HTR* 29, nos. 1-3 (1986): 247-53; Reuven Hammer, "A Rabbinic Response to the Post Bar Kochba Era: The Sifre to Ha-Azinu," *PAAJR* 52 (1985): 37-53. For additional bibliography, see Judith R. Baskin, "Rabbinic-Patristic Exegetical Contacts in Late Antiquity: A Bibliographical Reappraisal," in *Approaches*

to *Ancient Judaism*, ed. William Scott Green, vol. 5: *Studies in Judaism and its Greco-Roman Context* (Atlanta: Scholars Press, 1985), pp. 53-80. However, on the difficulty of identifying such polemics, see Chapter 2, notes 227-28, as well as my *Enosh and His Generation*, pp. 225-26.

36. See note 31.

37. In my analysis of the *Sifre*'s commentary to the opening words of the lection *Wa'ethannan* ("Sifre Deuteronomy 26 [Ad Deut. 3:23]: How Conscious the Composition? *HUCA* 54 [1983]: 245-301) I note much the same anticipatory phenomenon.

38. MS Berlin, *Midraš Ḥakamim*, and an interlinear gloss to a Geniza fragment (Oxford Heb. c10, not recorded by Finkelstein) add "your deeds."

39. MS Vatican and most of the other witnesses have *qilqĕlû lipnê*, as here translated. Only MS Berlin and *Midraš Ḥakamim* have *qilqēl bĕ-*, which is the reading adopted by Finkelstein and followed by Hammer ("did Israel rebuff God") and Basser ("did Israel subvert God"). The language clearly echoes that of the first interpretation, and therefore I have chosen to render the verb *qilqēl* here intransitively. However, the usage *qilqĕlû lipnê* introduces a slight change from the earlier usage. Perhaps, the use here of the expression *qilqĕlû bĕ-* would have conveyed the sense that Israel somehow involved God in its sinful deeds, as previously it had involved the natural and national witnesses. Following MS Vatican, the sense is that Israel became corrupt before, that is, they failed to fulfill their covenantal obligations to God.

40. In other words, who is to blame for the apparent degeneration of the covenantal relationship: Israel through its disobedience of God or God through His unfaithfulness to it? On the expression *šinnâ bĕ-* as an expression of unfaithfulness (*mĕ'îlâ*), see Saul Lieberman, *Hellenism in Jewish Palestine*, 2d. ed. (New York: Jewish Theological Seminary of America, 1962), pp. 49-50; Menaham Kahana, "'Ēn mĕ'îlâ 'ellā' šiqqûr/šinnûy," forthcoming in *Leshonenu*. Compare note 125.

41. §306 (F330.8-17).

42. The parallels of language are in the second part (B): the verb *qilqēl* and the phrase *'ătîdâ kĕnesset yiśrā'ēl*. On the former, see note 39. Neither of these expressions will recur in the successive interpretations.

43. §306 (F331.1-7).

44. Perhaps, this ambiguity is occasioned by the fact that in Deut. 31:19 God commands Moses to write the song, but it is Moses who specifically calls upon heaven and earth in 32:1.

45. Thus, they are like witnesses in capital cases who, according to rabbinic law, not only testify to the guilty party's deeds but implement the punishment. This association will be made explicit in the seventh interpretation, which cites Deut. 17:7 ("The hand of the witnesses shall be first upon him"). See note 29, as well as §151 (F205.5-7); *Sifre Num.* 114.

46. §306 (F331.8-11). Finkelstein follows MS Berlin alone in reading "heaven and earth" instead of "to heaven and earth" as in MS Vatican and a Geniza fragment (Ox. Heb. c10). The other witnesses have just *to heaven*. Thus, according to Finkelstein's text, the father begins his statement, addressed to

his son, with the exclamation *Heaven and earth!* But if we adopt, as I have, the better atttested reading, the father addresses heaven and earth and then addresses his son in the second person. The Editio Princeps (and not MS Vatican as Finkelstein records it) eliminates this difficulty by having "about him" instead of "about you." It may be that the father is so exasperated that he addresses his son while calling on heaven and earth. Moses, too, in his song, begins by addressing heaven and earth, even as his song is directed to Israel. In the biblical text Moses switches from third to second to third persons in speaking of and to Israel.

47. This is the text in MS Vatican and most of the other witnesses. Finkelstein (and Hammer, Basser, and Neusner) follows MS Berlin and a Geniza fragment (Oxford heb. c10) in reading, "When (*bizman šě-*) Israel performs God's will..."

48. This is the text in MS Vatican alone. Finkelstein (followed by Hammer, Basser, and Neusner) has instead, "When (*bizman/běšā'â šě-*) Israel do not perform God's will..." Although the text of MS Vatican is more difficult, it parallels better the "merit" (*zěkût*) of Israel when fulfilling God's will. See the previous note.

49. §306 (F331112-332.2).

50. This role of heaven and earth as witnesses was expressed in the fourth interpretation, also in the name of R. Judah. See note 45.

51. For other attempts to construe this passage, see the notes of Hammer (p. 300) and Basser (pp. 40-42), which, to my mind, are less clear, beginning with inferior versions of the text (see previous two notes).

52. I follow MS Vatican and the majority of witnesses: *lō' yākôl mâ la'ăśôt.* Finkelstein follows MS Berlin, *Midraš Ḥakamim*, and *Midraš Haggadol*: "it knows (*yôdē'a*) not what to do." In either case, the sense is the sea's impotence.

53. §306 (F332.3-333.3).

54. The commentary appears to paraphrase the lemma as, "Pay attention [Israel] to the heavens."

55. The following biblical passages stress that observation of nature, often divided between heavenly and earthly parts, will lead Israel to a recognition of God's might and majesty: Isa. 40:18-26; 44:23-24; Jer. 5:22; Ps. 29; 74:14-16; 104; 148; Job 38. Cf. Sira 43; Ep. Jer. 60-63; Matt. 6:25-33. On the animals at least knowing who their masters are, in contrast to Israel, see Isa. 1:3. For other Second Temple period parallels, see note 121.

56. The case of the sea is more ambiguous. On the one hand, it has chosen not to "rise and flood the world," yet on the other, its waves try to rise up but are constrained by the shore.

57. §306 (F333.4-10).

58. See notes 29 and 45.

59. The identity of this sage is uncertain. D. Ratner (*'Ahabat Ṣion* ad *p. Pesaḥ.* 5:1) argues that he is the brother of R. Joshua B. Hanahiah (ca. 120 C.E.).

60. §306 (F333.11-16).

61. On the sounds produced by the "revolutions" of the sun, see *b. Yoma* 20b, where it is said, in the name of R. Levi (ca. 300 *C.E.*), that the sound made by

the sun crossing the sky during the day makes it more difficult to hear human voices than at night. Furthermore, it is stated there in a *barayta* that the sound of the sun drowns out the tumult of Rome and vice versa. For heaven and earth singing God's praises and for Moses' need to silence them so his song could be heard, see the later expressions in *Deut. Rab.* 10:1-2; and *Yalquṭ Šimʿoni* 1.729 (from *Yelammedenu*). The idea that the heavenly bodies produce music through their movements is typically Pythagorean. On the sun standing still for Moses, see also the *barayta* in *b. ʿAbod. Zar.* 25a and its parallel in *b. Taʿan.* 20a. *Deut. Rab.* 10:1 (in the name of R. Levi) states, citing Deut. 32:1 as proof, that because Moses had attentively inclined his ear to the Torah, when he wished to speak words of Torah all the celestial and terrestrial creations listened in silence. Note that *Sib. Or.* 5:256-59 (late first century C.E.) speaks of a savior figure, "the best of the Hebrews," who will once again "cause the sun to stand, speaking with fair speech and holy lips" (*OTP* 1:399). This may be a reference to Joshua, or it may presume a tradition similar to that found in the *Sifre*, and refer to Moses. For other references to the sun standing still for Moses, see Louis Ginzberg, *Legends of the Jews*, vol. 6, pp. 25, note 146; 46, note 245; 160, note 947.

62. In §47 (F106.5-6), it is said that the righteous (*ṣaddîqîm*), like the stars, rule the whole world. On the idea that "righteous command [nature to change its ways] and God fulfills their command," see *Deut. Rab.* 10:2-3; and *Midr. Tan.* ad Deut. 33:1 (ed. Hoffmann, p. 208); both dealing with Moses.

63. The word *ṣaddîq* ("righteous") is often used to denote a type of rabbinic sage. See Chapter 2, note 157; Chapter 3, note 106.

64. For a broader exploration of this topic, in exegetical relation to Gen.1:28, see Jeremy Cohen, *"Be Fertile and Increase, Fill the Earth and Master It": The Ancient and Medieval Career of a Biblical Test* (Ithaca: Cornell University Press, 1989).

65. This phrase, *sāmak laddābār*, will recur twice more in the following interpretation. I have translated it identically in all three instances, even though its meaning shifts slightly, to convey the text's repetitiveness. The sense is that Isaiah, in adding his language to that of Moses, supported or expanded the significance of Moses' choice of words. On the relation of Isaiah's call to heaven and earth to that of Moses, see A. Kaminka, "*Mĕlîṣôt mōšeh ûmizmôrê tĕhillîm bĕpî yĕšaʿyāhû*," *Leshoneu* 1 (1928): 41; Harold Fisch, *Poetry with a Purpose*, pp. 55-79. See also *Mek. Pisḥaʾ* 7 (ed. Lauterbach, vol. 1, p. 91), where Isa. 1:2 is said to refer back specifically to Deut. 32:1.

66. §306 (F333.17-334.2). This interpretation is attributed to R. Akiba in *Tanḥ. Haʾazinu* 2 and *Deut. Rab.* (ed. Lieberman), p. 125. It is also given in the *Tgs. Pseudo-Jonathan, Neofiti*, and *Fragmentary*. The last will be discussed below as a countertext. On Moses' superiority to the other Israelite prophets, see for example, *Lev. Rab.* 1:14. For other explanations, see Basser, pp. 47-48.

67. Note Isa. 33:13: "Listen you that are far off.'

68. §306 (F334.2-9). I have included this within the tenth interpretation, even though it presents a distinct interpretation of the lemma, because it begins as a

direct response to the previously stated intepretation and not as "another interpretation." In effect, however, we have here three interpretations that attempt to explain the relation of Moses' words to those of Isaiah. As presently arranged in the commentary they may be said to constitute a subgroup of iterpretations with their own internal dynamic.

69. Rabbinic texts conceive of multiple heavens (as in the eighth interpretation, which speaks of "heavens and uppermost heavens"). The word for *heaven* in Hebrew (*šāmayîm*) is plural whereas that for *earth* (*ʾereṣ*) is singular, taken here to suggest the vastness of the former and the relative finitude of the latter.

70. See *m. Roš. Haš.* 2:6; *m. Sanh.* 5:4. See also the Book of Susanna 51:59.

71. Note that in the story of Susanna (see previous note) the two elders are differently examined by Daniel. In *m. Roš. Haš.* 2:6 it may be assumed that the two witnesses were identically questioned, but this is not stated. Alternatively, the commentary may construe "give ear" and "hear" out of context as the two ways that Moses (and then Isaiah) instructs heaven and earth as witnesses to pay attention to Israel's behavior.

72. Compare §342 (F392.17-19), in which Moses' blessing of the tribes in Deut. 33 is said to be a direct continuation of Jacob's blessing of his sons in Gen. 49, again because of their similar language.

73. Basser's rearranging of the last three interpretations (p. 50) is unwarranted, in my opinion, both text critically and rhetorically.

74. §306 (F334.10-12).

75. §306 (F334.12-16).

76. First interpretation.

77. Second and seventh interpretations.

78. Fifth interpretation.

79. Fourth interpretation.

80. Sixth interpretation.

81. Eleventh interpretation.

82. Tenth (B) and twelfth (implicitly) interpretations.

83. Ninth and tenth interpretations.

84. The text that follows from here through the next "for all eternity" in B2 is not found in MS Vatican (Finkelstein fails to record this) or MSS London and Oxford, *Yaluṭ Šimʿoni*, and the Editio Princeps. It does appear in MS Berlin, *Midraš Ḥakamim*, and *Midraš Haggadol*. This evidence alone would suggest omitting it, except that its omission from MS Vatican and the other major witnesses most likely originate as a scribal error of homoioteleuton, because the last words before the omission and the last words of the omission are identical. This is supported by the inclusion of this passage in a Hebrew Union College (Cincinnati) manuscript (#2026), which was kindly brought to my attention by Menahem Kahana, and a copy of which was kindly provided to Yale University's Sterling Memorial Library by the Hebrew Union College. This manuscript includes a Yemenite midrash that frequently quotes the *Sifre* to Deuteronomy, especially for the lections *Haʾazinu* and *Zot Habberakah*. See Kahana's discussion of this important manuscript in *Tarbiz* 57 (1987-88): 172-74. According to Kahana (personal letter of October 27, 1987), the fact

that this manuscript, representing an oriental textual stem, confirms the reading of MS Berlin, representing an Italian stem, supports my claim that the omission of the passage from the other manuscripts originated as a scribal error. See also Kahana's Ph.D. dissertation ("Prolegomena to a New Edition of the Sifre on Numbers,"[Hebrew Universtiy of Jerusalem, 1982], pp. 15-16), in which he shows that MS Berlin often preserves parts of texts omitted from MS Vatican due to the scribal error of homoioteleuton.

85. The Hebrew here (of MS Berlin) is *mĕqayyemet*. MS Cincinnati 2026 (see previous note) has: *ʿēdûtô šel mî mĕqayyemet ʾet šel mî* ("whose testimony validates whose"). For recent attempts at understanding our text see Basser (p. 54, note L9) and Hammer (p. 491, note 27). *Midraš Haggadol* has *makḥešet* ("disproves"), but Hammer (ibid.) is wrong in stating that this reading is "supported by several Sifre manuscripts." It is supported (in the next occurrence of the verb) only by *Midraš Ḥakamim*, which often agrees with *Midraš Haggadol*. This reading is presumably influenced by the later statement of Moses, "Who will refute them (*makḥîšām*)?" Nevertheless, I think the sense of *Midraš Haggadol*'s explanatory reading is correct. Because Moses and God have chosen different witnesses, in the event that they do not concur in their testimony, whose will prevail (be sustained)? For this understanding, see David Hoffman's note to the text of *Midraš Haggadol* in his *Midrasch Tannaïm zum Deuteronomium* (Berlin, 1909), p. 183, note 20.

86. In Deut. 31:20, the context in which the song will testify against them is one in which they grow fat from the abundance of the land, which may be understood to mean that heaven and earth had testified positively on their behalf (see the second, fifth, and seventh interpretations). It is possible that the Hebrew verb *ʿānĕtâ* in 31:21 is taken to mean that the song responded to the apparent testimony of heaven and earth.

87. The preceding two sentences follow MS Vatican, which is not fully recorded in Finkelstein's apparatus here. As far as I can tell, Finkelstein has misrecorded the readings of MSS Oxford and London, *Yalquṭ Šimʿoni* and the Editio Princeps, which essentially agree with MS Vatican.

88. §306 (F334.17-335.11).

89. This ambiguity derives from the ambiguous meaning here of the word *all* (*kōl*). Had Israel violated all commandments pertaining to heaven and earth (a more severe version of the previous interpretation) or had Israel violated only some of those commandments (an abbreviated restatement of the previous interpretation), thereby failing to observe them all? Alternatively, it has been suggested that in the present interpretation, in contrast to the preceding one, the phrases *from heaven* and *on the earth* should be understood literally as referring to those commandments received from heaven (scriptural) and those commandments received on earth (rabbinic). Thus, Israel is understood to be equally accountable for its compliance with both categories of law, that is, the entire rabbinic Torah ("written" and "oral"). This view is expressed by M. Friedmann in a note ad loc. (citing *Zayit Raʿanan*), and is followed by Hammer (p. 491 n. 25), who understands these as commandments from Sinai ("heaven") and "through Moses on earth."

Basser (pp. 52-53, note E27) similarly adopts Friedmann's interpretation, suggesting (without textual basis) that the order of the two interpretations was originally reversed: the previous interpretation was created to soften the indictment of the present one. These interpretations, as attractive as they may be, read more into the text, it seems to me, than is warranted. As seen in the previous two chapters, the *Sifre*, like other rabbinic texts, understands *both* scriptural and rabbinic laws to *derive* "from heaven."

90. Nowhere in the middle eleven interpretations is it explicitly stated whether Moses chose on his own to summon heaven and earth or whether he did so on God's behalf. It may be recalled that in the *mashal* of the second interpretation the king who appoints a tutor for his son represents Moses, whereas in the *mashal* of the third interpretation the king who entrusts his son to deputies represents God, as is the convention. In the *mashal* of third interpretation the king could be either (or both).

91. Compare Deut. 32:46, where Moses upon completing the song says to Israel: "Take to heart all the words which I have caused to testify against you (*me'id bākem*) today." This verse is never cited in the *Sifre*'s commentary to 32:1, perhaps so as not to dull its distinction between God's choice of the song and Moses' choice of heaven and earth as witnesses.

92. Compare Deut. 31:21: "This song shall respond to them as a witness as long as it is not lost [forgotten] from the mouths of their descendants." For similar imagery compare also Deut. 30:14: "For the teaching is very close to you; it is in your mouth and in your heart so as to perform it." Consider also the *Sifre*'s commentary to Deut. 6:7 (§34 [F60.8-9]): "'Impress [these teachings] (*wěšinnantām*) upon your children': They should be so well honed within your mouth that when someone inquires of you concerning a teaching you will not hesitate but will answer him immediately." Thus, the Torah is to be taught by constant repetition, so that it is ever sharp and "ready at hand" (that is, mouth). See also *Mek. Něziqîn* 1 (ed. Lauterbach, vol. 3, p. 1), where Deut. 31:19 is understood to refer to the learning of the Torah through its continual repetition. For other *Sifre* texts that stress the internalization of words of Torah through their constant study and review, and the ways in which such practices bot sustain Torah and benefit Israel, see Chapter 3.

93. We are never told why the song will prevail. Is it because it will last longer, because it is more trustworthy, because it is carried within Israel, or simply because it is God's choice?

94. For scholarly views of the relation of the song to its narrative context, see notes 22 and 101.

95. Not only will the song survive the created world but, according to well-known rabbinic traditions, it also preexisted creation. This latter view is expressed elsewhere in the *Sifre* (§37 [F70.5-6]): "Since the Torah is the most precious of anything, it was created before all else."

96. See notes 29, 45, and 71. Thus, *Midraš Haggadol* inserts the question: "Why did God [only] cause one witness to testify against them?"

97. Perhaps it is coincidental, but note that one verse is cited as evidence of Moses' choice of heaven and earth, two verses are cited as evidence of God's choice of

the song, and three verses are cited as evidence of God's being called a witness. Note as well that two of the three verses adduced for God's role as witness deal with the eschatological future.

98. See Ps. 50:4, where God calls heaven and earth to appear in court, presumably as witnesses, for the trial of his people. But cf. *m. ʾAbot* 4:22, where God is said to be the judge, witness, and plaintiff.

99. This was stressed in the sixth interpretation.

100. This point is made by David Hoffmann, *Midrasch Tannaïm zum Deuteronomium*, p. 183, note 20.

101. In addition to the sources cited in note 22, see Michael Fishbane, "Varia Deuteronomica," *ZAW* 84 (1972): 350-52, who argues for the identity of the *tôrâ* of 31:9, 12 and the song of 31:19 as covenantal witness.

102. For this rabbinic understanding of Deut. 31:19, see also the view of Rab Ḥisda (d. 309 C.E.) in *b. Ned.* 38a, with the commentaries of Rashi, Tosaphot, the Ran (R. Nissim ben Reuben of Gerona), and the Rosh (R. Asher b. Jehiel). For a similar view see R. Naftali Zvi Yehuda Berlin, in his commentary *Haʿameq Davar* (2d ed., Jerusalem, 1937) to Deut. 31:19. Cf. Maimonides, *Mishneh Torah, Hil. Sepher Torah* 7:1. For this understanding of the song as standing for the whole of the Torah within the continuation of the *Sifre's* commentary, see the following note. For the Torah as song, see also Jose Faur, *Golden Doves with Silver Dots: Semiotics and Textuality in Rabbinic Tradition* (Bloomington: Indiana University Press, 1986), pp. xxvi; 153, note 79.

103. For a sample of these interpretations, see Chapter 3 with note 156. The same identification of the song with Torah as a whole is presumed in the *Sifre's* commentary to Moses' remarks upon completing the song in 32:46 (§335). For the text and discussion, see Chapter 3.

104. For another example of this phenomenon, see my analysis of the *Sifre's* commentary to the opening words of the lection *Waʾethannan* ("Sifre Deuteronomy 26 [Ad Deut. 3:23]: How Conscious the Composition?" pp. 245-301), where I compare this to the later, more formally developed "proem" convention. See as well my treatment of §48 in Chapter 3, where I discerned a similar pattern. On the so-called circular proem and its antecedents, see Marc Bregman, "Circular Proems and Proems Beginning with the Formula 'Zo hi sheneʾemra beruaḥ haq-qodesh'," in *Studies in Aggadah, Targum and Jewish Liturgy in Memory of Joseph Heinemann*, ed. Jakob J. Petuchowski and Ezra Fleischer (Jerusalem: Magnes Press and Cincinnati: Hebrew Union College Press, 1981), pp. 34–51 (Hebrew section); Harry Fox, "The Circular Proem Composition: Terminology and Antecedents," *PAAJR* 49 (1982): 1-33.

105. See note 92.

106. See note 90.

107. Note how these are differentiated as two distinct future dialogues: "And, again in the future, she will say before him."

108. Another structural similarity may be noted between the first and final interpretations. In both cases denouement follows dejection: in the first

interpretation the sudden shift to eschatological reconciliation follows notice of Israel's inability to learn even from the ant, whereas in the final interpretation the establishment of the song as witness follows notice of Israel's having violated *all* the heavenly and earthly commandments. But on the latter, see note 89.

109. In the middle eleven interpretations God stands, as it were, somewhere offstage. He appears only twice, and these appearances are themselves suggestive of my point. In the third interpretation, God is represented by the king of the *mashal*, who assigns deputies to carry out his will. Similarly, in the sixth interpretation, God tells Moses to tell the people to observe nature so as to learn from its obedience to His laws. By contrast, in the first interpretation, God is portrayed eschatologically in direct dialogue with the "congregation of Israel," whereas in the final interpretation, He declares, in his own "voice," that He will serve as one of the witnesses to the covenant.

110. For "longue durée" used in this dual literary and historical sense, see David Carroll, "The Times of History and the Order of Discourse," pp. 122-26, who adapts the term from Fernand Braudel. Compare Peter Brooks's use of "dilatory space" as "textual middle," in "The Idea of a Psychoanalytic Literary Criticism," *Critical Inquiry* 13 (1987): 339. Brooks adapts this psychoanalytical terminology to textual dynamics from Roland Barthes (*S/Z*, e.g., p. 77).

111. We noted one exception to this pattern in the eighth interpretation, where the commentary stresses the power of the righteous over heaven and earth, as over nature in general.

112. §§335-36 (F384.15-385.13). I treated the first part much more fully in Chapter 3. For a similar but slightly different version of the second part, see *Gen. Rab.* 1:14 (ed. Theodor-Albeck, p. 12). The *Sifre*'s commenatary continues by showing that even apparently "empty" verses (Gen. 36:22; 36:12) can be found to be full of meaning. See also note 92.

113. For other *Sifre* passages that stress that the fulfillment of the covenantal promises are contingent upon Israel's study of Torah, see §§41 (F87.5; 88.11-13); 46 (F104.8-9); 48 (F113.18-114.2); 49 (F115.5); 336 (F385.13-14).

114. *The Sense of an Ending*, p. 25.

115. For the idea that union with God can be achieved through the rabbinic study of Torah, see §49, treated in Chapter 3. See also §33 (F59.5-8), where the same is said of love of God.

116. The *Fragmentary Targum* (also known as *Targum Yerushaimi*) is so called because, unlike most of the other extant *targumim*, it translates only select scriptural passages or phrases. The dating of extant targum texts is a very thorny issue. I presume a third or fourth century date for the present text, although its dating for my present purposes is not crucial. For an extensive discussion of rabbinic views of the place and function of targum as biblical explication, see my *Targum and Torah: Early Rabbinic Views of Scriptural Translation in a Multilingual Setting*. I have translated the following passage from MS Vatican Ebr. 440, as printed in Michael L. Klein, *The Fragment-Targum of the Pentateuch According to their Extant Sources*, 2 vols. (Rome:

Biblical Institute Press, 1980), vol. 1, pp. 224-25. The same text appears with slight variations in MS Paris (ibid., p. 113), as well as in MSS Nürnberg and Leipzig as recorded by Klein in his critical aparatus, ad loc. My translation differs only slightly from Klein's (ibid, vol. 2, pp. 85, 181-82). Although *Tg. Pseudo-Jonathan* is almost identical, *Tg. Neofiti* contains some interesting variations, none of which affect the argument that will follow.

117. *Tg. Neofiti* has: "Moses thought in his heart and said: 'Woe now to me, for I am being gathered from the midst of the world without having admonished [*ashèd* = testified against] the children of the Lord. If I admonish them before people who die and taste the cup of death, when those people die their decrees [= testimony to my admonition] will become void. Therefore I will admonish them before heaven and earth which never die and which do not taste the cup of death.'" *Targum Neofiti* continues much as does the *Fragmentary Targum*.

118. The most common rabbinic scheme places the day of judgment after the resurrection of the dead but before the world to come. However, there are enough variations to this scheme that I hesitate to presume, even though it is most likely, that the targum understands that heaven and earth will perish only after Israel has been judged.

119. This ending is virtually identical to the more "literal" translation of the verse as found in *Tg. Onqelos*. I emphasize that the words of the lemma have not been translated until now.

120. In presenting the comparison in this fashion I do not wish to suggest that the targumic arrangement is historically anterior to that of the *Sifre*. Neither this nor its converse, it seems to me, can be demonstrated. My purpose is simply to highlight the redactional reliefs of the *Sifre*'s commenary by comparing it with another rabbinic document that clearly drew from the same traditional font, but shaped and arranged what it drew to suit a different genre to different rhetorical effects.

121. I realize that the correspondences between the constituent parts of the targum and their parallels in the commentary are only approximate. Nevertheless, it may be useful to visualize the targumic arrangement as A-B-C-D, and that of the corresponding parts of the commentary (using the targum designations to factilitate comparison) as D . . . C + B . . . A.

122. This similarity between the two texts is also noted by Lars Hartman, *Asking for a Meaning: A Study of 1 Enoch 1-5* (Lund: Gleerup, 1979), pp. 29-30.

123. The following translation is from Michael A. Knibb, *The Ethiopic Book of Enoch: A New Edition in the Light of the Aramaic Dead Sea Fragments*, vol. 2 (Oxford: Clarendon Press, 1978), pp. 60-66. Aramaic fragments containing this passage are 4QEn[a] 1 ii (ed. Milik, pp. 145-46) and 4 QEn[c] 1 i (ed. Milik, pp. 184-85). To facilitate comparison with the sixth interpretation of the *Sifre* commentary, I have divided the *1 Enoch* passage into three sections (A, B, C), corresponding to my division of that interpretation in the commentary.

124. The Aramaic fragments here and below have *ḥzw'* in combination with *'tbwnnh*: look and contemplate.

125. The Aramaic in 4QEn[a] 1 ii 12 is *w'ntn šnytn 'bdkn*. Matthew Black (*The Book of Enoch or 1 Enoch: A New English Translation* [Leiden: E. J. Brill, 1985], p.

27) renders the contrast between sea and sinners as follows: "See how the seas and rivers together perform and do not change their tasks by abandoning his commands. But you have changed your works, and have not been steadfast nor done according to his commandments..."

126. For other Second Temple texts that draw moral lessons from the orderliness of "heaven and earth," see *1 Enoch* 41:5-8; 101:1-8; *T. Naph.* 3:2-4; *Vit. Ad.* 29:7; *2 Apoc. Bar.* 48:9-10; 1Q34^{bis} *II.1-7* (DJD I:154); *T. Moses* 12:9; *Pss. Sol.* 18:10-12; *Sir.* 16:26-28. But this literature also speaks of heaven and earth as witnesses that testify against the wicked: *1 Enoch* 100:10-11; 1QDM (1Q22). In the former, "heaven" not only testifies against the wicked, but withholds its rain and dew from them as punishment (cf. our third interpretation).

127. In the commentary the Hebrew is *histakkĕlû*, meaning both "look" and "reflect upon." In the apocalypse, the Aramaic fragments have similar expressions. See note 124. In both passages this is repeated, once for heaven (A) and once for earth (B).

128. See Michael Stone, "The Parabolic Use of Natural Order in Judaism of the Second Temple Age," in *Gilgul: Essays on Transformation, Revolution and Permanence in the History of Religions*, ed. S. Shaked et al. (Leiden: E. J. Brill, 1987), pp. 298-308. Stone notes that this tendency to attribute individual personality to the various forces of nature for the purpose of deriving moral lessons from their obedience to God is widespread in Second Temple sources. It is to be distinguished from the treatment of nature in the earlier biblical writings, where the emphasis is simply on the fixed regularity of God's plan for creation. According to Stone, this reflects a tendency among Second Temple Jewish groups to retreat from history. In the earlier biblical books history is the primary arena for God's plan (and humanity's participation in it), whereas in Second Temple sources nature (cosmos) increasingly becomes that arena. He calls this the *remythologization* of nature. For biblical sources, see note 55. For Second Temple sources, see note 126.

129. For a note of pessimism, recall the first interpretation in which Israel is said to be unable to learn even from the ant. On nature and history, see the previous note. Compare *Jub.* 1:7–14, where God at Mt. Sinai commands Moses to record His words in anticipation that the people will forsake Him and His commands once they enter and become satiated in the land; the written testimony will be there to testify against them. But this alone will not cause the people to repent their apostasy. God will next send other witnesses (presumably the prophets) to witness to the people, who will not only ignore the reproof of those witnesses, but kill them. Only the sufferings of destruction and Exile will finally cause the people to return.

130. The Syriac word for "Law" is *nāmûsāʾ*, which is the Peshiṭta's customary translation of the Hebrew word *tôrâ*, including its occurrences in Deut. 31. The Syriac simply follows the Greek of the Septuagint that almost always (91 percent) employs a form of *nomos* for *tôrâ*. Thus, it is quite likely that a Hebrew original of *2 Baruch* (if in fact that was its original language) would have had here and in what follows *tôrâ*.

131 The text of the apocalypse is extant in a single Syriac manuscript that is a translation from Greek, which may in turn have been a translation of a Semitic original. In rendering the following passage, I have followed the critical text of S. Dedering (*The Old Testament in Syriac, Part IV, Fasc. 3, Apocalypse of Baruch* [Leiden: E. J. Brill, 1973], p. 9), and have consulted the following translations: *The Old Testament Pseudepigrapha*, ed. James H. Charlesworth, vol. 1 (Garden City, NY: Doubleday, 1983), p. 627; *The Apocryphal Old Testament*, ed. H. F. D. Sparks (Oxford: Clarendon Press, 1984), p. 851; *Apocalypse de Baruch*, trans Pierre Bogaert, vol. 1, Sources Chrétiennes 144 (Paris: Éditions du Cert, 1969), pp. 482-83.

132. It is unclear whether this light (*nûhārā*) is the Law, as previously, or a heavenly light, presumably the sun.

133. There are some small but significant differences. The targum has Moses reason that heaven and earth will not taste death in *this world*, but will expire in the world to come, somewhat like, but still significantly different from the *Sifre*, which has heaven and earth removed and replaced by God at Israel's request prior to the latter's judgment. The *Sifre* has Moses worry that after his death the Israelites will go so far as to deny ever having received the Torah at all. As noted earlier, all of these explanations can be seen as elaborations of Deut. 31:29: "For I know that, after I die, you will act wickedly and turn away from the path which I enjoined upon you." Cf. §26 (F36.4), where Moses fears that after his death people will accuse him of having falsified the Torah or of having included something that had not actually been commanded.

134. For the combination of Torah and God as witnesses, note also *2 Baruch* 15:5: "Certainly, man might not have understood my judgment if he had not received the Law (*nāmûsā*), and if I [God] had not instructed him in understanding." Whereas the earth is mentioned in 1 and 2, it does not appear again in 3; in 3 I assume the celestial spheres are the same as heaven and "the light which nothing could deceive" is ambiguous. See note 132. In the *Sifre*'s commentary heavenly luminaries exemplify the witnessing function of "heaven" of Deut. 32:1 in the sixth, eighth, and twelfth interpretations. But the *Sifre* knows of other witnessing functions of "heaven," not mentioned in *2 Baruch* (or in the parallel from *1 Enoch* previously mentioned): releasing and withholding rain (third, fifth, and seventh interpretations). Likewise, whereas the *Sifre* specifies ways in which the earth functions as witness, *2 Baruch* does not. This focus by the latter on the heavens, and especially on the heavenly spheres, may be said to be reflective of *2 Baruch*'s apocalyptic, and hence astral, orientation: the heavenly lights, in their orderly array and movements, reveal a divinely ordered cosmos (unlike the seeming disorder on earth) in synchronization with which the elect live their lives.

135. See note 108.

136. This is not to deny the presence of dialogical commentary in the middle eleven interpretations. Rhetorical questioning and answering occurs in the second, third, fifth, sixth, seventh, and twelfth interpretations. However, in those, unlike the final interpretation, God does not participate directly in the commentary's exegetical give and take.

137. See note 112.
138. For the paramount importance of directing one's eyes, ears, and heart to "words of Torah," see §335 (F384.15-385.4), cited and discussed in Chapter 3. On the contrast between apocalypse and midrash with regard to their attitudes to time, see James Kugel, "Two Introductions to Midrash," in *Midrash and Literature,* ed. Geoffrey H. Hartman and Sanford Budick (New Haven: Yale University Press, 1986), pp. 84-90; and my comments in "Interpreting Midrash 2: Midrash and its Literary Contexts," *Prooftexts* 7 (1988): 295-96.
139. For this distinction between "imminence" and immanence" in apocalyptic and postapocalyptic fictions, see Frank Kermode, *The Sense of an Ending,* p. 6 and passim.
140. §333 (F383.16-17). This is the text according to the better witnesses. Finkelstein (followed by Hammer, Basser, and Neusner) has "this song" (*šîrâ zû*), adopting the reading of *Midraš Ḥakamim* and *Midraš Haggadol.* A gloss to MS Berlin has "this song of *Haʾazinu.*" For parallels, see Basser, p. 259, note E10. But the indefinite form of the preferred text suggests that, whereas this confluence of times is a characteristic of the Song of Moses in particular, it also may be said to characterize Torah (and its commentary?) as a whole. The sense is that all of time is signified by the song, and therefore included within it, at least in exegetical potential. Compare the same expression (*yēš bô*) used in §313 (F355.9-11) to denote the multiplicity (both in kind and in number) of teaching that Israel could discern in each divine utterance as it issued at Sinai. See Chapter 2, note 188.
141. The countertext of the *Fragmentary Targum* may be said to fall somewhere between the apocalypses and the *Sifre*'s commentary, agreeing with the *Sifre* that heaven and earth will eventually expire, but being ambiguous whether they will do so before or after Israel's final judgment. For further sources and discussion of the idea of heavenly bodies in particular bearing witness against humanity, see also L. Ginzberg, *Legends of the Jews,* vol. 5, pp. 37-38, note 105.
142. See note 128.
143. See the postbiblical sources listed in note 121, with which compare the biblical ones listed in note 55. See also my *Enosh and His Generation* (note 33), for a treatment of rabbinic sources that speak of God's employment of the ocean, which did not deviate from its assigned ways, to punish the Generation of Enosh, which did.
144. Compare, for example, Aeschylus' *Prometheus Bound* (88-92, 1091-93), where Prometheus begins and ends his monologue with a call to the elements of nature (including heaven and earth) to hear his words and to witness his suffering. As one recent commentator (Mark Griffith, ed., *Aeschylus' Prometheus Bound* [Cambridge University Press, 1983], pp. 101-102) remarks: "Prometheus appeals in indignation to the only available witnesses, the elements themselves: sky, wind, rivers and sea, earth and sun." Compare the *Sifre*'s fourth interpretation. But Aeschylus' ambivalent attitude to nature is also noted: "Prometheus can expect to find no comfort here—indeed these

are the same unfeeling elements which are to torture him in the years ahead" (cf. 22-27, 1043 ff, 1091). For other examples of this motif in Greco-Roman literature, see Griffith's notes ad loc. For secondary bibliography, see D. J. Conacher, *Aeschylus' Prometheus Bound: A Literary Commentary* (London: University of Toronto Press, 1980), p. 35.

145. Note how Jewish prayer appears to one of the Jew's earliest outside observers, Theophrastus (372-288 B.C.E.): "Being philosophers by race, they converse with each other about the deity, and at night-time they make observations of the stars, gazing at them and calling on God by prayer." For the text and translation, see Menaham Stern, ed. and trans., *Greek and Latin Authors on Jews and Judaism*, vol. 1 (Jerusalem: Israel Academy of Sciences and Humanities, 1976), p. 10.

146. Compare the following two texts, in which the testimony of "nature," is specifically rejected in favor of the authority of the sages, in the first case to decide matters of ritual purity and in the second to determine the intercalation of the year: *b. B. Meṣ.* 59b; *b.Sanh.* 18b. For the ability of a polyphonous text of commentary to express Israel's ambivalent perceptions of and relationships to the past event of revelation and the present reality of the non-Jewish nations, see Chapter 2. On the question of the interrelation of literary and sociohistorical heterogeneity more generally, see Chapter 1, especially at note 68.

147. For example, the three king parables of the second, third, and fourth interpretations are grouped together, with each suggesting something different about the identity of the king (Moses, God, ambiguous), and the role of the witnesses (overseers, dispensers of reward and punishment, audience). Similarly, the three explanations of how Isaiah's call to heaven and earth complements that of Moses (ninth and tenth interpretations), work together as a group, a sort of subplot. The eleventh and twelfth interpretations (and the beginning of the thirteenth) also seem to function well together. The fifth through eighth interpretations do not seem to follow any particular order.

148. As noted, not only does the final interpretation echo some of the language and structure of the first interpretation, but the beginning of the middle section echoes language of the first interpretation, whereas the end of middle section is echoed at the beginning of the final interpretation. All of this notwithstanding the striking thematic differences between these three sections.

149. In this way the whole of the commentary to Deut. 32:1 is like the first part (A1-12) of the first interpretation, where I argued that there is a temporal progression defined by the beginning and end even though the arrangement of the middle items is not linear but determined by other associative principles. See notes 31 and 36.

150. For the disciple of the sages as a sifter of discordant teachings, see §48 (F109.13-110.3), cited and discussed in Chapter 3.

151. For references see the introduction to this chapter, some of which are treated at length in Chapter 2.

152. The *Sifre's* commentary to the Song of Moses as a whole ends with reference to the "world to come" (§333 [F383.15-17], cited earlier).

Bibliographic References

Primary Sources

Sifre Deuteronomy, Printed Editions

Siphre ad Deuteronomium, ed. Louis Finkelstein. Corpus Tannaiticum 3:3:2. Berlin, 1939. Reprint, New York: Jewish Theological Seminary of America, 1969.

Siphre debe rab, ed. Meir Friedman. Vienna, 1864.

Sipre bemidbar debarim. With emendations and commentary listed below. Vilna, 1866.

Sipre. Venice, 1546 (Editio Princeps). Facsimile edition, Jerusalem: Makor, 1970-71.

Sifre Deuteronomy, Manuscripts

Cairo Geniza fragments:
Ox. Heb. c10 (Bodleian Library).
TS C6 113 (Cambridge University).
TS C2 182 (Cambridge University).
TS C2 211 (Cambridge University).

MS Berlin: Staatsbibliothek, Preussischer—Kulturbesitz (E. Berlin), 1594.33 (Acc. Or. 1928.328).

MS Casanata (Rome): H. 2736.

MS Cincinnati: Hebrew Union College 2026 (a Yemenite midrash that cites extensive sections of the *Sifre*).

MS London: British Museum, Margoliouth 341.3.

MS Oxford: Bodleian, Neubauer 151.

MS Vatican: Ebr. 32. Facsimile edition; Jerusalem: Makor, 1972.

Sifre Deuteronomy, Translations

Sifre: The Tannaitic Commentary on the Book of Deuteronomy, trans.

Reuven Hammer. Yale Judaica Series 24. New Haven: Yale University Press, 1986.

Sifre to Deuteronomy: An Analytical Translation, trans. Jacob Neusner, 3 vols. Atlanta: Scholars Press, 1987.

Der tannaitische Midrasch Sifre Deuteronomium, trans. Hans Bietenhard. Berlin, New York: Peter Lang, 1984.

Basser, Herbert W. *Midrashic Interpretations of the Song of Moses,* New York: Peter Lang, 1984. Includes a translation of the lection *Ha'azinu* (§§306-341).

Sifre Deuteronomy, Commentaries

Abraham Yequti'el Zalman Lichtstein. *Sipre ʿim peruš . . . zeraʿ 'abraham,* vol. 2. Radweil, 1819-20.

Anonymous (falsely ascribed to R. Hillel): MS Sasson (JTS) 593; MS Oxford 425.

David Pardo. In *Sipre debe rab.* Salonika, 1798-99.

Elijah of Vila (emendations). In *Sipre bemidbar debarim.* Vilna, 1866.

Hillel ben Eliakim. *Sifre,* ed. Shachne Koleditzky. Jerusalem, 1947-48.

Hillel ben Eliakim. *Sifre,* ed. Shachne Koleditzky. Jerusalem, 1982-83 (employs more manuscripts that the preceding).

Judah Najar. *Seper 'ohale yehuda.* Lemberg, 1822-23.

Moses David Abraham Treves Ashkenazy. *Sipre ʿim peruš toledot 'adam,* vol. 2. Jerusalem: Mossad Harav Kook, 1974.

Naphtali Zvi Judah Berlin. *Sipre . . . ʿim . . . ʿemeq hanneṣi"b,* vol. 3. Jerusalem, 1960-61

Suleiman of Safed. In *Sipre bemidbar debarim.* Vilna, 1866.

Yedaiah Happenini. MS Enelow (JTS) 148.

Other Rabbinic Writings

Abot de Rabbi Nathan [Hebrew], ed. Solomon Schechter. Vienna, 1887. Reprint with corrections, New York: Feldheim. 1967.

Agadath Shir Hashirim [Hebrew], ed. Solomon Schechter. Cambridge, 1896.

Babylonian Talmud Codex Munich (95) [Hebrew], facsimile ed. Jerusalem: Kedem, 1970.

The Fathers According to Rabbi Nathan, trans. Judah Goldin. Yale Judaica Series 10. New Haven: Yale University Press, 1955.

Lekach-Tob (Pesikta sutarta) [Hebrew], ed. S. Buber, 5 vols. in 2. Vilna: Romm, 1880-84. Reprint, Jerusalem, 1960.

Mechilta D'Rabbi Ismael [Hebrew], ed. H. S. Horovitz and I. A. Rabin, 2d ed. Jerusalem: Wahrmann, 1970.

Mekhilta D'Rabbi Šimʿon b. Jochai [Hebrew], ed. J. N. Epstein and E. Z. Melamed. Jerusalem: Mekize Nirdamim, 1955.

Mekilta de-Rabbi Ishmael [Hebrew], ed. and trans. Jacob Lauterbach, 3 vols. Philadelphia: Jewish Publication Society, 1933-35.

Menorat Ha-Maor of R. Israel ibn Al-Nahawa [Hebrew], ed. H. G. Enelow, 4 vols. New York: Bloch, 1929-32.

Midrasch Echa Rabbati [Hebrew], ed. S. Buber. Vilna: Romm, 1899. Reprint, Tel Aviv, 1963-64.

Midrasch Schir ha-Schirim [Hebrew], ed. L. Grünhut. Jerusalem, 1896-97.

Midrasch Tanchuma: Ein agadischer Commentar zum Pentateuch von Rabbi Tanchuma ben Rabbi Abba [Hebrew], ed. S. Buber. Vilna: Romm, 1885. Reprint, in 2 vols., Jerusalem, 1964.

Midrasche Tannaïm zum Deuteronomium [Hebrew], ed. D. Hoffmann, 2 vols. Berlin, 1908-09.

Midrasch Tehillim (Schocher Tob) [Hebrew], ed. S. Buber. Vilna: Romm, 1891. Reprint, Jerusalem. 1965-66.

Midrash Bereshit Rabba: Critical Edition with Notes and Commentary [Hebrew], ed. J. Theodor and Ch. Albeck, 3 vols. Berlin, 1903-36. Reprint with corrections, Jerusalem: Wahrmann, 1965.

Midrash Debarim Rabbah [Hebrew], ed. Saul Lieberman, 3d. ed. Jerusalem: Wahrmann, 1974.

Midrash Haggadol on the Pentateuch [Hebrew], ed. M. Margulies et al. Jerusalem: Mossad Harav Kook, 1947-75.

Midrash Seder ʿOlam [Rabbah] [Hebrew], ed. B. Ratner. Vilna: Romm, 1894-97. Reprint with intro. by S. Mirsky. Jerusalem. 1987-88.

Midrash Wayyikra Rabbah [Hebrew], ed. M. Margulies, 5 vols. Jerusalem, 1953-60. Reprint, 5 vols. in 3, Jerusalem: Wahrmann, 1972.

Midraš ʿăśeret haddibbĕrôt. In *Bet ha-Midrasch,* ed. A. Jellinek, vol. 1, pp. 62-90, 3d ed., Jerusalem: Wahrman, 1967.

Midraš ḥakamim. MS JTS R 2170 (Mic 4937).

Midraš rabba ʿal ḥamiššа ḥummeše tora weḥameš megillot, 2 vols. Vilna: Romm: 1884-87. Reprint, Jerusalem, 1960-61.

Midraš rabba: šir hašširim, ed. Shimshon Dunski. Jerusalem and Tel-Aviv: Dvir, 1980.

Midraš šeloša weʾarbaʿa. In *Batei Midrashot,* ed. Shlomo Aharon Wertheimer, vol. 2, pp. 47-73, 2d ed. Jerusalem: Ktab Wasepher, 1967-68.

Midraš šemuʾel, ed. S. Buber. Krakow, 1893. Reprint, Jerusalem, 1964-65.

Midraš tanḥumaʾ ʿal ḥamiššа ḥummeše tora. Jerusalem: Lewin-Epstein, 1973-74.

Mischnacodex Kaufmann, facsimile ed., ed. G. Beer, 2 vols. Haag, 1929. Reprint, Jerusalem: Makor, 1967-68.

The Mishnah of R. Eliezer; or the Midrash of Thirty-Two Hermeneutical Rules [Hebrew], ed. H. G. Enelow. New York: Bloch, 1933.

The Passover Haggadah [Hebrew], ed. E. D. Goldschmidt. Reprint, Jerusalem: Bialik Institute, 1977.

Pesikta Rabbati: Midrasch für den Fest-cyclus und die ausgezeichneten Sabbathe [Hebrew], ed. M. Friedmann. Vienna, 1880.

Pesikta, die älteste Hagada, redigirt in Palästina von Rab Kahana [Hebrew], ed. S. Buber. Lyck, 1868.

Pesiqta de Rab Kahana [Hebrew], ed. B. Mandelbaum, 2 vols. New York: Jewish Theological Seminary of America, 1962.

Seder Eliahu Rabba und Seder Eliahu Zuta (Tanna d'be Eliahu) [Hebrew], ed. M. Friedmann. Vienna 1904. Reprint, Jerusalem: Wahrmann, 1969.

"Seder Olam: A Rabbinic Chronology," ed. and trans. Chaim Milikowsky. Ph.D. diss., Yale University, 1981.

Sifra on Leviticus [Hebrew], ed. L. Finkelstein, vols. 2-3. New York: Jewish Theological Seminary of America, 1983.

Siphre ad Numeros adjecto Siphre zutta [Hebrew]. Ed. H. S. Horovitz. Corpus Tannaiticum 3:3:1. Leipzig, 1917. Reprint, Jerusalem: Wahrmann, 1966.

Sipraʾ debe rab huʾ seper torat kohanim, ed. I. H. Weiss. Vienna, 1862. Reprint, New York: Om Publishing, 1947.

Šiššā sidre mišna, ed. Chanoch Albeck, 6 vols. Jerusalem and Tel-Aviv: Bialik Institute-Dvir, 1952-56.

Talmud babli, 20 vols. Vilna: Romm, 1886. Reprint, Jerusalem, n.d.

Talmud yerušalmi ʾo talmud hammaʿarab...usebibo perušim ḥiqre halakot girsaʾsot wenusḥaʾot šonot, 7 vols. Vilna: Romm, 1922. Reprint, New York: M. P. Press, 1976.

Talmud yerušalmi. Venice: Bomberg, 1523-24. Reprint, Jerusalem. n.d.

The Tosefta: According to Codex Vienna [Hebrew], ed. S. Lieberman, vols. 1-5. New York: Jewish Theological Seminary of America, 1955-88.

Tosephta Based on the Erfurt and Vienna Codixes [Hebrew], ed. M. S. Zuckermandel, with a supplement by Saul Lieberman. Jerusalem, 1937. Reprint, Jerusalem: Wahrman, 1970.

Yalquṭ hammakiri ʿal yišaʿyahu, ed. J. Spira. Berlin, 1923. Reprint, Jerusalem. 1963-64.

Yalquṭ šimʿoni ʿal hattora, 5 vols. Salonika, 1526-27. Facsimile ed., Jerusalem: Makor, 1967-68.

Yalquṭ šimʿoni ʿal hattora. MS Oxford 2637.

Yalquṭ šimʿoni: neviʾim uketubim, 2 vols. Salonika, 1521. Facsimile ed., Jerusalem: Makor, 1973.

Yelammedenu. In *Bet Ha-Midrasch,* ed. A. Jellinek, vol. 6, pp. 79-90, 3d ed. Jerusalem: Wahrman, 1967.

Post-Talmudic Rabbinic Commentators, Philosophers, and Codes

Abraham ben Samuel Gedaliah. *Brît ʾabraham* to *Yalquṭ šimʿoni,* 2 vols. Leghorn. 1650-57.

Abraham Gombiner. *Zayit raʿanan* to *Yalquṭ šimʿoni.* Venice, 1742-43. Reprint, Jerusalem: "Hatam Sofer", 1970-71.

Abraham ibn Ezra. *Peruše hattora,* ed. A Vizer, 3 vols. Jerusalem: Mossad Harav Kook, 1976.

Beṣalel Ashkenazi, *Šiṭṭah mequbbeṣet,* 4 vols. New York. 1966.

David Qimḥi (RaDaQ). Commentary to the Prophets. In *Miqraʾot gedolot ʿim lʾʾb perušim,* 10 vols. New York: Pardes, 1950-51.

The Living Talmud: The Wisdom of the Fathers and Its Classical Commentaries, ed. and trans. Judah Goldin. New Haven: Yale

University Press, 1955.

Joseph Karo. *Šulḥan ʿaruk.* Venice, 1564-65. Reprint with commentaries, 10 vols., Jerusalem, 1967.

Meir ben Baruch Rothenberg (MaHaraM). Commentary in *Talmud Babli* (see earlier).

Moses ben Maimon. *Mishneh Torah* [Hebrew], ed. M. Hyamson, 2 vols. New York: Bloch, 1937-42.

Moses ben Naḥman (Naḥmanides). *Peruše hattora,* ed. Ch. Chavel, 2 vols., rev. ed. Jerusalem: Mossad Harav Kook, 1976.

Moses Margalit. *Pĕnê mōšeh.* In *Talmud yerušalmi* (see earlier).

Naftali Zvi Yehuda Berlin. *Haʿameq davar,* 2d ed. Jerusalem, 1937.

Solomon B. Isaac (Rashi). Commentary in *Talmud babli* (see above).
Solomon b. Isaac (Rashi). *Raši ʿal hattora,* ed. A. Berliner, 2d ed. Frankfurt, 1905. Rev. ed. with additions of Ch. Chavel, Jerusalem and New York: Feldheim, 1969.

Solomon Luria (Maharshal). *Ḥidduše maharshal.* In *Talmud Babli* (see earlier).

Tosaphot. Commentary in *Talmud babli* (see earlier).

Hebrew Bible and Versions

The Bible in Aramaic, ed. Alexander Sperber, 4 vols. Leiden: E. J. Brill, 1959-73.

Biblia Sacra: Iuxta vulgatam versionem, ed. Robert Weber, 2 vols. Stuttgart: Württembergische Bibelanstalt, 1975.

Biblio Hebraica Stuttgartensia, ed. K. Elliger and W. Rudolph et al. Stuttgart: Deutsche Bibelstiftung, 1976-77.

The Fragment-Targums of the Pentateuch According to their Extant Sources, ed. Michael L. Klein, 2 vols. Rome: Biblical Institute Press, 1980.

Der Hebräische Pentateuch der Samaritaner, ed. August von Gall. Giessen: A Töpelmann, 1914-18.

Neophyti I, ed. A. Diez Macho, 6 vols. Madrid and Barcelona. Consejo Superior de Investigaciones Cientificas, 1968-79.

Origenis Hexaplorum, ed. F. Field, 2 vols. Oxford: Clarendon, 1875.

The Palestinian Targum to the Pentateuch: Codex Vatican (Tg. Neofiti). Facsimile ed., Jerusalem: Makor, 1970.

Pentateuchus Syriace, ed. G. F. Barnes. London: Societas Bibliophilorum Britannicam et Externam, 1914.

The Prophets: Neviʾim. A New Translation of the Holy Scriptures According to the Masoretic Text. Philadelphia: Jewish Publication Society of America, 1978.

Septuaginta: id est Vetus Testamentum Graece iuxta LXX interpretes, ed. Alfred Rahlfs. 2 vols. Stuttgart: Württembergische Bibelanstalt, 1935, reprint, 1962.

Targum Pseudo-Jonathan of the Pentateuch: Text and Concordance, ed. E. G. Clarke et al. Hoboken, N. J.: Ktav, 1984.

The Torah: The Five Books of Moses, 2d. ed. Philadelphia: Jewish Publication Society of America, 1962.

The Writings: Kethubim. A New Translation of the Holy Scriptures According to the Masoretic Text. Philadelphia: Jewish Publication Society of America, 1982.

Apocrypha and Pseudegpigrapha

Apocalypse de Baruch, trans. Pierre Bogaert, vol. 1. Sources Chrétiennes 144. Paris: Éditions du Cerf, 1969.

The Apocryphal Old Testament, ed. H. F. D. Sparks. Oxford: Clarendon Press, 1984.

The Book of Enoch or 1 Enoch: A New English Translation, trans. Matthew Black. Leiden: E. J. Brill, 1985.

The Ethiopic Book of Enoch: A New Edition in the Light of the Aramaic Dead Sea Fragments, ed. and trans. Michael A. Knibb, 2 vols. Oxford: Clarendon Press, 1978.

The Old Testament in Syriac, Part IV, Fasc. 3, Apocalypse of Baruch, ed. S. Dedering. Leiden: E. J. Brill, 1973.

The Old Testament Pseudepigrapha, ed. James H. Charlesworth, 2 vols. Garden City, N. Y.: Doubleday, 1983-85.

Josephus, Philo, and Pseudo—Philo

Josephus. *Complete Works,* ed. and trans. H. St. J. Thackeray, Ralph Marcus, Allen Wikgren, and L. H. Feldman. Loeb Classical Library. 9

vols. London and Cambridge, Mass.: W. Heinemann and Harvard University Press, 1926-65.

Philo Alexandrini: Opera quae supersunt, ed. Leopold Cohn and Paul Wendland, 7 vols. in 8. Berlin: G. Reimer, 1896-1930.

Philo. *Complete Works,* ed. and trans. F. H. Colson, Ralph Marcus, and C. H. Whitaker. Loeb Classical Library. 10 vols. and 2 supp. vols. London and Cambridge, Mass.: W. Heinemann and Harvard University Press, 1929-62.

Pseudo-Philo. *Les Antiquites Bibliques,* ed. Daniel J. Harrington, trans. Jacques Cazeaus, with a commentary by Charles Perrot and Pierre-Maurice Bogaert. SC 229, 230. Paris: Les Édition du Cerf, 1976.

Pseudo-Philo. *The Biblical Antiquities of [Pseudo-] Philo,* trans. M. R. James. London: SPCK, 1917. Reprint, with a prolegomenon by Louis H. Feldman. New York: Ktav. 1971.

Dead Sea Scrolls and Texts from Wadi Murabba^cat

The Dead Sea Scrolls of St. Mark's Monastery, ed. Millar Burrows, vol. 1. New Haven: American Schools of Oriental Research, 1950.

The Genesis Apocryphon of Qumran Cave I: A Commentary, ed. and trans. Joseph Fitzmyer, 2d ed. Biblica et Orientalia 18a. Rome: Biblical Institute Press, 1966.

Grottes de Murabba^cat. Ed. P. Benoit et al. 2 vols. DJD 2. Oxford: Oxford University Press, 1961.

Les "petites grottes" de Qumrân: exploration de la falaise, les grottes 2Q, 3Q, 5Q, 6Q, 7Q, 10Q, le rouleau de cuivre, ed. M. Baillet, J. T. Milik, and R. de Vaux, 2 vols. DJD 3. Oxford: Clarendon, 1962.

Qumran Cave I, ed. D. Barthélemy and J. T. Milik. DJD 1. Oxford: Clarendon Press, 1955.

Qumran Cave 4, ed. John M. Allegro, vol. 1. DJD 5. Oxford: Clarendon, 1968.

The Temple Scroll, ed. and trans. Yigael Yadin, 3 vols. plus supplement. Jerusalem: Israel Exploration Society, 1977-83.

Yadin, Yigael. "Expedition D." *IEJ* 12 (1962): 227-57.

The Zadokite Documents (Damascus Document), ed. and trans. Chaim Rabin, 2d ed. Oxford: Clarendon, 1958.

Ancient Christian Sources

Eusebius Pamphili. *Die Praeparatio evangelica*, ed. Karl Mras, 2 vols. GCS 43. Berlin, 1954-56.

Heracleon. *The Fragments of Heracleon*, ed. A. E. Brooke. Cambridge, 1891.

Hippolytus of Rome. *Bénédictions de Moise*, ed. and trans. from Armenian and Georgian by M. Brière et al. PO 27:1-2. Paris: Turnhout, 1954.

Irenaeus. *Irénée de Lyon. Contre les hérésiees, livre 3*, ed. A. Rousseau and L. Doutreleau. SC 211. Paris: Cerf, 1974.

Irenaeus. *Irénée de Lyon. Contre les hérésies, livre 3*, ed. A. Rousseau, B. Hemmerdinger, L. Doutreleau, and C. Mercier. SC 100. Paris: Cerf, 1965.

Justin Martyr. *Dialogue with Trypho*. In *Die ältesten Apologeten*, ed. E. J. Goodspeed, pp. 90-265. Göttingen: Vandenhoeck & Ruprecht, 1915.

Novum Testamentum Graece, cum apparata critico curavit, ed. Erwin Nestle and Kurt Aland, 26th ed. Stuttgart: Deutsche Bibelstiftung, 1979.

Origen. *Commentarii in Canticum canticorum*. In *Origenes Werke*, ed. W. A. Baehrens. GCS 33. Leipzig-Teubner, 1925.

Origen. *Homiliae in Exodum*. In *Origenes Werke*, ed. W. A. Baehrens, vol. 6. GCS 29. Leipzig: Teubner, 1920.

Patrologiae cursus completus. Series Graeca, ed. J. Migne, 221 vols. Paris, 1844-66.

Theodore of Mopsuestia. *Commentary on John*, ed. J. M. Vosté. CSCO 3. Louvain, 1940.

Greco-Roman Pagan Sources

Aeschylus' Prometheus Bound, ed. Mark Griffith. Cambridge: Cambridge University Press, 1983.

Anonymer Kommentar zu Platons Theaetet (Papyrus 9782), ed. H. Diels and W. Schubart. Berlin, 1905.

Greek and Latin Authors on Jew and Judaism, ed. and Trans. Menahem Stern, 3 vols. Jerusalem: Israel Academy of Sciences and Humanities, 1976-84.

Héraclite. *Allégories d'Homère,* ed. and trans. Félix Buffière. Paris: Société d'édition "Les belles lettres", 1962.

Porphyrii Quaestionum Homericarum ad Iliadem Pertinentium Religuias, ed. Herman Ludwig Schrader. Leipzig: Teubner, 1890-92.

Secondary Sources

Abramson, Shraga. "*Millešon ḥakamim.*" *Leshoneu* 19 (1954): 61-71.

Agnon, S. Y. ʾ*Attem Rěʾîtem,* vol. 1 (the only volume completed). *Pārāšat Mattan Tôrâ.* Jerusalem: Schocken: 1959.

Albeck, Shalom. *Law Courts in Talmudic Times* [Hebrew]. Ramat-Gan: Bar-Ilan University Press, 1980.

Alexander, Philip S. "Retelling the Old Testament." In *It is Written: Scripture Citing Scripture. Essays in Honor of Barnabas Lindars,* ed. D. A. Carson and H. G. M. Williamson, pp. 99-121. Cambridge: Cambridge University Press, 1988.

Alon, Gedaliah. *Tôlĕdôt Hayyĕhûdîm Bĕʾereṣ Yiśrāʾēl Bitqûpat Hammišnâ Wĕhattalmûd,* 2 vols. Tel Aviv: Hakibutz Hameuchad, 1967-70.

Alon, Gedaliah. *The Jews in Their Land in the Talmudic Age,* trans. Gershon Levi, 2 vols. Jerusalem: Magnes, 1984. Translation of the preceding.

Alon, Gedalyahu. *Jews, Judaism and the Classical World: Studies in Jewish History in the Times of the Second Temple and Talmud,* trans. Israel Abrahams. Jerusalem: Magnes, 1977.

Ankersmit, F. R. *Narrative Logic: A Semantic Analysis of the Historian's Language.* The Hague: Martinus Nijhoff, 1983.

Aptowitzer, Victor. "Notes of the Sifre" [Hebrew]. *Tarbiz* 3 (1932): 462-66.

Austin, J. L. *How to Do Things with Words,* 2d ed. Cambridge: Harvard University Press, 1975.

Avi-Yonah, Michael. *The Jews under Roman and Byzantine Rule: A Political History of Palestine from the Bar Kochba War to the Arab Conquest.* Jerusalem: Magnes, 1984.

Baer, Yitzhak F. "Israel, the Christian Church and the Roman Empire from the Days of Septimus Severus to the 'Edict of Toleration' of 313 C.E." *Zion* 21 (1956): 1-49.

Bakhtin, Mikhail. *The Dialogic Imagination,* ed. Michael Holquist. Austin: University of Texas Press, 1981.

Bar-Asher, Moshe. "A Preliminary Study of Mishnaic Hebrew as Reflected in Codex Vatican 32 of Sifre Bemidbar" [Hebrew]. *Te'uda* 3 (1983): 139-164.

Barthes, Roland. *S/Z.* trans. Richard Miller. New York: Hill and Wang, 1974.

Baskin, Judith R. "Rabinic-Patristic Exegetical Contacts in Late Antiquity: A Bibliographical Reappraisal." In *Approaches to Ancient Judaism,* ed. William Scott Green, vol. 5: *Studies in Judaism and Its Greco-Roman Context,* pp. 53-80. BJS 32. Atlanta: Scholars Press, 1985.

Basser, Herbert W. *Midrashic Interpretations of the Song of Moses.* New York: Peter Lang, 1984.

Basser, Herbert. "Pesher Hadavar: The Truth of the Matter." *RevQ* 13 (1988): 389-406.

Basser, Herbert W. Review of Reuven Hammer, trans., *Sifre: The Tannaitic Commentary on the Book of Deutronomy* (New Haven: Yale University Press, 1986). *JBL* 107 (1988): 152-53.

Beer, Moshe. "The Hereditary Principle in Jewish Leadership." *Immanuel* 10 (Spring 1980): 57-61.

Beer, Moshe. "The Sons of Moses in Rabbinic Lore" [Hebrew]. *Bar-Ilan University Yearbook of Judaic Studies and the Humanities* 13 (1976): 149-57.

Ben Yehuda, Eliezer. *A Complete Dictionary of Ancient and Modern Hebrew,* vol. 10 (Jerusalem, 1944).

Berman, Saul. "Noachide Laws." *EncJud* 12 (1971): 1189-91.

Biblia Patristica: Index citations et allusions bibliques dans la littérature patristique, 4 vols. Paris: Centre national de la recherche scientifique, 1975-87.

Bickerman, Elias. "La chaine de la tradition Pharisienne." *RB* 59 (1951): 153-65

Borgen, Peder, and Roald Skarsten. "Quaestiones et Solutiones: Some Observations on the Form of Philo's Exegesis." *Studia Philonica* 4 (1976-77): 1-15.

Borges, Jorge Luis. *Labyrinths: Selected Stories and Other Writings,* ed.

Donald A. Yates and James E. Irby. New York: New Directions, 1962.

Boston, J. R. "The Wisdom Influence upon the Song of Moses." *JBL* 87 (1968): 198-202.

Boyancé, Pierre. "Études philoniennes." *Revue des Études Grecques* 76 (1963): 64-110.

Boyarin, Daniel. "'Language Inscribed by History on the Bodies of Living Beings': Midrash and Martyrdom." *Representations* 25 (Winter 1989): 139-51.

Boyarin, Daniel. "On the Identification of the *Dorshei Reshumot:* A Lexicographical Study," *Beer-Sheva* 3 (1988): 23-35.

Bregman, Marc. "Circular Proems and Proems Beginning with the Formula '*Zo hi shene'emra beruaḥ haq-qodesh*'." In *Studies in Aggadah, Targum and Jewish Liturgy in Memory of Joseph Heinemann,* ed. Jakob J. Petuchowski and Ezra Fleischer, pp. 34–51 (Hebrew section). Jerusalem: Magnes Press and Cincinnati: Hebrew Union College Press, 1981.

Bregman, Marc. "Past and Present in Midrashic Literature." *Hebrew Annual Review* 2 (1978): 45-59.

Brooks, Peter. "The Idea of a Psychoanalytic Literary Criticism." *Critical Inquiry* 13 (1987): 334-48.

Brooks, Peter. *Reading for the Plot: Design and Intention in Narrative.* New York: Alfred A. Knopf, 1984.

Carr, David. Review of Paul Ricoeur, *Temps et récit*, vol. 1 (Paris: Seuil, 1983). *History and Theory* 23 (1984): 357-70.

Carr, David. "Narrative and the Real World: An Argument for Continuity." *History and Theory* 25 (1986): 117-31.

Carr, David. *Time, Narrative, and History.* Bloomington: Indiana University Press, 1986.

Carroll, David. "Narrative, Heterogeneity, and the Question of the Political: Bakhtin and Lyotard." In *The Aims of Representation,* ed. Murray Kireger, pp. 69-106. New York: Columbia University Press, 1987.

Carroll, David. *The Subject in Question: The Languages of Theory and the Strategies of Fiction.* Chicago: University of Chicago Press, 1982.

Cazeaux, J. *La trame et la chaîne: ou les structures litéraires et l'exégèse dans cinq des traités de Philon d'Alexandrie.* ALGHJ 15. Leiden: E. J. Brill, 1983.

Chartier, Roger. *Cultural History: Between Practices and Representations.* Ithaca: Cornell University Press, 1988.

Chatman, Seymour. *Story and Discourse: Narrative Structure in Fiction and Film.* Ithaca: Cornell University Press, 1978.

Clark, Katerina and Michael Holquist. *Mikhail Bakhtin.* Cambridge: Harvard University Press, 1984.

Cohen, Boaz. *Jewish and Roman Law: A Comparative Study,* vol. 1. New York: Jewish Theological Seminary of America, 1966.

Cohen, Gerson D. "Esau as Symbol in Early Medieval Thought." In *Jewish Medieval and Renaissance Studies,* ed. A. Altmann, pp. 19-48. Cambridge: Harvard University Press, 1967.

Cohen, Gerson D. "The Song of Songs and the Jewish Religious Mentality." *The Samuel Friedland Lectures, 1960-66,* pp. 1-21. New York: Jewish Theological Seminary of America, 1966.

Cohen, Jeremy, *"Be Fertile and Increase, Fill the Earth and Master It ": The Ancient and Medieval Career of a Biblical Text.* Ithaca: Cornell University Press, 1989.

Cohen, Norman J. "Analysis of an Exegetical Tradition in the *Mekilta de-Rabbi Ishmael:* The Meaning of *ʾAmanah* in the Second and Third Centuries." *AJS Review* 9, no. 1 (1984): 1-25.

Cohen, Shaye J. D. *From the Maccabees to the Mishnah.* Philadelphia: Westminster, 1987.

Cohen, Shaye J. D. "Epigraphical Rabbis." *JQR* 72 (1981): 1-17.

Cohen, Shaye J. D. "The Significance of Yavneh: Pharisees, Rabbis, and the End of Sectarianism." *HUCA* 55 (1984) 27-53.

Conacher, D. J. *Aeschylus' Prometheus Bound: A Literary Commentary.* London: University of Toronto Press, 1980.

Craigie, Peter C. *The Book of Deuteronomy.* London: Hodder and Stoughton, 1976.

Cross, F. M., and D. N. Freedman. "The Blessing of Moses." *JBL* 67 (1948): 191-201.

Culler, Jonathan. *The Pursuit of Signs: Semiotics, Literature, Deconstructionism.* Ithaca: Cornell University Press, 1981.

Daube, David. "Alexandrian Methods of Interpretation and the Rabbis." In *Festschrift H. Lewald,* pp. 27-44. Basel: Helbring & Lichtenholm, 1953.

Daube, David. "Rabbinic Methods of Interpretation and Hellenistic Rhetoric." *HUCA* 22 (1949): 239-65.

Dawson, John David. "Ancient Alexandrian Interpretation of Scripture." Ph.D. dissertation, Yale University, 1988.

Dillon, John. "The Formal Structure of Philo's Allegorical Exegesis." In *Two Treatises of Philo of Alexandria: A Commentary on De Gigantibus and Quod Deus Sit Immutabilis,* ed. David Winston and John Dillon, pp. 77-87, BJS 25. Chico, Calif.: Scholars Press, 1983.

Dillon, John. *The Middle Platonists: A Study of Platonism, 80 B.C.-A.D. 200.* London: Duckworth, 1977.

Dörrie, Heinrich. "Erotapokriseis A (Nichtchristlich)." *RAC* 6 (1966): 342-347.

Dörrie, Heinrich. "Zur Methodik antiker Exegese." *ZNW* 65 (1974): 121-38.

Driver, S. R. *A Critical and Exegetical Commentary on Deuteronomy,* 3d ed. International Critical Commentary. Edinburgh: T. & T. Clark, 1901.

Eagleton, Terry. *Literary Theory: An Introduction.* Minneapolis: University of Minnesota Press, 1983.

Elbaum, Yaakov. "From Sermon to Story: The Transformation of the Akedah." *Prooftexts* 6 (1986): 97-116.

Epstein, Jacob N. Review of Louis Finkelstein, ed., *Siphre zu Deuteronomium,* fascs. 1-4 (Breslau, 1935-37) [Hebrew]. *Tarbiz* 8 (1936-37): 375-92.

Faur, Jose. *Golden Doves with Silver Dots: Semiotics and Textuality in Rabbinic Tradition.* Bloomington: Indiana University Press, 1986.

Finkelstein, Louis. "A Difficult Baraita and the Light It Sheds on the History of the Sanhedrin" [Hebrew]. *PAAJR* 46-7 (1979-80): 97-109.

Finkelstein, Louis. "Midrash, Halakhah and Aggadot" [Hebrew]. In *Yitzhak F. Baer Jubilee Volume on the Occasion of His Seventieth Birthday,* ed. S. W. Baron et al., pp. 28-47. Jerusalem: Historical Society of Israel, 1960.

Finkelstein, Louis. *New Light from the Prophets.* London: Valentine Mitchell, 1969.

Finkelstein, Louis. *"'Od 'al mupla' šebbebet din."* In *Studies in Rabbinic Literature, Bible, and Jewish History (in Honor or E. Z. Melamed),* ed. Y. D. Gilat, Ch. Levine, and Z. M. Rabinowitz, pp. 75-79. Ramat Gan: Bar-Ilan University Press, 1982.

Finkelstein, Louis. "Studies in the Tannaitic Midrashim." *PAAJR* 6 (1934-35): 189-228.

Finley, M. I. *Ancient History: Evidence and Models.* New York: Viking Press, 1986.

Finnegan, Ruth. Literacy and Orality: Studies in the Technology of Communication. Oxford: Blackwell, 1988.

Fisch, Harold. *Poetry with a Purpose: Biblical Poetics and Interpretation.* Bloomington: Indiana University Press, 1988.

Fischel, Henry. "Story and History: Observations on Greco-Roman Rhetoric and Pharisaism." In *American Oriental Society, Middle West Branch, Semi-Centennial Volume,* ed. Denis Sinor, pp. 59-88. Bloomington: Indiana University Press, 1969.

Fish, Stanley. *Doing What Comes Naturally: Change, Rhetoric, and the Practice of Theory in Literary and Legal Studies.* Durham: Duke University Press, 1989.

Fishbane, Michael. *Biblical Interpretation in Ancient Israel.* Oxford: Clarendon Press, 1985.

Fishbane, Michael. "The Qumran Pesher and Traits of Ancient Hermeneutics." In *Proceedings of the Sixth World Congress of Jewish Studies,* vol. 1, pp. 97-114. Jerusalem: World Union of Jewish Studies, 1977.

Fishbane, Michael. "Use, Authority and Interpretation of Mikra at Qumran." In *Mikra: Text, Translation, Reading and Inyterpretation of the Hebrew Bible in Ancient Judaism and Early Christianity,* ed. Martin Jan Mulder, CRINT 2, no. 1, pp. 339-77. Assen/Maastricht: Van Gorcum; Philadelphia: Fortress, 1988.

Fishbane, Michael. "Varia Deuteronomica." *ZAW* 84 (1972): 349-52.

Foucault, Michel. *The Archeology of Knowledge,* trans. Sheridan Smith. New York: Pantheon Books, 1972.

Fox, Harry. "The Circular Proem Composition: Terminology and Antecedents." *PAAJR* 49 (1982): 1-33.

Fraade, Steven D. "Ascetical Aspects of Ancient Judaism." In *Jewish Spirituality from the Bible through the Middle Ages,* ed. Arthur Green, pp. 253-88. Vol. 13 of *World Spirituality.* New York: Crossroad Publishing, 1986.

Fraade, Steven D. *Enosh and His Generation: Pre-Israelite Hero and History in Post-Biblical Interpretation.* SBLMS 30. Chico, Calif.: Scholars Press, 1984.

Fraade, Steven D. "Interpreting Midrash 1: Midrash and the History of Judaism." *Prooftexts* 7 (1987): 179-94.

Fraade, Steven D. "Interpreting Midrash 2: Midrash and its Literary Contexts." *Prooftexts* 7 (1987): 284-300 (with corrigenda in 7, no. 4 [January 1988]: 159-60).

Fraade, Steven D. "Of Priests, Scribes, and Sages in Second Temple Times." Forthcoming in *JBL.*

Fraade, Steven D. "Sifre Deuteronomy 26 (ad Deut. 3:23): How Conscious the Composition?" *HUCA* 54 (1983): 245-301.

Fraade, Steven D. *Targum and Torah: Early Rabbinic Views of Scriptural Translation in a Multilingual Setting.* Forthcoming.

Fraenkel, Jonah. "Hermeneutical Questions in the Study of the Aggadic Narrative" [Hebrew]. *Tarbiz* 47 (1977-78): 139-172.

Fraenkel, Jonah. "Time and Its Shaping in Aggadic Narrative" [Hebrew]. In *Studies in Aggadah, Targum and Jewish Liturgy in Memory of Joseph Heinemann,* pp. 133-62. Jerusalem: Magnes Press and Hebrew Union College Press, 1981.

Gadamer, Hans-Georg. *Truth and Method,* trans. from the German (*Wahrheit und Method* [Tübingen, 1960]) by G. Barden and J. Cumming. New York: Crossroad Publishing, 1986.

Gafni, Isaiah. "'Scepter and Staff': Concerning New Forms of Leadership in the Period of the Talmud in the Land of Israel and Babylonia" [Hebrew]. In *Kěhūnnâ ûmělûkâ: yaḥăsè dāt ûmědînâ běyiśāʾēl ûbāʿammîm,* ed. I. Gafni and G. Motzkin, pp. 79-91. Jerusalem: Zalman Shazar Center, 1986-87.

Gammie, John G., and Leo G. Perdue, eds. *The Sage in Israel and the Ancient Near East.* Winona Lake, Ind.: Eisenbraun's, 1990.

Gaster, T. H. "An Ancient Eulogy on Israel." *JBL* 66 (1947): 53-62.

Genette, Gérard. *Narrative Discourse: An Essay in Method,* trans. Jane E. Lewin. Ithaca: Cornell University Press, 1980.

Genette, Gérard. *Narrative Discourse Revisited,* trans. Jane E. Lewin. Ithaca: Cornell University Press, 1988.

Gentili, Bruno. *Poetry and Its Public in Ancient Greece: From Homer to the Fifth Century,* trans. A. Thomas Cole. Baltimore: Johns Hopkins University Press, 1988.

Ginzberg, Louis. *Legends of the Jews,* trans. Henrietta Szold, 7 vols. Philadelphia: Jewish Publication Society of America, 1913-38.

Goldberg, Abraham. "The School of Rabbi Akiba and the School of Rabbi Ishmael in Sifre Deuteronomy Pericopes 1-54" [Hebrew]. *Te'uda* 3 (1983): 9-16.

Goldenberg, Robert. "The Deposition of Rabban Gamaliel II: An Examination of the Sources." *JJS* 23 (1972): 167-90.

Goldenberg, Robert. "History and Ideology in Talmudic Narrative." In *Approaches to Ancient Judaism,* vol. 4: *Studies in Liturgy, Exegesis, and Talmudic Narrative,* ed. William Scott Green, pp. 159-71. BJS 27. Chico, Calif.: Scholars Press, 1983.

Goldin, Judah. "The First Pair (Yose ben Yoezer and Yose ben Yohanan) or the Home of a Pharisee." *AJS Review* 5 (1980): 41-62.

Goldin, Judah. "The Freedom and Restraint of Haggadah." In *Midrash and Literature,* ed. Geoffrey H. Hartman and Sanford Budick, pp. 57-76. New Haven: Yale University Press, 1986.

Goldin, Judah. "Not by Means of an Angel and Not by Means of a Messenger." In *Religions in Antiquity: Essays in Memory of Edwin Ramsdell Goodenough,* ed. Jacob Neusner, pp. 412-24. Leiden: E. J. Brill, 1968.

Goldin, Judah. *The Song at the Sea: Being a Commentary in Two Parts.* New Haven: Yale University Press, 1971.

Goodblatt, David M. *Rabbinic Instruction in Sasanian Babylonia.* SJLA 9. Leiden: E. J. Brill, 1975.

Goodblatt, David. *"Yĕhûdê 'ereṣ-yiśrā'ēl baśśānîm 70-132."* In *Hāhîsṭôryâ šel 'am yiśrā'ēl: yĕhûdâ wĕrômâ—mĕrîdôt hayyĕhûdîm,* ed. Uriel Rappaport, pp. 155-184. Jerusalem: Alexander Peli, 1983-84.

Goodblatt, David. "Sanhedrin." *Encyclopedia of Religion* 13 (1987): 60-63.

Goodman, Martin. *State and Society in Roman Galilee, A.D.* 132-212. Totowa, N.J.: Rowman and Allanheld, 1983.

Goody, Jack. *The Interface Between the Written and the Oral.* Cambridge: Cambridge University Press, 1987.

Gottlieb, Isaac Boaz. "Language Understanding in Sifre Deuteronomy: A Study of Language Consciousness in Rabbinic Exegesis." Ph.D. dissertation, New York University, 1972.

Graetz, Heinrich. *Geschichte der Juden.* 11 vols. Leipzig, 1860-78.

Green, William Scott. "Romancing the Tome: Rabbinic Hermeneutics and the Theory of Literature." *Semeia* 40 (1987): 147-68.

Green, William Scott. "What's in a Name? The Problematic of Rabbinic Biography." In *Approaches to Ancient Judaism: Theory and Practice,* vol. 1, pp. 77-96. Missoula, Mont.: Scholars Press, 1978.

Greenberg, Moshe. *Ezekiel 1-20.* AB 22. Garden City, N.Y.: Doubleday, 1983.

Greenberg, Stephen J., ed.. *Allegory and Representation: Selected Papers from the English Institute 1979-80.* Baltimore and London: Johns Hopkins University Press, 1981.

Greenblatt, Stephen J. "Capitalist Culture and the Circulatory System." In *The Aims of Representation: Subject/Text/History,* ed. Murray Krieger, pp. 257-73. New York: Columbia University Press, 1987.

Gruenwald, Ithamar. *Apocalyptic and Merkavah Mysticism.* Leiden: E. J. Brill, 1980.

Hadot, Pierre. "Théologie, exégèse, révélation, écriture, dans la philosophie Grecque." In *Les règles de l'interprétation,* ed. Michel Tardieu, pp. 13-34. Paris: Cerf, 1987.

Halevy, Isaak. *Dorot Hariʾšonim: Die Geschichte und Literatur Israels,* 4 vols. Berlin-Vienna, 1897; reprint 1923.

Hallewy, E. E. "Biblical Midrash and Homeric Exegesis"[Hebrew]. *Tarbiz* 31 (1961): 157-69.

Halperin, David J. *The Faces of the Chariot: Early Jewish Responses to Ezekiel's Vision.* Tübingen: J. C. B. Mohr (Paul Siebeck), 1988.

Halperin, David J. *The Merkabah in Rabbinic Literature.* New Haven: American Oriental Society, 1980.

Hammer, Reuben. "A Rabbinic Response to the Post Bar Kochba Era: Sifre Haʾazinu." *PAAJR* 52 (1985): 37-53.

Harper, G. McLean Jr. "Village Administration in the Roman Province of Syria." *Yale Classical Studies* 1 (1928): 102-68.

Hartman, Lars. *Asking For a Meaning: A Study of 1 Enoch 1-5.* Lund: Gleerup, 1979.

Hay, David M. "Philo's references to Other Allegorists." *Studia Philonica* 6 (1979-80): 41-75.

Heinemann, Isaak. *Darke haʾaggada.* 3d ed. Jerusalem: Magnes Press, 1970.

Heinemann, Joseph. ʾAggādôt wĕtôlĕdôtêhen. Jerusalem: Keter, 1974.

Herr, Moshe D. "Continuum in the Chain of Torah Transmission" [Hebrew]. *Zion* 44 (1979): 43-56.

Herrr, Moshe D. "The Historical Significance of the Dialogues between Jewish Sages and Roman Dignitaries." In *Studies in Aggadah and Folk-Literature,* ed. Joseph Heinemann and Dov Noy, vol. 22 of *Scripta Hierosolymitana,* pp. 123-150. Jerusalem: Magnes, 1971.

Herr, Moshe D. "Persecution and Martyrdom in Hadrianic Days." In *Scripta Hierosolymitana* 23 (1972): 85-125.

Heschel, Abraham Joshua. *Theology of Ancient Judaism* [Hebrew], 2 vols. London and New York: Soncino, 1962-65.

Himmelfarb, Martha. *Apoclyptic Ascent and the Heavenly Temple.* Forthcoming.

Himmelfarb, Martha. *Tours of Hell: An Apocalyptic Form in Jewish and Christian Literature.* Philadelphia: University of Pennsylvania Press, 1983.

Horgan, Maurya P. *Pesharim: Qumran Interpretation of Biblical Books.* CBQMS 8. Washington, D.C.: Catholic Biblical Association of America, 1979.

Hoy, David. "Jacques Derrida." In *The Return of the Grand Theory in the Human Sciences,* ed. Quentin Skinner, pp. 43-64. Cambridge: Cambridge University Press, 1985.

Huffmon, Herbert B. "The Covenant Lawsuit in the Prophets." *JBL* 78 (1959): 285-95.

Hunt, Lynn, ed. *The New Cultural History.* Berkeley: University of

California Press, 1989.

Ingarden, Roman. *The Cognition of the Literary Work of Art*, trans. Ruth Ann Crowley and Kenneth R. Olson. Evanston: Northwestern University Press, 1973.

Ingarden, Roman. *The Literary Work of Art: An Investigation on the Borderlines of Ontology, Logic, and the Theory of Literature*, trans. George G. Grabowicz. Evanston: Northwestern University Press, 1973.

Iser, Wolfgang. *The Act of Reading: A Theory of Aesthetic Response.* Baltimore: Johns Hopkins University Press, 1979.

Jaffee, Martin S. "Introduction" to *The Talmud of Babylonia: An American Translation, XXVI: Tractate Horayot*, pp. 8-45. BJS 90. Atlanta: Scholars Press, 1987.

Jameson, Frederic. *The Political Unconscious: Narrative as a Socially Symbolic Act.* Ithaca: Cornell University Press, 1981.

Jastrow, Marcus. *A Dictionary of the Targum, the Talmud Babli and Jerushalmi, and the Midrashic Literature*, 2 vols. New York: Choreb, 1926.

Jauss, Hans Robert. *Toward an Aesthetic of Reception*, trans. Timothy Bahti. Minneapolis: University of Minnesota Press, 1982.

Kahana, Menahem. "Commentaries to the Sifre which Are Concealed in Manuscripts"[Hebrew]. In *Seper Zikkaron to Rab Yiṣḥaq Nissim*, ed. Meir Banehu, vol. 2, pp. 95-118. Jerusalem: Yad Harab Nissim, 1984-85.

Kahana, Menahem. "The Critical Edition of *Mekilta de-Rabbi Ishmael* in the Light of the Geniza Fragments." *Tarbiz* 55 (1986): 489-524.

Kahana, Menahem. "*Dappîm min hamměkîltāʾ lidbārîm pārāšôt haʾăzînû wězōʾt habběrākâ.*" *Tarbiz* 57 (1988): 165-201.

Kahana, Menahem. "ʾÊn měʿîlâ ʾellāʾ šîqqûr/šinnûy." Forthcoming in *Leshonenu*.

Kahana, Menahem. "Prolegomena to a New Edition of the Sifre on Numbers"[Hebrew]. Ph.D. dissertation, Hebrew University of Jerusalem, 1982.

Kaminka, A. "*Měliṣôt mōšeh ûmizmôrê těhillîm běpî yěšaʿyāhû,*" *Leshoneu* 1 (1928-29): 40-43.

Kellner, Hans. "Narrativity in History: Post-Structuralism and Since." In *The Representation of Historical Events,* Beiheft 26 of *History and Theory* (1988): 1-29.

Kermode, Frank. "Endings, Continued." In *Languags of the Unsayable: The Play of Negativity in Literature and Literary Theory,* ed. Sanford Budick and Wolfgang Iser, pp. 71-94. New York: Columbia University Press, 1989.

Kermode, Frank. *The Genesis of Secrecy: On the Interpretation of Narrative.* Cambridge: Harvard University Press, 1979.

Kermode, Frank. *The Sense of an Ending.* Oxford: Oxford University Press, 1967.

Kimelman, Reuven. "The Conflict between the Priestly Oligarchy and the Sages in the Talmudic Period" [Hebrew]. *Zion* 48 (1983): 135-48.

Kimelman, Reuven. "Rabbi Yohanan and Origen on the Song of Songs: A Third-Century Jewish-Christian Disputation." *HTR* 73 (1980): 567-95.

Kohut, Alexander, ed. *Aruch Completum* of R. Nathan ben Yeḥiel, 8 cols. 1878-92.

Kook, S. C. "Additional Notes to Emendations to the Sifre" [Hebrew]. *Tarbiz* 3 (1932): 466-67.

Koselleck, Reinhard. *Futures Past: The Semantics of Historical Time,* trans. Keith Tribe. Cambridge: MIT Press, 1985.

Kosovsky, Biniamin. *Otzar Leshon Hatanna'im: Thesaurus "Sifrei" Concordantiae Verborum.* 5 vols. Jerusalem: Jewish Theological Seminary of America, 1970-75.

Krecher, J. "Kommentare." *Reallexikon der Assyriologie und vorder-asiatischen Archaeologie* 6, no. 3-4 (1981): 188-91.

Krieger, Murray, ed. *The Aims of Representation: Subject/Text/History.* New York: Columbia University Press, 1987.

Kugel, James. "Two Introductions to Midrash." In *Midrash and Literature,* ed. Geoffrey H. Hartman and Sanford Budick, pp. 77-103. New Haven: Yale University Press, 1986.

Kuhn, Karl Georg. *Konkordanz zu den Qumrantexten.* Göttingen: Vandenhoeck and Ruprecht, 1960.

LaCapra, Dominick. *History and Criticism.* Ithaca: Cornell University Press, 1985.

LaCapra, Dominick. *History, Politics, and the Novel.* Ithaca: Cornell University Press, 1987.

LaCapra, Dominique. *Rethinking Intellectual History: Texts, Contexts, Language.* Ithaca: Cornell University, 1983.

Levine, Lee I. "The Jewish Patriarch (Nasi) in Third Century Palestine." *ANRW* II.19, no. 2, 649-88.

Levine, Lee I. *The Rabbinic Class in Palestine during the Talmudic Period* [Hebrew]. Jerusalem: Yad Izhak ben Zvi, 1985.

Levy, Jacob. *Wörteruch über die Talmudim und Midraschim,* rev. L. Goldschmidt, 4 vols. Berlin: B. Harz, 1924.

Lieberman, Saul. "Achievements and Aspirations of Modern Jewish Scholarship." *PAAJR 46-47 (Jubilee Volume)* (1980): 369-80.

Lieberman, Saul. *Hellenism in Jewish Palestine.* 2d ed. New York: Jewish Theological Seminary of America, 1962.

Lieberman, Saul. "The Martyrs of Caesarea." *Annuaire de l'Institut de Philologie et d'Histoire Orientales et Slaves* 7 (1939-44): 395-446.

Lieberman, Saul. "On Persecution of the Jewish Religion" [Hebrew]. In *Salo Wittmayer Baron Jubilee Volume,* ed. Saul Lieberman, vol. 3, pp. 213-45. Jerusalem: American Academy for Jewish Research, 1975

Lieberman, Saul. Review of Louis Finkelstein, ed., *Siphre zu Deuteronomium, fasc. 1 (Breslau, 1937) [Hebrew].* Kiryat Sefer 14 (1937-38): 323-36.

Lieberman, Saul. "Roman Legal Institutions in Early Rabbinics and in the Acta Martyrum." *JQR* 35 (1944-45): 1-57.

Lieberman, Saul. *Siphre Zutta.* New York: Jewish Theological Seminary, 1968.

Lieberman, Saul. *The Talmud of Caesarea: Jerusalem Tractate Neziqin* (= Supplement to *Tarbiz* II.4) [Hebrew]. Jerusalem, 1931.

Lieberman, Saul. *Tosefta Ki-Fschuṭah,* vol. 9. New York: Jewish Theological Seminary of America, 1988.

Lohse, E. "*Rabbi, rabbouni.*" *TDNT* 6 (1968): 961-65.

Lyotard, Jean-François. *Le Différend.* Paris: Minuit, 1983.

Lyotard, Jean-François. *Instructions païennes.* Paris: Éditions Galilee, 1977.

Lyotard, Jean-François. *The Postmodern Condition: A Report on Knowledge,* trans. Geoff Bennington and Brian Massumi. Minneapolis: University of Minnesota Press, 1984.

Mach, Rudolf. *Der Zaddiq in Talmud und Midrasch.* Leiden: E. J. Brill, 1957.

Mack, Burton. "Argumentation in Philo's *De Sacrificiis.*" Forthcoming in a volume on *De Sacrificiis* in *Studies in Hellenistic Judaism.*

Mack, Burton L. "Philo Judaeus and Exegetical Traditions in Alexandria." *ANRW* II.21, no. 1 (1984): 227-71.

Mantel, Hugo. *Studies in the History of the Sanhedrin.* Cambridge: Harvard University Press, 1961.

Marcovich, Miroslav. "Hippolyt von Rom." *TRE* 15 (1986): 381-87.

Margulis, B. "Gen. 49:10/Deut. 33:2-3." *VT* 19 (1969): 202-210.

Martin, Wallace. *Recent Theories of Narrative.* Ithaca: Cornell University Press, 1986.

McGann, Jerome J. *Social Values and Poetic Acts: The Historical Judgment of Literary Work.* Cambridge: Harvard University Press, 1988.

Melamed, E. Z. *Halachic Midrashim of the Tannaim in the Babylonian Talmud* [Hebrew]. 2d. ed. Jerusalem: Magnes Press, 1988.

Melamed, E. Z. *Pirqè mābōʾ lesiprût hattalmûd.* Jerusalem, 1973.

Mendèlow, A. A. *Time and the Novel.* New York: Humanities Press, 1965.

Mildenberg, Leo. "The Eleazar Coins of the Bar Kochba Rebellion." *Historia Judaica* 11 (1949): 77-108.

Miller, J. Hillis. "The Figure in the Carpet." *Poetics Today* 1.3 (1980): 107-118.

Milik, J. T. "Deux documents inédits du désert de Judah." *Biblica* 38 (1957): 245-54.

Miller, P. D. "A Critical Note on Deut. 33:2b-3a." *HTR* 57 (1964): 241-43.

Miller, Stuart S. *Studies in the History and Traditions of Sepphoris.* SJLA 37. Leiden: E. J. Brill, 1984.

Moran, W. L. "Some Remarks on the Song of Moses." *Biblica* 43 (1962): 317-27.

Naveh, Joseph. *On Stone and Mosiac: The Aramaic and Hebrew Inscriptions from Ancient Synagogues.* Jerusalem: Israel Exploration Society, 1978.

Neusner, Jacob. "The Formation of Rabbinic Judaism: Yavneh (Jamnia) from A.D. 70-100." *ANRW* II.19, no. 2 (1984): 3-42.

Neusner, Jacob. *A History of the Jews in Babylonia,* 5 vols. Leiden: E. J. Brill, 1965-70.

Neusner, Jacob. *Judaism and Christianity in the Age of Constantine: History, Messiah, Israel, and the Initial Confrontation.* Chicago: University of Chicago, 1987.

Neusner, Jacob. *Judaism and Scripture: The Evidence of Leviticus Rabbah.* Chicago: University of Chicago Press, 1986.

Neusner, Jacob. *Judaism in Society: The Evidence of the Jerushalmi: Toward a Natural History of Religion.* Chicago: University of Chicago, 1983.

Neusner, Jacob. *Judiasm: The Evidence of the Mishnah.* Chicago: University of Chicago, 1981.

Neusner, Jacob. "The Present State of Rabbinic Biography." In *Hommage Georges Vajda: études d'histoire et de pensée juives,* ed. Gérard Nahon and Charles Touati, pp. 85-91. Louvain: Peeters, 1980.

Neusner, Jacob. *Sifre to Deuteronomy: An Introduction to the Rhetorical, Logical, and Topical Program.* BJS 124. Atlanta: Scholars Press, 1987.

Neusner, Jacob. *Torah: From Scroll to Symbol in Formative Judaism.* Part Three of *The Foundations of Judaism: Method, Teleology, Doctrine.* Philadelphia: Fortress, 1985.

Newsom, Carol A. "The Sage in the Literature of Qumran: The Function of the *Maskil.*" In *The Sage in Israel and the Ancient Near East,* ed. John G. Gammie and Leo G. Perdue. Winona Lake, Ind.: Eisenbraun's, 1990.

Nikiprowetzky, Valentin. *Le commentaire de l'Écriturem chez Philon d'Aleandrie.* ALGHJ 11. Leiden: E. J. Brill, 1977.

Nikiprowetzky, Valentin. "L'Exégèse de Philon d'Alexandrie dans le *De Gigantibus* et le *Quod Deus sit Immutabilis.*" In *Two Treatises of Philo of Alexandria: A Commentary on De Gigantibus and Quod*

Deus sit Immutabilis, ed. David Winston and John Dillon, pp. 5-75. BJS 25. Chico, Calif.: Scholars Press, 1983.

Nitzan, Bilha. *Pesher Habakkuk: A Scroll from the Wilderness of Judaea (1 Qp Hab)* [Hebrew]. Jerusalem: Bialik Institute, 1986.

Novak, David. *The Image of the Non-Jew in Judaism: An Historical and Constructive Study of the Noahide Laws.* New York: E. Mellen, 1983.

Oppenheimer, Benjamin. *"Maʿămād Har Sînay: Hannĕbûʾâ Ûbĕḥîrat Yiśrāʾēl Bĕpôlmôs Ḥazal."* *Molad* 8, nos. 39-40 (249-50) (1980): 91-110.

Orlinsky, Harry M. *Notes on the New Translation of the Torah.* Philadelphia: Jewish Publication Society of America, 1970.

Pagels, Elaine H. *The Johannine Gospel in Gnostic Exegesis: Heracleon's Commentary on John.* Nashville: Abington, 1973.

Pépin, Jean. *Mythe et allégorie: les origenes grecques et les contestations judéo-chrétiennes,* rev. and enl. ed. Paris: Études Augustinennes, 1976.

Pépin, Jean. "Remargues sur la théorie de l'exégèse allégorique chez Philon." In *Philon d'Alexandrie,* ed. Roger Arnaldez et al., pp. 138-68. Colloques nationaux du Centre National de la Recherche Scientifique, Lyon, 11-15 Sept. 1966. Paris: Éditions du Centre National de la Recherche Scientifique, 1967.

Perry, Menakhem. "Literary Dynamics: How the Order of a Text Creates its Meanings." *Poetics Today* 1, no. 1 (1979-80): 35-64, 311-361.

Perry, Menakhem, and Meir Sternberg. "The King through Ironic Eyes: The Narrator's Devices in the Biblical Story of David and Bathsheba and Two Excursuses on the Theory of the Narrative Text" [Hebrew]. *Hasifrut* 1 (1986): 263-92.

Pfeiffer, Rudolf. *History of Classical Scholarship from the Beginnings to the End of the Hellenistic Age.* Oxford: Clarendon, 1968.

Pockock, J. G. A. *Politics, Language, and Time: Essays on Political Thought and History.* New York: Atheneun, 1971.

Rappel, Dov. *"Šîrat 'Haʾăzînû'."* *Beth Mikra* 12, no. 3 (31) (1966-67): 3-26; 13, no. 1 (32) (1967-68): 14-23; 13, no. 2 (33) (1967-68): 28-47.

Ratner, D. *Seper ʾAhabat Ṣion,* 12 vols. Wilna, 1901-17.

Richard, Marcel. "Hippolyte de Rome." *Dictionnaire de spiritualité, ascétique et mystique, doctrine et histoire* 7, no. 1 (1968): 531-71.

Ricoeur, Paul. *Time and Narrative*, 3 vols., trans. Kathleen Blamey and David Pellauer. Chicago: University of Chicago Press, 1984-88.

Riffatere, Michael. *Semiotics of Poetry*. Bloomington: Indiana University Press, 1978.

Rimmon-Kenan, Shlomith. *Narrative Fiction: Contemporary Poetics*. London: Mehtuen, 1983.

Rotenberg, Mordechai. *Re-biographing and Deviance: Psychotherapeutic Narrativism and the Midrash*. New York: Praeger Publishers, 1987.

Runia, David T. "Further Observations on the Structure of Philo's Allegorical Treatises." *VC* 41 (1987): 131-133.

Runia, David T. *Philo of Alexandria and the Timaeus of Plato*. Leiden: E. J. Brill, 1986.

Runia, David T. "The Structure of Philo's Allegorical Treatises: A Review of Two Recent Studies and Some Additional Comments." *VC* 38 (1984): 209-56.

Satran, David. "Hippolytus of Rome: The Origens of Christian Biblical Commentary." Chapter 4 of *Nebuchadnezzar Dethroned: The Interpretation of Daniel 4 in Early Jewish and Christian Literature*. Harvard Semitic Monographs. Atlanta: Scholars Press, 1991.

Schechter, Solomon. "Geniza Specimens." *JQR* 10 (1898): 654-59.

Scholem, Gershom. *Jewish Gnosticism, Merkabah Mysticism and Talmudic Tradition*, 2d ed. New York: Jewish Theological Seminary of America, 1965.

Scott, R. B. Y. "The Literary Structure of Isaiah's Oracles." In *Studies in Old Testament Prophecy*, ed. H. H. Rowley, pp. 175-86. Edinburgh: T. and T. Clark, 1950).

Searle, John. *Expression and Meaning: Studies in the Theory of Speech Acts*. Cambridge: Cambridge University Press, 1979.

Seeligmann, I. L. "A Psalm from Pre-Regal Times." *VT* 14 (1964): 75-92.

Shanks, Hershel. "Is the Title 'Rabbi' Anachronistic in the Gospels?" *JQR* 53 (1963): 337-45.

Shanks, Hershel. "Origins of the Title 'Rabbi.'" *JQR* 59 (1968): 152-57.

Shils, Edward. *Tradition*. Chicago: University of Chicago Press, 1981.

Shinan, Avigdor. "*Siprût hāʾaggādâ bên higgûd ʿal peh ûmĕsôret kĕtûbâ.*" In *Meḥqĕrê yĕrûšālayim bĕpôqlôr yĕhûdî* 1 (1981): 44-60.

Silberman, Lou H. "Challenge and Response: Pesiqta Derab Kahana, Chapter 26 As an Oblique Reply to Christian Claims." *HTR* 29, no. 1-3 (1986): 247-53.

Silberman, Lou H. "Unriddling the Riddle: A Study in the Structure and Language of the Habakkuk Pesher (1QpHab)." *RevQ* 3 (1961): 323-64.

Simpson, David. "Literary Criticism and the Return to 'History'." *Critical Inquiry* 14 (1988): 721-47.

Skehan, Patrick W. "A Fragment of the 'Song of Moses' (Deut. 32) from Qumran." *BASOR* 136 (1954): 12-15.

Skehan, Patrick W. "The Structure of the Song of Moses in Deuteronomy (Deut. 32:1-43)." *CBQ* 13 (1951): 153-63.

Skura, Meredith Anne. *The Literary Use of the Psychoanalytic Process.* New Haven: Yale University Press, 1981.

Smallwood, E. Mary. *The Jews under Roman Rule From Pompey to Diocletian: A Study in Political Relations.* SJLA 20. Leiden: E. J. Brill, 1981.

Sparks, H. F. D. "Jerome as Biblical Scholar." In *The Cambridge History of the Bible,* vol. 1, *From the Beginnings to Jerome,* ed. P. R. Ackroyd and C. F. Evans, pp. 510-41. Cambridge, Mass.: Cambridge University Press, 1970.

Steiner, George. *After Babel: Aspects of Language and Translation.* Oxford: Oxford University Press, 1985.

Steinfeld, Zvi Aryeh. "The Mufla of the Court" [Hebrew]. *Sinai* 82 (1978): 24-40.

Stern, David. "Midrash and Indeterminacy." *Critical Inquiry* 15 (1988): 132-61.

Sternberg, Meir. *Expositional Modes and Temporal Order in Fiction.* Baltimore: Johns Hopkins University Press, 1978.

Sternberg, Meir. *The Poetics of Biblical Narrative: Ideological Literature and the Drama of Reading.* Bloomington: Indiana University Press, 1985.

Stone, Michael. "The Parabolic Use of Natural Order in Judaism of the Second Temple Age." In *Gilgul: Essays on Transformation, Revolution and Permanence in the History of Religions,* ed. S. Shaked et all., pp. 298-308. Leiden: E. J. Brill, 1987.

Svenbro, Jesper. *Phrasikleia: Anthropologie de la lecture en Grèce ancienne.* Paris: Editions La Découverte, 1988.

Tobin, Thomas H. *The Creation of Man: Philo and the History of Interpretation.* CBQMS 14. Washington, D. C.: Catholic Biblical Association, 1983.

Todorov, Tzvetan. *Mikhail Bakhtin: The Dialogical Principle.* Trans. Wlad Godzich. Minneapolis: University of Minnesota Press, 1984.

Toews, John E. "Intellectual History after the Linguistic Turn: The Autonomy of Meaning and the Irreducibility of Experience." *American Historical Review* 92 (1987): 879-907.

Torjesen, Karen Jo. *Hermeneutical Procedure and Theological Method in Origen's Exegesis.* Patristische Texte und Studien 28. Berlin: De Gruyter, 1986.

Towner, Wayne Sibley. *The Rabbinic Enumeration of Scriptural Examples.* Leiden: E. J. Brill, 1973.

Trifon, Dalia Ben-Hayim. "The Priests After the Destruction of the Second Temple" [Hebrew]. Ph.D. dissertation, Tel-Aviv University, 1985.

Urbach, Ephraim E. "Class-Status and Leadership in the World of the Palestinian Sages." *Proceedings of the Israel Academy of Sciences and Humanities* 2, no. 4 (1966): 38-74.

Urbach, Ephraim E. "The Homiletical Interpretations of the Sages and the Expositions of Origen on Canticles, and the Jewish-Christian Disputation." *Scripta Hierosolymitana* 22 (1971): 247-75.

Urbach, Ephraim E. "*Mishmarot* and *Ma'amadot.*" *Tarbiz* 42 (1972-73): 304-27.

Urbach, Ephraim E. "The Response of the People of Ninveh and the Jewish-Christian Dispute" [Hebrew]. *Tarbiz* 20 (1949): 118-122.

Urbach, Ephriam E. *The Sages: Their Concepts and Beliefs,* trans. Israel Abrahams, 2 vols. Jerusalem: Magnes, 1979.

Urbach, Ephraim E. "Talmudic Sage: Character and Authority," In *Jewish Society through the Ages,* ed. H. H. Ben-Sasson and S. Ettinger, pp. 116-47. New York: Schocken Books, 1969.

Vansina, John. *Oral Tradition: A Study in Historical Methodology.* Chicago: University of Chicago Press, 1961.

Vermes, Geza. *Scripture and Tradition in Judaism,* rev. ed. Leiden: E. J. Brill, 1973.

Wacholder, Ben Zion. "The Date of the Mekilta De-Rabbi Ishmael." *HUCA* 39 (1968): 117-144.

Walter, Nicolaus. *Der Thorausleger Aristobulos: Untersuchungen zu seinen Fragmenten und zu pseudepigraphischen Resten der jüdisch hellenistischen Literatur.* Berlin: Akademie-Verlag, 1964.

Warnke, Georgia. *Hermeneutics, Tradition and Reason.* Stanford: Stanford University Press, 1987.

Weinsheimer, Joel C. *Gadamer's Hermeneutics: A Reading of Truth and Method.* New Haven: Yale University Press, 1985.

Weiss, P. R. "The Office of the Mufla." *JJS* 1 (1949): 172-77.

Whibley, Leonard ed. *A Companion to Greek Studies,* 4th ed. Cambridge: Cambridge University Press, 1931.

White, Hayden. *The Content of the Form: Narrative Discourse and Historical Representation.* Baltimore: Johns Hopkins University Press, 1987.

White, Hayden. "The Question of Narrative in Contemporary Historical Theory." *History and Theory* 23 (1984): 1-33.

White, James Boyd. *When Words Lose Their Meaning: Constitutions and Reconstitutions of Language, Character, and Community.* Chicago: University of Chicago Press, 1984.

White, John. "Introduction" to *The Scholia on the Aves of Aristophanes.* Boston and London: Ginn and Co., 1914.

Whitman, Jon. *Allegory: The Dynamics of an Ancient and Medieval Technique.* Cambridge: Harvard University Press, 1987.

Wilken, Robert. *John Chrysostom and the Jews: Rhetoric and Reality in the Late Fourth Century.* Berkeley: University of California Press, 1983.

Winston, David. "Two Types of Mosaic Prophecy According to Philo," In *Society of Biblical Literature 1988 Seminar Papers,* ed. David J. Lull, pp. 442-55. Atlanta: Scholars Press, 1988.

Wolfson, Harry Austryn. *Philo: Foundations of Religious Philosophy in Judaism, Christianity, and Islam,* 2 vols. Cambridge: Harvard University Press. 1947.

Wright, G. E. "The Lawsuit of God: A Form-Critical Study of Deuter-onomy 32." In *Israel's Prophetic Heritage: Essays in Honor of James Muilenburg,* ed. Bernhard W. Anderson & Walter Harrelson, pp. 26-67. New York: Harper and Bros., 1962.

Yerushalmi, Yosef Hayim. *Zakhor: Jewish History and Jewish Memory.* Seattle: University of Washington Press, 1982.

Zeitlin, S. "A Reply [to Hershel Shanks]." *JQR* 53 (1963): 345-49.

Zeitlin, S. "The Title Rabbi in the Gospels Is Anachronistic." *JQR* 59 (1968): 158-60.

Index of Primary Sources

Hebrew Bible

Genesis
1:14: 141
1:26: 180
1:28: 270
2:15: 89, 90, 239
5:24: 153
9:15: 37
12:1: 9
12:2: 9
15:15: 9
16:12: 34
19:36: 34
20:18: 136
21:21: 195
25:26: 38
25:27: 39
27: 201
27:22: 32
27:40: 32, 34
29:31: 135
32:4: 195
36:12: 275
36:22: 275
40:15: 34
41:31: 248
41:39: 248
49: 271

Exodus
1:10: 100, 247
12:16: 243
15:2: 42, 44, 205, 212
18:13–26: 75, 77, 246, 247
18:21: 248

19: 209
19–20: 47, 210
19–24: 26
19:12: 60, 61, 223
19:18, 20: 195
19:18: 46
19:23: 223
20:2: 33, 199
20:13: 32, 33, 34
20:14: 216
20:15: 37, 45, 223
20:18: 260
20:19: 46, 140
21:35: 216, 217
24:1: 75, 76
24:7: 34, 49, 51, 54, 140, 141
24:9–11: 78
24:9: 75
31:14: 219
32:32: 49

Leviticus
4:13: 237
5:21: 217
13–14: 239
18:4: 254
18:5: 221
23:7–8: 243
23:36: 95
26:46: 239

Numbers
5:11–31: 87
11:16–25: 75, 77, 246

311

1 Chronicles
21:17: 49
23:4: 258

2 Chronicles
5:5: 238

6:14: 29
6:28: 29
6:41: 29
30:27: 238
34:14–28: 114
36:16: 128

Ancient Versions

Samaritan Pentateuch
Deut. 11:14: 235
Deut. 33:2: 196
Deut. 33:10: 239

Septuagint
Deut. 1:13: 249
Deut. 11:14: 235
Deut. 32:10: 224
Deut. 33:2–3: 202
Deut. 33:2: 196, 206
Deut. 33:3: 211

Aquila
Ps. 48(47):15: 203

Vulgate
Deut. 11:14: 235
Deut. 33:2: 196, 206
Ezek. 44:15: 238

Peshiṭta
Deut. 17:9: 238
Deut. 33:2: 196, 206
Deut. 33:3: 211
Deut. 33:10: 239
Ezek. 44:15: 238

Targum Onqelos
Num. 25:4: 246, 276
Deut. 33:2: 196, 206
Deut. 33:3: 211, 212, 213, 223
Deut. 32:10: 224

Targum Pseudo-Jonathan
Exod. 20:2: 207, 212, 223, 270, 276
Deut. 33:2: 196, 197, 206
Deut. 33:3: 213
Deut. 33:10: 224, 239, 246, 249

Fragmentary Targum
Gen. 2:15: 239
Exod. 20:2: 207
Deut. 32:1: 150–153, 197, 246
Deut. 32:10: 223, 224
Deut. 33:2: 196, 206
Deut. 33:3: 196, 206, 212, 213, 270

Targum Neofiti
Gen. 2:15: 239
Exod. 20:2: 207
Deut. 32:1: 270, 276
Deut. 32:10: 223, 224
Deut. 33:2: 196, 197, 206
Deut. 33:3: 212, 213, 238

Targum of the Prophets
Isa. 1:2: 150
Isa. 51:6: 150
Isa. 65:17: 150
Jer. 18:18: 234
Ezek. 7:26: 234

Targum of the Writings
Ps. 68:19: 242
Cant. 5:10–16: 206

Apocrypha and Pseudepigrapha

Dead Sea Scrolls

Philo

Josephus

Pseudo-Philo

Rabbinic Sources

Mishnah and Talmud

Midrashic Literature

§343 (F398.10–13): 41
§343 (F399.7): 215
§343 (F399.11–15): 45
§343 (F399.11–400.6): 242
§343 (F399.16–400.6): 46, 242
§343 (F400.2–4): 258
§343 (F400.5–6): 255
§343 (F400.6): 243
§344 (F400.8–14): 49, 54
§344 (F400.10): 244
§344 (F400.15–401.11): 51
§344 (F401.2–6): 239
§344 (F401.3–4): 224
§344 (F401.4): 243
§344 (F401.15): 223
§345 (F402.3–5): 56, 57, 58
§345 (F402.6–8): 235, 255
§345 (F402.8): 256
§346 (F403.1–6): 99, 233, 250, 257
§346 (F403.4): 233
§346 (F403.4–6): 236
§346 (F403.7–404.4): 227, 246
§351 (F408.12–409.2): 214
§351 (F408.14–17): 185
§351 (F408.15): 224
§352 (F410.17–18): 238
§352 (F411.1–16): 265
§355 (F418.11–14): 234, 246
§355 (F418.12–13): 243
§356 (F424.15): 200
§357 (F427.4): 219
§357 (F428.13–15): 219
§357 (F429.2): 215
§357 (F429.6–14): 245, 262

Midraš Tanna'im
Deut. 20:14: 217
Deut. 33:1: 270

Mekilta to Deuteronomy
(ed. Kahana)
Deut. 33:3–4: 208, 209, 211, 212,
213, 214, 217, 228

AMORAIC AND POST-AMORAIC COLLECTIONS

Agadath Shir Hashirim
(ed. Schechter)
p. 39: 205

Deuteronomy Rabbah
10:1–2: 270
10:1: 270

Deuteronomy Rabbah
(ed. Lieberman)
p. 15: 203, 212, 270

Ecclesiastes Rabbah
12:11: 235

Exodus Rabbah
1:9: 247
5:9: 196, 259
27:9: 197
28:1: 242
28:6: 196, 259
30:5: 242
33:2: 242
33:7: 221
34:7: 222

Genesis Rabbah
1:14: 252, 275
2:4: 210
16:5: 240

Lamentations Rabbah
2:1: 247

Leviticus Rabbah
11:14: 270
13:2: 197

Menorat Ha-Maor (ed. Enelow)
vol. 3, p. 331: 201, 202
vol. 3, p. 332: 203, 204, 208, 214

Post-Talmudic Rabbinic Commentators and Philosophers

Christian Sources

NEW TESTAMENT

Matthew
1:22: 175
2:17: 175
6:25-33: 269
7:13-14: 210

Luke
4:16-21: 173
4:16-28: 172

John
6:59: 172

Acts
7: 172
7:38: 202
7:53: 202
13:13-16: 173
13:16-41: 172
13:27: 173
15:21: 173

Galatians
3:19: 202

Hebrews
2:2: 202

CHURCH FATHERS

Eusebius, *Historia Ecclesiastica*
2.18.1: 178

Hippolytus of Rome, *Bénédictions de Moise* (ed. Brière)
p. 128: 195, 218

Irenaeus, *Adversus Haereses*
3.20.4: 228
4.33.11: 228

Jerome, *Apologia contra Rufinum*
1.16: 188

Justin Martyr, *Dialogue with Trypho*
131: 212

Origen, *Commentarii in Canticum Canicorum*
1.1: 205

Origen, *Homiliae in Exodum*
9.4: 228

Origen, *Scolia in Canticum Canticorum*
PG 17:373-76: 204
PG 17:253 B4: 228

Origen, *Selecta in Deuteronomium*
PG 12:817A: 196

Theodore of Mopsuestia, *Commentary on John*
intro.: 173

Greco-Roman Pagan Sources

Index of Names and Subjects

Qumran community: 102

R. Abbahu: 52, 216
R. Akiba: 72, 98, 111, 113, 114, 186,
204, 205, 207, 213, 217, 224, 241,
244, 255, 259, 262, 270
R. Bannaya: 137, 185, 209
R. Eleazar b. R. Judah: 120
R. Eleazar b. R. Zadoq: 118
R. Eliezer: 243
R. Eliezer b. Hyrcanus: 209, 253,
257, 258
R. Eliezer b. Jacob: 89, 90, 240
R. Elisha b. Abuyah: 252, 253
R. Gamaliel II; 51, 52, 53, 63, 87, 88,
214, 225, 227, 239, 250
R. Ḥelbo: 207
R. Hezekiah: 52
R. Issac Nappaḥa: 245
R. Ishmael: 95, 106, 192, 207
school of: 123
R. Jacob b. R. Ḥanilai: 252
R. Joḥanan: 52, 186, 216, 221, 224,
240, 245
R. Joḥanan ben Zakkai: 70, 72, 98,
244, 257, 262
R. Jose: 101, 210, 221
R. Jose b. Ḥanina: 52, 260
R. Jose b. R. Judah bar Ilai: 120
R. Jose the Galilean: 86
R. Joshua: 243, 260
R. Joshua b. Ḥananiah: 269
R. Judah b. Ḥananiah: 138
R. Judah b. Ilai: 110, 134, 135, 225,
250
R. Judah the Patriach: 72, 95, 120,
186, 224, 236, 242, 250, 252, 260
R. Levi: 269, 270
R. Meir: 128, 221
R. Naftali Zvi Yehuda Berlin: 274
R. Nehemiah: 135
R. Simeon b. Eleazar: 34, 35, 129,
131
R. Simeon b. Gamaliel II; 103, 214

R. Simeon b. Laqish (Resh Laqish):
250
R. Simeon b. Menasya: 109, 110,
116, 219
R. Simeon b. Yoḥai: 107, 110, 115,
186, 192, 207, 213
R. Simeon b. Zoma: 210, 234
R. Simeon the Pious: 217
R. Tarfon: 241
Rab: 52
Rab Ḥisda: 274
Raba: 146
Rabbenu Tam: 259
Rabbi
as title or term of address: 229
Rabbinic literature
as a source for historiography and
biography: 231
Rabbinic sages: 17, 46, 49, 69, 72,
81, 82, 114, 121, 227, 242, 243. *See
also* Disciples of the Sages;
Ḥākām; Master-disciple
relationship
antecedents to: 72
appointments of as judges: 82, 86,
98, 105, 118, 249, 250, 251
appointments of to administrative
positions: 98, 118
as *parnāsîm:* 50
as distinctive class: 255
as embodying Torah teaching and
practice: 96
as intermediaries between Israel
and God: 81
class of: 18, 187
declaring pure and impure: 108,
109, 115
hereditary offices among: 245, 255
history of: 71, 74
in relation to larger Israel: 66
in relation to the biblical elders:
100
in relation to the priests: 74, 87,
220
legislative authority of: 95, 96